Georgia Governors
in an Age of Change

Georgia Governors

IN AN AGE OF CHANGE

FROM ELLIS ARNALL TO GEORGE BUSBEE

Edited by Harold P. Henderson & Gary L. Roberts

The University of Georgia Press / Athens & London

© 1988 by the University of Georgia Press
Athens, Georgia 30602

Set in 9-1/2 on 12 Mergenthaler Trump Medieval

The paper in this book meets the guidelines for
permanence and durability of the Committee on
Production Guidelines for Book Longevity of the
Council on Library Resources.

Printed in the United States of America

92 91 90 89 88 5 4 3 2 1

Library of Congress Cataloging in Publication Data

Georgia governors in an age of change: From Ellis Arnall to George
Busbee / edited by Harold P. Henderson and Gary L. Roberts.
     p.   cm.
Includes bibliographies and index.
ISBN 0-8203-1004-2 (alk. paper). ISBN 0-8203-1005-0 (pbk.: alk. paper)
  1. Georgia—Governors—History—20th century. 2. Georgia—Politics and
government—1865–1950. 3. Georgia—Politics and government—1951–
I. Henderson, Harold P. II. Roberts, Gary L. F291.G43 1988
973.8'043—dc19   87-23293
                                                                CIP

British Library Cataloging in Publication Data available

Ellis G. Arnall, photograph courtesy of Wide World
Photos; George D. Busbee, photograph courtesy of
George Busbee; S. Marvin Griffin, Lester G.
Maddox, Carl E. Sanders, and Ernest Vandiver,
photographs courtesy of Georgia Department of
Archives and History; Jimmy Carter, photograph
courtesy of Ford and Ruby Lee Spinks; Herman E.
Talmadge, copyrighted photograph courtesy of Herb
Pilcher; M. E. Thompson, photograph courtesy of
Atlanta *Journal and Constitution.*

To

Mara Dare, Hank, and Teena Ann Henderson

and to the memory of

Leland H. and Helen T. Roberts

CONTENTS

GEORGE D. BUSBEE
1975–1983

GEORGIA POLITICS:
RETROSPECT AND PROSPECT

PREFACE

During the four decades that followed the inauguration of Ellis G. Arnall as governor, the state of Georgia moved through complex, often troubled, but fundamentally important changes that literally transformed the social, economic, and political order. Those years witnessed an end to the county unit system, a shift from rural domination to urban influence, the industrialization of Georgia, the civil rights revolution, the first stirrings of a two-party system, and the election of one former governor to the presidency of the United States. Georgia was a vastly different place when George Busbee left office in 1983 than it had been when Ellis Arnall took office in 1943.

This is the first book to focus exclusively on the modern period of Georgia state politics and to present a clear overview of gubernatorial leadership during the critical post–World War II years. The book is unique because it brings together in one place scholarly evaluations of the administrations of the nine men who held the office of governor between 1943 and 1983 and assessments of the same administrations by the men themselves. The pieces included are the products of a symposium held at Abraham Baldwin Agricultural College in the autumn of 1985 under the auspices of the Social Science Division of the college with the support of the ABAC Foundation, the Georgia Endowment for the Humanities, the National Endowment for the Humanities, and the Georgia State Department of Archives and History.

The first Abraham Baldwin Symposium on History and Government brought together scholars, former governors, and a sizable cross section of Georgia citizens for the purpose of reviewing the years of change in terms of gubernatorial leadership. That within itself made it an important meeting, but the sessions had an unusual twist. Scholars are used to presenting papers, and politicians are used to making speeches, but neither group is used to doing either under the close scrutiny of the other—especially with an attentive public close at hand and able to raise its own questions on the spot. The result was a rare opportunity to see the historical process up close and to preserve a vital piece of Georgia's recent past.

Most of the essays that follow were presented at the conference, although many of them were revised and extended following the meeting. The introductory essay was drawn from the papers in an effort to provide some overall sense of direction, the paper on M. E. Thompson is entirely new, and the essay on Marvin Griffin by his son Sam Griffin is also a new addition. Taken together, the materials presented represent the most exhaustive examination of the four decades of Georgia politics between the terms of Ellis Arnall and George Busbee yet written. Every effort has been made to ensure high academic standards, but we have also sought to provide readable prose for the general reader who may be interested in state politics.

Our purpose is simply to provide a readable introduction to gubernatorial leadership in modern Georgia. Each of the scholarly essays critically examines the administration of one of the governors within the context of the larger issues that faced him during his term. Each essay focuses on the high points of the governor's tenure, emphasizing his influence—or lack of it—on the evolution of modern Georgia. Major initiatives, important legislation, notable controversies, political style, and personality are stressed to provide an analytic evaluation of each governor's administration.

The authors vary in their perspectives and styles, and we have made no effort to impose any restrictions on them beyond suggesting that they consider critical historical developments—rural-urban rivalry, industrialization, race relations, party politics, and governmental policy—within the context of the overall themes of continuity and change. Perhaps the most striking feature of the essays, taken together, is the way that they lay out an unmistakable pattern of political evolution in which tradition and consensus have been maintained even while larger forces—the federal government, the civil rights revolution, the changing economic order—have worked to modify and redefine the meaning of tradition and consensus.

The essays not only fill gaps in historical coverage and provide detailed coverage of the modern era of Georgia politics, but also they provide a synthesis of an era which heretofore has been treated generally in published works. Of all the governors included, only Lester Maddox and Jimmy Carter have been the subjects of biographies. Other books are in the works (by, we should point out, contributors to this volume), but until they are published, these essays will be the most complete assessments of the governors extant outside of a few theses and dissertations, which are generally unavailable to the public.

The absence of substantial bodies of private papers complicated the research in critical areas. Only the personal papers of Marvin Griffin, M. E. Thompson, and Carl Sanders have been available for scholarly use. Other papers either remain in the confidential care of the governors themselves or have been destroyed. As a result, some of the scholars have had to rely primarily on public documents, news coverage, and interviews without the more intimate view afforded by personal papers.

The remarks of the governors naturally cover much of the same ground as the scholarly essays, and they vary in scope and candor. Yet even the most self-serving commentaries provide some sense of their authors' perceptions of their roles in the history of the state and some glimpse of what they believe to be important. They provide a kind of balance that is useful in contrasting the perspectives of participants and observers.

Without the contributions of many individuals, this book would not have been possible. Our greatest debt is to the governors who are the subjects of the essays. We are especially grateful to the seven living ex-governors who participated in the project, and to Joe Frank Harris, the present governor of Georgia, who enthusiastically supported our efforts. The scholars who contributed essays deserve high praise for their professionalism and cooperation throughout the project as well as for their scholarship. The unflagging support of Thomas R. Milam, chairman of the Social Science Division at Abraham Baldwin Agricultural College, was crucial to our efforts.

The following individuals and groups contributed significantly to the project: Frederick Allen, political editor of the Atlanta *Constitution* and the Atlanta *Journal*; Secretary of State Max Cleland; Marian Holmes and Virginia Shadron of the Georgia State Department of Archives and History; Richard Ottinger of Georgia Public Television for permission to use excerpts from interviews with Marvin Griffin and M. E. Thompson originally taped by GPTV; Ronald E. Benson, executive director of the Georgia Endowment for the Humanities; Brenda Sellers, reference librarian, Abraham Baldwin Agricultural College; and the members of the board of the Abraham Baldwin Agricultural College Foundation.

Hazel Purvis, who typed the final version of the manuscript, deserves special thanks for her tireless efforts on our behalf. Finally, we wish to acknowledge the conviviality, trust, and professionalism of our colleagues in the Social Science Division, which creates an environment that encourages the pursuit of excellence.

Harold P. Henderson
Gary L. Roberts

Georgia Governors in an Age of Change

Tradition and Consensus:
An Introduction to
Gubernatorial Leadership
in Georgia, 1943–1983

GARY L. ROBERTS

The "redemption" of Georgia from Radical Reconstruction in 1871 ushered in a new age that was somewhat schizophrenic in nature. The Redeemers rode to power on the votes of poor whites who shared with them a determination to keep the South a white man's country, but they were basically elitists who represented the genteel paternalism of the old planter class in racial matters and a mixed commitment to the old plantation economy (with its emphasis on a plentiful supply of subservient labor) and to economic policies of low taxes and reduced services designed to encourage business opportunities and undo Reconstruction reforms. The Redeemers maintained their power with a balance of fear—playing the concerns of poor whites and poor blacks against each other—and subordinated debate on economic questions by appealing to tradition and the principle of white solidarity.

The legacy of the Bourbon Redeemers was a system which emphasized a stable social order based on white supremacy, a closed political order based on one-party politics, states' rights (which translated into home rule for the state and no interference from the federal government), and economic conservatism. Not even the efforts of some Bourbons to promote increased industrialization shook this fundamental program. The only serious challenge to the assumptions of redemption came from the radical populist vision of Thomas E. Watson. For a time, Watson waged unrelenting war upon the economic and social policies which virtually enslaved small farmers and sharecroppers, even denouncing the race question as a political ploy designed to deflect attention from more important issues. In the end, Bourbon Democracy submitted to pressure from the small white farmers and won a Pyrrhic victory that opened the door for "Jim Crow" and a retrenched plantation economy with all of the elements that that implied.

Throughout the early years of the twentieth century, Georgia enjoyed a reputation for demagogic "wool hat" politics, racism, and backwardness. Tom Watson eventually capitulated to racism and salvaged a strong, if extreme, voice in Georgia politics. The Progressive Era confirmed the forces which would dominate political debate in Georgia for the first half of the twentieth century: the redneck tradition vs. the genteel tradition, rural interests vs. urban interests, race, and the county unit system of voting. Ultimately, Progressivism in Georgia merely reinforced the racist elitism of Georgia politics, and proved to be so conservative that Watson's "outs" realized few gains. By the 1920s Georgia's politics was largely divorced from the state's considerable economic and social problems.

The key to political success was the county unit system of voting in the Democratic Party's primary elections. The system emerged out of the old party convention system which assigned the counties two votes for each representative in the lower house of the state legislature. When Georgia Democrats adopted the direct primary at the turn of the century, they kept the county unit concept. As Georgia's cities grew, the system increasingly discriminated against them. Hoke Smith, an urban progressive, managed to abolish the approach following the 1906 election, but only the 1908 election was decided by popular vote. Joseph Mackey Brown's rural supporters reinstated the practice in time for the election of 1910, and in 1917 the legislature made the system mandatory in the Neill Primary Act.

The 1917 law maintained the rule of two county unit votes for each representative in the House of Representatives. In practice that meant that the 8 most populous counties, each with three representatives, had 48 county unit votes; that the next 30 counties, each with two representatives, had 120 county unit votes; and that the remaining 121 counties, with only one representative each, had 242 votes. Under the law, the candidate with a plurality of votes in each county received all of the county unit votes. Gubernatorial candidates and candidates for the U.S. Senate had to have a majority of county unit votes (206) to win, while all other candidates had to have a plurality of unit votes.

The county unit system guaranteed the supremacy of rural interests through the barren nadir of the 1920s and provided the critical advantage for the new champion of the "wool hat boys," Eugene Talmadge, who emerged out of the misery of the Great Depression. Talmadge, who was elected governor in 1932, the same year that Franklin D. Roosevelt promised a "New Deal" to the American people, picked up the mantle of Tom Watson and dominated Georgia politics for more than a decade after that. "The wild man from Sugar Creek" won the support of rural Georgians with a flamboyant style that appealed to their sense of identity. "Ole Gene" piled up impressive victories, taking full advantage of the county unit system. His folksy stories, red galluses, and racist rhet-

oric proved to be a formidable combination, and yet, for all his popularity, Talmadge produced few changes in the lives of Georgia's people.

While he inherited Tom Watson's constituency, he lacked Watson's
commitment to the social and economic reforms badly needed by poverty-
stricken rural Georgians. His principles were the principles of tradition.
He favored the county unit system (which guaranteed rural domination
over urban centers), states' rights (which protected home rule and es-
chewed outside interference), white supremacy (which assured his popularity in rural areas), and—considering his base of voters—an oddly conservative approach to social and economic issues (which sustained the
rural elites and created few problems for him among business leaders who
favored low taxes and minimal government services). The county-seat
gangs profited more than the "good ole boys" who cheered him on the
hustings. Talmadge fervently opposed the New Deal, with all its programs designed to help the very folks he relied upon. He warned against
the dangers of such programs and even entertained hopes of running for
president.

In 1936 this distraction cleared the field for an open challenge to Talmadge. Conditions in Georgia were desperate. The plantation economy
was in a shambles, and enough of Talmadge's followers were disen-
chanted to defeat his choice for the Democratic gubernatorial nomination. Eurith D. "Ed" Rivers, an unabashed Roosevelt supporter, swept
into office along with FDR. Rivers then launched a "little New Deal" in
Georgia. After ridding state government of Talmadge cronies, he sought
and got a wide range of federal projects that greatly improved the quality
of life in the state. Under his leadership Georgia led the nation in rural
electrification and set up the first low-cost housing program for rural
Americans. Rivers worked hard to improve education, the state's highway system, the penal system, conservation, and mental health. He initiated the first welfare system in Georgia, greatly enhanced medical
care, and managed to get around constitutional provisions that prohib-
ited state borrowing.

Unfortunately, during his second administration, charges of corruption in the Highway Department, a bloody controversy with the chairman of the Highway Board, revenue problems, and complaints about a
pardon racket marred his record. He was himself tried for embezzle-
ment in a case that ended with a hung jury. He also incurred the enmity
of business conservatives who disapproved of his reforms and alienated
the county-seat cliques who saw in his approach a threat to local control. Rivers left office with many of his goals unmet and a state debt of
$29 million. In 1941 Eugene Talmadge returned to office.

But not for long. The tide had turned in Georgia politics. Soon after he
returned to the governor's mansion, Talmadge sought to remove two

prominent educators in the university system whom he accused of advocating racial integration. When the Board of Regents refused to dismiss them, the governor turned on the board, replacing several members and firing not only the two officials he had previously attacked but also several others, including the vice-chancellor of the university system. While Talmadge ranted about liberals, foreigners (anyone from outside Georgia), and "race mixers" in the colleges who were trying to destroy Georgia's traditions, Ellis Gibbs Arnall, the state attorney general, announced that no governor had the right to interfere so flagrantly with the educational institutions of the state. The Southern Association of Colleges and Secondary Schools revoked the accreditation of ten schools in the university system. The controversy attracted national attention. Talmadge tried to belittle the criticism, but too many Georgians were aroused. The controversy provided Ellis Arnall with the major issue in his campaign for governor in 1942. With the backing of former Governor Ed Rivers, former Speaker of the Georgia House of Representatives Roy Harris, concerned students, faculty, and parents, an anti-Talmadge coalition was forged that gave Arnall a stunning upset victory over Talmadge.

With the election of Arnall, the changes initiated under Rivers were validated and the modern era of Georgia politics began in earnest. Demagoguery, racism, and chicanery did not disappear, but a new age began which eventually saw the old order shunted aside. Arnall moved into office with a crowded agenda of reform. He ended the educational controversy, appointed a new Board of Regents, regained accreditation for the university system, and changed both the Board of Regents and the State Board of Education into constitutional bodies. Responding to a negative image of Georgia's system of justice, Arnall set about reforming the state's penal code. He abolished the chain gang and followed Rivers's lead in bringing professionals into the administration of Georgia's prisons for the first time. The new governor also expanded the State Merit System for government employees instituted during the Rivers administration.

Arnall also sought reforms that democratized the state. He engineered an end to the poll tax and made Georgia the first state to give eighteen-year-olds the right to vote. He developed a soldiers' rights bill that was widely copied during those days of World War II. He brought suit against twenty railroad companies before the United States Supreme Court, charging them with conspiring to fix rates which discriminated against the South in violation of the Sherman Anti-Trust Act. And he supervised the writing of a new state constitution which was adopted before he left office. He managed to accomplish these things without any new taxes and paid off a state debt of $36 million in the process. These progressive reforms directly benefited Georgia's citizens and gave Arnall broad support in the growing business community as well as among urban and suburban voters.

In 1944 the U.S. Supreme Court struck down the white primary. The ruling threw Georgia politicos into a frenzy and added more than a hundred thousand black voters to the rolls in time for the campaign of 1946. The Talmadge faction wanted to sidestep the court's decision by repealing state laws regulating elections, as white supremacists were able to do in several other Southern states, but Arnall refused to cooperate and the move failed. The controversy split the anti-Talmadge faction, however, and drove some former Arnall supporters like Roy Harris into the Talmadge camp.

Those most distressed by the changes were the local political elites of rural Georgia. Their hope rested on the poor white farmers and sharecroppers whose lives had begun to improve under the reforms of Rivers and Arnall. To blunt the appeal of change, the defenders of the old order relied on the tactic they had used successfully again and again—white supremacy—and turned once more to "good ole Gene" to raise the cry as only he could. But, significantly, even he was forced to offer for the first time in his career a program of social and economic proposals which confirmed the impact of Rivers and Arnall on state politics.

Arnall wanted a rematch. He was the first governor to serve a four-year term, but the constitution prevented him from succeeding himself. Two efforts to persuade the legislature to initiate an amendment to remove that prohibition failed, and Arnall was forced to step aside. In the Democratic primary of 1946 Eugene Talmadge defeated James V. Carmichael, the Arnall-backed candidate. While Carmichael polled a plurality of over 16,000 votes, Talmadge won the nomination with a majority of the county unit votes. Talmadge was elected governor of Georgia for the fourth time in November. However, Talmadge's death on December 21, 1946, created pandemonium in the state. Had he died after taking office, the issue would have been resolved easily. Melvin E. Thompson, the new lieutenant governor, would have taken office as provided under the Constitution of 1945. But Talmadge died before taking office. Both Arnall and Thompson insisted that Thompson should succeed to the governor's chair as soon as he took the oath of office as lieutenant governor, but the legislature assumed the right to choose the next governor from the two other candidates for governor who polled the most votes in the general election. As matters developed, Eugene Talmadge's son Herman had received a few more write-in votes than Carmichael, and on the strength of those votes the General Assembly elected Herman Talmadge governor.

Arnall refused to recognize the legality of the legislative vote, and Thompson insisted that he was entitled to the office. When Arnall refused to turn the governor's office over to the man he called "the pretender," Talmadge locked Arnall out of the governor's office in the state capitol while the national press gleefully enjoyed the "three-governors controversy." Once Thompson was sworn in as lieutenant governor, Arnall resigned as governor in his favor. Talmadge occupied the governor's chair through a bitter session of the General Assembly until the Georgia Supreme Court ruled that Thompson should serve as governor until the 1948 general election, when the people would choose a new governor to serve out the balance of the term.

For a moment that spring of 1947, Thompson's victory seemed to herald a new era. Liberals and moderates rejoiced. The national media reported a revolution among the down-home folks of Georgia against the usurpations of Talmadge. But in Georgia most people knew the truth. The Talmadge faction was still the most powerful force in Georgia politics, and its rural base was secure behind the picket line of the county unit system.

Thompson did not seize leadership of the suddenly vocal moderate element. Political realities made it impractical for him to challenge the existing order brashly. He had no dependable political base in the state, and he lacked the finesse to gain any advantage from the situation. Perhaps more important, Thompson did not share the liberal vision of those who saw his fight as an opportunity to change the direction of Georgia politics. He was prepared to lead Georgia down the roads charted by Rivers and Arnall, but he was not inclined to challenge the social traditions of his native state.

By the time the Supreme Court acted, the legislative term was almost over. The legislature had accomplished little because of the controversy, and it would not meet again until after the 1948 election. Although he could have called a special session, Thompson refused, fearing that nothing would be accomplished. Despite this difficult situation, Thompson built roads and bridges, spent more money than the legislature had proposed for education, improved the state's park system, and purchased Jekyll Island. While doing these things, he insisted that no new taxes were needed and promised to carry out the Democratic Party's platform, including the restoration of the white primary. The accomplishments were enough to unify the anti-Talmadge forces in the state, but not enough to win. Although the popular vote was close, Herman Talmadge overwhelmed Thompson in county unit votes and won the right to complete his father's term.

During the campaign Talmadge emulated his father's style, denounced Thompson as a liberal, and promised lifetime drivers' licenses for veterans. He had the stump speaker's appeal of his father, and he rode the prejudices of his constituency for all they were worth. But Herman Talmadge was not a mere imitation of Gene Talmadge. He had a program for improving Georgia's services to its people that put everyone on notice that he had caught the spirit of economic progress.

Talmadge's plans to improve the state's schools, hospitals, and highways were stymied when the voters disapproved a tax increase in a special referendum in 1949. Despite this setback, Talmadge boldly called a special session of the legislature and asked for tax increases on hunting and fishing licenses and on cigarettes and gasoline. While these actions damaged his popularity temporarily, he defeated Thompson in the 1950 election when he was elected for a full four-year term.

Talmadge surprised many of his critics during the next four years, proving to be a capable administrator who made substantial improvements in state government. For all of the old rhetoric, he had read the handwriting on the wall and he knew that the people who elected him would demand the kind of economic services that Rivers and Arnall had brought to Georgia. He increased state spending for education, created the Minimum Foundation Program, which revolutionized public education in Georgia, and made substantial improvements in higher education. He created the State Forestry Commission and reorganized the State Highway Department. To fund the expansion of state services, Talmadge abandoned a stand both he and his father had taken and implemented a sales tax.

Talmadge still embraced the principle of states' rights, and he railed against the intrusions of the federal government into the affairs of the states. But federal grants and government programs were realities no governor could afford to ignore. He could not hope to reject federal dollars and federal benefits in the way that his father had done. While he never wavered in his criticism of the federal intrusion into state life and warned of its consequences, Talmadge sought federal funds for a variety of programs. He was especially successful in garnering grants to build hospitals under the Hill-Burton Act.

A staunch segregationist, Talmadge stoutly defended states' rights with the same fervor and skill that his father had used on the wool hat boys a generation earlier. He even helped to articulate the legal case for segregation. While unable to restore the white primary, he managed to leave the resolution of the race issue to his successors. He left office in 1955 an immensely popular and powerful figure in Georgia. He had managed to marry tradition and progress in ways that won approval among the conservative power elite.

In 1954 Marvin Griffin, Talmadge's lieutenant governor, won the gubernatorial nomination with only 36 percent of the popular vote but with a majority of county unit votes. He assumed the governorship in 1955, just in time to fight the first skirmishes in a struggle that would eventually transform the state of Georgia. He became the new champion of states' rights, the county unit system, and racial segregation—in short, of the old order in Georgia—against the intrusion of federal power and the rumbles of social change. In the process, he won the reputation of a rustic and hard-nosed fighter, the master of the old-time stump speech, and a gregarious fellow who loved a good story. Among rural Georgians, Griffin's style was familiar and engaging. He spoke frequently, turned phrases with great skill, and defended the established order vigorously. He was at home at the barbecues and fish fries that became his trademark, and he won the heart of the voters with down-home humor, laughter, and an "I'm one of you" approach that proved irresistible.

Griffin did not quibble in his defense of segregation and the county unit system, which he called the state's "two great traditions." To maintain the racial status quo he supported an amendment to the constitution which would allow the state to meet its obligations to education by making tuition grants to students in private schools. In the aftermath of *Brown v. Board of Education,* racial segregation remained one of the dominant themes of Griffin's administration, although he stopped short of utter defiance of the federal government. Beyond the race question, he kept his campaign promises of fiscal restraint and, helped immensely by Herman Talmadge's sales tax, still managed to move the state forward in critical areas such as education, highway construction, and tourism.

Griffin's commitment to education was particularly notable. He was a former teacher himself and, despite his folksy image, a man of intellectual interests. Public schools were improved, library construction was increased, teachers' salaries were raised, and additional teachers were hired. Appropriations for higher education leaped during his term. He placed a nuclear reactor at Georgia Tech and built a huge science complex at the University of Georgia, developments which brought Georgia's universities onto a competitive footing with other institutions of higher learning.

Nor did Griffin abandon his interest in history or economic progress. He thought the unfinished sculpture on Stone Mountain a disgrace and worked hard to purchase the Georgia landmark as a state park. When he met resistance in the General Assembly, he warned state legislators that, while they might get away with opposing him, running against Robert E. Lee, Jeff Davis, and Stonewall Jackson would be more difficult. The legislature capitulated. Other accomplishments included a program for building rural roads, the construction of a farmers' market in Atlanta, the development of facilities that turned Bainbridge into a port city on the Flint River, and improvements of the state docks at Brunswick.

By 1958 Griffin had built an impressive record, but like Rivers he left office under a cloud. Charges of corruption in the State Purchasing Department and the Highway Department, complaints about cronyism and nepotism, embarrassments involving his brother, and allegations of questionable activities on the part of the governor himself overshadowed the accomplishments of his administration.

Griffin left office in 1959 just in time to avoid the real confrontations over segregation, but during his administration the groundwork for resistance was laid. The strategy was simple—throw the weight of state government behind the segregated order and defend the position with the time-honored arguments of states' rights. In the beginning the fight was largely rhetorical. Griffin swore that there would be no race mixing while he was governor, and he was able to make that declaration stick.

Most of the legal maneuvers were defensive and precautionary. Griffin shored up traditional bulwarks of Georgia politics. For example, his effort to strengthen the county unit system was not only a means of assuring rural domination of state politics but also a means of diluting the black vote, especially in the cities, which were thought to be the hotbeds of racial agitation. The educational reforms of the period included some efforts to improve black schools as a means of heading off the criticism that educational opportunities were unequal. More directly, in 1955 the General Assembly passed legislation which promised to deny funds to any school system that integrated its classrooms.

S. Ernest Vandiver, Griffin's lieutenant governor, assumed the office of governor with the time-honored assumptions of Georgia under siege. The battle over segregation. so far delayed, evaded, and filibustered, was about to be joined. The county unit system was under attack. The mild-mannered, honest, and essentially moderate Vandiver donned the armor of states' rights and stepped into the gap as the unlikely champion of the old order. The gubernatorial contest in 1958 focused on the issue of segregation. The candidates agreed on the race issue, but the campaign turned bitter, with Vandiver's opponents characterizing him as weak on that critical question. To counter the charge, Vandiver pledged that black children would not be enrolled in the white public schools of Georgia while he was governor. "No, not one!" became a campaign slogan, and Vandiver won the Democratic primary in the greatest landslide in the history of the state.

Vandiver took office confidently. He promised three things—honesty, fiscal restraint, and the preservation of racial segregation and the county unit system. The first two he accomplished. The pall that had hung over state government at the end of the Griffin years was removed. Vandiver cleaned up state agencies, instituted competitive bidding, and improved management of state business. Although he remained a fiscal conservative, he made significant improvements in state services, in providing leadership in the construction of a new state archives building, rescuing mental health services from the abominable condition that years of neglect had created, and increasing support of education, welfare, and tourism. Vandiver was one of the first governors of Georgia to promote foreign trade.

For all of these accomplishments, he still faced the civil rights revolution. Strident voices inside government and out called for a fight to the finish, but Vandiver was cautious. In 1960 he appointed a special committee headed by John A. Sibley which recommended that each school district decide for itself whether to integrate or to close its schools. Vandiver sold the proposal to the General Assembly and thwarted those who wanted to close the schools altogether.

While Vandiver moved to protect the public schools, the crisis broke on another front. Early in January 1961 a federal judge ordered that two black students, Charlayne Hunter and Hamilton Holmes, be admitted to the University of Georgia. White reaction threatened to destroy Vandiver's moderate course. Mobs roamed the campus at Athens, and threats of violence were so ominous that the governor at first ordered the two students removed from the campus for their own protection. But when a federal court directed that they be admitted to the university immediately, Vandiver faced a real crisis. He could hardly be called an advocate of social change, but he recognized the political and social realities. Faced with the alternative of obeying a federal court order or blindly resisting federal authority as the governors of Arkansas, Mississippi, and Alabama had done, he told Georgians they must obey the law, and in difficult times earned a statesman's laurels. In the fall nine black students entered formerly all-white high schools in Atlanta, and the desegregation process began in Georgia's public schools.

Vandiver also saw another sacred cow, the county unit system, destroyed. Trends in U.S. Supreme Court decisions threatened the system, and even its defenders admitted that it was grossly unfair to urban voters. In order to forestall federal intervention, Vandiver called a special session of the legislature in 1962 to modify the state's primary election laws to give urban voters a greater voice in the system, and although the General Assembly produced a new law which corrected the most obvious injustices, one day after Vandiver signed the bill into law the federal district court for the northern district of Georgia held that the new law did not go far enough. The case sounded the death knell of the county unit system. Reapportionment was moving toward the "one person, one vote" concept. Vandiver would be the last governor nominated under the county unit system.

The Vandiver term was a watershed in Georgia politics. It saw the demolition of the superstructure of the old order. Resistance to integration cracked, and the collapse of the county unit system threatened rural domination, undermined traditional leadership, and left the one-party system more vulnerable than it had ever been. Perhaps equally important, Vandiver had confronted the power of the federal government and found it doggedly determined to bring change. He realized the folly of resistance, grudgingly accepted the fact, and perhaps even recognized some justice and benefit in the change. After Vandiver, "massive resistance" was abandoned as a tactic. But if tradition were threatened on a broad front, the groundwork had been laid for a new politics based on a commitment to "bread and butter" issues like roads, education, mental health, and business development.

The nature of the changes was underscored in the election of 1962, which pitted former Governor Marvin Griffin, "the stump king," against a young urban senator named Carl E. Sanders. Here was a classic showdown between the old politics and the new. Carl Sanders challenged not only the formidable Marvin Griffin, but also the style and substance of the Georgia politics of the past. Sanders paid homage to the past, but he made it clear that he was more interested in Georgia's future. His program included the kind of promises that had already become standard by that time—promises of better education, better roads, better health care, better farm programs—but it also included an emphasis on jobs and industry, welfare and youth programs, recreation and tourism.

The winds of change elsewhere aided him. In 1960 John Fitzgerald Kennedy brought glamour, youth, and idealism to national politics, a combination which also served Sanders well. Like Kennedy, he was young. Like Kennedy, he had an attractive wife and young children. Like Kennedy, he was handsome and likable. Like Kennedy, he was idealistic and optimistic. Like Kennedy, he understood the importance of image and the potential power of the mass media. When Marvin Griffin remarked afterwards that "a lot of people ate my barbecue that didn't vote for me," it was a commentary on more than Griffin's strategy. Sanders's base of support also confirmed the change. Not only did he have the backing of business interests, urban and suburban voters, and the state's young people, but also he had the support of key members of the rural leadership and the support of Herman Talmadge. Perhaps more significant, Sanders would have defeated Griffin even if the county unit system had been in place.

Sanders moved into the governor's mansion determined to make good his promises, and he accomplished most of what he set out to do. Sanders understood the importance of image. His progressive image, his racial moderation, as well as his participation in regional and national associations, commissions, and conferences, brought Georgia a reputation for progress it had not known since the days of Ellis Arnall. Within the state, his greatest achievement came in the field of education. Sanders built classrooms, raised teachers' salaries, and used the Minimum Foundation Program to establish uniform standards for education and to require communities to pay 20 percent of the costs of local schools. He was convinced that the quality of education depended upon a strong system of higher education, and he spent more money on the construction of new facilities on college campuses than had been spent in the entire history of the university system before he took office. He pushed the expansion of the state's community colleges to bring higher education within reach of everyone who wanted it, regardless of where they lived in Georgia.

Aided by prosperity and new taxes on tobacco and alcohol, Sanders also initiated mental health and prison reforms. He created several new agencies including a Commission on Science and Technology, the Water Quality Control Board, the state's first police academy, and youth development centers for youthful offenders. The youthful governor also reorganized the Parks Department and the Game and Fish Commission.

Initially, Sanders was remarkably successful in maintaining good relations with the legislature and the people. In the beginning he was able to keep conservative backing despite his support of the Kennedy administration. But when he prevented George Wallace from speaking to the General Assembly after the legislature had invited Wallace to appear, he lost much conservative support, and his open support of Lyndon Johnson in 1964 alienated many more Georgians. When Georgia supported Barry Goldwater in the presidential election that year—the first time the state had ever gone Republican—it was a serious defeat for Carl Sanders.

Soon after taking office Sanders became convinced that the state's constitution was unwieldy. The document, adopted in 1945, had been amended more than 380 times. In 1963 the General Assembly took up the issue and authorized a commission to revise the constitution. In a special session that lasted two months, the legislature approved a new constitution and a new election code. However, the lingering effects of reapportionment derailed the project. The federal district court in Atlanta stepped in and prevented the state from putting the constitution on the ballot because the legislature which had approved it was malapportioned. Ironically, the court accepted the election code drawn up by the same legislature. By the time the U.S. Supreme Court reversed the lower court's decision on the proposed constitution, the election had been held. It was Sanders's most serious defeat, and constitutional reform would be delayed for more than a decade. Still, Sanders sustained the image of a stable, optimistic modern governor, and the new politics seemed vindicated as his administration neared its conclusion. Then came the shock of the election of 1966.

Few people took Lester Garfield Maddox seriously when he announced as a gubernatorial candidate that year. He had a reputation as a right-wing extremist even in Georgia, and, besides, he faced several of the state's most venerated politicos, including two ex-governors, in the race for the Democratic nomination. Even he quipped that the only thing he had to do to win was "to defeat the Democrats, the Republicans—on the state and national level—159 courthouses, more than 400 city halls, the railroads, the utility companies, major industry, and all the daily papers and TV stations in Georgia." Nobody accused him of overstating the case, and when he was elected governor in one of the most bizarre elections in the history of Georgia, it was a national event.

Maddox said all along that the "people" were behind him (hardly a new refrain in politics), but in the end the legislature, not the people, handed him the governorship, to the delight and consternation of a broad American audience. Outside the state, some people laughed, some cried, and some expressed dismay that Georgia had chosen a man for governor who was best known for chasing blacks away from his restaurant with a pick handle. Inside the state, blacks panicked, liberals predicted disaster, moderates shuddered, and conservatives held their breath. The extreme right—archsegregationists, Ku Kluxers, and John Birchers—rejoiced. The only other people who seemed pleased were the "plain folks," lots of them, who saw Lester Maddox as a voice for those who had no voice. He expressed their frustrations, their fears, their discontent.

To many white Southerners, he appeared to be a martyr to the causes of tradition and property rights. Lester Maddox had become a folk hero to embattled segregationists. People supported him both in Atlanta and in rural communities, not merely because they shared his racial views but because he seemed to defend the "little guy." Here was a man who had never finished high school, a man who had had to work all his life, a man with courage to speak out even if it cost him his business. As improbable as it seemed to political observers, Lester Maddox reached people with his populist appeal.

In 1966 Maddox faced former Governor Ellis Arnall, former Governor Ernest Vandiver, former Lieutenant Governor Garland T. Byrd, Albany newsman and former head of the State Democratic Party James Gray, State Senator Jimmy Carter, and Hoke O'Kelley, who told Georgians that the 1966 election would be the last chance they would have to elect a World War I veteran. Vandiver withdrew for health reasons, and the rest fought a hard campaign. In the Democratic primary Ellis Arnall came in first, Lester Maddox a surprising second, and Jimmy Carter third.

A runoff was required. And Georgia's Republicans were delighted. For the first time in recent history they had an attractive candidate themselves, Howard "Bo" Callaway, a congressman from west Georgia with solid conservative credentials and a well-filled campaign fund. Rumor had it that Republican headquarters was encouraging Republicans to vote for Maddox in the runoff because he would be easier to beat in the general election. If that was indeed their strategy, it backfired. To be sure, Maddox won the runoff, but many Democrats were furious over the alleged Republican involvement in the result. In the general election in November, Callaway received more votes than Maddox, but not the majority he needed. More than 52,000 Georgians had written in Ellis Arnall's name and gained their revenge. The matter now went to the General Assembly, overwhelmingly Democratic, and on the first ballot Lester Maddox was elected governor and the state did not fall apart.

In fact, the state fared surprisingly well. In his inaugural address, Maddox declared that Georgia had no room for "those who advocate extremism or violence." He appointed more blacks to public office than any governor in Georgia's history to that time. Maddox ran an honest administration, notable for its openness, and appointed distinguished and capable men to key positions. He made believers of thousands of Georgia teachers with substantial pay raises, opened the governor's office to anyone who wanted to see him, and pursued initiatives in penal and welfare reform.

The older, more familiar Lester Maddox did not disappear altogether. The right-wing rhetoric soon returned. The inconsistencies continued. He rode bicycles—backwards, of course—and indulged in the kind of antics that had characterized him in the past. Some of his aides left him, and he appointed a few people with known Klan connections. The most substantial criticism leveled at Maddox was that he had no program, no clearly defined objectives. This criticism reflected his lack of experience more than anything else, and it probably contributed substantially to the most important political development of the Maddox years—the growing independence of the General Assembly.

Some observers had seen in Maddox's election a rejection of the new politics, of the button-down style of Carl Sanders. Others saw it as the last gasp of the old order. In fact, it was neither. Maddox's victory was an anomaly, a fluke that ultimately confirmed rather than deposed the new trends in Georgia's political life. Although he ran strongly among the rural people who had sustained the Talmadges and Marvin Griffin, he was himself from urban, blue-collar roots. He was a political outsider with few connections to the local Democratic elites. Perhaps equally important, his election shattered Republican hopes in Georgia, assured continued one-party domination of state politics, and enabled the trends begun under Sanders to continue.

The impact of Maddox's populist vision was felt in 1970 when Jimmy Carter was elected governor. Carter had little in common with his predecessor, but he did learn from the Maddox years. In 1970 he faced a formidable opponent. Carl Sanders was shrewd, articulate, and still immensely popular in Georgia. Beating him would be a major upset. Carter never wavered. He took a conservative position on social and economic issues, portrayed himself as a man of the people who understood the needs of farmers and small businessmen, and assailed Sanders as "Cuff Links Carl," a former governor who had parlayed his term in office into a personal fortune. He openly courted Maddox and Wallace supporters, attacking Sanders for his refusal to allow Wallace to speak and praising Maddox as "the essence of the Democratic Party" in his "compassion for the ordinary man." The approach was short on facts but long on effectiveness. He had to face Sanders in a runoff, but in the end he won the Democratic nomination and beat Republican Hal Suit in November.

Carter immediately shocked some of his more conservative supporters. On inauguration day he announced that "the time for racial discrimination is over." He added, "No poor, rural, weak, or black person should ever have to bear the additional burden of being deprived of the opportunity of an education, a job, or simple justice." It was an auspicious beginning which put everyone on notice that Carter's vision was broader than his campaign platform.

Carter soon demonstrated that he would be an active governor. Like his predecessors in the fifties and sixties, he had to deal with racial issues. He tackled the problem head-on. He appointed a biracial Civil Disorder Unit to help communities with racial troubles. He created a Council of Human Relations, and he appointed a black judge. His most dramatic exercise of symbolic politics came when he refused to reappoint Roy Harris, a prominent segregationist, to the university system Board of Regents, and replaced him with a black man. He included a black state trooper in the four-man team that served as his security, and appointed blacks to other important state jobs. In 1973 he proclaimed January 15 to be Martin Luther King, Jr., Day, and a year later he hung King's portrait in the state capitol, while Lester Maddox fumed and the Ku Klux Klan held a protest rally outside.

Still, Carter's first priority was the reorganization of the executive branch of state government. He put together a reorganization committee which solicited the assistance of both state agencies and major businesses. Eventually, with the assistance of a statewide campaign for support, he succeeded in reducing the number of state agencies from three hundred to twenty-two. Carter also introduced "zero-based budgeting" to state government, a move that forced state agencies to monitor their expenditures more closely. The reorganization plan was altered in the years that followed—especially the unwieldy Human Resources Department—but, like him or not, Carter profoundly affected the future course of state government.

He also tackled the criminal justice system in Georgia, carrying out extensive reforms in the judicial system, creating a merit system for choosing judges, a unified court system, and a constitutional means of regulating judicial behavior. He was less successful in penal reform, although he did initiate several reforms that improved prison education, prison treatment programs, and educational standards for prison employees.

Governor Carter was also vitally interested in the environment and in historic preservation. He created the Georgia Heritage Trust, which allowed the state to obtain sites of historical, archeological, geological, or recreational importance. Before he left office, more than two thousand sites had been earmarked and nineteen of them (amounting to 20,000 acres) had been acquired. He prevented the construction of a dam on the Flint River and thwarted developers on the Chattahoochee in the Atlanta area. His commitment to environmental issues was unmistakable.

Carter undertook initiatives in other areas as well—welfare, tax policy, consumer issues, and education—but they were less successful. In education, he introduced a number of needed reforms but incurred the ire of the state's teachers by opposing salary increases. He pushed a property-tax relief bill, but it was so altered in the General Assembly that he vetoed it when the legislature voted to extend it the next year. He got nowhere with his plans for consumer legislation.

Carter's accomplishments as governor were impressive, especially in light of the tragicomic battle between himself and his lieutenant governor and the constant criticism of the Atlanta *Constitution*. Carter had been a hardworking, progressive governor and a fiscal conservative who managed to leave a surplus in the state treasury when he departed from the governor's office, and still he left the post as an unpopular man. The reasons were largely matters of style. While many Georgians applauded Carter's more liberal approach once he reached the governor's office, others pointed out the inconsistencies between his performance and his campaign promises. Carter nurtured the image of the friendly, approachable governor, but those who dealt with him often complained of his aloofness. Opponents complained that he ran state government like the captain of a ship at sea, with an authoritarian hand. He found it difficult to compromise and hard to admit an error. He had trouble dealing with the legislative leadership, and some complained that he relied too heavily on a close cadre of advisers outside of government. His constant bickering with Maddox also contributed to disillusionment with the man from Plains. So, ironically, while Carter made significant changes in Georgia that moved the state forward, he emerged from the office less respected than his record justified.

Of all the governors in Georgia's recent past, the man who succeeded Carter, former State Representative George D. Busbee, assumed the office with the greatest knowledge of the inner workings of state government and more practical political experience. No recent governor had a more intimate understanding of the day-to-day operation of the legislative process nor greater prospects for developing a close working relationship with the legislature. During the campaign he billed himself as a "workhorse, not a showhorse," and the slogan fit. Never flamboyant or dramatic, he captured the voters with a simple promise to work hard, and he went on to serve two terms with such skill that when he left office even skeptics were forced to admit that he would be "a tough act to follow."

In 1974 Busbee was one of twelve men to announce for the governorship. Jimmy Carter's blessing went to Bert Lance, the Calhoun banker who had served as head of the Highway Department under Carter. In the primary Busbee finished second behind Maddox. However, Maddox's obstructionist role in the Carter years and his image as a single-issue (race) candidate had seriously eroded his voter base, and Busbee's masterful campaign took advantage of the shift. He trounced Maddox in the runoff with almost 60 percent of the vote. He then went on to devastate Ronnie Thompson, the Republican candidate, in November.

The Busbee approach was outlined in his inaugural address. He advocated government by consensus. The time had come, he said, to end the childish bickering and political shenanigans that had characterized government in the past. The problems were much too serious. He demanded legislative-executive cooperation, and for the most part he got it. Busbee recognized the changes that the state faced. He saw the rapid urbanization of Georgia and the increasing demands for jobs and services. He foresaw the devastating effects of inflation and anticipated a shift in the character of federal-state relations. To a large degree, these realities determined his agenda.

Busbee emphasized education as a first priority, initiating a statewide kindergarten program, emphasizing vocational education, and increasing the number of comprehensive high schools which provided vocational training as well as college prep curricula. He worked at increasing student aid, made special contributions to medical education, increased research funds to the universities, and sought to stall the exodus of college professors from Georgia with increased salaries.

His battles in the field of education were frequently bitter. His statewide kindergarten program became entangled with a tax-relief program.

Caught in a serious recession, the Carter surplus evaporated and Busbee faced hard choices. Late in 1975 he called a special session of the legislature which rescinded a major property tax relief program and raises for teachers. College and university teachers took the matter of raises to court, and the Georgia State Supreme Court ruled in their favor. Their raises were restored, but in subsequent years Busbee kept the percentage of raises down, defending his stance as an anti-inflation device. Not surprisingly, his position cost him some support among educators.

Busbee's second priority was economic development. He worked harder than any previous governor to attract new business to Georgia, especially industries requiring skilled workers. Sensitive to the changing rural economy, he sought to distribute industry throughout the state. His program encouraged "freeport" legislation to exempt certain products from taxation on a county and city option basis. Georgia's environmental protection program and highway construction received Busbee's active support. The governor worked for improvements at the Hartsfield International Airport in Atlanta. The aggressive chief executive encouraged efforts to make Georgia a leader in the movie industry, courted banking interests, and worked for a program of grants to local communities to help them with water and sewer systems. He traveled widely, both in the United States and abroad, to attract investment in Georgia. He worked for the creation of the World Congress Center in Atlanta.

Closely related to economic development was Busbee's emphasis on improving intergovernmental relations. Working closely with the Georgia congressional delegation to obtain funds and to eliminate practices that restricted economic growth, he led efforts to advance the interests of the Sunbelt and prevent discrimination against Sunbelt states through organizations like the National Governors' Association, an organization he chaired in 1981. Busbee supported Ronald Reagan's "new federalism."

Busbee also made constitutional revision a top priority. He moved on this question early in his first administration, and was able to have a new edition of the 1945 constitution drafted in time for the 1976 general election. This updated version of the old constitution was designed to simplify the process of real revision, but Busbee had to face the reality that changing the constitution would be a long, hard fight. In the summer of 1981 he chastised the General Assembly for its lack of statesmanship in dealing with the issue. Yet, following a sometimes acrimonious special session, Georgia had a new constitution.

Perhaps his greatest challenge in the first administration was to achieve his goals in light of the financial crisis. He rejected the notion of solving the problem simply by firing employees and cutting services. He undertook a restructuring of the Department of Human Resources and worked to modify Medicaid. He claimed that he cut the state budget by $176 million without reducing jobs or services.

In 1976 the constitution of Georgia was amended to allow a governor to succeed himself, and in 1978 Busbee easily won reelection, which allowed him to complete the work he had begun in his first administration. He increased the state's support of the arts, worked hard to reform the prison system (the area which he still regards as the most perplexing state problem), and supported a program to educate more doctors and to place doctors in rural areas.

In 1983, when Busbee left office, he was the "new model" governor. He personified the transformation which had taken place in Georgia politics. The old politics lingered on, but it was clearly an anachronism. The bitterness of the politics of race, with all of the fears it implied, had somehow given way to the politics of economic development. During the Busbee years modernization took the upper hand over tradition because, at last, most Georgians accepted it. Many of the old attitudes survived, but the blatant excesses of the past would no longer be tolerated. New approaches and new rhetoric were required to sustain power.

And yet, ironically, the new politics became the bastion of tradition itself. Georgia's political vision had become a businessman's vision, deeply rooted in a conservative business ethos more attuned to progress and growth in industrial terms than to a primary consideration of human needs. The only apparent aberration was the unvarnished populism of Lester Maddox, but even his defense of the "little guy" was couched in work-ethic rhetoric that the business community could applaud. So far, Georgia governors have been able to convince their constituents that the road to social progress is tied to economic progress. And economic progress, by definition, is tied to a conservative economic philosophy.

The new consensus is committed to less government regulation of business, opposed to big government in general, for lower taxes and local control, and supportive of state efforts to attract new business—all merely modern variations on the themes of states' rights and Henry Grady's "New South." Moreover, the consensus sustains the one-party system in Georgia. Georgia's Democratic leadership effectively took the Republicans' high ground and stands well entrenched on the very economic and political issues that Republicans might be expected to defend. The election of several Republican congressmen, the election of a Republican senator in 1980, and Georgia's support of Republican presidential candidates in three of the six elections since 1964 suggest that the Democratic hold is weakening. George Wallace's third-party movement carried the state in 1968, and the Democratic victories in 1976 and 1980 owed much to Jimmy Carter's native-son status. Still, Georgia's Republicans have made few inroads into the local politics of rural Georgia. The Republican Party in Georgia remains confined largely to suburban communities in the state's larger metropolitan areas. The debacle of 1966 still looms over Georgia Republicans, and the conservative, business-minded orientation of Georgia Democrats seems unlikely to provide the opportunity for a major shift. Equally important, the local courthouse elites are still Democratic, still committed to the status quo, and still potent within the system.

The politics of race is now camouflaged in discussions of welfare, jobs, criminal justice, education, and housing. Blacks have joined the Democratic consensus, and the Democratic Party has welcomed them, if not with open arms, then at least with the certain knowledge that they are essential to continued Democratic hegemony in the state. Democratic politicians move through carefully orchestrated relationships to solidify the alliance without alienating rural and blue-collar constituencies, and black leaders tolerate a certain amount of the old posturing in the knowledge that when the chips are down the party will make concessions.

Yet, even here, the traditions have not been discarded entirely. The edifice is one of sanitized traditions, enshrined, remembered, molded into a congenial metaphor of Georgia's "good life." If white Georgians have begun to come to grips with the arrant racism of the past, they have done so while romanticizing the Old South and defending the virtues of the rural past. In practical terms, tradition has been wedded to the business ethos to ensure the support of the older order so that free market individualism seems as venerable as states' rights or Southern hospitality. This mythologizing process serves a determined boosterism. Tradition has become the ally of the new vision—something to be preserved, honored, even revered, but something which must be used ultimately to promote the modern vision of Georgia as a congenial and genteel environment for families, communities, and industries.

Consensus politics takes advantage of the essential conservatism of Georgia voters exactly as the old order did. The governors since Ellis Arnall have moved Georgia forward with a progressive approach that has emphasized bread-and-butter issues like education, roads, penal reform, conservation, and the environment. They have not all been great leaders. Some were propelled toward change by the times in which they served. A few genuinely led the state in new directions. But, for the most part, Georgia's governors have been essentially conservative, pragmatic men, motivated more by the values of the gradually changing power elite than by idealistic visions. The federal government forced the great changes in the old order which enabled Georgia governors to transcend the more controversial issues of race and reapportionment and to sustain the consensus despite the changing configuration of state politics. Past governors were able to rail against the federal influence even when they secretly applauded the changes, a tactic which preserved traditional Democratic constituencies while the party sought to build new alliances among blacks, labor, urban voters, and top business and financial interests.

The consensus politics of the 1980s is not as colorful as the stump politics of the past. Many who remember the old times look back longingly to the barbecues, fish fries, and personal politics of the good old days, but not even they—most of them, at least—would bring back the bitterness and hatred that were parts of that brand of politics. For the moment, given the essentially conservative—and apathetic—character of Georgia's voters, the consensus seems secure. And yet, if the more flagrant ugliness of the old order has disappeared, the new business-dominated politics has within it enough blemishes to ensure that the future will be as fraught with problems as the past. Clearly the state has not come to grips with all of the issues that divide its people.

Coalition politics is always flammable. For it to succeed, party leaders must maintain loyalty and control. Any dissent, any challenge, even problem-solving proposals which take shape outside the agenda of the consensus, are likely to be seen as threats to the coalition, however well meaning they are. Consensus hides conflicts within the party, stifles debate, and encourages the use of raw political power. Rumblings of discontent among agricultural interests, economic policies that cater to corporations and industry, black disillusionment, and increasing rhetoric about "two Georgias" (a concept which implies a political bias toward Atlanta and the surrounding counties at the expense of the rest of the state) suggest that Georgia's "era of good feelings" is more illusion than reality. Ironically, as the 1980s move toward conclusion, the key issue facing Georgia's political leadership is the same one the Bourbons faced a century ago: Can the politically and economically conservative leaders sustain a coalition of disparate elements, some of which do not share their vision?

Ellis G. Arnall

1943 – 1947

Ellis Arnall
and the Politics
of Progress

HAROLD P. HENDERSON

In the 1942 primary election in Georgia, Ellis Arnall defeated Governor Eugene Talmadge for the gubernatorial nomination of his party.[1] Talmadge had served three terms as commissioner of agriculture and three two-year terms as governor prior to this defeat. While he had suffered three losses in previous campaigns, no opponent had ever denied him the governor's chair until 1942 when Arnall, then only thirty-five years old, defeated the fifty-eight-year-old Talmadge, considered by some as one of the most successful vote-getters in Georgia's history.[2]

Critics denounced Talmadge as a demagogue, a dictator, or as "the wild man from Sugar Creek." Strong executive action such as removing uncooperative state officials, calling out the state militia, and ruling by executive decree had characterized the Talmadge administrations. When the Public Service Commission refused to lower utility rates to his satisfaction, Talmadge fired the entire commission and installed more cooperative members. When the state treasurer and state comptroller general refused to cooperate with him in spending money without an appropriation bill, Talmadge removed them from office. When the State Highway Board refused his request to fire some engineers, he proclaimed martial law and removed the uncooperative board members.[3]

Even the Board of Regents failed to avoid Talmadge's domination. In 1941 Talmadge, who served as an ex officio member of the board, sought the dismissal of Dr. Marvin S. Pittman, president of Georgia Teachers College, and Dr. Walter D. Cocking, dean of the College of Education at the University of Georgia. He contended that these two educators favored coeducation of the races in Georgia. When the board refused by a close vote to comply with Talmadge's request, he replaced three of the regents. The board eventually removed ten employees of the university system, including Vice-Chancellor J. Curtis Dixon, President Pittman, and Dean Cocking. Taking a dim view of Regent Talmadge's educational activities, the Southern Association of Colleges and Secondary Schools withdrew accreditation from ten units of the university system. Claiming that the issue was racial and not educational, a stubborn Talmadge refused to concede that he had done anything improper. Ellis Arnall, in the midst of the growing controversy, formally announced his candidacy for the Democratic gubernatorial nomination on November 1, 1941.[4]

Born into a prominent mercantile-textile family in Newnan, Arnall attended Mercer University and later transferred to the University of the South, where he graduated with a degree in Greek. In 1931 he graduated from law school at the University of Georgia, where he served as president of his class as well as president of the Interfraternity Council, the legal fraternity, the student body, and the Gridiron Club. Arnall returned to Newnan to practice law. In 1932 the voters of Coweta County overwhelmingly elected Arnall, then twenty-five years old, to a seat in the Georgia House of Representatives. Not content just to be a member of the House, he successfully ran for the second highest position in the body—that of speaker pro tempore. During his two terms as state representative (1933–37) Arnall generally supported the legislative proposals of Talmadge, who then served as governor. However, he began to drift away from the governor as a result of Talmadge's dictatorial manner and his opposition to social welfare legislation. In 1937 Governor Eurith D. Rivers appointed Arnall assistant attorney general and, two years later, attorney general. In 1940 Arnall ran unopposed for the attorney generalship.[5]

Arnall had long contemplated running for governor, but his plans did not have him entering the 1942 race. However, he later admitted that the Pittman-Cocking affair altered his plans because it provided him with an excellent issue to use against Talmadge.[6] Arnall effectively capitalized on the idealistic and democratic sentiments of a nation at war with dictatorship. Denouncing Talmadge as Georgia's own version of Hitler, he maintained that the paramount issue in the campaign was "efficient, honest, democratic administration of public affairs versus tyrannical political domination of the state government." He called upon all Georgians to join him in a crusade to eliminate "gubernatorial dictatorship."[7]

In his campaign's kickoff address in 1941, Arnall unveiled a platform of governmental reform aimed at restricted gubernatorial power. He insisted that the reputation and honor of the state could be redeemed only by reforming the governor's office. Not surprisingly, two of his major reforms dealt with education. Arnall promised to remove "the slimy hands of dictatorial governors" by the creation of a constitutional Board of Regents and a constitutional State Board of Education.[8] He received 57 percent of the popular vote and 64 percent of the county unit vote in the 1942 primary. Both Arnall and Talmadge agreed that the educational issue was the major factor in Talmadge's defeat.[9]

The Arnall administration undertook an ambitious reform program, and one observer contended that by 1945 Arnall had succeeded "in lifting his state from the benightedness of Tobacco Road to the position of runner-up to North Carolina for the title of 'Most Progressive Southern State.'"[10] The accomplishments of the Arnall administration were numerous. They included a new state constitution as well as the creation of a constitutional Board of Regents, State Board of Education, State Board of Pardon and Paroles, and State Game and Fish Commission. During the Arnall years Georgia became the first state to pass a soldier voting law, the first state to lower the voting age to eighteen, and the fourth Southern state to abolish the poll tax. The Arnall administration also substantially increased state appropriations for education, initiated a teacher-retirement system, established a State Agricultural and Industrial Development Board, created the State Ports Authority, instituted a State Merit System, initiated reforms in the state's infamous penal system, and liquidated the long-existing state debt without raising taxes. Arnall also successfully argued Georgia's case before the United States Supreme Court that the state could sue the railroads because their rate-fixing practices violated federal antitrust legislation.[11] One historian observed a less tangible achievement in that prior to Arnall's administration national attention had often been directed toward Georgia "for her sins and the sins of her leaders, and feature writers in their articles for national magazines had brought Georgia in shame and disrepute. Now the picture was completely reversed. It seemed none came to Georgia but to praise—to praise the state and its governor."[12]

The Arnall administration has been highly praised by the academic community. In a 1985 Georgia Association of Historians survey, respondents gave Arnall the most positive ranking of the governors who served from 1943 to 1983 in the categories of exercising effective political leadership, earning a positive national reputation, and addressing the major issues of his term in office.[13] (See Appendix.) Numan V. Bartley concluded that Arnall's "tenure in the governor's office was the most progressive and probably the most effective in modern Georgia history."[14] James F. Cook contended that "only the administrations of Hoke Smith and Richard Russell could rival Arnall's in the magnitude of reform legislation."[15] V. O. Key, Jr., asserted that "many Georgians and most outsiders consider his administration (1943–1947) the most competent given the state in several decades."[16] E. Merton Coulter wrote that "Arnall was the most dynamically constructive governor Georgia had had within the memory of its oldest inhabitants."[17] In the opinion of Thomas E. Taylor, "Arnall was one of the most noteworthy individuals to come out of the South this century."[18]

It is beyond the scope of this paper to discuss the numerous accomplishments of the Arnall administration. Instead, it will concentrate on Arnall's influence in four key areas: the 1943 reforms, the Constitution of 1945, penal reforms, and race relations during his administration.

In his inaugural address in January 1943, Governor Arnall urged the legislature to enact his campaign reform program. Specifically, he asked the legislature to reorganize the Board of Regents and to submit to the voters an amendment making the board a constitutional body. Arnall contended that only by placing the regents under the protection of the constitution could the board be removed from future political interference. He also emphasized that such action would hasten the reaccreditation of the university system. Among other things, House Bill One created a new board, removed the governor as a member, and lengthened the term of the regents from six to seven years. Both houses unanimously supported the proposed legislation. The legislature also unanimously voted to submit an amendment to the voters changing the board to a constitutional body. Shortly thereafter the executive committee of the Southern Association of Colleges and Secondary Schools voted to recertify the unaccredited units of the university system. Georgia voters ratified the amendment with an affirmative vote of 81 percent.[19]

Arnall also urged the conversion of the State Board of Education into a constitutional board. The legislature unanimously created a new board, removed the governor as a member, and lengthened the term of office from six to seven years. The legislature also unanimously proposed a constitutional amendment changing the body to a constitutional board. The voters ratified this amendment with an affirmative vote of 81 percent.[20]

In addition, the governor called upon the legislature to remove the pardoning power from the governor's office.[21] Both of Arnall's immediate predecessors, Talmadge and Rivers, had been criticized for abusing the clemency power.[22] Arnall proposed a constitutional amendment transferring such power from the governor to a constitutional board. With only three dissenting votes, the General Assembly agreed and created the State Board of Pardon and Paroles. In addition, the legislature proposed an amendment to make the new agency a constitutional body, and it was ratified by an affirmative vote of 82 percent.[23]

Arnall's reform program called for the legislature to remove the governor's power to suspend the state treasurer and the state comptroller general. The legislature unanimously agreed.[24] He also requested that the power of the governor to appoint the state auditor be transferred to the legislature, and the lawmakers unanimously complied.[25] They also agreed without dissent to remove the governor as a member of the governing board of state agencies in order to "democratize" their operations.[26]

In the area of finance Arnall called for the creation of a Finance Commission whose purpose would be to hear appeals from state agencies when their requests for funding were disapproved by the Budget Bureau. The legislature approved the proposed legislation unanimously.[27] Arnall further proposed that the legislature abolish the allocations system by which state revenue obtained from certain taxes went to specific governmental agencies. Approximately 60 percent of the state budget was predetermined by the allocation system. Arnall requested the replacement of the system with a system of specific appropriations for each state agency. The legislature not only unanimously agreed to Arnall's request but passed two appropriation bills of over $70 million without a dissenting vote. Arnall claimed that passage of his appropriations bills without amendments and with unanimous support was "without parallel or equal in Georgia's long legislative history."[28]

In addition to his campaign reform program, Arnall urged the 1943 legislature to create a teacher retirement system because the teachers "certainly deserve special consideration at the hands of the state." With only two dissenting votes, lawmakers created the State Teachers' Retirement System. The legislature also proposed two constitutional amendments pertaining to the system. One provided that the taxing power of the state and local governments could be used to pay benefits, and the other changed the constitution to authorize the payment of benefits. The voters overwhelmingly approved both amendments and the system began operation in January 1945. Arnall said that the establishment of the retirement system gave him "more satisfaction than any other accomplishment of my administration."[29]

He asked the General Assembly to limit campaign expenses for the governor because, he said, "We must not let it get where only rich men can run for governor." The legislature expanded his request and limited the expenditures of a candidate for any state office to $25,000. Arnall also asked the 1943 legislature to enlarge the power of the attorney general "to investigate irregularities in State Departments and to stop corruption in state government wherever it shows its ugly head." The legislature, with only four dissenting votes, supported the governor's request. Arnall pledged to the people that he would have an honest administration and promised to expose anyone "who profits, racketeers, or thrives on unjust gains or 'deals' at the state's expense." Years later he recalled that, while he had been called many things in public life, "Nobody ever accused me of any financial irresponsibility or wrong doing."[30]

At Arnall's request, the legislature abolished the Wildlife Division in the Department of Natural Resources and replaced it with a "nonpolitical" Game and Fish Commission. The legislature also proposed a constitutional amendment making the commission a constitutional body. Georgia voters approved the amendment with an affirmative vote of 78 percent.[31]

During the campaign Arnall had promised to create a statewide merit system to replace a merit system which existed on a departmental basis with no overall state supervision. The legislature gave him the authority to create a state merit system directed by a Merit System Council. The governor had the authority to appoint the council, which had the power to appoint a merit system director. Initially, the system included only employees in the state and county departments of welfare, the State Employment Security Agency, the State Department of Labor, and the state and county departments of health.[32]

Arnall's efforts to remove the influence of the governor from the operation of state agencies did not extend to the Highway Department. He favored the abolition of the three-man Highway Board that had been created in the last Talmadge administration. In its place, he supported the creation of a state highway director who would serve at the pleasure of the governor and a twelve-member Highway Commission appointed by the governor. With only seventeen votes in opposition, the legislature approved the governor's request. Arnall resisted efforts to make the governing body of the Highway Department a constitutional body, claiming that "highway construction is purely political and it ought to be." He admitted that he "used the highway department to get through a lot of things that I couldn't have gotten through unless I controlled it." Arnall explained that what he did was "remove the influence of the governor from the agencies that ought to be left alone and should be based on technical knowledge and expertise—such as the merit system, such as education, such as the prison system. I don't think that these are political, but I think highway building is purely political."[33]

The strongest opposition to his reform program in the 1943 legislature came from his request to lower the voting age to eighteen. Arnall contended that "any man old enough to fight for us in the deserts of

North Africa or the swamps of New Guinea is old enough to take part in our government." Despite former Governor Talmadge's opposition, the Senate voted 39 to 8, three votes more than the constitutional two-thirds majority required, in support of a constitutional amendment lowering the voting age. However, the House vote fell short of the required majority by thirteen votes. Upon reconsideration the following day, the House approved the amendment by a vote of 140 to 43. The voters ratified this amendment by an affirmative vote of 68 percent.[34]

Arnall called the 1943 legislature "the finest that has ever assembled under the dome of the State Capitol."[35] The Atlanta *Journal* commended the work of the lawmakers for restoring democratic government to Georgia. The Atlanta *Constitution* praised the legislature for its record of accomplishments "that has rarely, if ever, been equalled by a previous assembly session."[36] One observer compared Arnall's success with the 1943 legislative session to that of President Roosevelt's famous "100 Days."[37] Walter Davenport dubbed the governor "Unanimous Arnall" because of his success with the legislature and contended that the passage of Arnall's ten-point reform program within twenty-four days after assuming office was "a political record breaker anywhere and a miracle in Georgia."[38] One out-of-state newspaper editorialized that "both Talmadge's abuses of power and the speedy correction of those abuses are unique in state affairs."[39]

Under Arnall's leadership the state received a new constitution to replace the Constitution of 1877, which by 1943 had been amended over three hundred times.[40] In March 1943 the legislature passed a resolution creating a commission to write a new state constitution, with the stipulation that the legislature must approve the document prior to its submission to the people.[41] The resolution designated the governor as a member of the commission, which elected Arnall as its chairman. Arnall informed commission members that he wanted the new constitution to be "the capstone of this administration."[42]

The commission spent more than a year in revising the constitution before submitting its work to the 1945 session of the legislature for its deliberations.[43] The commission produced no major revisions of the old constitution. Arnall defended its work by declaring that "had we put into this document too many radical departures from custom or procedure, it would have, in my judgement, met defeat."[44] The Georgia League of Women Voters had supported the inclusion of eight major reforms in the revised charter. However, the revision contained only one of these eight.[45] Over thirty newspapers expressed disappointment in the work of the commission. Stung by this criticism, Arnall reconvened the body for an additional two-day session. This session proposed additional revisions, including a liberalized home rule, the creation of a constitutional State Board of Corrections, the provision of constitutional protection for the State Merit System, and the creation of a constitutional State Veterans Board.[46] The Georgia League of Women Voters supported the revision as "an improvement over the present constitution."[47]

One scholar of Georgia constitutional history, Albert B. Saye, concluded that "fully ninety percent" of the new constitution was taken from the amended Constitution of 1877 and that the commission's work "was confined primarily to a revision of form and organization." However, fifty changes were made in the revision, and even Saye conceded that "some of the changes in structure were of great significance."[48] The revisions included the creation of the office of lieutenant governor and the incorporation of the Veterans Service Board, the State Board of Corrections, and the State Personnel Board into the constitution.[49]

After revising the commission's final product, the legislature submitted the new charter to the voters. Arnall contended that the 1945 legislature's greatest accomplishment was its passage of the new constitution and its submission to the people for ratification.[50] Lauding the work of the commission, the Atlanta *Constitution* declared that it had done "a commendable job of streamlining and modernizing the state's archaic organic law." The *Journal* praised Arnall for his statesmanship in guiding the new constitution by "the rocks of destruction."[51] Governor Arnall, joined by former Governor Rivers and House Speaker Roy V. Harris, campaigned throughout the state in favor of the new constitution, while former Governor Talmadge led the opposition to its ratification. Voters ratified the proposed constitution in August 1945 by a favorable vote of 64 percent.[52]

The Arnall administration had provided the state with a new constitution. However, by 1962 amendments to the 1945 constitution had surpassed the number of amendments to the Constitution of 1877. As a result, Carl Sanders promised constitutional revision in his successful quest for the Democratic gubernatorial nomination that year. However, a federal district court thwarted the Sanders administration's efforts to provide the state with a new constitution. Finally, during the George Busbee administration, the voters replaced Arnall's "capstone" constitution.[53]

After obtaining the passage of his campaign reform program, Arnall turned his attention toward Georgia's infamous penal system. The system stood in need of reform. One observer ranked it "second only to racial problems in causing infamy to be heaped on the state by the northern press."[54] Arnall did not address the penal system in his inaugural address. Instead, after the regular session in 1943 he requested that appropriate committees in both houses investigate the problem. He also asked that House Speaker Harris and Senate President Frank C. Gross compare the state's penal system with those of surrounding states. After visiting nine Southern states, Harris and Gross concluded that Georgia had "the worst system we have seen anywhere." Their report criticized the system for its harsh treatment of prisoners and its lack of efforts toward rehabilitation. Arnall contended that the publicity which resulted from these reports produced a climate in the state receptive to penal reform.[55]

As a result, the governor convened the legislature in September 1943 to deal with the prison problem. In an address to the lawmakers Arnall condemned Georgia's penal system as punitive in purpose, archaic in method, and burdensome to the taxpayers. Basing his reforms on the legislative reports, he called for a complete reorganization of the system. What he had in mind was a coordinated penal system headed by a single executive official with authority to make rules and regulations with guidelines set by the legislature. The governor's request for action included prohibiting whippings, eliminating the use of manacles and leg irons, segregating juvenile first-offenders from other inmates, housing male and female inmates at different facilities, providing proper vocational training for the prisoners, eliminating striped uniforms, segregating the mentally ill from other inmates, and providing for state supervision of county work camps. Arnall reminded the lawmakers that no "true reform" of the system had occurred since Georgia abolished the lease system almost fifty years earlier. In one of the most eloquent statements of his administration he told the lawmakers:

I know that we live in a practical day. We hear a great deal of talk about being practical, being efficient, doing what is wise and prudent. I think it is high time that we talk some once again about doing what is right.

It is not right to shut a man like a mad dog in a cage and whip him with a rubber hose and work him as a brutal drayman might work a sick horse. And when I think of boys huddled with professional criminals obtaining no education and no religious instruction, I am disgusted and I know that you are; but when I think of men—men made in the image of the most high God—dying in prison without the consolation of a man of God at their side, I am heart-sick. These things must not continue in our state.[56]

The legislature overwhelmingly supported Arnall's reforms by a vote of 147 to 25 in the House and 32 to 4 in the Senate. While conceding that it would take several years to fully implement his penal reforms, Arnall contended that at least prison reform had begun in Georgia.[57]

Arnall never posed a threat to the Southern racial orthodoxy, whether as a state legislator, as attorney general, or as a gubernatorial candidate. In fact, William Anderson, in his biography of Eugene Talmadge, concluded that in 1942 "two racists [Talmadge and Arnall] opposed each other; one identified with closing the colleges, the other with keeping them open and accredited."[58] On one occasion during the 1942 campaign Arnall asserted that no "intelligent or decent type person" believed in racial coeducation in Georgia.[59] On another occasion he assured the voters that "our southern tradition, customs, and ideals will always prohibit co-education of the white and Negro races."[60] Moreover, during the heat of the campaign, Arnall resorted to demagoguery when he said: "Over in west Georgia where I live, we don't need any governor to keep Negroes out of our white schools. We know how to handle a thing like that without any help. . . . Why, if a Negro ever tried to get into a white school in the section where I live the sun would not set on his head. And we wouldn't call on the governor or the State Guard either."[61]

Since the passage of poll tax laws in the South in the latter part of the nineteenth century and the first decade of the twentieth century, critics had attacked that tax as undemocratic and as a deterrent to black participation in Southern elections. During the 1942 campaign Arnall opposed abolishing the poll tax.[62] According to him, several of his liberal supporters urged him to campaign against the tax, but he refused to do so, telling them, "Hell, if I do, I'll get beat."[63] Nor did he advocate any legislative action in 1943 dealing with the poll tax. The constitutional revision commission of which Arnall served as chairman discussed the poll tax issue shortly after the U.S. Supreme Court struck down the white primary in Texas. Arnall stated that as a result of that decision "my own mind is not quite clear as to what properly should be done in Georgia, and at the moment the Chair has no deepseated convictions on it." In fact, Arnall declared that he would like to study the effect that abolishing the poll tax would have on the state.[64]

In December 1944 the commission voted 9 to 7 to retain the poll tax in the new constitution. Arnall did not vote since the vote was not a tie, nor did he express his views on the subject at that time.[65] According to an Associated Press survey, the overwhelming majority of Georgia legislators did not believe the poll tax should be abolished by the legislature.[66] In December 1944 Arnall called for a year-long study of the effect of the poll tax since "no careful study of that tax in operation has been made." He indicated that he would take a stand on the issue after the study's completion. Up to this point he had avoided taking a leadership role in abolishing the poll tax.[67]

Prior to the opening session of the 1945 legislature, House Speaker

Harris and Senate President Gross indicated their support for repealing the tax. Both of Georgia's U.S. senators, Richard B. Russell, Jr., and Walter F. George, had gone on record favoring repeal. Neither Russell, George, Harris, nor Gross viewed the elimination of the poll tax as a race-related issue.[68] In addition, a new convert, former Governor Talmadge, came out in opposition to the tax, contending that it deterred white voting participation. Talmadge concluded that abolishing the poll tax would not allow Negroes to vote in Georgia because they "as a class don't care to vote anyway, unless they are encouraged by some communistic element."[69]

Despite broad support for abolishing the tax, Arnall merely asked in his address to the 1945 legislature on January 7 that the body "ponder" the value of the poll tax.[70] However, on January 23 a more aggressive Arnall spoke to the legislature and recommended that the lawmakers repeal the state's poll tax because it served "no possible good." Furthermore, he informed the legislature that if it failed to act he would suspend collection of the poll tax by executive order. Arnall assured the lawmakers that he saw "no danger" of blacks participating in the state's elections as long as the white primary was retained.[71] He engaged in a vigorous lobbying effort to get the poll tax repealed.[72] Calling legislators into the governor's office, he told them,

> When you adjourn and you haven't done away with the poll tax, then by executive order I can do away with it until the next meeting of the legislature. So you will be running without any poll tax. So when you go to ask somebody to vote for you, they say, "Hell if it hadn't been for Governor Arnall, I couldn't vote, I'm against you." Whereas if you take full credit on it and you go home and tell it— put it in the local paper that you supported doing away with it— you wanted a broad franchise—you'll get elected.[73]

The day after the governor's second address, the Senate voted 31 to 19 to repeal the poll tax. Senator Spence Grayson, a poll tax opponent, declared that up until the governor's address "this bill faced certain defeat in the Senate. The governor's influence and nothing else passed it." The Senate even passed a resolution complaining of the "heat" generated by the governor's office on this issue. Led by Speaker Harris, the House voted 141 to 51 to repeal the poll tax.[74]

As a result of the repeal of the tax, voting did increase in the next state election. The vote in the 1942 Democratic primary (303,151) was more than doubled in the 1946 primary (691,881). However, this increased turnout may be attributed to the demise of the white primary and the lowering of the voting age as well as the repeal of the poll tax. Nevertheless, under Arnall's leadership Georgia joined the ranks of the other Southern states—Florida, Louisiana, and North Carolina—that had repealed the poll tax.[75] Arnall's belated leadership on the issue came under criticism. In fact, Frederick D. Odgen, in his *The Poll Tax in the South*, attributed Arnall's study-to-action conversion to a telephone call from President Roosevelt urging him to take a more positive action on the subject.[76] On the other hand, the Atlanta *Journal*, while praising all of those who brought about the repeal, contended that "if there is one to whom particular credit is due, it is Governor Ellis Arnall. At the crucial moment when the tides of battle wavered, he entered the issue with a forthrightness and courage that were altogether admirable. It is safe to predict that repeal of the poll tax will be counted, in the long perspective years, among the finest fruits of his progressive and constructive administration."[77]

The white primary issue proved to be even more controversial than the poll tax issue because the white primary served as the major legal deterrent to effective black participation in Southern politics.[78] Arnall's 1943 reform program did not include opening the primary to blacks. In fact, as late as January 1944 Arnall contended that Georgia's black military personnel, unlike their white counterparts, could not participate in the state's primary elections.[79]

A U.S. Supreme Court decision in 1944 invalidating the white primary in Texas led to a series of events that resulted in the demise of the white primary in Georgia.[80] In October 1945 a federal district court invalidated the state's white primary, and the U.S. Fifth Circuit Court of Appeals upheld the decision.[81] However, the appellate court seemed to provide a way in which the white primary could be saved. The salvation of the white primary required the repeal of all state primary laws and the conversion of the state's Democratic Party into a private organization with no state regulation. Thus, a white primary sponsored by a "private" organization would be beyond the scope of the *Smith v. Allwright* decision.[82] Former Governor Talmadge proposed immediate action to save the white primary. He called upon the State Democratic Executive Committee to convene and incorporate all state primary laws into the rules and regulations of the Georgia Democratic Party. Then Talmadge urged the legislature to repeal all state primary laws, including the Neill Primary Act of 1917 requiring the county unit system in primary elections. Speaker Harris advocated similar action.[83]

Despite such pressure, Arnall announced on April 4 that he would abide by the decision of the federal courts, reminding Georgians that "it is our duty as good citizens to uphold the courts, the Constitution, and laws of our land." He warned that the county unit system could be discarded if the state's primary laws were repealed.[84] Arnall feared that repeal of primary laws against fraud and corruption would allow the unscrupulous to steal elections. Furthermore, he declared that even in the absence of state regulation the federal courts would still prohibit white primaries.[85] The governor refused to call a special session of the legislature to repeal the state's primary laws as requested by Talmadge and Harris. Moreover, Arnall threatened to veto any legislation repealing the state's primary laws passed by a session convened by the legislators themselves. After Arnall's decision, the Georgia Democratic Party amended its regulations to permit black participation in the primaries.[86]

Arnall's decision on the white primary resulted in the political revival of Eugene Talmadge. Unlike the 1942 campaign, the white primary issue allowed Talmadge to take the offensive on a political issue, and he wasted no time in denouncing Ellis "Benedict" Arnall for opening "the breach in the dike that has protected Southern manhood, Southern womanhood, and Southern childhood for three quarters of a century."[87] He accused Arnall of doing more to promote racial equality in America than any other man.[88] Two days after Arnall's statement on the white primary, Talmadge made his announcement of his candidacy for governor, in which he promised to restore the white primary.[89]

Arnall's stand on the white primary damaged him politically because it put him on the defensive on the emotional issue of race. Arnall claimed that he could have controlled Georgia politics for the "next forty years" if he had led the fight to save the white primary. However, he emphasized that he could not do it "because it's a violation of my inborn concepts of first class citizenship for all the people." Anticipating that he would be condemned as a "nigger lover" and a "traitor to the South," Arnall nevertheless believed that permitting blacks to vote in the Democratic primary was "morally right and legally right."[90] Certainly, his stand on the white primary earned him the contempt of die-hard segregationists. Talmadge contended that Arnall's decision made him the most despised governor since Rufus Brown Bullock, Georgia's Republican Reconstruction governor.[91]

While Arnall and Talmadge both considered themselves segregationists, Arnall's version of segregation stood in contrast to Talmadge's. Perhaps Talmadge's philosophy of segregation is best summed up by his statement: "I want to deal with the nigger this way: he must come to my back door, take off his hat, and say, 'Yes sir.' "[92] Arnall, unlike Talmadge, expected the South to comply with the separate-but-equal doctrine. Arnall contended that blacks were entitled to equal protection of the law, equal educational, vocational, and professional opportunities, the right to vote, and the same public services as whites. He agreed that blacks had "inadequate" educational opportunities in the South. He viewed the race problem as basically an economic problem which could be solved by improved economic opportunities for all Southerners. According to Arnall, "The poverty of the South created racial hatred since there was only a half a loaf of bread for both races." He believed that "economic opportunity solves racial problems, solves the problems of ignorance, the problems of poverty," but that economics was not the entire answer to the race problem, "for part of the answer must be found within the human heart."[93]

Ellis Arnall's political ascendancy was one of the most remarkable chapters in Georgia's political history. The voters of Coweta County sent him to the State House of Representatives when he was only twenty-five. The members of the House twice elected him speaker pro tempore. Governor Rivers appointed him attorney general when he was thirty. Arnall obtained his state's highest political office when he was only thirty-five. As governor, he achieved a remarkable record of accomplishment. As a result, the national media found themselves in the unusual position of praising rather than condemning a governor of Georgia. However, in the later half of his term the Arnall luster began to fade as a result of several major defeats. At the 1944 National Democratic Convention, Arnall unsuccessfully led the fight to renominate President Roosevelt's liberal vice-president, Henry A. Wallace.[94] Arnall suffered a major defeat on the state level when the House of Representatives refused in 1945 and 1946 to propose a constitutional amendment permitting gubernatorial succession. Since he could not succeed himself, Arnall supported James V. Carmichael in the 1946 Democratic gubernatorial primary. While Carmichael led in popular votes, Eugene Talmadge received the nomination because of his majority vote in the county unit system. When Talmadge died before he could be sworn in, the legislature, overruling Arnall's objections, elected Herman Talmadge governor.[95]

The decline of Arnall's popular support in the later years of his administration may be attributed to several factors. Many white Georgians believed that he was too liberal on the race issue. Others believed that he was too liberal for Georgia. Arnall's numerous out-of-state speaking engagements, his two successful books, his numerous articles, and a nationwide lecture tour after leaving the governor's office damaged him politically in Georgia. Many Georgians did not want their governors or their former governors discussing their problems with outsiders. As V. O. Key put it:

A native son's popularity all too often varies inversely with his prestige in the rest of the land. This is especially true when he excites the admiration of the "northern press" and draws plaudits from commentators who annoy the folks back home with meddling ob-

servations on southern life. Arnall was accused by his opponents of
"smug snobbery" and portrayed as having traded his loyalty to
Georgia for the pottage of outside approval.[96]

After leaving the governor's office, Arnall continued to display an interest in politics. For a brief period he served in the Truman administration as director of the Office of Price Stabilization. President Truman
offered him the position of United States solicitor general, but Arnall
declined.[97] In the 1948 gubernatorial campaign Arnall supported the
unsuccessful candidacy of Melvin E. Thompson against Herman Talmadge. Arnall considered seeking the governor's office in 1950 but finally decided not to do so. At one point he strongly hinted that he might
run for governor in the 1954 election. He did not. In 1958 he reluctantly
withdrew his name from consideration as a gubernatorial candidate.
During the desegregation crisis in Georgia, Arnall threatened to be a
candidate for governor in 1962 if the public schools were not kept open.
The schools remained open, and Arnall did not enter the 1962 campaign.[98]

Arnall returned to Georgia politics as a gubernatorial candidate in
1966 after being out of office for almost two decades. He received a
plurality of 29.4 percent of the vote in the Democratic primary in which
six candidates entered. Prior to the 1966 primary, Arnall would have
been the nominee, since state law required only a plurality vote for
nomination; however, the state's election code had been changed in the
Sanders administration to require a majority vote for nomination. In a
run-off election, Lester G. Maddox defeated Arnall by receiving 54.3
percent of the vote.[99]

Arnall provided Georgia with responsible and capable leadership as
governor. His aborted political career was not only his personal loss but
a loss for his state as well. Arnall had much to offer. Unfortunately, the
opportunity to serve Georgia never came his way again.

Governor You Will Be

ELLIS G. ARNALL

I have the happy privilege of having been the youngest governor in the nation when I became chief executive of Georgia, and according to the statistics and figures I am now the oldest living former Georgia governor, being seventy-eight years of age. However, age is not to be reckoned by the calendar, but by the spirit, by the attitude, by the concepts which one has.

I like to tell that I became governor of this great state by reasons of a fortune-telling contest. Having been born in Newnan at 48 Wesley Street, I went to the public schools there, and in the first grade grammar school, on Halloween, our beloved teacher, Miss Maggie Brown, had a fortune-telling contest. She took a chalk box and emptied the chalk out of it and wrote on slips of paper what we children, who drew slips from the box, would be—what profession, what business, what vocation we would follow . . ."Fireman you will be," "Banker you will be," "Policeman you will be" . . . and I drew one that said, "Governor you will be." I had no idea of what a governor was, but I took it home to Mother and she explained to me what a governor was. And, from that day on, it became my lot in life, my fate, my predestination, my luck, my privilege, God's will—whatever you may call it—to serve as chief executive of Georgia. So I like to think that my career was shaped by an incident that happened there in the first grade grammar school in my hometown, Newnan.

I became governor much sooner than I thought I would. Having attended Mercer, the University of the South, and the University of Georgia Law School, I undertook to get into public affairs because that was

my privilege and my lot. So I ran for the legislature from Coweta
County. There were five in the contest and I fortunately led the ticket
and was elected to the legislature, at the time the youngest member of
the Georgia General Assembly. Before going to the legislature I inquired
of some of my older friends who had served there, and from some of the
lawyers there in Newnan, what was the highest privileged office in the
House of Representatives, and they explained to me that the speaker of
the House was the most important but the next most important was
speaker pro tempore. So I decided that I would be speaker pro tempore.
To this end, I got in my old jalopy and went into each county in Georgia,
visiting the legislators there and listening to them talk and talking with
them. They were rather amused that a brash young freshman representative aspired to be speaker pro tempore of the House. Nevertheless, a
great majority agreed to vote for me. When the legislature convened,
there were three other candidates in the race for speaker pro tempore, all
of whom had served and were serving in the General Assembly. I, as a
neophyte, was elected speaker pro tem on the first ballot. I shall never
forget that on the opening day the speaker of the House, who was then
Ed Rivers, later governor of Georgia, threw me the gavel and asked me to
preside over the House. I had never read *Robert's Rules of Order*, knew
nothing about the procedure, but anyway, we got through the session
and I became the assistant presiding officer of the House.

My next entry into politics was after I had served two terms there as
speaker pro tem. I was appointed special assistant attorney general by
the late Governor Eugene Talmadge. In those days we were close friends.
Later we became arch political rivals. There came a vacancy in the Office of Attorney General. Governor Rivers appointed me attorney general of Georgia, the youngest in the state's history, and I ran for the full
term without opposition.

Then the prophecy of becoming governor became nearer and nearer at
hand. Governor Talmadge made the greatest political mistake in his life
when he undertook to involve himself in controversy with the Board of
Regents as to who could teach what in the schools. Because Dr. Marvin
Pittman, who was the president of the Georgia Teachers College at
Statesboro, and Dr. Walter Cocking, who was the dean of the College of
Education at the University of Georgia, were said to be teaching things
that Talmadge did not believe were true, proper, or right, he forced them
out of office by dictatorially controlling the Board of Regents. At the
time, my family and I were vacationing at Sea Island. I picked up the
Atlanta *Constitution* one morning and read where an assistant attorney
general, in my absence, had rendered an opinion that Talmadge was
perfectly right in removing the Board of Regents members to obtain a

majority so as to remove these two distinguished educators. So I was confronted with a situation. Either I remained silent and said nothing, or else I repudiated the opinion of the assistant attorney general to the effect that Talmadge was within his legal rights. I called the Associated Press and announced that the assistant attorney general's opinion was erroneous and wrong; that the governor had no right to interfere with or to meddle with educational establishments, concepts, or principles; and that he had acted illegally. Well, overnight that projected me into the race for governor, against the late Eugene Talmadge.

So I campaigned and was elected to the office of governor. At the time I was thirty-five. I was in and out of the office of governor before I was forty, and it was a lot of pleasure. It was a great privilege to serve as chief executive of Georgia. Now, at that time the war was in progress and I became the wartime governor. I am by nature a mover and a shaker. I think holding public office, just sitting there keeping the seat warm, would not be much fun. I was constantly in fights and issues, constantly shocking people, constantly having a good time, leading the state into ways that had never been envisioned, but which, by reason of the times, were on the horizon.

The first thing I did was to create a constitutional Board of Regents and a constitutional Board of Education, staggering members' terms so that no governor could control the educational institutions of the state. I insisted that the withering hand of the politician must be removed from the throats of the educators, that in proper education you are free to teach any issue and present any position. It's up to the student to embrace it or not to embrace it.

Georgia was reaccredited by the Southern Association of Colleges and Secondary Schools, since, under the Talmadge order, we had lost our standing. The Board of Regents and the State Board of Education were constitutionally created when I was governor of Georgia. I am proud to say we spent more of the state's income for education, percentage-wise, than has ever before or since been spent. We spent a majority of the money that came into the state treasury on the cause of education. Education is the hope of today and tomorrow. It is the cure for ignorance, the cure for prejudice, the cure for disease, the cure for poverty; it holds the future, not only of the individuals, but of our entire state. It is the most important thing in state government. Incidentally, in connection with education, my administration created the Teacher Retirement System. Another thing that we did was to create the program of educating doctors at the state's expense who would agree to go into rural Georgia and serve the health needs of the people. That program was efficient and well conceived. I am proud of that contribution.

I undertook to fiscally straighten out our state. For the first time and the only time in Georgia's history, we paid the state completely out of debt without raising taxes a penny. Before that time and since that time Georgia has never been out of debt.

Another thing that we did in which I take great pride is that the legislature enacted each of the platform pledges that I had made to the people without a single vote against a single one. As a matter of fact, this is the only time in the history of the state that every proposal of a governor in his original campaign platform was enacted without a vote against a single proposal; all were enacted unanimously. I have always realized that the strength of democracy is the will of the people, that all of the ills of government can be readily cured by a larger dose of democracy! So I wanted to expand the voting rights of the people of this state and to that end we set out to do so.

The first thing I wanted was to do away with the poll tax. The poll tax was deep in the hearts of many people, and I remember when I went up to the legislature to ask the members to do away with it I thought I would be lynched because there was so much feeling against my concept. Then I went back to the legislature and I told the members that they had to run in the middle of my four-year term, because their terms were for only two years, and that I loved all the legislators. They were good to me. They had enacted my program without a vote against it and now I had a new program and I wanted them to do away with the poll tax and because I wanted them reelected. I had an opinion from the attorney general which I read to them. It held that if the legislature failed to remove the poll tax I, as governor, had the right to suspend the payment of the tax until the next meeting of the General Assembly. So I said to them, "I don't want to have to do this, because if I do, when you are running for reelection, they'll say that if it wasn't for Governor Arnall they couldn't even vote. I want to give you full credit, I want you to return to the legislature because you are good men, good women and we need you." So when my message got across, the legislature did away very quickly with the poll tax. That was the end of Georgia's requirement that it was necessary to pay for the right to vote.

Then, the next thing I wanted was to drop the voting age to eighteen because so many young people had helped me in my campaign for governor. I was very near and dear to them and they were very near and dear to me and I wanted them to have the franchise right. So I proposed that we do away with the twenty-one-year-old requirement and let everyone at eighteen vote. Now, we were at war, so I arranged with the Veterans Hospital to send over to the legislature, when I spoke, all of the cripples, all of those who had been maimed and injured in the war who were in the hospital here, and we filled the gallery with wounded men, some in wheelchairs, who had suffered injuries from the war and they completely filled the halls of the capitol. So, when I made my speech, here were these young men whom we had called upon to fight for our liberties and yet they couldn't vote. We of this over-wise and cynical generation had plunged our nation into war and now we had called on these young people to save our souls, save our lives, and save our country. It was only right that they have the franchise privilege. With that great outpouring of veterans strength, the legislature very quickly dropped the voting age to eighteen. Georgia became the first state in the Union to lower the voting age to eighteen. We did it more than two decades before the national government did it and it has worked fine. We need to get more young people interested in politics. We need the idealism of youth in politics. We enacted the best soldier vote law in the nation, and though we had been restricted to only about 500,000 Georgia voters, with the stroke of the pen and with the help of the legislature we increased the registered vote in Georgia to over a million! We moved Georgia forward! There is nothing wrong with government that a participation of the young people won't cure.

Another thing that happened to Georgia, back before I was governor: our state had gotten a bad name for the fact that we were inhumane in our prison system. I saw a great movie, *I Am a Fugitive from a Georgia Chain Gang*. I said then, when I saw the picture, that when I got to be governor we were going to do something about the reformation of our prison system, and we did that. We did away with barbaric and inhumane treatment, we did away with the stripes, we did away with the shackles and the iron cages. We undertook to bring about reformation in the prisons and teaching the inmates in the prisons how they could become gainful employees and good citizens after they had served their prison terms. The prison reform program gave Georgia a good name throughout the nation.

From the time of the Civil War, the War Between the States, we in the South had been economically penalized. It cost on an average of 39 percent more to ship manufactured goods the same distance from the South to the North as it did from the North to the South. As a result, we had little industry in the South. We were drawers of water and hewers of timber. We in the South were merely a colonial appendage, somewhat like Ireland is to the United Kingdom. I decided then that when this prophecy that I would be governor was fulfilled I was going to do something effective and drastic to readmit the South into the Union on the basis of full fellowship and full equality. So Georgia, first of all, brought suit against the Ku Klux Klan and the asphalt companies for conspiracy. We were denied the right to do that because the state was not "a person," but we took the case to the Supreme Court of the United States and with the help of the attorneys general from other states, who filed *amicus curia* briefs, the Supreme Court held that Georgia was "a person" under the antitrust law and could bring suit.

I filed the case as attorney general and argued the case in the U.S. Supreme Court as governor against twenty-two of the nation's leading railroads, accusing them of conspiracy to violate the Sherman Antitrust Act. The result was that Georgia for the first time in its history was able to compete with the North in the shipment of manufactured goods. We have witnessed a great movement of industry from the North to the South. We have congenial people here, the climate is good, and now that we can compete on equal terms the Sunbelt is the fastest growing section of our nation.

Illustrative of this is that there was a peanut butter factory down in Dawson, Georgia. It made Cinderella Peanut Butter, but it was cheaper to send the raw peanuts from Dawson to Chicago and have them made into peanut butter and send the peanut butter back to Atlanta than it was to ship the finished peanut butter from Dawson to Atlanta. There was a disparity of over 1,200 miles. That's what we were up against.

When I look out of my window today and see the great buildings here in Atlanta, see the industrialization and thrust of our state and realize that our income is up, that the welfare of the people is up, I can't help but take pride in the fact that we did, through the case of *Georgia vs. Pennsylvania Railroad et al.*, readmit the South and Georgia to the Union with complete equality. Georgia is God's Garden Spot now! I take great pride in the fact that they had talked about freight rate inequality for years, but no one had been able to do anything effective about it, and yet our concept was such that we were able to force the Interstate Commerce Commission to equalize rates by going directly to the United States Supreme Court and obtaining the results we wanted. So, when I look out today, I would have to say that of all the things that I was able to do with the help of the people, the legislature, and the news media, the thing that is the most lasting, that will be the hallmark of the Arnall administration for all time, is that we broke the freight-rate shackles that had so long bound and impoverished the South. That was why we had bigotry and poverty in the South. There were not enough jobs to go around. We only had half of a loaf of bread for all of our people. We kept the black man in the ditch along with the white man because they were fighting, one with the other, for economic survival. I'm glad that Georgia's industrialization and economy, due to this great move, has expanded so that today we are moving forward and have overcome to a large extent the bigotry and poverty that had haunted our state.

There were many other things that we did that were important. For example, our Supreme Court had six justices. We created another justice so there would be seven on the court and there could no longer be divided opinions. We wrote a new constitution in 1945 and undertook to create greater home rule. Another thing that we did was that we created and installed the merit system for state employees so that no longer could the politicians fire efficient people just to put some political friend in a job. We have the merit system and I take pride in having been the sponsor and founder of that system which has worked so well. We improved the facilities at Milledgeville to afford better treatment for those there, and I am proud of the fact that one of the buildings at Central State Hospital is named the Arnall Building. I have always believed that the underprivileged and those with infirmities should receive proper attention from the state.

Georgia became, under our administration, the model of state government. There was scarcely a day that newspaper people weren't here from Los Angeles or New York to see what was making Georgia "tick." Up until I became governor, unfortunately, they wrote about the sins of our state and our people and they had very little to say or do about praising us. But, due to the fact that we moved Georgia forward at a time during the war when we could do so, when these changes were inevitable and had to come, we pushed Georgia out in front and it became a leader. And so it was that Dr. E. Merton Coulter in his history of Georgia said, "Arnall was the most dramatically constuctive governor Georgia had had within the memory of its oldest inhabitant. Too often previously, the attention of the nation had been directed toward Georgia and her ills and sins and the sins of her leaders. And feature writers came here to write articles discrediting our state, but now everyone who came came to praise Georgia and her young governor." And so it is that Georgia gained the spotlight of favorable, commendable, and progressive history.

So it was fun being governor. I look back on my service with great pleasure. I don't know of anything that I would do differently than what I did. I was criticized, but that's the price of progress. Any leader who takes the initiative is going to get opposition. The strength of your progress is largely measured by the strength of your opposition.

So I am very happy and glad that in the first grade grammar school, Temple Avenue School in Newnan, Georgia, on Halloween, Miss Maggie Brown, our teacher, had a fortune-telling contest and I drew a slip that said, "Governor you will be," and I have appreciated that privilege. I have appreciated the faith, the confidence, the vote of the people who made that possible.

M. E. Thompson

1947 – 1948

M. E. Thompson
and the Politics
of Succession

HAROLD P. HENDERSON

In November 1946 Melvin Ernest Thompson was elected Georgia's first lieutenant governor. Although Thompson's election was historic in itself, the moment was dwarfed by Eugene Talmadge's election to a fourth gubernatorial term.[1] Thompson seemed destined to serve in the shadow of Georgia's legendary "wild man from Sugar Creek," but Talmadge's unexpected death in December 1946, prior to his inauguration, dramatically altered Thompson's future and thrust him into the center of one of the most controversial episodes in Georgia political history.[2]

Unfortunately for the state, the Constitution of 1945 failed to specify who would assume executive authority in January if a governor-elect died before taking the oath of office. Article v, section 1 of the constitution provided three possible interpretations as to who Arnall's successor should be. Paragraph 1 provided that the incumbent governor would hold office for four years "and until his successor shall be chosen and qualified." Paragraph vii stipulated that "in case of the death, resignation or disability of the Governor, the Lieutenant Governor shall exercise the executive power." Paragraph iv provided that the person receiving the majority vote in the general election would be governor, "but, if no person shall have such majority, then from the two persons having the highest number of votes, who shall be in life, and shall not decline an election at the time appointed for the General Assembly to elect, the General Assembly shall immediately elect a Governor."

Talmadge's demise created an instantaneous debate concerning which of these provisions applied. Thompson, as lieutenant governor-elect, found himself at the center of the controversy. The mild-mannered Thompson seemed unsuited for the political Donnybrook which lay ahead. Born in Millen, Georgia, on May 1, 1903, Thompson spent his youth in rural Georgia and made a decision to enter the education profession. He graduated from Emory University in 1926 and began an educational career as a high school principal and coach at Emanuel County Institute. He earned a master's degree from the University of Georgia and completed most of the requirements for a doctorate. In 1927 Thompson became superintendent of the Hawkinsville public school system, where he served until 1933. In 1933 he became a state school supervisor, a position he held until 1937 when Governor E. D. Rivers appointed him assistant state school superintendent. Thompson served in that capacity until 1943.[3]

His role at the state level encouraged his interest in politics. Thompson actively supported Ellis Arnall's successful gubernatorial campaign in 1942, and Arnall rewarded him by naming him his executive secretary. Later, Arnall appointed him to the position of state revenue commissioner. As the 1946 Democratic primary neared, Thompson planned to run for state school superintendent. Arnall agreed to support his candidacy. Frank C. Gross, who had served as presiding officer of the State Senate during the Arnall administration, sought and received Arnall's promise of support in his campaign for the lieutenant governorship. In the meantime, Thompson changed his mind about running for the superintendency and decided to run for the lieutenant governorship. By then, Arnall was committed to Gross, who had been instrumental in getting his legislative program through the upper house. Thus, despite his close association with Arnall, Thompson ran without his benefactor's support.[4]

During the primary Thompson avoided identifying himself with any of the gubernatorial candidates—Talmadge, Rivers, or James V. Carmichael. Instead, he promised to work with whomever the people elected governor. Thompson apparently avoided taking a stand on the white primary, which was a major issue in the governor's race. Prior to the 1946 primary the federal courts had invalidated the state-regulated Democratic Party's white primary. Talmadge, among others, sought to salvage the white primary by converting the state's Democratic Party into a private association with its primaries unregulated by state law. Citing the possibility of massive fraud and corruption in unregulated primaries, Arnall refused to go along with this effort and urged compliance with the federal rulings. Arnall's decision permitted blacks to vote in the 1946 primary. While Talmadge promised to restore the white primary, Carmichael (who was supported by Arnall) and Rivers sided with Arnall on the issue.[5]

The gubernatorial contest naturally overshadowed the quest for the state's second highest office, but the battle for the lieutenant governorship was hard fought. Six candidates sought the nomination for the new office, which had been created by the Constitution of 1945. Thompson won the crowded primary with 29.6 percent of the popular vote and 46.8 percent of the county unit vote.[6] With no opposition in the general election, he began immediately to prepare for his new responsibilities. Eugene Talmadge's unexpected death in December forced him to consider a larger duty. He assumed that he would succeed to the governor's chair, as though Talmadge had already taken office, but events quickly dispelled the notion that others accepted this view.

Governor Arnall made his position known on December 24. Arnall contended he could stay in office for another four years because of the death of the governor-elect. However, he explained that he had no desire to continue in office under those conditions. Like Thompson, he argued that the people had chosen a lieutenant governor to succeed to the governorship if the governor elected were unable to serve. Arnall concluded that it was his constitutional duty to remain in office until "the lieutenant governor has been installed in office and he can succeed under constitutional provision."[7]

Speaker of the House Roy Vincent Harris and six other prominent Talmadge leaders issued a statement concerning succession on December 26. They contended that Eugene Talmadge had been elected because of his platform to restore the white primary, retain the county unit system, and expand state services. The Talmadge leaders accused Arnall of trying to dictate his successor in the present situation as he had in the recent primary, when he supported Carmichael against Eugene Talmadge in order to destroy the white primary. Fortunately, they declared, the constitution provided a way to elect a governor who would carry out Talmadge's platform. They claimed the General Assembly had the duty of choosing the next governor from the two candidates receiving the highest number of write-in votes in the general election.[8]

Several individuals had received write-in votes for governor in the 1946 election. The majority of these went to three persons: Herman E. Talmadge, the governor-elect's son, who received 675 votes; Carmichael, the governor-elect's major primary opponent, who received 669 votes, and D. Talmadge Bowers, who received 637 votes. The Talmadge leaders called upon all Georgians interested in expanding state services, maintaining the county unit system, and restoring the white primary to join them "in a campaign for the election of Herman Talmadge as Governor of this State by the Legislature."[9]

Herman Talmadge issued his first statement on the question on December 27. "My father gave his life," Talmadge said, "fighting for those principles which he believed best for the people of Georgia." He considered it his duty to carry on his father's fight for these principles. Unfortunately, he explained, the state constitution did not provide for a special election in the circumstances which the state faced. Therefore, Talmadge contended that it was mandatory for the General Assembly to elect a governor from the two candidates receiving the highest number of write-in votes. He urged all Georgians to inform their representatives in the General Assembly whom they desired for their governor.[10]

Shortly after Eugene Talmadge's funeral, Thompson made his position known. He announced that he intended to assume executive authority because the people had elected him lieutenant governor for the purpose of succeeding to the governorship in the event of death, disability, or resignation of the governor. "Unfortunately for all concerned," Thompson stated, "the people's choice for Governor has died. They [the people], therefore expect me to take his place. I shall not shirk this responsibility." Thompson expressed the hope "that no one will dare resort to trickery or legal technicalities in order to thwart the expressed will of the people."[11]

To counter the Herman Talmadge claim that only he could carry out the Democratic Party's platform, Thompson sent telegrams to all lawmakers emphasizing his commitment to implement the platform. He insisted the platform "can best and more quickly be adopted by the Legislature permitting the law of succession to operate without hindrance." Moreover, Thompson argued that the only thing the General Assembly could do concerning the succession question was to declare the results of the general election.[12]

Talmadge immediately attacked Thompson's claim to the governorship. "The opposition has no more claim on the governor's office," he stated, "than any other man or woman in Georgia." Talmadge charged that the forces which had opposed his father in the primary were using Thompson as a "stalking horse" to destroy the county unit system and the white primary.[13] He claimed the issue in the present "race" was the same as in the recent primary. "All the forces who destroyed the white primary in Georgia and fought its return last summer," Talmadge stated, "are now supporting Mr. Thompson." Among these supporters he listed "the Negro press and Henry A. Wallace and his crowd of pinks."[14] Furthermore, he accused former Governor Rivers, who supported Thompson's claim, Arnall, and the Atlanta *Journal* of joining together "to foist M. E. Thompson on the people of Georgia and destroy forever in this state the white primary."[15] Talmadge reminded Georgians that "the fight I am making is a white man's fight to keep Georgia a white man's state."[16]

Refuting Talmadge's charges that he would sabotage the Democratic Party's platform, Thompson promised to carry it out "without changing the simple dotting of an 'i' or the crossing of a 't.'" He even claimed to have assisted in drafting the white primary bill. In defending his loyalty to the platform, Thompson went so far as to pledge to appoint only persons "who sincerely believe in preserving the white primary and the county unit system and expanding state services."[17] He expressed hope that once he took office the legislature would immediately enact into law every plank of the Democratic platform. "I hope that the first bill I have the privilege of signing as acting governor," Thompson added, "will be the one guaranteeing a Democratic white primary."[18]

While Thompson and Talmadge argued over who could best carry out the Democratic Party's platform, Arnall sought aid from the state attorney general in the succession question. Attorney General Eugene Cook responded with a ruling on January 3, upholding Arnall's right to remain in office until his successor qualified. Designating the lieutenant governor-elect as Arnall's successor, Cook held that Thompson would assume the executive power of the state upon his qualification and Arnall's resignation. The attorney general held that the constitutional provision authorizing the legislature to elect a governor applied only when a candidate failed to receive a majority of the votes cast for governor and that the legislature could not disregard a majority of votes "simply because the person receiving same was at that time or subsequently became incapacitated to fill said office."[19]

Talmadge immediately denounced Cook's ruling as a political decision that was not binding on the legislature. Contending that the legislature was a sovereign body, he claimed its decision in this matter was not reviewable by the courts.[20]

As early as December 21 Frederick Barrow Hand, who was Eugene Talmadge's choice for speaker of the House, had called for a special election to determine Arnall's successor. However, Arnall pointed out that there was no provision for such an election in the 1945 constitution. He contended that the quickest way for the people to decide the governorship was to allow Thompson to become acting governor.[21] However, on January 6 six freshman solons announced that they had found a way to hold a special election legally. They cited a provision of the Constitution of 1945 that provided the legislature had the power to fill unexpired terms by special elections. The lawmakers called upon both claimants to state whether they would abide by the results of such an election.[22]

Talmadge responded by declaring that he would participate in a special election provided the General Assembly elected him governor first. If defeated in the special election, Talmadge promised to resign. He explained that such a procedure was "the only plan that will insure the people . . . an opportunity to name their own governor for the next four years."[23]

Thompson argued that a special election would be illegal. If the legislature elected Talmadge, he maintained, Talmadge supporters could file suit against an illegal special election and the courts would have to rule in favor of such a suit. As a result, Thompson argued, Talmadge, once elected by the legislature, would be governor for four years. Thompson also expressed opposition to a special election because "Negroes would vote in such a special election, and it would be based on the popular vote and not on the county unit vote." He maintained those who "sincerely believed" in the county unit system and the white primary could not subscribe to such a procedure.[24]

Although Talmadge and Thompson were the main contenders for the governorship, other individuals also laid claim to the office. Denying that he was a Republican, Talmadge Bowers claimed the legislature should elect him governor.[25] James V. Carmichael, one of the recipients of write-in votes in the general election, removed himself from consideration in a legislative election. "I will not seek the office," he stated on December 21, 1946, "and I would not accept it even if I were elected."[26] With the elimination of Carmichael, the Talmadge forces contended that the General Assembly had to choose between Bowers and the son of Eugene Talmadge. However, in a dinner speech before a group of 250 guests on January 13, 1947, Herman Talmadge went ever further, claiming that the legislature was not restricted to write-in candidates but could elect *anybody* governor.[27]

The legislature met in joint session on January 14 to resolve the issue. Prior to the session a resolution was introduced in the House inviting Talmadge and Thompson to appear and state whether they favored a special election. The resolution called upon each of the claimants to state whether he would call a special election when he assumed the governorship. The House defeated this resolution by a vote of 86 to 17.[28]

In the joint session Representative J. Robert Elliott, the Talmadge floor leader, introduced a resolution creating a committee to tabulate the returns of the general election. The resolution, providing that separate reports be made for each of the nine statehouse offices, stipulated that the report on the governor's office be considered first and that no action be taken on other returns until final action had been taken on the election of a governor. Representatives Charles L. Gowen and Adie N. Durden, Thompson supporters, sought to amend Elliott's resolution. The Durden-Gowen amendment provided for the publication of all general election returns "before any business is transacted." If the Durden-Gowen amendment had been adopted, Thompson's status would have changed from lieutenant governor-elect to lieutenant governor with an indisputable constitutional claim to the governorship. Elliott's resolution, on the other hand, sought to keep Thompson in the position of lieutenant governor-elect until after the governorship issue had been settled. The lawmakers voted on the Durden-Gowen amendment first and defeated it by a vote of 128 to 126, a narrow Talmadge victory. The legislature then unanimously passed Elliott's resolution. The presiding officer appointed a committee to tablulate the results of the governor's election. The results, to the amazement of many Talmadge supporters, showed that Carmichael had received 669 write-in votes, Bowers, 637, and Herman Talmadge, 617.[29]

With the report of the tabulating committee, Talmadge's hopes of becoming governor appeared doomed. The Talmadge supporters had insisted that the General Assembly had to elect a governor from the two recipients of the highest number of write-in votes in the general election. By that standard, Talmadge was out of the running, and the lawmakers had to choose between Bowers and Carmichael, providing either would accept such an election. Bowers had expressed his willingness to accept election as governor by the legislature, while Carmichael, in his statement on December 21, had denied any interest in assuming the governorship by legislative decision. However, Representative Pierre Howard claimed that as soon as the tabulating committee made its report "rumors flew thick and fast that Jimmie Carmichael was on the way to the Capitol to state that he would accept the Governorship." Howard, who had supported Carmichael in the primary, rushed to Arnall's office and questioned the governor about the rumors. Howard reported that Arnall confirmed the reports and declared, "We are reversing our position and we are going to elect him [Carmichael] and I will surrender the office to him."[30] However, Arnall denied that he had ever made such a statement to Howard. Furthermore, Arnall said, "I never undertook to persuade Carmichael to let the legislature elect him because I didn't think that they [the legislators] had the right to."[31]

If both Bowers and Carmichael were willing to accept a legislative election, Talmadge was eliminated from consideration by the General Assembly on the basis of the much-publicized arguments of the Talmadge faction. As noted earlier, Talmadge had claimed on January 13 that the legislature could elect anyone governor, whether a recipient of write-in votes or not. Whether he would have pushed this claim could have proven highly interesting, but events took a different turn.

Following the write-in tabulation, the Telfair County delegation immediately challenged as incorrect the number of write-in votes for Herman Talmadge from that county. Upon checking the returns, the committee found fifty-eight additional write-in votes for Talmadge. The Telfair County ordinary supposedly had incorrectly placed the fifty-eight votes in question in an envelope marked "Constitutional Officers" instead of one designated "Governor." This discovery gave Talmadge first place in write-in votes with 675.[32] Now, according to the Talmadge interpretation, he was eligible to be elected governor by the legislature. Talmadge's position was made stronger when Ralph McGill reported in the Atlanta *Constitution* that Carmichael had reiterated his opposition to being elected by the legislature.[33]

Resuming efforts for an immediate Talmadge election, Representative Elliott introduced a resolution declaring that due to the death of Eugene Talmadge no person had received a majority of the votes cast for governor. Since there had been no election, the resolution concluded that the legislature had the duty of electing the next governor. Representative Durden offered a substitute resolution contending that Eugene Talmadge had been elected governor. The lawmakers defeated Durden's resolution, 132 to 118, and adopted Elliott's, 137 to 114. Elliott then nominated Herman Talmadge for a four-year term as governor. At 1:50 A.M., January 15, 1947, 161 legislators elected Talmadge governor. Eighty-seven members of the General Assembly voted against his election by voting "present." Immediately, Talmadge took the oath of office and delivered an inaugural address. He promised that if the legislature passed a special election bill he would sign it and would be a candidate in the ensuing campaign. He emphasized that the restoration of the white primary was to be the chief objective of his administration.[34]

Following his address Talmadge, escorted by a committee of twenty-five legislators, proceeded to the governor's office, which was still occupied by Arnall. Harris, Eugene Talmadge's widow, and a host of Talmadge supporters also accompanied the newly elected governor. When Talmadge and his entourage reached the executive offices, they found the outer doors locked. Two Talmadge supporters quickly eliminated this obstacle by battering down the doors. Moments later Talmadge confronted Arnall and a brief exchange of words ensued. Talmadge asked Arnall whether he was aware of the legislature's action. Arnall replied that he was, and then told the delegation that "the governorship belongs to the people and cannot be decided by the Legislature." Arnall dubbed Talmadge a "pretender" and refused to yield the office of governor to him. Talmadge, declaring that his purpose was not to create disorder, turned and walked out of the governor's office. Before leaving the capitol, he appealed to his supporters to avoid violence and go home.[35]

Talmadge returned to the capitol on January 15 and set up his office in the reception room of the executive offices. Besides appointing an adjutant general on his first day as governor of the state of Georgia, Talmadge also appointed a highway patrol commander, a revenue commissioner, a highway director, and a parks commissioner. Officials who had been appointed to these same positions by Arnall refused to recognize the new appointments. The rival highway patrol commanders, claiming to be the best of friends, sat behind the same desk.[36]

On January 16 Thompson supporters in the legislature sought to adjourn the General Assembly until the courts had ruled on the dispute. Adjournment resolutions were introduced in both houses. Speaker Fred B. Hand, however, asserted that the legislature would not adjourn since "we know who is governor because we elected him."[37] The House defeated the adjournment resolution by a vote of 114 to 65. The Senate simply ignored the resolution and confirmed Talmadge nominees for commissioner of revenue, adjutant general, and highway director.[38]

Earlier the same day Talmadge took possession of the executive offices and had the locks changed before Arnall arrived. Once in the governor's office, he proclaimed, "I am now in full control of the State of Georgia. Georgia now has but one governor." Unable to gain entrance to the governor's office, Arnall announced his intentions to remain governor until the lieutenant governor-elect assumed the executive powers. He said he would set up his office at the information booth in the capitol rotunda. Admitting what he was doing was "unpleasant and distasteful," he nevertheless claimed it was his "duty to preserve the office for the Lieutenant Governor." Arnall eventually moved the "governor's office" to his Atlanta law office.[39]

Mass meetings were held throughout the state protesting and defending Herman Talmadge's legislative election. Many of the gatherings called for the controversy to be settled by the courts.[40] An organization founded as a result of one meeting, the Aroused Citizens of Georgia, called upon Talmadge and Thompson to go on record "as recognizing the power and authority of our courts to decide the issue."[41] As early as January 15 Arnall had ordered the attorney general to bring legal action against Talmadge's claim to the governorship.[42] Talmadge, when asked what he would do if the suit went against him, replied, "Nothing. The governorship is exclusively the province of the General Assembly."[43] On another occasion he declared that the legislature's "action in this matter is not subject to review by the courts, since it would be an encroachment by the judicial branch of the government upon the legislative branch."[44] Harris also contended that "this is one of those situations where the Legislature has jurisdiction and not the courts."[45]

Arnall accused the Talmadge forces of fearing court adjudication because "they know the courts will determine the issue against those who have usurped the office of governor."[46] Talmadge's position, the Atlanta

Journal observed, meant the judiciary "shall have no voice in deciding the most critical question that has faced Georgia in the last eighty years."[47] Talmadge denied having claimed that he would not abide by a court decision. Nevertheless, he reiterated his claim that the courts had no jurisdiction in the matter. "But should I be wrong," he admitted, "I will, of course, abide by the courts' decision."[48] Talmadge accused his opposition of boasting of having "stacked the Supreme Court of Georgia against us." Nevertheless, he said, the court would uphold his claim because "our legal position is correct and members of the Supreme Court are honorable men."[49]

So far, Thompson had kept silent—"quiet as a porcelain nest egg," according to *Time* magazine.[50] On January 18 he took the oath as lieutenant governor. He then announced his intentions of assuming the executive powers in the capacity of acting governor until the people could elect themselves a governor. Thompson also said he would call upon Talmadge to evacuate the executive office and mansion at a very early date. Attorney General Cook immediately recognized Thompson as acting governor. Thompson then appointed an executive secretary, an adjutant general, a revenue commissioner, a highway director, and members of the highway board.[51]

Upon hearing of Thompson's qualification, Arnall resigned and made a speech supporting Thompson.[52] When Talmadge learned that Thompson had taken the oath of office as lieutenant governor, he accused him of threatening to recruit an army and take the governor's office by force. Warning Thompson that he would not yield to force, Talmadge declared, "We are amply able to defend the governor's office and will do so if necessary." Thompson belittled the idea that he intended to use violence in the matter.[53] He contended the controversy should be settled by the courts and promised to abide by the courts' decision.[54]

On January 20 Thompson confronted Talmadge in the governor's office, where Talmadge told him, "You have no right to claim the office. There is no vacancy. The General Assembly of Georgia elected me governor."[55] Thompson left the executive offices and proceeded to the Senate chambers, where he took an oath to "faithfully exercise the executive power of the State."[56] Startled Talmadge supporters in the Senate reacted quickly. Senator Iris Faircloth Blitch thought it "ridiculous in the eyes of the nation for the Senate to join in electing Talmadge governor and then hear another man take the oath of executive office." She promised to lead an effort to remove Thompson's executive oath from the *Senate Journal*.[57]

On the same day, over the opposition of the Thompson legislative forces, Talmadge was invited to address a joint session of the General Assembly, by a vote of 29 to 20 in the Senate and 86 to 64 in the House.[58]

Representative Durden had unsuccessfully sought to include Thompson's name in the invitation, but Representative Elliott objected to hearing Thompson because "he is not the Governor." In response, Durden expressed his unwillingness to invite a man "who has only squatters rights to the governorship."[59]

Prior to Talmadge's address to the legislature on January 21, Thompson urged that body to adjourn until the courts had ruled in the dispute. He warned that if such a decision went against Talmadge, all legislative measures he had signed would be invalid. Thompson also challenged Talmadge to an electoral battle as soon as an election could be held under the constitution. When the time came for Talmadge to address that joint session, many representatives walked out of the House chambers. Senatorial opponents left the capitol instead of walking over to the House chambers. Observers estimated that no more than half of the lawmakers heard the speech.[60]

In his address Talmadge denied using force or executing a military coup d'etat to gain the governorship. He urged the legislature to enact the white primary bill and to provide additional revenue for the promised expansion of state services. Talmadge noted that the constitution provided for a special election within sixty days if both the governor and lieutenant governor resigned. He promised to resign as soon as the legislature enacted the Democratic Party's platform if Thompson did likewise, and to go before the people in a white primary.[61]

Talmadge's melodramatic speech provoked a response from Thompson almost immediately. For him to agree to Talmadge's proposal would be "an insult to the People," Thompson said. He explained that the governorship and the lieutenant governorship belonged "to the people and are not private property to be traded or trafficked in." Moreover, he insisted that the purpose behind the proposal was to avoid court adjudication. Talmadge replied, "He is afraid of the white people of Georgia."[62]

The day following his address, Talmadge suffered his first setback in the legislature. Efforts on the part of his supporters to remove Thompson's executive oath from the *Senate Journal* failed because of a tie vote.[63] Moreover, the Senate postponed consideration of a list of appointments from Talmadge.[64] Seeking to take advantage of these Talmadge setbacks, Thompson urged the legislature to adjourn. On January 27 the House defeated an adjournment resolution by a vote of 115 to 82 and the Senate confirmed eighteen Talmadge nominations.[65] Thompson refused to send any nominations to the Senate, "to spare my friends the embarrassment of not being paid."[66]

Despite Talmadge's strong support in the General Assembly, he encountered difficulty in enacting his legislative program. Talmadge considered the white primary bill, the appropriations bill, and a sales tax bill to finance expanded state services the most important measures before the legislature.[67]

On January 20 the white primary bill was introduced in the House. When hearings opened, the committee room was jammed with people who seemed determined to speak against the bill. They were not all Atlanta liberals. Helen D. Longstreet, the widow of Confederate General James Augustus Longstreet and a symbol of the Old South, told the committee to bury the bill "too deep for resurrection." The bill also came under bitter attack from the state's press.[68] Despite such opposition, the House passed the white primary bill by a vote of 133 to 62.[69]

The following day the House, by a vote of 133 to 6, approved the Talmadge administration's appropriations bill. The bill provided $77,658,538 for existing state services and $38,422,026 for the promised expanded state services. However, the latter sum was made contingent upon whether new taxes were raised to finance the new services.[70] On March 5 the House passed a sales tax measure by a vote of 121 to 71. Ignoring another Thompson appeal to adjourn, the Senate passed the white primary bill by a vote of 36 to 15.[71] After ironing out differences over a Senate amendment, the General Assembly presented Talmadge the first major bill of the 1947 session. On February 20, with Harris at his side, Talmadge signed the white primary bill.[72] With one of his three important bills enacted into law, the other two moved toward the same goal. On March 5 the Senate Finance Committee recommended passage of the Talmadge administration's appropriation bill. On March 13 another Senate committee approved the House-passed sales tax bill. Immediate Senate passage of both was expected.[73]

In the meantime, several suits had been filed in superior courts concerning the controversy. Eventually the issue reached the Georgia Supreme Court.[74] On March 19, 1947, the high court ended the sixty-three days of dual governorship when it upheld Thompson's claim to the executive office in a 5 to 2 decision. The majority opinion, written by Presiding Justice William Henry Duckworth, addressed two questions: did the courts have jurisdiction in the dispute and did the General Assembly exceed its authority in electing Talmadge? On the first question, counsel for Talmadge had argued the courts lacked jurisdiction for two reasons. First, the legislature's election of Talmadge was a "purely political question" over which the courts had no right of review. Second, the legislature, in electing Talmadge, was exercising powers conferred upon it by the constitution, which removed the action from court jurisdiction. Duckworth rejected these arguments. He held that the court did have jurisdiction because the dispute involved interpretation of the constitution regarding the authority of the legislature to elect a governor. Having disposed of the jurisdictional issue, Duckworth then dealt with the central question of whether the legislature had exceeded its authority in electing Talmadge governor. He declared that the power to elect a governor was reserved to the people with only one exception. When the voters failed to cast a majority of their votes for a gubernatorial candidate, Duckworth said, the constitution gave the legislature the power to elect a governor. In this case, he concluded, the legislature had erred in assuming elective power on January 15, 1947, because Eugene Talmadge had received a majority of the votes cast in the 1946 election. Therefore, any election conducted by the legislature was null and void. Once Arnall resigned, Duckworth said, Thompson automatically assumed the executive power of the state until the next general election.[75]

Arnall, upon learning of the decision, remarked, "Stealing is still unlawful in Georgia." He revealed later that he knew in advance how the Supreme Court would rule:

> Before I plunged the state into a banana republic war, I wanted to know that I was right. I knew I was right but I wanted it confirmed. So in violation of all law and legal ethics and everything else, I called one of the members of the Supreme Court down to my office and I said, "Look, if I make this fight and am wrong, I am a fool and will have embarrassed the state. If I am right in my view that I am governor for four more years and upon my resignation the lieutenant governor becomes governor, I want to know it before I pitch the battle." This dear friend of mine . . . that afternoon came back and said, "I have canvassed the reaction of the court and while they are not committed to this, I believe that a majority of the court support your view." So I wasn't just shooting in the dark and I felt that I had a right to violate the law and legal ethics because of the principle at stake, the highest office at the gift of the people was at stake, and I wanted to know that my procedure was right before I adopted the view that I did.[76]

Thompson expressed great elation over the decision and promised to begin his administration "with malice toward none and charity toward all."[77] Despite his objections to the decision, Talmadge immediately evacuated the governor's office. As he left the capitol he told reporters that "the court of last resort is the people of Georgia. This case will be taken to the court of last resort."[78] Harris, immediately announcing Talmadge's candidacy for 1948, predicted he would receive the support of three-fourths of the white people.[79]

News of the decision incited shouts of joy from Thompson supporters in the General Assembly. The Senate responded by rescinding confirmation of all Talmadge appointments.[80] Attorney General Eugene Cook ruled invalid all legislative measures signed by Talmadge. He suggested that these measures be returned to the legislature and submitted to Thompson for his approval or veto.[81] The press overwhelmingly approved the decision. The Macon *Telegraph* hailed it as "a great victory for constitutional government."[82] The Augusta *Chronicle* called it a victory for democracy over a "scheme to seize control of Georgia's electoral machinery—through the medium of the so-called 'White Primary Law'—and set up a political dictatorship."[83]

Acting Governor Thompson, speaking to a joint session of the General Assembly on March 20, proclaimed, "Today, again, law and order prevails in Georgia." He declared the effort of a small group to usurp the people's right to elect a governor had failed. While indicating a desire for a white primary, Thompson attacked the Talmadge white primary law because it would "allow fraud and stolen elections to run rampant in Georgia." Instead of that legislation, he urged the legislature to enact two bills recently introduced by his supporters. Thompson contended that these bills, if enacted into law, would result in a "fair" white primary. He reminded the legislators of the Democratic Party's platform promising expanded state services, and of the necessity to pass adequate revenue measures to carry out this promise.[84]

Thompson quickly learned that he faced a hostile opposition determined to obstruct his program, even at the risk of inconsistency. On the same day Senator Grady Coker, a Talmadge supporter, moved that the Senate postpone consideration of the sales tax bill indefinitely. By a vote of 31 to 16 the Senate agreed to the motion.[85] Senator George Everitt Millican accused Talmadge supporters, who previously had supported the sales tax bill, of now voting to kill the measure.[86] On March 20 the Senate also defeated the two measures advocated by Thompson in place of the Talmadge white primary law. The first, requiring segregation of the races at the polls, was defeated 25 to 24. The second, restoring the primary to state regulation and providing for educational requirements for voters, fell five votes short of the required majority for passage. The following day the Senate again refused to consider the sales tax bill.[87] Frustrated by this flagrant political vindictiveness, Thompson accused Talmadge supporters of voting against it "so that I cannot carry out all the pledges of the Democratic party."[88] Political factionalism had brought legislative action to a standstill.

Speaker Hand called for a special session to enact revenue measures to finance the promised expansion of state services. Thompson, however, expressed opposition to a special session. According to the Atlanta *Constitution*, Thompson leaders opposed the move because they did not think the two factions could cooperate in a special session any more than they had in the regular session. Furthermore, the Thompson leaders suspected Talmadge desired a special session as a "sounding board" for his 1948 gubernatorial campaign.[89]

As a result of the defeat of the sales tax bill, Senate President Pro Tem William T. Dean announced the appropriations bill would not be called up for further consideration by the Senate.[90] The 1945 constitution provided that if the legislature failed to pass an appropriations bill, the appropriations bill for the preceding year should be used. Dean's action sounded the death knell for the promised expanded state services, not because anyone opposed them, but simply because of political infighting.

The major issue remaining was the white primary bill. The bill, which had been signed by Talmadge, was submitted to Thompson for his consideration. Some of his close friends urged him to sign the bill to prevent Talmadge from using the white primary issue in the 1948 election. Despite such urging, Thompson vetoed the white primary bill. He claimed that the bill abolished all legal protection of elections and that it was the second step in a "conspiracy" to destroy the one-party system in Georgia. Thompson asserted the first step of this plot had been taken when Harris and "his cohorts bolted the [Democratic] party by conducting a write-in campaign against the party's nominee for governor."[91] While the Atlanta *Journal* praised Thompson for his "act of statesmanlike courage," Talmadge denounced Thompson and assured Georgians that they would have a white primary.[92]

Seldom had a governor of Georgia begun an administration under such trying conditions as Melvin Ernest Thompson did in March 1947. Two days before the General Assembly of Georgia adjourned, Thompson addressed it for the first time as chief executive. The legislature, divided by bitter factionalism, had failed to pass an appropriations bill or provide any additional revenue to implement the Democratic Party's platform of expanded state services. With Thompson's announced opposition to a special session, the legislature would not convene again until after the primary election in 1948. In the meantime, Thompson was left with the party's platform and no revenue measure to carry it out.

The General Assembly, after a historic seventy-day session, adjourned on March 22, 1947. The Atlanta *Journal* called the session, which had cost an estimated $360,000 and passed only five major bills, "fruitless and farcical."[93] Without support from the General Assembly, Thompson was forced to seek other means of fulfilling his party's promises. In this effort he did surprisingly well. By the time he entered the 1948 governor's race he could boast of a number of accomplishments. He argued that he had carried out the Democratic Party's 1946 platform without raising taxes. Instead of the $77 million in revenue that Talmadge had estimated the state would receive for the current fiscal year, Thompson contended that the state actually had received over $108 million. "Without any additional taxes," he said, "this administration has done substantially all of those things for the people that the opposition said couldn't be done without those additional levies." Thompson claimed that his administration had built more roads and bridges than any other administration over a comparable period of time. Even without new taxes, he said, his administration had spent more money for public education than the last General Assembly proposed with new taxes. Thompson proudly asserted that the state's park system had been improved and expanded for all Georgians.[94] This expansion included the acquisition of Jekyll Island as a state park, which Thompson called his proudest accomplishment.[95] He assured Georgians that there was no need for a tax increase and promised that if elected, "I'll keep a sales tax from being put on the people of Georgia."[96]

Unlike the 1946 campaign, when the leadership of the anti-Talmadge faction had been split, former Governors Rivers and Arnall united behind the Thompson candidacy. Both made speeches throughout the state on Thompson's behalf. In addition, Rivers planned campaign strategy and directed the campaign's operation.[97]

As promised, Talmadge entered the race, contending that he wanted "to continue the program that we won in '46 but lost at the hands of death."[98] Thompson found himself on the defensive because of the race issue in the 1948 campaign. Despite his opposition to the federal civil rights program and his own proposals to reinstitute the white primary and strengthen the county unit system, white Georgians committed to the racial status quo viewed Thompson with suspicion. The anti-Talmadge faction of the Georgia Democratic Party had aligned itself with the liberal wing of the national party, and Thompson actively supported President Truman. Thompson had vetoed the white primary bill in 1947 and had received many black votes in 1946.[99] In addition, two of Georgia's best-known liberal politicians, Ellis Arnall and Ed Rivers, actively supported him.

Talmadge conducted a vigorous white supremacy campaign. He promised Georgians a primary "as white as we can have" and reminded them that Thompson had vetoed the white primary bill passed in the previous session of the General Assembly.[100] He denounced the civil rights program of the Truman administration, particularly the proposed Federal Employment Practices Committee. If elected, he promised to "do all within my power to help defeat the passage of this oppressive, communistic, anti-South legislation." He assured voters that the most important plank in his platform was "my unalterable opposition to all forms of the [federal] civil rights' program."[101] On one occasion Talmadge told an audience, "I don't want your wives or your daughters to work under a Negro foreman or work beside a Negro."[102] He claimed that the "shotgun wedding" of Arnall and Rivers occurred because of their desire "to see the civil rights program thrust down the throat of the South."[103] Talmadge sought to portray Thompson as a racial liberal and a puppet of Rivers and Arnall. In other areas, especially issues relating to state services, Talmadge and Thompson took similar positions. Both favored a constitutional State Highway Board, an expanded road building program, an improved health program, increased welfare benefits, and a merit system for the state highway patrol.[104] But, ultimately, Thompson's strategy of running on his record could not compete with Talmadge's white supremacy appeal.[105]

After a bitter campaign Talmadge emerged victorious. Thompson stayed close in the popular vote, receiving 45 percent while Talmadge received almost 52 percent, but Talmadge garnered 76 percent of the county unit vote. Two years later Talmadge and Thompson squared off again over a full four-year gubernatorial term. Again, Talmadge emerged the victor, receiving 71 percent of the county unit vote.[106] In 1954 Thompson entered his last campaign for governor, coming in second to Marvin Griffin with only 14 percent of the county unit vote.[107] Thompson's final political effort occurred in 1956 when he unsuccessfully ran against Talmadge for a U.S. Senate seat. In this race he failed to receive any county unit votes and received less than 20 percent of the popular vote.[108]

Thompson's career as an elected state public official was brief. He served only two days as Georgia's first lieutenant governor and less than twenty-three months as acting governor. Because of an unanticipated increase in state revenue, Thompson managed to increase state spending during his administration without additional taxes. Unfortunately for him, he never convinced enough voters that he should ever be more than acting governor. Georgians will probably best remember Thompson because of the unusual circumstances by which he came to power and for the purchase of Jekyll Island as a state park during his administration. Joseph Tomberlin called him "a modest, low-key, perhaps even reluctant politician." Certainly, Thompson appeared modest and low-keyed when compared to the Talmadges, Ed Rivers, and Ellis Arnall, but his campaign for the lieutenant governorship, his political struggle with Herman Talmadge after the death of Eugene Talmadge, his three gubernatorial campaigns, and his senatorial campaign dispel the idea that he was a reluctant politician. However, Tomberlin correctly observed that Thompson "was largely an unsuccessful office seeker and probably never would have held center stage except for the fortuitous circumstances in late 1946 and early 1947."[109] Unfortunately for Thompson's political career, Talmadgeism proved too much of an obstacle for the acting governor to overcome.

M. E. Thompson:
Recollections

An Interview by
GENE-GABRIEL MOORE

Editors' Note: In 1976 Georgia Public Television conducted a series of interviews with former Georgia governors. The material which follows was edited from the interview with M. E. Thompson conducted at his home in Valdosta, and is published with the permission of Georgia Public Television.

MOORE: I think probably very few Georgians have had an opportunity to hear your side of the events of January 1947, when we had a very dramatic, extraordinary political episode in Georgia with two men, the lieutenant governor of the state and the son of the dead governor-elect, claiming the office of governor, and I would appreciate it if you would tell your version of those days.

THOMPSON: It was not a two-governor fight, it was a three-governor fight. Here's what happened: In 1946 I ran for lieutenant governor. Ellis Arnall did not support me; I was his executive secretary and then his revenue commissioner, but he supported Frank Gross from Toccoa, but I won. I took the position that I was elected for a vacancy that occurred. I was nominated by the Democrats at the same time Gene Talmadge was nominated and I was elected in the general election at the same time Gene Talmadge was elected.

Ellis Arnall took the position legally that there was no election because Gene Talmadge died between the time of his election and the time of his inauguration. Herman Talmadge took the position that since there was no election the legislature had a right to elect from one of the two in life who got the most votes in the general election. Now, Herman didn't get the most votes—wasn't even second in it—because part of the votes that he counted were write-in votes from people in the Helena precinct who voted in alphabetical order, though they'd been dead for years.

I took the position that I was elected for any vacancy that occurred. Ellis Arnall, for some reason, had seen fit to resign as soon as I was sworn in for lieutenant governor, creating a vacancy, so it ended up with a two-governor contest—either Herman or me—but it started off as a three-governor contest. The Georgia Supreme Court held by a 5 to 2 decision that Ellis Arnall was right and that he could have held office for four more years without any other election. Then I would have been lieutenant governor under him, but he, having resigned, created a vacancy. It would be unfair to Herman Talmadge or his position, or those who supported them, to say that he was opposed to me. That isn't right. He had a position that he thought was right; I had a position that I thought was right. Ellis Arnall had a position that he thought was right, and Ellis Arnall won. And as a result of Ellis winning, I won too. So the contest was really started off between three claiming to be governor instead of two.

MOORE: During that time you were lieutenant governor, what were you doing other than presiding over the Senate? I know you had a suit before the Supreme Court.

THOMPSON: I never did preside over the Senate a single day. I stayed in my room most of the time, at the Henry Grady Hotel, walking to and from the capitol by myself, unguarded. Others had guards around them; I didn't have any guards. I didn't need any.

MOORE: You became governor of the state. And immediately Herman Talmadge started running for the office in the 1948 primary. You were in office for almost twenty-one months as governor. The hallmark achievement of your two years in office was the purchase of Jekyll Island. That also became a campaign issue for Herman Talmadge, then a candidate for governor. He used it rather effectively, I thought, and it probably helped cost you the election in the September primary in 1948. Do you ever regret buying Jekyll Island?

THOMPSON: Not the slightest bit, and I honestly don't think it was much of a factor in that race. I think that the main issue in Herman Talmadge's opening campaign speech, and in all of his speeches, was that his father had been elected governor of Georgia but his friends and supporters had been denied the fruits of victory. Now, I tried to turn that on them by saying that they had been denied the *spoils* of victory . . . and I think that became the issue, not Jekyll Island.

MOORE: What about the white primary? Reports have it that you, at one point, were not opposed to the white primary, but when the General Assembly sent the bill to you, you vetoed it.

THOMPSON: I vetoed it because I said then, as I say now, that it was not a white primary but a "no" primary.

MOORE: You were linked, according to the speeches and accusations, to Ellis Arnall, who at that time was identified as a Southern liberal, and you had served in the Arnall administration as commissioner of revenue and as Arnall's executive secretary. Was this a burden when you went on the stump in 1948?

THOMPSON: I doubt it. Let me tell you what was. I was known as a Rosenwald scholar. The Rosenwald Foundation gave educational grants, and I got one the same year that Ralph McGill got one—he was with the Atlanta *Constitution*—and Dr. Carswell, chancellor of the university system, got one, and M. D. Mobley, head of the vocation education program in Georgia. Rosenwald was one of the founders of Sears, Roebuck, and he gave scholarships—mostly to Negroes who didn't have any other way of getting scholarships in the South—and he gave them for consolidated schools all over Georgia and everywhere else.

MOORE: It was a very animated race in the primary of 1948. How would you characterize that campaign?

THOMPSON: It was a hot one. Well, the best race I ever ran was when I ran for lieutenant governor. I spent about $12,000 on that campaign. I think I spent about $130,000 in my reelection efforts, both in 1948 and 1950. I don't know how much money Herman spent. I just don't know. I know this: he and I both signed statements that we spent only the $25,000 that we were allowed.

MOORE: Governor, we didn't have television in 1948—at least we didn't have television covering political campaigns in 1948—and the two major newspapers in Georgia were the Atlanta newspapers, the *Journal* and the *Constitution*. Neither one of them supported either Mr. Talmadge or Mr. Thompson in '48 and . . .

THOMPSON: Now, Gene, I don't believe that. I tell you what, I think the Atlanta *Constitution* supported Herman Talmadge; I think the Atlanta *Journal* supported M. E. Thompson.

MOORE: Mr. Talmadge came in as governor in November of 1948, after the general election. What were you doing between then and 1950 when you ran again?

THOMPSON: Partly campaigning and partly trying to make a living back here in Valdosta—not doing too well.

MOORE: Those were hard days. There's a question I've always

wanted to ask you. You were elected in '46 to a four-year term as lieutenant governor, and although you didn't win election to governor in
'48, weren't you still lieutenant governor? You hadn't resigned that
position.

THOMPSON: No, I don't think so. I think that the law was clear on
it. I was elected for a four-year term if I served as lieutenant governor,
but since I gave up the lieutenant governor's job to serve as governor, I
think my term was two years instead of four.

MOORE: I'm going to get back to January 1947. During most of this,
the Talmadge faction put most of its heat on Arnall as the liberal figure,
calculated to enrage the populace. For a while you were sort of sidelined,
at least you seemed to be from press reports. What was the atmosphere?
There were fights in the capitol, I know. Arnall was almost physically
evicted from the capitol.

THOMPSON: Well, I'm trying to be fair now when I say this. The
opposition between Arnall and Talmadge was more intense than it was
between Thompson and Talmadge. In 1946, when I was elected lieutenant governor, Ellis did not support me, but I carried his home county. I
carried Lanier County, home of Ed Rivers. I carried Telfair County, Eugene Talmadge's county, stronger than any county in Georgia. Now,
whether Gene Talmadge or Herman Talmadge voted for me or not, I just
don't know. I think that if they ever did it was in 1946 when I was first
elected lieutenant governor.

MOORE: Well, that night of January 14, 1947, were you in the
capitol?

THOMPSON: Yes, I was.

MOORE: Can you describe the events of that night?

THOMPSON: It was, I remember, about the night that the vote—the
critical vote—was taken, the time of electing Herman Talmadge or supposedly electing Herman Talmadge by the legislature. A man came running into my office—Rhodes Jordan—and running right behind him was
a fellow named Jim Mann, who was at that time a member of the legislature from Rockdale County. Mann had a knife open, and he was
threatening to kill Rhodes. No one ever got after me, and I can't honestly say that, other than that, I ever saw any act of violence. I heard
of it.

MOORE: Were you on hand, Governor, when Roy Harris and Herman
Talmadge presented themselves to Ellis Arnall's office that night?

THOMPSON: No, I wasn't. Ellis hadn't supported me for lieutenant
governor and I didn't figure I owed him anything. I owed my election to
the people of Georgia. Now, don't misunderstand me. I'm very fond of
Ellis Arnall. I'm one of his disciples.

MOORE: Let's move forward a little bit into your twenty months in office. I know teachers got a payroll raise in those short months, but you had a relationship with the General Assembly that cannot be characterized as warm during your twenty months in office.

THOMPSON: Well, they were always trying to have a special session. As a matter of fact, the courts acted after sixty-seven days. There were only three days left in the legislative session. I didn't have a chance to be in cooperation with the legislature unless I agreed to have a special session, at which time they would have tied my hands. I knew it and I didn't do it. The only special session I ever had was after the election in 1948.

MOORE: You campaigned and won on the planks of your platform when you ran for lieutenant governor. One of those planks was the 3 percent sales tax, and the General Assembly turned its back on the 3 percent sales tax, which in effect turned its back on your program as governor.

THOMPSON: Gene, that ain't exactly the truth. May I tell it as it is? All right, now, recently I received this citation about Jekyll Island given to me by the county commissioners in convention in Atlanta. On April 4 of this year I'd already written to them telling that I thought the finest thing I had done for Georgia was when I had courage enough to advocate a sales tax and that I knew they were going to give me a Jekyll Island award, but that I thought that was not the best thing I ever did, and I repeat to you today I don't think it was. Well, I went up there and they gave me the citation and imagine my somewhat embarrassment when they cited Herman for his sales tax, and I made this remark, and there are at least a thousand people in Georgia [who] will remember that I made it. I said, "Now, I'm glad that Herman Talmadge has his citation, and I think he deserves it, but there are people in this room who will remember in 1948 that I had courage enough to advocate his sales tax. Governor Talmadge said he would veto it, that . . . he would cut off his right arm before he'd ever sign a sales tax." I said, "I've seen him here tonight, and he still has his right arm." That happened. Now, I don't want to be misunderstood. I'm not against Herman, never have really been against him. I've been against some of the things he's for.

MOORE: What was Herman Talmadge like? You knew his father, Eugene, and you knew young Herman. . . . Comparing the two, what were they like?

THOMPSON: Well, now, old man Gene, I knew him quite well. Sometimes I voted for him, sometimes I voted against him, but old man Gene was a reactionary. Herman is a practical fellow. I think that Herman, in a sense, is smarter than his dad was. He's not quite so bullheaded. Herman is willing to admit sometimes that he's wrong. I don't think his dad would've. He'd have died and gone to hell before he'd ever admit he was wrong about anything.

MOORE: There's power, there's prerogative, there's privilege that the governor has, and you had all of this. You and Mrs. Thompson lived in the old governor's mansion in Atlanta, a huge stone house, forbidding in every aspect. Do you miss all that power, all that privilege of having a car at your disposal, having the state patrol at your elbow, huge office, secretary, being able to move things around?

THOMPSON: Now, that shows that you're younger than I am because the record will show that I never had a highway patrolman drive me anywhere. I drove my own car. We did not have guards at the mansion at that time, and I can tell you why—we never felt any need for it.

MOORE: I think we ought to say something about who the voters were in 1946 and 1948. There were not very many black Georgians at the polls.

THOMPSON: That's right, but on the other hand they would've been had they had somebody to vote for. They didn't have much choice between Herman Talmadge and me.

MOORE: For a long time in our state, Governor . . . there were two factions of the Democratic Party, and it was the only party Georgia had at the time that amounted to anything. One was the Talmadge faction and the other was the anti-Talmadge faction, and all through the late '40s and into the middle '50s you were the leader of the anti-Talmadge faction.

THOMPSON: The leader?

MOORE: Well, you practically were as far as the standard bearer is concerned. You were the candidate who ran against Talmadge and his allies.

THOMPSON: In 1950 Ellis Arnall and Ed Rivers, in my opinion, voted for Herman Talmadge instead of M. E. Thompson.

MOORE: What were the circumstances in 1950?

THOMPSON: Herman had some problems, and I was attacking him. The people believed that I was telling the truth, and on the night of the election, about eleven, I was ahead in the county unit vote and in popular vote. At that time the unit vote was the controlling factor. Then the returns just quit coming in. I had telephone calls from Meriwether, Terrell, and other counties telling me that I had carried those counties. The next morning they reported that Herman had carried those counties and there were about five hundred more votes in the race for governor than there were in any other race at that time, statewide race, leading me to believe that some shenanigans was done. Later on, I was talking to Roy Harris—incidentally, who's a good friend of mine. I don't agree with

Roy, and Roy doesn't agree with me all the time, but I told Roy, I said, "Roy, I know of at least fifty counties ya'll stole from me after the election." He laughed and chuckled as only Roy can do. He said, "Oh, M. E., it wasn't more than thirty-five."

MOORE: Your administration came after the Arnall administration, which has been described as a very progressive one for a Southern state. It seems to me . . . that the people would have been ready for still more of the same. You came in with a good program, and you did some good things. . . . What were the reasons why in 1948 and again in 1950 that the people rejected M. E. Thompson?

THOMPSON: Well, I guess the simplest answer is I didn't get enough votes.

MOORE: Right, but why didn't you?

THOMPSON: I just don't know. I'll tell you what I think. I think that the chances are that all during that time—'47 and '48 and '50—I seemed to dawdle around, I wasn't as positive as I am now, and I think that as a result I lost votes on both sides. That may be the explanation, and maybe it isn't.

MOORE: Do you think you might have been elected governor if you had stayed as lieutenant governor and let Herman Talmadge have the governorship for two years and then run, or stayed as lieutenant governor and run in '50 for governor?

THOMPSON: I couldn't have done that. I had to assume the responsibility, which I did. I had to do the best I could with what I had to do.

Herman E. Talmadge

1948–1955

Herman E. Talmadge and the Politics of Power

ROGER N. PAJARI

In the period following World War II major changes swept the South and the nation. Changes in race relations, legislative apportionment, education, industrialization, urbanization, commerce, agriculture, health, nutrition, and welfare and a sweeping set of changes emphasizing protection and broadening of civil liberties for all flew across Georgia with the force of a hurricane.[1] Governor Herman E. Talmadge was intimately involved in orchestrating Georgia's governmental response to these changes. He saw some of them as good for the people of Georgia, while some of the others he saw as menacing and potentially destructive to Southern traditions.

These changes can be grouped into two different but somewhat overlapping categories. First, there were those which affected the modernization and transformation of the state's economic base and which were of critical importance to the agricultural, industrial, banking, transportation, and commercial communities, not to mention the interest of labor. Higher profits, increased salaries and wages, and the economic well-being of all Georgians were at stake in the state's response to, success in attracting, developing, and building Georgia's industrial, banking, commercial, and agricultural bases. Governor Talmadge energetically and successfully committed himself and the government of Georgia to policies facilitating these changes. He scored his greatest successes and will probably leave his most lasting contribution in his efforts to modernize the state's economy.

A second category of changes brought forth the opposite response from Talmadge. These changes can be described as political and constitutional and have much to do with the modernization of Georgia's governmental, political, and constitutional systems. Political and constitutional modernization includes, among other things, an expansion of the electorate to include all citizens, development of a modern system of state taxation, development of open two-party competition, operating government in the sunshine with an expansion of a free press, development of an independent and professional legislature, a heightened respect for due process of law, and enhanced respect for the civil liberties of all people, regardless of race, sex, creed, or ethnic origin. The forces promoting political and constitutional modernization have had an impact on all states, but the responses of the states have varied. Georgia's response was highly negative and was shaped significantly by Talmadge. It was here where he succeeded the least in accomplishing his goals. The modernization of Georgia's state government and politics and its conformability with constitutional changes was slowed by his effort but was not stopped.

Simply stated, the administration of Herman E. Talmadge was extremely successful in promoting and setting in place state government policies which led to the economic modernization of Georgia, and it was least successful in stopping those legal and cultural changes which led to the modernization of Georgia's state politics, government, and conformity to constitutional principles. These two sets of changes were in progress prior to Talmadge's inauguration as governor, and they continued following his departure from the office.

The thesis of this paper suggests the existence of standards or criteria by which one can judge a governor's success and failure. Such generally accepted standards do not exist. How are governors in general evaluated as performers in state governments? Thad Beyle and Lynn Muchmore concluded in their study of the American governorship, "To date that is a relatively unresearched and analyzed question."[2] Scholars and citizens do not agree on what we want of a governor. Some people want a charismatic leader, a competent manager, an innovator, or an intergovernmental leader, while others may seek a governor who maintains the status quo, or one with other qualities which exemplify some other standard of performance. Often governors themselves become confused or victimized by these conflicting criteria.[3] But important criteria include the extent of a governor's political popularity; his conformity to an open, liberal, democratic model of government grounded in equalitarianism; and his compliance with the "active-positive" model of executive leadership. Other criteria examine whether the goals of his administration were accomplished; whether the governor was able to work cooperatively and constructively with the legislature, other state agencies, local governments, and the national government; whether his administration provides evidence of his effort to qualitatively improve the state's and its people's general welfare; and whether, under a particular governor's administration, the state followed good administrative procedures, including conformity to standards of due process and equal protection of the law.

Herman Talmadge was born in Telfair County, Georgia, on August 9, 1913. He attended public schools in McRae, the county seat of Telfair County, until 1930 when his family moved to Atlanta. Following graduation from the DeKalb County school system, he became the fourth generation of Talmadges to attend the University of Georgia. There he had an excellent academic record, was president of his social fraternity, and was a leading member of his debate team. Later he attended and graduated from the University of Georgia Law School in 1936 and then practiced law with his father in Atlanta until 1941, when he enlisted in the U.S. Navy and served in the Southwest Pacific during World War II. Following the completion of his tour of duty with the Navy in 1945 as a lieutenant commander, he returned to Georgia and got involved in his father's campaign for governor.[4]

James F. Cook quotes Herman Talmadge's explanation of how he got into politics:

> When I was in the Pacific [in World War II], I thought it was foolish to be in politics, and I thought I would never be active in that way again. But when I got back and my father launched his fourth campaign, I found it necessary to help him. After his death, circumstances forced me into the fight. Then when I was elected by the legislature and kicked out, of course I felt I had to be vindicated. Too, there was the pleasure of winning, and it's a great honor to be governor. Politics is a rough, mean, hard, vicious life.[5]

While circumstances, necessity, and family loyalty played a part in his entry into politics, the encouragement of Roy V. Harris, a powerful political leader from Augusta who was a former speaker of the Georgia House and a protégé of Eugene Talmadge, was also of critical importance. Harris was the experienced and successful campaign manager of many previous governors and was probably one of the most knowledgeable Georgians in organizing political campaigns.[6]

Talmadge was thirty-four years old when he first served as governor between January 14 and March 18, 1947, following his election by the General Assembly. The Georgia Supreme Court ruled his election unconstitutional. In a subsequent election he was formally elected by the people of the state, was inaugurated November 17, 1948, and then served the remaining portion of his father's unexpired term. He ran for reelection in 1950 and was elected for a four-year term that began with his inauguration as governor on January 9, 1951.[7] In 1956 he was elected to the U.S. Senate, succeeding Senator Walter F. George. He served in the Senate until 1980.

When Talmadge campaigned for governor in 1948 and in 1950, he followed his father's lead in advocating white supremacy.[8] In this sense he was submerged in the past traditions of the state and in character with his father. However, unlike his father, "he had a sense of urban and industrial progress."[9] In this regard Talmadge bridged the gap between the old and the new Georgia, and his years as governor were reflective of tensions between the past and the present and between the mores of rural and urban America.[10] His later appeal to the conservative, urban business vote stemmed from his "New South" programs for developing the state economically, while his stands on matters of race, civil rights, and democracy endeared him to the pro-Talmadge faction, its machines, and the organizations which his father had helped to establish in rural, especially south Georgia, counties.[11]

Talmadge's successes and failures are made more understandable not only when viewed in the context of his biography but also when viewed in the context of Georgia history. Politics and issues surrounding state government often tend to be responses to or reflections of social continuity and changes and tensions found in society generally. Georgia state politics in the 1940s and 1950s was no exception.

The county unit system was one of the most influential historic forces in shaping the state's politics, which transformed state party nominating elections into 159 separate elections with disproportionate electoral power being lodged in the rural counties. The county unit system indirectly supported racial segregation, another source of continuity during this period of Georgia history, which was more directly defended by family, church, and the law.[12]

A third force of continuity was the highly organized personal following that former Governor Eugene Talmadge had developed. During the course of his controversial career in Georgia politics, which included several terms as governor, he succeeded in cultivating a deep strain of personalism in the state's political system. His appeal was anchored in his strong call for continued racial segregation, low taxes, and little government and his anti-New Deal rhetoric directed against federal governmental programs and regulations. The effect of Eugene Talmadge's leadership was to divide Georgia state politics into two major factions within the Democratic Party. The county unit system and racial emotionalism tended to reinforce the bifactional pattern.[13]

Continuity and stability were also manifest in the ideology of Georgia voters. At least three distinct ideological groups were active in the political history of Herman Talmadge's years as governor. First, there were Georgia voters best described as neo-Populists. These were Georgia's liberals. Small in number and found in rural as well as urban areas, they tended to believe in democracy, individualism, and social justice. A second ideological group consisted of business conservatives. They were Southern moderates who desired to transform the South into an urban-industrial society similar to urban areas of the North except with some Southern biases. People in these first two categories tended to be more tolerant, genteel, and paternalistic. Finally, there were those Georgians often described as neo-Bourbons. They were people who sought to impose a Southern, rural ideological and social pattern of human relations on a developing Southern, urban industrial society. Neo-Bourbonism was the South's reaction to nationalization of the South's economy and sweeping constitutional and political reforms.[14]

Neo-Bourbons were the dominant leaders of Georgia politics in the 1950s and encouraged massive resistance to many of the changes sweeping the South. They were suspicious of the word "progress," opposed liberal education, and were hostile to the national government, its bureaucracy, its regulations, and its civil rights–related court rulings and legislation. The neo-Populists and business conservatives were often opponents of the neo-Bourbons and their social and political agendas.[15]

The governorship of Talmadge was most successful when judged from the perspective of his political popularity, his being an active and positive leader, and his record of putting in place programs, policies, and facilities which improved or helped to bring about improvements in the quality of life for Georgians. Many of these have been particularly instrumental in modernizing the state's economy. His political popularity and power as governor stemmed in large measure from his support in rural, poor, and largely black counties.[16] Although he denies this, he also received strong support from key corporate elites in the state's major cities.[17]

Governor Talmadge's electoral margins in the 1948 and 1950 Georgia Democratic Party primaries were 51.1 percent and 49.4 percent of the popular vote respectively. In each election his margin of victory based on county unit votes was overwhelming. (See Table 1.) His electoral success in 1948 was a by-product of several factors: a strong stand on the matter of race, a "surprisingly good" press, a well-organized campaign, good speaking ability and attractive personality, support from key state

TABLE I

Outcomes of 1948 and 1950 Georgia Democratic Primary Contests for Governor

	Year	
	1948	1950
Candidates		
Herman Talmadge	51.8%	49.4%
	(357,865 votes)	(287,637 votes)
	(312 county unit votes)	(295 county unit votes)
	(130 counties carried)	(124 1/2 counties carried)
M. E. Thompson	45.1%	47.9%
	(312,035 votes)	(279,137 votes)
	(98 county unit votes)	(115 county unit votes)
	(29 counties carried)	(34 1/2 counties carried)
Minor Candidates	3.1%	2.7%
	(21,000 votes)	(16,000 votes)
Total	100.0%	100.0%

and county officials, and Talmadge's not having many personal enemies. The slight decline in his popularity in the 1950 primary was a by-product of his failing to keep his promise not to seek increases in state taxes, the public's critical appraisal of his first two years as governor, and allegations of vote fraud in several counties.[18] The matter of state tax increases in 1949 was given special attention inasmuch as the governor had to call the General Assembly into special session to adopt new taxes to avert a financial crisis. He did this even though the voters, in a statewide referendum, rejected by a three-to-one margin a proposition calling for tax increases. Many voters also were unhappy about his lack of success in preventing blacks from registering to vote.[19]

Apart from being popular at the polls, Talmadge was personally popular with many groups and with key individuals. In 1953 representatives at the National 4-H Clubs of America's meeting in Chicago presented him with the prestigious 4-H Club Alumni Recognition Award for his work in establishing a regional 4-H camp at Rock Eagle, Georgia.[20] His popularity extended to individuals as well. Like his father, he had "an uncanny ability to dramatize issues in ways which . . . tapped the emotions of the masses," said Lieutenant Governor Zell Miller, writing in the 1980s about important people in Georgia history. Miller described Talmadge as "the most popular governor Georgia had ever had."[21]

Other standards that can be used to judge a governor's success are the extent to which he is actively involved in promoting state policies which address pressing state needs and the extent to which he enjoys his work as governor.[22] A review of Talmadge's record and behavior as governor suggests that he fits the "active-positive" model. He enjoyed being governor and has personally testified that being governor was a much more satisfying experience than being a senator.[23] Furthermore, he conspicuously set out to be an active governor. In his first inaugural address he stated that he did not want to be a caretaker-type governor, but wanted to be one who initiated and implemented needed state policies. He noted that there are two roads open to any man who assumes the executive authority of the state:

> He can just sit over there in the governor's office, directing routine affairs, taking no decisive stand on important public issues, just letting things go along in a slip-shod fashion and somehow muddle through his term of office. It is not enough to just be governor without any ambition or foresight for his state or its people who elected him. I tell you now, I do not intend to be that kind of governor. On the other hand, your governor can initiate progressive and constructive movements, and can take the lead in fighting for things that our people believe in and that the state really needs; he can create broad and comprehensive policies and can act as a leader in mapping out movements and expansion programs designed to further agriculture and industry in the state. He can work with the legislature toward enactment of forward looking legislation and with the department heads toward affectuating this legislation into reality. This is the kind of governor I want to make.[24]

His record of accomplishments suggests that he succeeded overwhelmingly in this endeavor.

A flood of initiatives undertaken by Talmadge are evidence of this activism. The most important of these were instrumental in facilitating the state's economic development. When he took office as governor, Georgia was generally recognized as a depressed state. Its per capita income, level of public education, state road system, level of health care and availability of health care facilities, and amounts and quality of social services generally were among the most poorly developed in all of the United States. Its prison system and correctional programs had a notoriously negative reputation. Not only was the state economically depressed, but its political culture also acted as a drag on the development of an activist state government which could help to change this. Talmadge, unlike his father, used the governorship to put Georgia on the path toward becoming a leading progressive state in the South. It was his dream that Georgians would have a per capita income equal to the national average by 1964.[25]

In 1947 the Georgia House of Representatives created a Committee on Tax Revision which issued a report on the eve of the opening of the 1951 session of the General Assembly.[26] While Talmadge had opposed legislative efforts to adopt a state sales tax in 1950, an election year, his stance on the sales tax and tax reform became centerpieces of his legislative agenda in 1951.[27] In his inaugural address of that year, he called for passage of a 3 percent sales tax, revision of the state income tax, abolition of the state property tax, and elimination of scores of nuisance professional and business taxes. He was highly successful in these tax reform efforts. By 1952 the sales tax revenues constituted about 30 percent of all state revenue. Talmadge's budgetary proposals and innovations also included a successful effort in 1952 to secure a constitutional amendment to earmark all motor fuel and auto tag tax revenues for building and maintaining state roadways and the development and use of state authorities to enable the state to circumvent the constitutional prohibition against spending more revenue than it takes in.[28] Such authorities have been instrumental in securing sale of bonds to fund needed long-term capital projects such as schools, highways, and state buildings.[29]

Talmadge promoted policies to develop and diversify the state's economy. He was instrumental in securing a major expansion in the state's Port Authority to promote increased trade and make the state a more attractive place for industrial development.[30] While promoting industrial development, he also pushed for improvements in Georgia's agricultural and forestry enterprises. He was an early advocate of the creation of the State Forestry Commission, helped build or expand twenty-eight farmer's markets, promoted the development of a statewide soil conservation program, and facilitated the expansion of the state's agricultural experiment stations and the building of the College of Veterinary Medicine at the University of Georgia.[31] His efforts resulted in a major reforestation effort and the placement of an additional one-half million acres of state forest land under state fire protection.

Major improvements were also undertaken in the state's highways and roads. Utilizing the earmarked auto fuel tax revenues, the state was able to construct over ten thousand miles of new roads and expand its efforts to build, replace, or improve bridges. In cooperation with the General Assembly, Talmadge also was successful in establishing a new Highway Board and in reorganizing the State Highway Department.[32]

Georgia's prison system also was improved during Talmadge's administration. The governor's promotion of the idea of juvenile corrections, his work for improvements in the state prisons, and his help in establishment of the state's crime lab in 1951 were also credits to his leadership.[33]

A variety of notable improvements in health care facilities and services were also outcomes of Governor Talmadge's efforts. As late as 1950 at least fifteen of the state's counties had no organized health services.[34] He was a strong advocate of expanding the capacity of the Medical College of Georgia so that it could graduate one hundred doctors a year rather than seventy-five as it was doing. In addition to his promotion of state scholarships to doctor and nurse trainees willing to accept work in rural areas of the state, he was a strong promoter of hospital construction.[35] When he left office, approximately sixty hospitals had been either built or approved for construction, including the state's first clinic for the treatment of alcoholism.[36] During the Talmadge administration, expenditures for state mental health facilities more than doubled.

While all of the latter improvements helped to create an environment conducive to economic development, they pale in importance when compared to improvements in education and training. During Talmadge's term as governor, the state of Georgia added a twelfth grade to all public schools, extended the length of the academic school year from seven to nine months, more than doubled the amount of public school teachers' salaries, started 1,036 school building projects at a cost of approximately $170 million, purchased over a thousand school buses, tripled the outlay for vocational rehabilitation, and increased state education expenditures to such an extent that more was spent on education in his six years as governor than was spent by all previous administrations in the state's history. When he left the office of governor, the state was spending a higher percentage of its budget on education (53 percent) than any other state in the Union.[37] A significant part of this increased effort in education was the funding of the Minimum Foundation Program, which the General Assembly had earlier established for all public schools in the state.

Another way to document the increased effort of Georgia state government under Talmadge's leadership is to examine state departmental income from state revenue allotments prior to, during, and at the completion of his term as governor. (See Table 2.) Between 1946 and 1954 expenditures of state revenues by various state departments increased dramatically. The largest percentage increases in expenditures were in Forestry (605 percent), Public Health (436 percent), Public Welfare (400 percent), Public Education (310 percent), and Corrections (205 percent).

TABLE 2

Summary of Revenue Distribution for Selected Georgia State Departments in 1946, 1950, and 1954

Departments	Year			Percent-Increase, 1946–1954
	1946	1950	1954	
Agriculture	$ 925,021	$ 1,302,987	$ 2,084,794	125%
Corrections	796,755	1,801,904	2,558,895	205%
Education	25,616,923	58,668,430	104,979,410	310%
Forestry	473,870	1,525,676	3,341,687	605%
Highways	3,964,279	43,569,974	56,749,417	67%
Pardons & Parole	97,647	114,383	187,817	92%
Public Health	2,340,260	9,761,656	12,555,293	436%
Public Safety	1,002,239	1,725,967	2,474,273	149%
Public Welfare	12,433,738	36,770,421	62,259,153	400%
University System	12,734,328	21,514,916	28,977,855	128%

Source: Report of the State Auditor of Georgia, 1946, 1950, 1954, Years Ending June 30. State Capitol: Atlanta, Ga. (B. E. Thrasher, Jr., Auditor.) Figures, rounded to the nearest whole number, represent departmental income from state revenue allotments only.

But public services such as higher education, public safety, and service to farmers also increased well over 100 percent.

Some may discount these numbers by noting the low level of per capita expenditures for such state services in 1946 and the fact that even small absolute increases could easily translate into huge percentage increases. That is not the interpretation advanced here. State government budgets normally change incrementally, and large percentage increases or decreases are exceptional. When they do occur, they are evidence of a crisis or, as in Georgia's case, of innovative and daring leadership. Changes of this magnitude were possible because of Talmadge's leadership and political support. These programs, coupled with his industrial recruitment and development efforts, produced more than 15,000 new jobs in the state and secured more than $50 million in new plant construction.[38]

Another measure of a governor's success is the extent to which he accomplishes his objectives. Viewed from this perspective, Talmadge was, with some exceptions, mostly successful. He was able to obtain support for tax reform and major advances in the level and quality of state services. He dominated the General Assembly and its leadership and therefore indirectly controlled its committee system. Even though the General Assembly held up, modified, or defeated some of his proposals, he was the "ultimate victor on the issues of importance."[39] He did not succeed in his effort to disenfranchise black voters by implementing a law requiring reregistration of all voters and the reinstitution of the poll tax. He was also unsuccessful in his effort to amend the state's constitution to require use of the county unit system in general elections.[40] He did succeed in amending the constitution to require closing of public schools in the event of court-ordered desegregation,[41] but this victory was short-lived, and his effort to forestall desegregation did not succeed.

A related measure of gubernatorial success is the extent to which a governor works cooperatively and successfully with other governmental entities and the press. Here again, the record of Talmadge is mixed. Working cooperatively did not mean giving in to every demand. For example, in 1953 he issued an order calling for an across-the-board 6 percent reduction in state spending. The State Department of Education responded by reorganizing itself and reducing its staff.[42] On other occasions there was pressure from teachers who threatened to strike if money was not provided to fund the Minimum Foundation Program and teacher pay raises. Similar threats came from medical doctors at the state's hospital in Milledgeville when they became unhappy with administrative appointments and policies there.[43] When such threats occurred, Governor Talmadge worked cooperatively with the parties involved and resolved the disputes. Generally he worked cooperatively with local governments, but he did not hesitate to veto local legislation when he disagreed with it. For example, despite strong appeals from Atlanta Mayor William B. Hartsfield, he vetoed a bill which would have created an Atlanta traffic court.[44] He dispensed spoils such as road-paving contracts to reward local communities and their representatives when they supported him. He also held up or denied such spoils when communities and their representatives worked against him. This pressure extended to local politicians' voting records as well as to their activities and stands on matters of race. He did not have to use the veto extensively because he dominated the General Assembly. In 1951 and 1952 he vetoed seventeen bills. In 1953 he vetoed twenty-three.[45]

His record of cooperation with the General Assembly is a record which approaches dominance. Legislators routinely granted sweeping budgetary discretion to him. In 1949, when he told the General Assembly that he did not think "any one man should be entrusted with this much authority," the legislature responded by doubling the size of the contingency budget.[46] Following the adoption of the sales tax and the huge influx of new state revenue, he continued to exercise sweeping control over the spending of state funds. In other words, he continued a pattern of gubernatorial dominance begun in 1933.[47]

Talmadge's record of his dealings with federal authorities is filled with many examples of contention and conflict, but he also encouraged cooperation with the federal government. For example, he urged expansion of cooperative efforts in hospital construction, economic development, and agriculture. But these efforts are overshadowed by the conflict he fostered in areas of civil rights and federal labor law. He fought the activities of the Federal Fair Employment Practices Commission and described members of the Warren court as "not fit to empty the waste baskets of earlier Supreme Court justices."[48] He did everything in his power to preserve a system of segregated schools and public institutions, and he attacked the federal courts for invading the political thicket of reapportionment, which eventually undermined the county unit system.

Talmadge's relationship with the press and his record of having operated an open, nonsecretive governor's office also indicate some successes and some failures. Some writers describe him as being very open and available to newspaper reporters and citizens. One reporter described him as "being willing to talk with you about anything on God's earth at any time. He'll never dodge a question, or mouth around about it."[49] The same writer reported that it was not uncommon for Talmadge to answer his own phone at the governor's mansion and that he never put off people who wanted to meet him. Yet another journalist described him as lacking candor and openness when dealing with the press. This person described Talmadge's answers to journalists' questions as often vague and contradictory.[50]

Governor Talmadge's statements and actions are reflective of such contradictions. For example, in a 1951 speech before an association of Georgia newspapermen he praised the press for its coverage of his administration's record.[51] Yet state government documents indicate that he attempted to intimidate the press by having administration leaders in the General Assembly introduce legislation which would have subjected newspapers to state regulation and forced them to publish responses from state officials when such officials had been accused of public misconduct or malfeasance. The proposed laws did not receive legislative approval, however.[52] Talmadge "outlived the animosity" of the press and generally had its support during the last two years of his governorship.

Though he was highly or partially successful in most of his endeavors as governor, he conspicuously failed in at least three areas. First, he tried mightily to subvert generally accepted standards of due process and equal protection of the law. Second, he espoused and attempted to legislatively and constitutionally mandate a standard of political philosophy grounded on now discredited assumptions about race. Finally, it seems clear that he did not add any new role dimension or new expectations to the office of governor. Had he succeeded in the first two of the latter endeavors, Georgia's political development would have been set back at the very time his domestic policy agenda was putting Georgia on track for the most sweeping period of economic development in the state's history. In other words, his failures in the realm of political modernization have been real victories for the state, just as his successes in health, transportation, education, welfare, and other domestic areas were to become bulwarks of victory for the state's future economic development.

Talmadge's entry into Georgia politics began in 1946 when voters, responding to the fears of Eugene Talmadge's declining health, wrote his son's name in for governor. The election returns showed Eugene Talmadge the winner, but the press reported that 675 write-in votes were cast for Herman E. Talmadge, 669 for James V. Carmichael, and 637 for D. Talmadge Bowers. Prior to his inauguration, Eugene Talmadge died. On the strength of the press reports, Herman Talmadge saw a chance to become governor. He argued that the General Assembly must choose the next governor from the two highest living vote-getters, but when the tabulating committee counted the write-in votes he had only 617, which seemed to take him out of the running. However, 58 newly discovered, some say fraudulent, write-in votes for Herman Talmadge were brought in from his home county of Telfair. These votes, added to those previously counted, made him the top vote-getter. The General Assembly proceeded to elect him governor.

Anti-Talmadge forces disputed the legislative election. They interpreted the Georgia constitution to mean that M. E. Thompson, the lieutenant governor-elect, should succeed to the governorship, but only if the outgoing governor, Ellis Arnall, resigned his office. Upon Thompson taking the oath as lieutenant governor, Arnall resigned. However, before Thompson could occupy the office as acting governor, Talmadge and his supporters forcefully occupied both the governor's office and the mansion. Refusing to accept this outcome, Thompson set up an acting governor's office in downtown Atlanta and challenged Talmadge's legislative election. Fifty-six days passed before the Georgia Supreme Court ruled that M. E. Thompson was the rightful occupant of the office of governor until the next general election. Faced with this ruling, Talmadge surrendered the office but won election to the governorship in the general election held in 1948. Many scholars and students of law see Talmadge's forceful takeover of the governor's office as a major violation of due process and an event which brought much bad publicity to the state.[53]

A variety of other due-process indiscretions also characterized Talmadge's gubernatorial administration. Allegations of vote fraud in the 1946 gubernatorial election had counterparts in 1950. Jack Tarver, a writer for the Atlanta *Constitution*, in analyzing the outcome of the 1950 primary contest between Talmadge and Thompson, described a "morning after scramble" to find necessary votes to keep many county election outcomes in the Talmadge column. This was apparently made more feasible because of the close vote totals in many counties.[54]

Another example of due-process violations encouraged by Governor Talmadge was his effort to disenfranchise black Georgia voters. He was able to obtain General Assembly passage of the Voters' Qualification Act in 1949, which required that voters reregister every four years and that each person seeking reregistration should correctly answer thirty questions. When it became clear that more whites than blacks were being disenfranchised because of the process, the law ceased to be enforced. It was repealed in 1951 when it became apparent that voters resented the law and that it was constitutionally suspect because of the literacy test.[55]

Still another due-process related indiscretion was Talmadge's successful effort to secure legislation from the General Assembly that gave his handpicked Democratic Party Executive Committee authority to determine the qualifications of future candidates for governor, the makeup of ballots, the deadlines for filing for candidacy, and the dates for coordinating the Democratic primary.[56] One very positive piece of due-process legislation promoted by Talmadge and passed by the General Assembly in 1949 required a secret ballot.[57]

Several other due-process indiscretions can be found in Talmadge's governorship. On numerous occasions Talmadge spoke out against gubernatorial dominance and political use of the state's highway building and maintenance programs. He believed that highway politics was undesirable in the running of the governor's office as well as in gubernatorial campaigns, and to ameliorate the problem he advocated placement of the highway programs under the control of an independently appointed board. However, following the passage of a compromise highway bill providing for a three-member legislatively appointed board, the legislature proceeded to appoint three Talmadge-approved protégés to serve on the board. Talmadge also sought to control some of the state's constitutional boards. For example, he used his influence over members of the State Board of Corrections to secure their vote to replace Director of Prisons C. A. Williams with a Talmadge supporter.[58]

Although he denies it, some scholars, investigative reporters, and state legislators accused Talmadge of tampering with the state's merit system by placing it under the leadership of a political supporter and by transforming the system into a patronage dispensing agency. Accusations included allegations that merit system personnel administered "early-service" merit exams orally and used merit system employees to campaign for the extension of the county unit system to general elections.[59]

Finally, some critics accuse Talmadge of violating the spirit of due process when he pushed for the adoption of a state sales tax after saying he would submit tax-increase measures to the voters of the state. Georgia voters rejected such a proposal by a three-to-one margin, yet this did not deter the governor from accepting such a tax when passed by the General Assembly. He justified his switch on the matter by arguing that the money was needed to upgrade public schools for both blacks and whites; he reasoned that a major upgrading of the public schools for black students would forestall federal desegregation efforts.[60]

Talmadge also pushed for a number of policies which would have had the effect of denying people equal protection of the law. In each of these efforts he failed. Although he was successful in getting the General Assembly to pass a law cutting off appropriations to any public school system enrolling blacks in white schools, the law was ultimately declared invalid by the United States Supreme Court.[61] The most important equal-protection setback for Talmadge related to expansion and preservation of the county unit system. In 1950 and 1952 he vigorously campaigned for passage of a constitutional amendment making the system part of the state constitution and applicable to general elections. Some members of the General Assembly described his pressures on lawmakers as intimidating. He threatened to deny opposition legislators state patronage, road building, and other benefits. The Senate vote on the proposed amendment was thirty-six votes for and sixteen votes against the proposed amendment. This was the exact number of "yes" votes needed for the resolution to pass. Talmadge reportedly posted the names of the sixteen senators who voted "no" on his office wall and said, "This will hang here for years."

Later he stumped the state urging Georgians to vote for the amendment. In his speeches before such groups as the Georgia Prison Wardens Association and the Georgia Peace Officers Association he said that "only the county unit system would ensure Georgia against a gangster ridden political machine operating from Atlanta." Wearing the familiar red suspenders commonly worn by his father, he told his audiences that "the corrupting tentacles of organized crime and its gangster leaders" could be stopped at the county line with the system. Talmadge described those criminal elements as including civil rights activists, foreign agitators, the Communist Party, the National Association for the Advancement of Colored People, the race-mixing Southern Regional Council, people affiliated with "the notorious Rosenwald Foundation," individuals promoting the Federal Fair Employment Practices Commission, and those who "frequently participate in mixed meetings and mixed social gatherings." Although the General Assembly passed the proposal, the voters were not convinced by his rhetoric and failed to adopt the amendment.[62]

When initially established in 1917, the county unit system allocated electoral power in rough proportion to the distribution of the state's population, but by Talmadge's time, with Georgia's urbanizing population, the system increasingly diluted the voting power of the state's urban citizens and accentuated the voting power of its rural citizens. The United States Supreme Court eventually dealt a deadly blow to its use in primaries.[63]

Talmadge's actions not only mirrored his personal philosophy, but also one held by many Georgians at that time. In 1955 he published a book describing this philosophy, which was grounded in a belief in white supremacy, racial segregation, elitism, states' rights, representative—as opposed to direct—democracy, and a state-fostered free-enterprise system, as well as a firm commitment to defend individual property rights. In an interview thirty years later he denied any regrets over the book's publication, since it was in keeping with the mores of the time.[64] He was not a political opportunist devoid of a political philosophy, but his philosophy was characterized by a flawed set of assumptions and a curious linkage of various idea systems into a prescription for maintaining the state's political and social culture while simultaneously encouraging its modernization, urbanization, and industrialization.

The core of Talmadge's belief system was the ethnological and theological assumption that God created five races of people and that his intention was to keep them separate from each other. The fact that different regions of the world were home for different races, he believed, illustrated God's intention to segregate people. Buttressing these assumptions was his questionable reading of world history, which he believed provided evidence that nations composed of several races which were socially integrated inevitably became mongrelized, weak, lazy, indifferent, and subject to conquest by other states. The price of violating God's plan of segregation, he wrote, was biological degradation and then political destruction.

Another theme linking the elements of this belief system was his reading of American constitutional law and his understanding of the legal and political beliefs of America's founding fathers and many of its later leaders. In his view, the Constitution and the founding fathers never intended for the United States to become an integrated society. He believed that leaders such as Thomas Jefferson and Abraham Lincoln favored segregation, and that amalgamation of the races was inevitable if blacks and whites were allowed to integrate in social settings.

Finally, he believed the major forces pushing the United States toward integration were part of an internationally organized Communist conspiracy which included journalists and news commentators. He viewed liberals, the AFL-CIO, the NAACP, and foreigners as unwitting accomplices of the Communists, whose intention was to weaken the United States by promoting race mixing. He also noted that the conspiracy encompassed other tactics such as promotion of registration and voting rights for blacks, demolition of the county unit system, destruction of states' rights, and the undermining of our republican form of government by promoting powers, regulations, and controls over people at the federal level. At stake in this fight were Southern traditions, the values of private property, the republican form of government, white supremacy, and the people's constitutionally guaranteed civil liberties.[65]

Talmadge's belief system appealed to many people in the 1940s, 1950s, and 1960s, but time eventually discredited it, even among most Southerners. If convincing people that his philosophy was a correct philosophy is used as a criterion of gubernatorial success, then Talmadge did not succeed as a governor.

Talmadge was most successful when judged by his political popularity, his record of being an active and positive leader, and in his success in putting in place a large number of extremely important domestic programs to enhance the general welfare of the people of Georgia. These diverse programs were in such fields as transportation, education, welfare, health, tax reform, agriculture and conservation, port development, and commerce. Most have remained in place for forty years and have been a bedrock on which the state's economic development is based. When judged by his ability to work cooperatively and successfully with other state organizations, local governments and the federal government, Talmadge gets mixed reviews. In some instances the relationships were cooperative and productive, while in others the record is one of complete lack of cooperation. The same conclusion can be drawn when he is judged by his record of agenda accomplishments and his relationships with the press.

Talmadge's most glaring failures were in the constitutional and political realm. He was not successful in getting acceptance of his standards of due process and equal protection of the law, and his views on race and democracy were ultimately rejected by the courts and the people of the state and nation. Finally, Talmadge was not an innovator in the office of governor. Rather, he continued in the tradition of strong, aggressive twentieth-century Georgia governors. While he succeeded in promoting the general economic welfare of the state, he failed to stop the state's progress toward constitutional and political modernization. The people were the big winners where he succeeded and where he did not succeed.

Reflections on
the Gubernatorial
Years

HERMAN E. TALMADGE

From 1937 to 1941 Ed Rivers served as governor of Georgia. In those days before inflation there were hotels all over the state, bellboys in great abundance, and a dime was considered a great tip. Right after Ed Rivers went out of office, he said a former governor couldn't even get a bellboy to carry his bag to his car. And that's substantially correct.

One of my friends had a son. He suggested that he go out and listen to a former governor speak. The son got back and he said, "What did the governor say?" The son replied, "He recommended himself most highly." Well, I assume now we would be classified as elder statesmen. An elder statesman, you know, is an unemployed politician. That's the way they get that title.

Anyway, I have found that there is life after leaving office. Most politicians, when they're in office, don't realize that fact. You know, people fawn over governors. They fawn over senators. They're looking for favors. When I was governor of Georgia I would have hundreds and hundreds of people pass through my office every day. They wanted appointments as judges, as solicitors, or some member of the family on the payroll, or they wanted a road, or health center, a bridge, or something like that. And, of course, the first thing they do is start off running you for president of the United States, or United States senator, or president of the World Court, or some highly laudatory office of that nature. And

93

then, as soon as they get through with that, they bring up the business at hand, which is a road, or bridge, or schoolhouse, a job, a pension.

It got to the point where I wouldn't even talk politics with people who came through my office, particularly if I knew they were in the business of doing things like that. The same people passed through every governor's office as long as they lived, regardless of their political preferment, and they came there for the same reason. But now and then someone would come in with corns on his hands, someone who had worked for a living, and you knew you could ask him a question and he would give you an honest answer. He didn't think there was any political preferment that you could give to him. There were no rewards that you could give him and no punishments that you could give him. And I have long since learned that you will get facts primarily from those sources rather than the influential and the affluent who represent counties, municipalities, congressional districts, and things of that nature. But, you know, one of the greatest blessings about being out of office is that a lot of people want to test your memory. You met some fellow at Moultrie, Georgia, about twenty years ago when you were campaigning, and there were ten thousand people there, and he'd walk up to you and say, "Hello, Herman, I bet you don't remember my name, do you?" And now you can answer frankly, "No, and I don't give a damn."

I served as governor for a little over six years, United States senator for twenty-four years. During all that period of time I had an abundance of secretaries and they would answer my mail. Some of it I would have to sign. Deposits were made in the bank, then they would give me the bank balances occasionally—particularly when they were running low. And bills would come in and they would prepare the checks and put them on my desk for my signature. And then, right after I left the Senate, I came back to Lovejoy and I didn't have any secretary there, and my secretary hadn't sent me my bank records, and I started getting some bills and I figured, well, I better pay these bills—I don't want to ruin my credit rating. So I'd been banking with the Trust Company of Georgia for some forty years and they'd started branch banking throughout the state and the Trust Company bought a bank in Clayton County and they expanded faster than hot dog and hamburger stands. And they had a little bank up there about six miles north of my farm by the side of the road. I went in there one morning in my fatigue clothes that I wear on the farm, and a couple of young ladies at the counter recognized me and they said, "What can we do for you, Senator?"

I said, "I want some blank checks." You'd have thought I'd held up a gun and said give me your money.

They said, "What?"

I said, "I want some blank checks."

They said, "What sort of checks do you want?"

I said, "Some counter checks, so I can pay some bills."

One of them said, "Do you do business with us?"

I said, "I've been banking at the Trust Company of Georgia, your main office in Atlanta, for more than forty years."

She said, "What's your number?"

I said, "I don't know, I didn't know I had a number. Why?"

So she got on the telephone, called the Trust Company in Atlanta, and apparently tried to get my number, and she evidently got some young lady on the phone as inexperienced as she was. Meanwhile, my blood pressure was rising. I knew I could write a check on a guano sack and if I had money in the bank to pay they had to honor it. So I finally said, "If you'll get Mr. Strickland, the chairman of the board of that bank, on the phone, I believe he and I can handle the matter right quick."

So she finally got my number and she said, "How many checks you want, Senator?"

I said, "A dozen or so."

So she got the checks, and then I saw her go back to a little machine and stamp numbers on it. I found out why about three months later when they cashed one of my checks I hadn't even signed. They do everything by machinery now. So after you go out of office, there are a lot of those little simple things you have to relearn. And I have been enjoying doing it.

Dr. Pajari visited with me at Lovejoy several weeks ago, and I spent two or three hours with him. I have long since found that history depends on who writes it. I've got no complaint with Dr. Pajari. He did one of the most astounding jobs of research I have ever seen. He sent me an advance copy of his paper. I think he revised it a time or two. And I was amazed that he gave the source of practically every statement. I looked at the source. If there was something favorable in the paper, it was usually someone that I considered a fair-minded reporter. If there was something unfavorable, I knew it was written by some villain who had been denouncing me for twenty-five years. That's the way history is written. It is written by the sources. We live in a diverse society with over five million people in Georgia now. And thank God not all of us have the same opinion, like they had in Germany under Adolph Hitler and Italy under Benito Mussolini.

When I left the office of governor I foolishly threw my papers away. I had no idea of their historical significance. I had no place to store them. I think every modern governor of Georgia except Dick Russell has done the same thing. Dick Russell kept every paper from the time he served in the Georgia legislature, not only his, but his father's also, who was chief justice of the Georgia Supreme Court. Now, after I went to the Senate I had sense enough to keep my papers, and when I left the Senate I sent over 1,600 boxes to the University of Georgia Library. So that will be a source of information for future historians.

I have long since learned that history is written by whatever the source was. If the source was favorable, you get a good report; if the source was unfavorable, you get a bad report. That's no reflection on scholars. Of course, scholars pursue the only leads that they have. Dr. Pajari has done an admirable job in that respect and I commend him for it. He was kind enough to make many generous remarks about my administration. I think I came along at a time when the people of Georgia and the General Assembly had reached a consensus to make progress in this state. You know, it took us one hundred years, from 1860 to 1960, to get our tax digest back to what it was before the War Between the States. We were extremely poor.

I was born and reared in Telfair County, where everybody was poor and thought that was the way everybody lived. They didn't know there was any other way of life. Grown people and families went barefooted twelve months of the year. Of course, they had no shoes to wear. Overalls were the common thing that people wore. Lots of people in the state at that time had no suits of clothes whatsoever. Those times were poor, and the people of Georgia were poor even when I took office as governor, following World War II. But at that time they had reached a consensus where they were not content to brag that Georgia was the Empire State of the South—they were ready to make it the Empire State of the South. I served as the catalyst.

I had a General Assembly that was working with me, and we instituted programs at that time that set the pattern for the remarkable progress Georgia has made over the past three decades. If you study statistics now, you will find Georgia not at the bottom of the list, where it was in 1948, but near the top in nearly every index. I want to give you just one example. I was born and reared on a farm. All of our neighbors burned their timber every year, trying to get early wiregrass grazing for the cattle, trying to kill rattlesnakes, and some of them setting a fire just for the hell of it. And when I was elected, the total income from forest resources in this state, everything—raw material, fiber and everything else—was $300 million a year.

When I campaigned over the state, frequently at any time from the fall of the year to the spring you'd have to stop your car on the highway to let the smoke clear away so you could see the road. We were burning up the greatest natural resource that we had. We don't have petroleum, we don't have an abundance of mineral wealth except the clays, little or no gold, no lead, no zinc whatever, but the great natural resource that we have in this state is our renewable trees, our soil. Having been a farm boy with some interest in forestry, I recognized that. And we immediately brought Georgia from next to the last in the nation in forestry to number one. You know what the result is today? Our timber resources bring into Georgia, now combined—finished and everything else— more than $7 billion annually. That's a far cry from $300 million that it was in 1948.

I am very proud of those achievements. I don't take credit for all of them, of course. I was the catalyst that precipitated the forward advancement of this state. Every governor of Georgia and every General Assembly that succeeded me has followed the pattern that we set forth and improved on it. Every one of them has continued it, and our progress has been undiminished since that time.

S. Marvin Griffin

1955 – 1959

Marvin Griffin
and the Politics
of the Stump

ROBERT W. DUBAY

Late on election night in September 1962, when it was obvious that former Governor Marvin Griffin had been thoroughly trounced in his bid for a political comeback in the Georgia Democratic primary, a supporter in Griffin's campaign headquarters brought a bit of levity to an otherwise somber setting when he remarked: "Someone's been eatin' Marvin's barbecue and not votin' for him."[1] But Griffin had a more insightful explanation for his landslide loss, saying: "It seems to be a trend of the times."[2] Griffin's words were prophetic indeed because that election was in many ways a milestone in Georgia history. For one thing, it was the first statewide electoral contest in nearly fifty years where winners were determined by popular vote rather than by the indirect county unit system method.[3]

Stylistically and substantively, the 1962 primary served as another kind of dividing line as well. Griffin's campaign was a carbon copy of the way such proceedings had been scripted for generations—there were plenty of barbecues, bird suppers, motorcades, fish fries, gospel singers, and fiery speeches punctuated with Griffin's special brand of folksy humor and vaudevillian antics. When it came to oratorical ability and effectively "shelling down the corn" out on the stump before live audiences, the ex-governor had few peers.

Griffin personified the last of those fast-fading days when, for reasons of reverence, obligation, momentary escape from boredom, or the promise of a free "feed," droves of dilapidated pickup trucks, rod-knocking Ford automobiles, and even an occasional tractor or two could be seen bouncing precariously over dusty potholed roads carrying entire families to worship at those sweltering summer Saturday campaign rituals where they heard the stump man's preacherlike tongue crucify the opposition. Communion between onlooker and aspirant was absolute. Each nourished the other, and during the course of a standard thirty-minute political sermon already impassioned believers became further inflamed when told how the money changers and the Jezebels and the Beelzebubs would be driven from beneath the capitol dome if the savior standing before them was elected on Judgment Day.

But by 1962 conditions, attitudes, and tastes had shifted decidedly in Georgia, or were on the verge of doing so. The state had become urbanized (meaning that a majority of the population lived in communities of 2,500 or more residents) and many citizens were more interested in jobs, the state's public image, and social harmony than they were in fighting for lost causes like restoring the county unit system, trying to reestablish segregated schools, and preventing court-ordered legislative reapportionment. Indeed, Marvin Griffin manifested the "old ways"—blatant racism, Washington-baiting, violations of human and constitutional rights, and government by cronyism, courthouse clique, backroom deal, and, some said, out-and-out theft.[4]

The victor that year was Carl E. Sanders, a bright young state senator from Augusta. Throughout his highly polished campaign, which included the first large-scale use of television in state history and helicopter visits to shopping malls, Sanders projected an image of moderation on racial matters and emphasized economic progress.[5] Voters apparently liked what they saw and heard and decided that what was needed was a "New Georgia."[6]

The fourth of six children, Samuel Marvin Griffin was born in the small southwest Georgia town of Bainbridge on September 4, 1907. After high school he enrolled at The Citadel in Charleston, South Carolina. Upon graduation in 1929, he secured a teaching position at Randolph-Macon Academy in Virginia and taught social and military sciences for the next four years.[7]

Due to the illness of his father, Ernest Howard "Pat" Griffin, Marvin returned to Bainbridge in 1933 to help run the family newspaper, the *Post-Searchlight*. Pat, who was also a state legislator, died the following year, and this turn of events enabled Marvin to enter the political arena by successfully offering for his father's vacant seat in the General Assembly's lower house. Rather than seek reelection two years later, Griffin attempted to unseat six-term incumbent Congressman Edward

"The Judge" Cox and was soundly defeated. Recalling Cox as a gifted orator of the old school, Griffin remembered how his opponent tongue-lashed him at a joint rally in Colquitt one afternoon: "When The Judge got through flaying me from Dan to Beersheba, there wasn't enough political hide left on me to cover a postage stamp."[8]

Capitalizing on the friends and contacts he had made during his legislative term, Marvin Griffin found employment with the State Revenue Department and a state-owned radio station until late 1939, when he became an aide and then executive secretary to then-Governor Eurith D. Rivers. For a variety of reasons this Rivers administration (his second) is not remembered as being among the most virtuous in Georgia history. Part of the responsibility for this view is traceable to the role played by Marvin Griffin in processing an abnormally high number of pardons and paroles. For from mid-1940 until Rivers left office the next January, there were strong and serious public allegations that Griffin and the governor's chauffeur had received money in return for such documents. Although a combination of circumstances prevented proper legal analysis of these charges, interesting facts are known: (1) Several of the certificates contained either the governor's stamped signature or Griffin's signature for Rivers; (2) Some of the documents were executed while the governor was out of the state; (3) During this episode, Griffin acquired a personal pardon for himself for a contempt of court citation and accompanying $200 fine he had received back in December 1939.[9]

Almost immediately after the close of the Rivers administration, numerous investigations were launched into areas of suspected misconduct. However, before pardon and parole affairs could be probed, Griffin resigned his commission in the Army Reserves and joined a newly federalized National Guard unit as a private. The unit was soon on out-of-state maneuvers.[10]

When the U.S. entered World War II, Griffin was made a captain and placed in charge of an all-Georgia antiaircraft battalion which was stationed in New Guinea throughout the war. Ironically, the outfit, known more for hijinks than heroics, bore the official code name "One Corrupt Group."[11] Having contracted malaria, Griffin returned to Georgia in the summer of 1944. His arrival happened to coincide with the resignation of State Adjutant General Clark Howell. Since the war was not yet over, the current governor, Ellis Arnall, made several telephone calls seeking a replacement for Howell. Griffin's name soon surfaced, and since Arnall and Griffin had served together in the legislature, the governor offered Griffin the post.[12]

In those days the adjutant generalship transcended its normal significance, for once the war ended the adjutant general decided which towns would have active National Guard groups, a matter of local pride and one which also brought economic benefits to the communities involved. Many of Griffin's subsequent choices were politically motivated.[13] Hoping that his newfound public name recognition and decisions regarding the location of Guard units would pay dividends at the polls, he announced for the governorship in the spring of 1946.[14] His electioneering efforts were supervised in part by James Dallas Pippen of Dry Branch, Georgia. Pippen knew state politics well and offered valuable advice on everything from tactics to wearing apparel—even to the point of having Griffin always dress in a navy blue suit, polka-dot tie, and white Panama hat.[15]

Griffin's campaign never really ignited, due in large measure to his being overshadowed by such formidable figures as Eugene Talmadge, James Carmichael, and Ed Rivers, who had entered the field. When it was clear that he could not win the governor's race, Griffin withdrew and immediately began stumping for the newly created post of lieutenant governor. He finished a respectable second, losing to Melvin E. Thompson, a former state school superintendent and revenue commissioner.[16]

Gene Talmadge won both the Democratic primary and the general election for governor in 1946, but died before being sworn into office, and this triggered a power struggle for the governorship which lasted several months and at one time or another saw no less than six individuals and their supporters claim the governor's chair.[17] Throughout this protracted episode, Griffin pledged the support of the adjutant general's office to his boss, outgoing Governor Arnall. But behind the scenes Griffin, who also had been designated as Gene Talmadge's adjutant general, used his influence and authority to assist Herman Talmadge's efforts to become chief executive. In this capacity, Griffin was responsible for physically locking Arnall out of his office.[18]

Once the courts decided that Thompson should serve as acting governor until the next election, Griffin returned to Bainbridge to chart plans for a reentry onto the political stage and to mourn the death of his daughter Patsy, who had tragically perished in the famous Winecoff Hotel fire in Atlanta on December 7, 1946.[19]

Griffin's electoral preparations were more extensive and thorough when the time arrived for the summer primary of 1948. Since Herman Talmadge and Acting Governor Thompson were the major contenders for the governorship, Griffin entered the contest for lieutenant governor and had no trouble in winning the post. Two years later he won the office again by an even wider margin—in part because he was closely identified with the popular Talmadge, who had won the chief executive spot in 1948 and 1950.[20]

Marvin Griffin made maximum use of his six years as lieutenant governor and presiding officer of the Senate. His fundamental objective, of course, was to lay the groundwork for his long-postponed bid for the executive mansion. Accordingly, Griffin availed himself of every opportunity to make some sort of public appearance, be it ceremonial or a speaking engagement.[21] Even though the 1954 primary attracted an array of political standouts, including House Speaker Fred Hand, Agricultural Commissioner Tom Linder, and former Governor Thompson, Griffin was recognized as the man to beat. And since the campaign took place on the heels of the United States Supreme Court's landmark *Brown* ruling, it was inevitable that segregation would be a central concern that political season. Griffin lost no time in monopolizing the white supremacy issue.

But there were three other reasons why voters followed the Griffin banner. First, he had the backing of the Talmadge crowd. Second, his rallies were spectacular extravaganzas laced with heavy doses of showmanship—such as his campaign opener in Moultrie when he plucked dried animal pelts from a feed sack and designated each skin as symbolizing an opponent. Then, with great fanfare, the hides were nailed to a wooden door that had been removed from someone's smokehouse.[22] A third factor in Griffin's appeal stemmed from a sizable number of progressive platform planks which pledged no tax increases and promised industrial expansion, farm-to-market roads, educational expenditures, improvements in social and recreational services, and honesty in government in the form of an end to influence-peddling.[23]

When the ballots were counted in early September, Griffin led the field with but 37 percent of the popular vote, yet he was the winner by virtue of receiving a plurality in enough counties to garner a majority of the county unit vote.[24] Few governors in modern Georgia history have entered office with more control over the legislature than did Marvin Griffin, and for the first three years of his term he had little difficulty in getting the General Assembly to see things his way. How is this explained? It goes without saying, of course, that Griffin accumulated a substantial storehouse of debts and favors by virtue of his previous positions. If circumstances warranted, political IOUs could be cashed in.

Working with lawmakers was also easier in those days. Issues were fewer and clearer. Besides, Griffin possessed a powerful personality and most state solons shared an ideological kinship with the governor. Two other things likewise kept legislators in line. In each of those areas, the role played by one of Marvin's brothers, Robert A. "Cheney" Griffin, was prominent, for even before the administration took office in January 1955 Cheney Griffin was placed in charge of patronage power and ultimately succeeded in giving new meaning to the term "spoils system." With skill and dispatch, the Griffin brothers solidified their hold on state government. Thousands of jobs were quickly filled with loyal supporters while public funds were transferred to "pet" banks and $60 million worth of state insurance coverage was doled out to those who had voted the right ticket. Such activities, while not illegal, made many an officeholder part of the Griffin team in more ways than one.[25]

Cheney Griffin also accidentally stumbled onto another means of exerting pressure on legislators when he discovered the existence of a "secretarial pool" in nearby East Point. "I went out there and found about fifty women and only one typewriter in the place," he remembered. In short order he fired several of the women and soon learned that the secretaries were the "gal friends" of certain senators and representatives. The women were reinstated.[26]

Basically, the Griffin administration is a study in paradox, irony, and deviousness. On the other hand, there were a number of profound and positive achievements which occurred between the years 1955 and 1959. But many of those signs and symbols of progress were either the result of someone else's thinking, an extension of the previous administration's program (Talmadge's), or the by-product of national and regional forces and trends which probably would have continued to unfold no matter who sat in the governor's chair. In short and on balance, while Griffin was never a particularly creative or original individual, he was receptive to ideas—motivations notwithstanding. Griffin always felt that his single greatest accomplishment was road paving. While the quality, location, and circumstances surrounding the construction of those highways became subjects of controversy during and after his term, the fact was that 12,000 miles of roads were hard-surfaced in four years, and this represented one-third of the grand total of all such state roads in history. Nevertheless, Herman Talmadge's administration produced a better record on both a mileage and percentage basis.[27]

All levels of education fared well under Griffin, partly because he believed in its value and partly because he was obligated to continue the Minimum Foundation Program implemented by Governor Talmadge.[28] In terms of higher education, the facts and figures are impressive. The state university system's annual budget more than doubled between 1955 and 1959. Further, there were shining symbols of progress over and above operating appropriations, such as a $13 million science center for the University of Georgia and a $5 million nuclear reactor for Georgia Institute of Technology.[29] Despite earlier initiatives to improve the quality of elementary and secondary education in Georgia, the state still ranked last in the Deep South in respect to per capita student expenditure when Griffin entered office. To reverse this trend and maintain the momentum begun under Talmadge, the governor poured vast sums into the public school system. By 1959 fifty-three cents of every tax dollar went to support learning. Within four years, annual appropriations had increased by 50 percent and teacher salaries went from $2,888 to $3,625 per year.[30] And along similar lines there were related advances, including the beginning of educational television programming, expansion of bookmobile services into rural areas, construction of new classrooms at a rate second only to that of California, and the virtual elimination of one-room schoolhouses.[31]

While Governor Griffin's educational endeavors were commendable indeed, certain questions arise as to the depth of his commitment to such enterprises. On the one hand, several of the bigger and more visible examples of his generosity had decided political purposes designed to be used in future campaigns. Much of the funding for special projects came from a contingency or stabilization account which enabled the chief executive to spend the revenue as he saw fit.[32] It was no accident that members of the Board of Regents were on the speaker's platform with Griffin in 1962.[33]

To finance his entire program, the governor was forced to summon the legislature into special session to approve multiple tax increases— something he had pledged not to do during the campaign. To get the General Assembly to pass the necessary revenue bills, the governor played heavily on the need to upgrade black education in order to preserve racially segregated schools, the hope being that if this were done Negroes would be less inclined to press the integration question. Indeed, once tax legislation was on the books, insofar as appropriations to black schools were concerned, this is precisely what happened. During the Griffin era 54 percent of capital outlay and approximately 52 percent of new school plants went to black facilities. Additionally, teacher salary discrimination between the races was greatly reduced.[34]

In other sectors as well the Griffin years proved beneficial and impressive. Social services pushed forward. Georgia led the nation in the number of individuals vocationally rehabilitated. The state's first alcohol-abuse clinic was opened, twenty-seven new public health centers were erected, and a wide variety of medical, children's, and old-age programs received additional funding or underwent modernization.[35]

Of a more far-reaching impact were the economic advances of the Griffin administration. No fewer than one thousand new manufacturing plants opened their doors in Georgia between 1955 and 1959. And there is little doubt that Griffin's many industry-seeking trips to Northern commercial centers aided in bringing these businesses South. At least some corporate leaders were influenced by the "able and effective" way in which the chief executive "sold" the state, telling audiences that there was no place "where the peaches [were] sweeter, the watermelons redder, the fish hungrier, or the girls prettier."[36] Business executives, of

course, made their decisions to move to Georgia based on their considerations too, such as low taxes, right-to-work laws, and the chief executive's record of using state troopers to intimidate labor unions.[37]

In other quarters, Griffin-backed economic plans resulted in significant improvements to the state-owned docks at the ports of Brunswick
and Savannah and the development of an inland port system which was
designed to connect interior areas to the state with overseas shipping
commerce by utilizing the Flint and Chattahoochee rivers.[38] Additionally, claiming that it was "easier to milk a tourist than a cow," the
chief executive deserves credit for spearheading the legislative purchase
of Stone Mountain and revitalizing Jekyll Island to make it a more attractive resort.[39]

On a less dramatic scale, there were other types of noteworthy accomplishments. In the four years Griffin held office, a new state archives
building was authorized, more parks were built than during any previous administration, historical sites were purchased or restored, 1,700
roadside markers were erected, a badly needed refurbishing of the governor's mansion and state capitol and dome took place, and numerous
farmers markets were put into operation.[40]

In spite of its many merits, however, the Griffin regime is fully deserving of its reputation as one of the most corrupt, amoral, mismanaged,
and inefficient administrations in Georgia history. And Griffin, as chief
executive, must be held accountable, directly and indirectly, for such
shortcomings and violations of the public trust. Even a cursory analysis
of the period between 1955 and 1961 will reveal an abnormally high
number of incidents, both proven and alleged, of official wrongdoing.
Certainly, no subsequent administration compiled such a negative record. How, then, can the assertion made in a contemporary issue of *Reader's Digest* be explained?: "Never in Georgia history had so many stolen
so much."[41]

In the first place, the Griffin administration happened to coincide
with the arrival of modern investigative journalism on the Georgia
scene. By the mid-fifties the Atlanta newspapers were staffed by a group
of talented, energetic, and resourceful young editors and reporters. Further, with more people on the state payroll than ever before, it was also
easier for newsmen to gain access to information. And in an atmosphere
where the spoils system was so ruthlessly and randomly practiced, disgruntled officeholders and disappointed businessmen (who were sometimes prevented from doing business with the state because of favoritism or the failure to provide kickbacks) were readily available to tell
their stories to anyone who would listen.

Along similar lines, the relationship between Griffin and the news
media was seldom cordial during his entire public career. In large mea-

sure, this was a by-product of a time-honored tradition among Georgia politicians: make the big-city press a whipping boy and an issue during campaigns.[42] But the real issue between the politicians and the press was rural versus urban, progressivism versus status quo. Griffin likewise hardly endeared himself to the larger Georgia newspapers by attempting to prohibit alcoholic beverage advertisements from appearing in such sheets and by sponsoring drastic changes in state libel laws so as to permit easier lawsuits against the papers. Both of these thinly-veiled efforts to stifle First Amendment guarantees through intimidation and threats failed, however.[43] Given such an adversarial atmosphere, there is little doubt that at least a few news stories were exaggerated or, when later proven to be inaccurate, never received the benefit of retraction.

On a personal basis Griffin also contributed to the shadow of suspicion which would forever haunt his administration. For one thing, he can be blamed for placing too much trust and reliance in close associates, including relatives, friends, and political appointees, some of whom misused their positions for personal gain.[44] Except for serious incidents of criminal activity (which were multiple), a number of lesser instances of official misconduct and cheap crookedness might have gone unnoticed had they not been so downright comical—like the legendary case of how a Savannah grocery store owner received over $10,000 in state insurance premiums without having written a single policy because he had no insurance license.[45] Even the *Wall Street Journal* found it funny that an individual "submitted two bids from two companies he owned" for wheelbarrow sales to the state and then simply bought the items in a local hardware store and had them delivered.[46]

Of all the revelations concerning the flawed Griffin years, none were more telling than those which smacked of executive impropriety or malfeasance. While a certain number of these accusations were obviously the handiwork of political opponents and amounted to little more than nit-picking, a constant flow of questions about matters ranging from the construction of private boathouses and the clearing of personal land by prison labor to unauthorized use of state aircraft and non-reimbursed state expenses for private travel to hunting and vacation sites proved embarrassing and probably caused many Georgians to at least wonder about the true cut of the man sitting beneath the capitol dome.[47]

Two incidents did more to undermine the governor's credibility than anything else. One was the discovery of the fact that he owned part interest in a steamship line. When it was likewise learned that several other high-ranking state officials also held stock in the same company, members of the press corps and ordinary citizens began questioning why Griffin had been so supportive of state port projects.[48]

Undoubtedly the most damaging blow to Griffin's reputation came in late 1960 when the attorney general's office sought an indictment against him from a Fulton County grand jury. The basis for the investigation was that the now ex-governor had allegedly conspired with four other individuals "to defraud, cheat, and illegally obtain from the State of Georgia" the sum of $19,350 through the sale of metal buildings to the boy's training school, the Welfare Department, and the Forestry Commission. Evidence presented to the grand jury indicated that a felonious scheme may have transpired during 1957 and 1958 whereby the governor would provide funds for the purchases, which would be by rigged bid. Everyone involved would share in the kickbacks, and according to one sworn affidavit, Griffin had on two occasions personally been handed $3,500 in cash—transactions which took place in the executive bathroom.[49]

Although the grand jury declined to indict him, the subsequent publication of affidavits, invoices, purchase orders, correspondence, and related materials caused many Georgians to reevaluate their opinion regarding the former chief magistrate.[50] In the end, however, another Fulton County grand jury, which had examined a wide spectrum of dishonesty relating to the Griffin administration a year earlier, may have come close to summing up those scandalous times when it concluded that an "amoral climate" had existed during Griffin's tenure in office and that this made it possible for "cronyism" and other levels of lawlessness to run rampant.[51]

Any assessment of Griffin's governorship would be incomplete without reference to race relations and constitutional issues, both of which were frequently intertwined. But what is most troublesome, and yet imperative to comprehend, is the reprehensible disregard of human and civil rights which occurred between 1955 and 1959.

It goes without saying, of course, that when Griffin came to power no Deep South politician could have been elected to office without being a segregationist. But Griffin's racist views were extreme, and he seemingly left no stone unturned to keep the racial situation at a confrontational level, both inside and outside Georgia. In the latter regard, Griffin made numerous forays beyond state soil to preach his demagogic message of massive resistance to integration. Seemingly, everywhere he went racial tensions were further inflamed by his rhetoric. Perhaps the best illustration of what his diatribe could trigger came in the late summer of 1957 when he visited Little Rock, Arkansas, on the eve of that city's dramatic school desegregation crisis.[52] Given this kind of behavior, it was no small wonder that one historian labeled the governor a "roving ambassador of turmoil."[53]

Griffin's antiblack attitudes and actions often bordered on ludicrousness and frequently brought national ridicule to the state. Certainly the most embarrassing episode came in late 1955 when he attempted to prevent Georgia Tech from playing against the University of Pittsburgh in the Sugar Bowl because Pitt had a black player on its squad.[54] A few years later another press field day was in the offing when a group of Canadian coal miners who had been freed from a cave-in were invited to Georgia for a free vacation. When one of the miners turned out to be black, the news media had a joyful time printing stories on how segregation was maintained amid the integrated gathering of rescued souls.[55]

At least in part, some of what Governor Griffin did regarding racial matters is understandable, perhaps pardonable, considering constituent pressures, the context of those troubled times, his personal background, and the legitimate right to raise constitutional issues. To begin to acquire an understanding of Griffin's racial views and policies, one must remember that he was a product of his past. Considering that his father was a member of the Ku Klux Klan and that racial bigotry was deep-rooted in Georgia during his formative years and that state laws required separation of the races, it is easy to see how such feelings and attitudes developed.[56] Moreover, recently released documents from Federal Bureau of Investigation files shed supplementary light on Griffin's actions. These materials reveal, among other things, that the governor received a series of death threats between 1955 and 1957 from an organization calling itself the National Negro Congress.[57]

In related matters, basic constitutional and civil rights were not safe in Georgia during Marvin Griffin's tenure as chief executive. Ironically, the state's official float in the second inaugural parade of President Dwight D. Eisenhower in January 1957 carried the caption: "The Right to Express Our Views." But when it came to practicing those rights at home, Georgians did not always have their guarantees protected while Griffin was in power.

The activities of various government agencies such as the Georgia Commission on Education, the Georgia Bureau of Investigation, and the attorney general's office are significant in determining the extent to which personal and First Amendment rights were jeopardized. The case of the Georgia Commission on Education is especially illuminating. That organization's executive secretary, for instance, was known to have acquired "a dreamy assortment of private-eye equipment" (pocket microphones, a camera with a telescopic lens, a telephone wiretap apparatus, etc.) which was utilized to conduct clandestine investigations of suspected integrationist plots. The same group also participated in similar work in Tennessee and Louisiana. Governor Griffin knew of such intrigue but did nothing to retard it, except to say that the commission director might have been a bit "overenthusiastic."[58]

Throughout these years the Georgia Bureau of Investigation was also busy on a variety of fronts, ranging from investigating the Koinonia Farm Community near Americus for its integrated life-style and racially mixed Bible school camp to spying on NAACP personnel, photographing black voters at polling places, and preparing dossiers on the families of black students who applied for admission to Georgia colleges. While it is not entirely clear what purpose such information would serve, judging from some of the reports it would seem like the motive might have been character assassination or attempting to establish an imaginary link between communism and those who sought enforcement of the law of the land.[59]

For all its faults and defects, the Griffin administration should remain one of the most important governorships since World War II. The legacy of progressive accomplishments is long indeed. And even in terms of negative features, there is much to be said on a positive level because the stridency of racism and the magnitude of governmental wrongdoing probably served to hasten reform in both areas.

S. Marvin Griffin:
Georgia's 72nd Governor

SAM M. GRIFFIN, JR., &

ROY F. CHALKER, SR.

Editors' Note: When the symposium was scheduled, Sam Griffin was invited to speak on behalf of his late father. He declined to participate, but he did submit the following paper on his father's record.

On a hot day in early July 1981 Marvin Griffin sat and spoke intently into a portable tape recorder, using the measured cadence and diction of the experienced teacher lecturing on a favorite and familiar subject. Speaking extemporaneously, in a few moments he had traced the paternal lineage of his ancestors back to his great-great-great-grandfather, James Griffin, of Edgecombe County, North Carolina, through his service during and after the Revolutionary War, then down to Montgomery County, Georgia, around 1804, and finally over to Irwin County, where he is buried.

With the same familiarity and precision, Griffin recounted the history of his beloved state and of the Griffin family and traced the boundaries of Georgia with precision and clarity. The entire recitation of family and state heritage was conducted without the benefit of charts, maps, or notes. Nor was it done from a podium or at a round-table discussion. On this particular day Marvin Griffin was seated upright in bed in a Tallahassee hospital. He had just discovered that he had inoperable lung cancer, and he was under no illusions as to what lay ahead.

What Marvin Griffin demonstrated that day was not a remarkable knowledge of his ancestry and the history of his state, nor even courage and personal presence in a time of stress. Instead, what he did was the manifestation of a total and continuing love of a place and its people—all of its people—present and past. It was a part of him. That sort of love is not created—not even understood—by mere knowledge, research, clinical analysis, or scholarly works. It comes from within, and it must be felt to be understood.

The year 1907 was just over forty years after the War Between the States and the Reconstruction Act which divided the Southern states into five military districts and allowed the people and what remained of the area's devastated resources to be exploited. It was the year before Henry Ford produced his Model T, and it was a year of economic panic—though in south Georgia it was hardly remarkable in the context of economic hardships which had plagued Georgians, especially those in the extreme rural reaches of the state, for more than half a century. Marvin Griffin was born on September 4 of that year to, as he styled it, "a family of moderate means."

His father, Ernest Howard "Pat" Griffin, had left his native Quitman, in Brooks County, at age eighteen and moved to Camilla, in Mitchell County. There he worked as a clerk in Brimberry's store and in 1898 married Josie Butler. He entered the grocery business in Camilla, briefly and unsuccessfully, and then moved to Pelham and founded a weekly newspaper, the Pelham *Free-Lance*. In 1907 he moved to Bainbridge with his three children—Louis Howard, Miranda Lou, and Josie May—and founded the Bainbridge *Post*. In 1915 he bought the *Searchlight*, another weekly newspaper, and combined them into the *Post-Searchlight*.

Samuel Marvin Griffin was the fourth of the family's children and the first to be born in Bainbridge, Decatur County, followed by Iverson Carlisle and Robert Alwyn "Cheney" Griffin. For Marvin Griffin, as the son of a weekly newspaper editor, the courageous daily struggle of the average Georgia cracker—the battle of his family, friends, and neighbors, black and white, to fight the poverty, disease, and insularity that recycled itself without hope or promise—was a familiar part of his life. Equally familiar were the meager armaments for the battle: dirt roads, makeshift one-room schoolhouses, inadequate medical services, and remote colleges. Out of this familiarity with and affection for the ordinary man (whom he later collectively symbolized in the figure of "Willie Highgrass") was born the desire to excel, to do something to make a difference in the lives of these people. Politics and newspapering were natural, environmental channels for this desire, as they were for his father.

Few things were more interesting than politics to the elder Griffin, a red-haired country newspaper editor of Scotch-Irish descent. Pat Griffin was elected to the legislature in 1915, and in 1920 helped create Seminole County from Decatur County. That this partitioning coincided with his defeat for the next term was not coincidental. However, he was reelected in 1924, and again in 1928, 1930, and 1932. He died during the 1933–34 term.

Marvin Griffin's first experience with politics began as a boy of ten in 1917, as he described it in the first chapter of an unfinished autobiography:

> I was privileged to go to Atlanta with my late father, who was one of Decatur County's two representatives in the General Assembly. At that time his colleague was the late A. B. Conger, a prominent Bainbridge attorney, who later served as a United States District Judge for the Middle District of Georgia. I drew my first political perquisites of office as a page in the legislature and received two dollars a day for my services.
>
> After the legislature adjourned in the afternoon, standing committees of the House held meetings or public hearings on bills before the body for consideration, and I was privileged to go sightseeing in the City of Atlanta without the restriction of an adult. I had money, at least $5, and the city was mine. We stayed in the old Kimball House while in Atlanta. In fact, most members of the General Assembly and practically all politicians "put up" at the Kimball House. Some rural members of the General Assembly thought all legislation was passed at the Kimball House, and the truth of the matter is, most of it was passed there.
>
> I have a vivid recollection of Uncle Joe Hall of Bibb County, who sat in the lobby of the Kimball House with a coterie of friends and colleagues about him, talking about legislation before the House, and other stalwarts of the General Assembly such as the late John Wesley Culpepper of Fayette County, Cecil Neill of Muscogee County, and William Burrell of Hancock, taking turns to relate the activities of the time.
>
> I recall one afternoon when I was on my own I left the Kimball House and strolled up Peachtree Street to see the sights north of the Winecoff Hotel, which was later to be the scene of such a tragedy to more than one hundred Georgia families.
>
> The Executive Mansion in those days was located where the Henry Grady Hotel is today. It was a red brick, two-story home set back about 75 feet from the sidewalk, and it was enclosed with a

black, iron-picket fence. The gate of the fence had a large, shiny brass plate with the words, "Executive Mansion," and much to my surprise, it was not locked.

I opened the gate, but did not go in. I did, however, stand up on the bottom rail of the gate, and "swung" on it a time or two.

A city policeman came along and said, "Young man, do you realize you are swinging on the Governor's gate? He wouldn't like that if he saw you." He next asked me where I lived, and I told him down at Bainbridge, Georgia. It seemed he knew a number of Bainbridge people, including my father, and he scolded me no more, perhaps realizing that I had never been to the city before, which I hadn't.

On my return to the Kimball House I related my experience to my father, and he asked the question, "Well, do you think you would like to live in that mansion?" I replied that it seemed to me to be hard to get into, and he made the observation that it was extremely difficult to get into, and that many Georgians had tried for years to live in it, but few had ever made it.

Even before that initiation into the mysteries of politics, Marvin Griffin had begun to accept the mantle of leadership which would eventually lead to the executive mansion. His teachers recognized in him an academic and intellectual excellence, his friends and classmates looked to him for leadership, and his family became accustomed to the expectation of achievement. And Griffin carried the responsibility with fortitude, but without diminishing his boyish exuberance or humor.

"We were not what one would call 'bad,'" he said of himself and the boys in his neighborhood, "but we did not get any gold stars for exemplary conduct. One Atlanta friend of my father's asked him one time, 'Pat, are these boys of yours rough?' My father replied without batting an eye, 'Well, let's put it this way: If a cat is discovered in our neighborhood with a whole tail, he is a tourist.'"

Griffin attended the Bainbridge public schools and graduated from Bainbridge High School in 1925. In the fall he enrolled in the freshman class at The Citadel, the Military College of South Carolina. He had exhibited considerable athletic talent as a high school baseball pitcher. At The Citadel he pitched for the college baseball team during the school year, and in the summer earned school money working for his sister's brother-in-law, Russ Davis, a Lake City, Florida, pharmacist. He jerked sodas in the mornings and pitched baseball for the local team in the afternoons.

Griffin graduated from The Citadel in 1929 with an A.B. in history and political science, distinguishing himself with the cadet rank of major, commanding the 1st Battalion of the Corps of Cadets, the highest military achievement possible. In September of that year, just before the catastrophic stock market crash, he was offered and accepted a position as commandant of cadets at Randolph-Macon Military Academy in Front Royal, Virginia, a boarding school and college preparatory institute in the upper Shenandoah Valley.

For the next four years he taught history, Spanish, and military science, and it was during this time that he met Mary Elizabeth Smith of neighboring Winchester, Virginia. "Lib," as she was called, was secretary to the principal of Handley High School and the daughter of the county treasurer (tax commissioner) of Frederick County. On July 11, 1931, they were married in the Methodist church at Kernstown, a few miles from her home.

Though named Samuel Marvin, the young Griffin had always been called Marvin by his family and by friends in Bainbridge. In later public life he settled upon "S. Marvin Griffin" as a signature, quipping, "I part my hair on the side, not in the middle." However, his Citadel schoolmates chose to call him "Pat," the nickname bestowed upon his father. It followed him to Randolph-Macon, and it was this name that Lib and his Virginia friends always used. On July 10, 1932, their first child, a daughter, was born in Winchester, and she was christened Patricia Ann.

In June 1933, after Marvin Griffin had been in Virginia nearly four years, his father became extremely ill. In those dismal depression days, as his health failed, so did the economic vitality of his newspaper. Griffin resigned his position at Randolph-Macon and returned to Bainbridge to become editor and try to salvage the business. On January 6, 1934, E. H. "Pat" Griffin died at age fifty-five. He was at the time beginning the second year of a two-year term in the legislature, and Marvin Griffin ran for and was elected to the seat vacated by his father. He served one two-year term, 1935–36, but his attention was divided. He had inherited the newspaper, the *Post-Searchlight*, but outside of the nameplate, the subscription list, the simple newspaper equipment of the day, and the obligation to a tradition, his inheritance consisted mostly of a large string of unpaid bills and uncollectible receivables. He and Lib put in long hours at the task of settling accounts, salvaging assets, and rebuilding a business—which wasn't easy in the mid-1930s, for friends, neighbors, and the business people of the community upon which the newspaper relied for its subsistence had little to offer but hope, promise, and good intentions.

A second child, Samuel Marvin, Jr., was born on February 12, 1936, and that same year Griffin decided to challenge U.S. Representative E. E. "Gene" Cox for his Second District congressional seat. It was a baptism by fire into the realities of politics. Griffin discovered that nothing—including the fact that his grandfather had been a postmaster in Brooks

County under a Republican Reconstruction administration—was insignificant or unfair game in a political campaign. At a tricounty forum in Colquitt, Georgia, he learned that a candidate should either speak last or vacate the platform when he has finished if there is no rebuttal allowed. He delivered a speech in which he "exhorted everybody to do good, and admonished those who would do evil," and returned to his seat on the platform while Cox delivered his address. The congressman used him as a convenient clinical chart at which to point, with accusing finger, to illustrate the specimen archenemy of Franklin Delano Roosevelt and all he represented. It was both a humiliating and an enlightening experience, and one which he never forgot.

Neither did Lib, who was deeply hurt when she watched as the wife of a prominent attorney—whom she had previously thought a close friend—sat in the Cox ranks on the platform and applauded and laughed with obvious approval at Marvin's dissection. Years later it was this experience to which she would most often mention when explaining her aversion to politics. Cox soundly trounced him in the election.

However, his defeat did not sour Marvin Griffin on politics. On the contrary, it seasoned him and honed his appetite. The place for a young man with political aspirations was Atlanta, of course, and an opportunity for a job with the State Revenue Department was irresistible. It met the criteria of being at the center of Georgia's political world and providing an additional paycheck for a struggling weekly newspaper editor. Griffin became a part of the administration of Governor E. D. Rivers. It was during these years that he made the acquaintance and friendship of M. E. Thompson, another young man seeking a political career. Though they would become vigorous political opponents in later years, he and "Fess" retained a personal friendship and mutual respect.

Griffin became an executive aide to Governor Rivers, and he also received appointments to the State Radio Commission, the Library Commission, and the Aeronautics Advisory Board. Finally, on June 6, 1940, he was named executive secretary to replace Downing Musgrove, who had been appointed comptroller general. He continued to serve as Rivers's executive secretary until Eugene Talmadge was inaugurated as governor in January 1941.

Two factors which would significantly affect his political career were established during the Rivers years. One was the experience in the executive branch of government, and the other was the beginning of an adversarial relationship with the Atlanta newspapers. The first would combine with his cultural background, his education, his teaching experience, and his legislative service to begin forming a political philosophy and an agenda which would manifest itself in his later campaigns and administration. And, added to his future experience as a military commander, adjutant general, lieutenant governor, and president of the Senate, it would make him one of the most qualified men to ever be elected governor. The second would ensure the presence of a constant but changing coalition of powerful political enemies formed around the nucleus of a hostile newspaper empire that would daily oppose, criticize, condemn, harass, belittle, or distort every program, action, statement, or position he would take—regardless of merit—as long as he lived.

The Rivers administration was not on the best of terms with the Atlanta newspapers prior to Griffin's appointment as executive aide. Later, as executive secretary, he inherited part of the adversarial relationship. The remainder of it likely grew from the Rivers-Miller and executive clemency disputes. Rivers had reappointed W. L. "Lint" Miller of his hometown of Lakeland to the Highway Commission and made him chairman in 1937. With the assistance of the legislature, he abolished the previous board to do it. However, Miller considered himself an independent agent, and a split occurred. One of the differences concerned the school fund emergency of 1939. Sufficient monies were not appropriated to meet teacher salaries, and many systems were facing a shutdown. Rivers wanted to use highway funds until the shortfall could be solved; Miller didn't. The situation offended Griffin's sense of reason, and he wrote an editorial urging that the schools should be permanently funded and not rely upon the legislature for annual largess.

Rivers sought to remove Miller, acting on the premise that whomever he had appointed he could certainly fire, but Miller refused to step down gracefully and took the matter to court. Griffin, acting on Rivers's orders and with the militia, evicted Miller in defiance of the court order and was found in contempt of court and fined $200 for carrying out Rivers's directive. Miller was finally upheld by the court and returned to the board, but the episode formed the basis for a seamy-sounding allusion often voiced by Griffin critics. Griffin later asked for and received a gubernatorial pardon for the citation.

In an open letter to Gene Talmadge on March 28, 1946, while Griffin intended running for governor, he replied to editorial attacks that Talmadge had made in his political weekly, the *Statesman*, and addressed the matter of pardons:

> You know that a secretary to a Governor never did have the authority to grant a pardon to a single soul in Georgia, and that no pardon would be valid without the Governor's signature, unless you permitted that to be done while you were Governor. When you were Governor, the record will show that you issued several hundred more pardons than I was ever privileged to certify as to the sig-

nature. Many people say you are dishonest, but since I can't prove it, I will not be ungentlemanly enough to say it is so.

In spite of this political give-and-take and earlier spats, Talmadge and Griffin reconciled their differences, and Talmadge had enough respect for him to ask him to serve as his adjutant general after Talmadge won the 1946 governor's race.

Griffin critics often allude to his having been pardoned by Rivers for contempt, usually implying that he pardoned himself for some personal wrongdoing. They seldom tell how the contempt charge originated. The contempt citation as it relates to the so-called pardon scandals of the Rivers administration was not the only connection the Miller situation played in the general Griffin/newspaper enmity that was to plague him throughout his career.

The Atlanta *Journal* was bought by former Ohio Governor James Cox about that time, but the Atlanta *Constitution* was published by the respected Major Clark Howell. However, one L. A. Farrell, a special correspondent for the *Constitution*, wrote a story saying that Rivers had called his adjutant general, Jack Stoddard, back from a trip to Washington and had plans for the militia to march on the federal court in Macon, where a contempt case was pending against him arising out of Miller's removal. Farrell said Rivers would resist federal court action by military force should the court rule against him. Rivers objected. Farrell was questioned but insisted on his story, and the paper elected to reassert its correctness, despite the demonstrable fact that Stoddard was still in Washington and had never left. Griffin opined in an editorial that "articles in the *Constitution* for sometime will be taken with a grain a salt."

Use of executive clemency had been a newspaper topic for many years. The Georgia House of Representatives ordered a probe of pardons and paroles in February 1939, asking for a list of pardons granted, attorneys, etc., dating back to February 1938, predating Griffin's appointment as executive secretary by more than two years. It was a continual bone of contention with every governor. Some light is shed on the foundation of the Griffin/newspaper pardons controversy, however, in an editorial letter he wrote. On November 7, 1940, Griffin addressed a letter to the Atlanta *Journal* concerning the newspaper's continuous criticism of Rivers, and specifically editorial condemnations for a pardon granted to one E. T. "Pee Wee" Randall, who had run afoul of the law and been sentenced to six to eight years for possession of burglary tools. Rivers pardoned him less than one year later by commuting his sentence to time served. The newspaper attacked the pardon as evidence of "a racket." Griffin wrote the editors and published the letter in his paper:

I am perfectly familiar with the policy of the Atlanta *Journal* and have watched closely your continued unwarranted attack on the Governor of Georgia using executive clemency as a basis for your criticism. The Atlanta *Journal* recently changed hands, but this policy of continued destructive criticism of the Governor began about the time the Chief Executive refused to issue a conditional pardon to one Richard Gallogly, in whom the Journal is critically interested.

"Dapper Dick" Gallogly had served twelve years as "thrill killer" of drugstore clerk Willard Smith in a holdup in 1928. In October 1939 Gallogly was hospitalized and claimed his health had been ruined by his years in prison. On the trip from the hospital to Tattnall prison, accompanied by his wife and mother, he commandeered the guards' car, left his mother on the roadside with the guards, and escaped to Texas with his wife. He was finally caught and returned to prison in Georgia. The *Journal* had campaigned for clemency and Rivers had refused.

Press criticism about the Randall pardon had included complaints that executive clemency was poorly administered by Rivers because it bypassed judicial input. Griffin quoted a letter Rivers had received from the sentencing judge in the case, Judge Paul Etheridge, prior to granting the pardon. The judge said he had opposed earlier pleas for clemency, but he had since been given additional evidence, and he recommended that Randall's sentence be reduced to time presently served. He chided the paper for ignoring the fact that Rivers's acting on the recommendation of the sentencing judge was hardly precipitous, nor evidence of "a racket," unless the paper thought the judge was guilty too.

Even after his death, Griffin critics refer to the pardon scandals publicity of the Rivers administration as though it furnishes proof positive of Griffin's dishonesty. In fact, Griffin was never charged, indicted, tried, or convicted of any wrongdoing concerning pardons or anything else in the Rivers administration.

Griffin had retained the reserve officer's commission earned as a Citadel graduate. By mid-1940 the Nazis had begun their sack of Europe and Japanese imperialism in Asia and the Pacific was well underway. On September 27, 1940, Germany, Italy, and Japan signed a ten-year military and economic pact. National Guard units were being formed across the nation, with units being called into federal service for a year's training shortly after organization. Marvin Griffin resigned his reserve commission and enlisted in the Georgia National Guard as a private. A coast artillery/antiaircraft unit was formed in Bainbridge on October 14. Griffin was appointed captain in command of this unit, which was designated Battery D of the 101st Separate Battalion.

Gene Talmadge won his 1940 governor's race, and on January 14, 1941, was inaugurated. On January 23 Griffin wound up his duties as executive secretary of the now-ended Rivers administration and wrote a column in which he wished the new Talmadge administration well, "without bitterness" for the criticisms it had heaped on Rivers, declared he would not be active in politics for the next twelve months, and said farewell to home in preparation for a year's active duty in training. On February 9, 1941, Battery D left Bainbridge to report to Camp Stewart in Hinesville for induction into federal service. Ten months later, on December 7, 1941, the Japanese attack on Pearl Harbor and the subsequent declaration of war changed the training plans, and on February 12, 1942, the 101st embarked on the former liner *Queen Mary* at Boston harbor to go overseas. The unit disembarked in Australia, and on April 28 was ordered from Brisbane to Port Moresby, New Guinea.

Japanese forces occupied the territory north of the Owen Stanley mountain range as Allied forces struggled to establish air bases on the south side. Because stragglers and AWOLs from other units were rounded up for transfer to New Guinea along with the 101st, the code name "One Corrupt Group" was assigned for the purposes of this movement. Once there, the unit provided antiaircraft coverage for the port, and then moved onto the north coast with invading troops. The 101st received two Presidential Unit Citations and served in three major campaigns—the Netherlands East Indies, Papua, and New Guinea.

Griffin was promoted to major and then to lieutenant colonel, and placed in command of the 101st Battalion. He commanded the battalion until he was rotated back to the U.S. with other members of the battalion in July 1944 after nearly thirty months in the jungles of New Guinea.

While Griffin was overseas, Ellis Arnall, who had been attorney general at the time Rivers was governor, was himself elected governor, and on January 12, 1943, was inaugurated. Arnall's adjutant general, Clark Howell, had resigned and Arnall offered Griffin the position. Griffin accepted and began the process of reorganizing the Georgia National Guard. In view of the fact that Arnall had been attorney general and in a position to know Griffin as executive secretary to Rivers, his appointment would seem to indicate a confidence in Griffin's integrity and ability in disagreement with the allegations and suspicions voiced by his political enemies and the Atlanta newspapers.

With Griffin back in Atlanta and once again in the Georgia mainstream, politics beckoned again. He had been elected vice-president of the Georgia Press Association in September 1945, but he resigned the position to seek public office. He first intended to make the 1946 race for governor, but with E. D. Rivers, Gene Talmadge, Jimmy Carmichael, and Hoke O'Kelly in the wings, he decided he would fare better in the race for lieutenant governor, an office that had been created by the Georgia Constitution of 1945.

Politics and political campaigning were more an extension of Griffin's way of life than they were a design. From early days he was accustomed to stop at every crossroads and country store, buy a package of peanuts and a cold drink, introduce himself, and find out all about the proprietor and his family. And he remembered. It was not a contrived political tactic. It was a sincere desire to know and to learn about people, a desire to bond with them, and he thoroughly enjoyed it. His campaign for lieutenant governor had actually been underway for a lifetime. In 1946 it was merely beginning to take direction. However, in the July 17 primary he ran second in a field of six candidates. His old friend Melvin E. Thompson was elected lieutenant governor, and Gene Talmadge was elected governor.

Having patched up old wounds—and perhaps because in their earlier scraps Talmadge was able to take the measure of the younger man and liked what he saw—Talmadge asked him to continue as adjutant general under his administration. Griffin informed Arnall of the request and said if Arnall had any objections he would resign for the remainder of the term. Arnall told him he had none, and said he was flattered that Talmadge would give his selection a vote of approval by asking Griffin to continue. On December 5 Herman Talmadge announced for his father that Marvin would continue as adjutant general.

Talmadge, of course, died before being sworn in. Griffin concluded that Talmadge, elected by the legislature, was the legitimate governor and that he owed him his support while at the same time providing for Arnall's safety by furnishing him an escort of field-grade National Guard officers in plain clothes. Some of Talmadge's less patient supporters wanted to forcibly eject Arnall from the governor's office, but Griffin would not allow it.

However, Talmadge stalwart Roy V. Harris had the locks to the governor's office changed once Arnall had gone for the day, giving Talmadge control of the office. Denied access to the governor's office, Arnall set up his office in the capitol rotunda the next morning. The Georgia Supreme Court finally decided the matter in Thompson's favor, resulting in a two-year term with a special election for 1948. Griffin served as adjutant general until March 22, 1947, two days after Thompson was ruled the legal governor by the court.

In early December 1946 the state Y-Clubs were holding an assembly in Atlanta and Griffin's daughter Patsy, then fourteen, was a delegate. The Bainbridge delegation was staying at the Winecoff Hotel on Peachtree, one block down from the Henry Grady, where those years ago young Marvin had swung on the governor's gate. Griffin had a room at the Piedmont Hotel, several blocks down the street. He took Patsy out to dinner that evening and returned her to her hotel before retiring himself. He was awakened by the sirens and noise and ran up the street to the fire. When he discovered how bad it was, he began to check the hospitals.

Griffin thought he had found his daughter at Grady Hospital, and called his wife in Bainbridge. She was rushed to Atlanta by his brother, Cheney, while Griffin sat by the bedside of a badly injured child who had been tentatively identified as Patsy. Before Lib arrived, the child's identity was determined, and it was not their daughter. Griffin renewed his search, and with the help of friends her body was finally located and identified in a funeral home in Decatur. Even thirty-five years later, it was extremely difficult and painful for him to recall it.

By 1948 Griffin had made the necessary preparations to run for lieutenant governor, and he was successful in a field of six without a runoff. Herman Talmadge defeated M. E. Thompson in the governor's race, and both Talmadge and Griffin were inaugurated on January 10, 1949. Griffin was, incidentally, the first lieutenant governor to serve under the Constitution of 1945, since Thompson served as acting governor instead of in the position of lieutenant governor to which he had been elected in 1946.

Griffin was reelected in 1950—this time carrying 156 out of 159 counties and receiving 57 percent of the popular vote. He ran better than his unofficial running mate in the governor's race, Herman Talmadge. His success may have marked him as a potential political rival, with future consequences.

Then came 1954 and the campaign for governor. As adjutant general, Griffin had made the acquaintance of a young man on Ellis Arnall's staff who would become one of his most loved and loyal friends. He was also one of the best practical politicians in Georgia history. James D. Pippen was articulate, debonair, had an extraordinary understanding of human nature, excellent powers of observation, and the finest memory for names, faces, and details of any politician in Georgia. His advice and counsel were invaluable. Another plus factor was the organizational ability of Marvin's brother Cheney, who ran the state headquarters.

The campaign of 1954 was, as Griffin put it, a baseball team because nine candidates qualified. These included M. E. Thompson, Fred Hand, Tom Linder, Charlie Gowen, Ben Garland, Edmund Barfield, Mrs. Grace W. Thomas, and Arthur Neeson. It was a long, hot summer. Both Hand and Griffin were Talmadge affiliates, which threatened to split that support and favor Thompson. Linder had a substantial following as agriculture commissioner. The Atlanta newspapers invested considerable time and flattery encouraging Hand to enter the race and split the Talmadge vote.

The issues were divided into two groups: (1) The standard issues of the day, which included vows to support segregation, states' rights, and the county unit system and pledges of no additional taxes; and (2) The creative issues, which included whatever innovative programs the candidates devised to intrigue the voters, and attacks on the reliability of the other candidates, together with whatever reasons one candidate could think of to substantiate why another candidate should not be relied upon to protect the matters mentioned in the standard issues.

Segregation and the county unit system could hardly be called issues, however, for none of the major candidates opposed them. With at least five major candidates, focus would understandably be a problem in campaigning. Thompson and Griffin realized that if they would concentrate on each other throughout the campaign they could dominate the public attention and would stand a better chance of one of the two of them being elected. This they did, effectively shutting the other candidates out in the cold and leaving them to share leftovers. Of course, they each had their strategies aimed at the other, too, and Griffin was successful.

Out of a field of nine, Griffin carried 115 counties (including Fulton), tallied 302 county unit votes, and received 36.3 percent of the total popular vote. Thompson ran second with 26 counties, 56 unit votes, and 25 percent of the popular vote. Griffin received 234,690 popular votes and Thompson got 162,007, out of a total vote of 646,235. The other seven candidates had to share the remaining 249,538 popular votes, and the next highest vote-getter was Tom Linder, with 87,240. Ernest Vandiver, who had succeeded Griffin as adjutant general, was elected lieutenant governor.

Marvin Griffin does not need a defense for his administration. The statistical and factual data of his accomplishments are a matter of record which no amount of belittling, criticism, or nit-picking can erase. The man who is entitled to receive the blame for the failure is equally entitled to receive the credit for the successes. The educational improvements, the additions to higher education, the roads, the programs, the encouragement and financial support to teachers and other state employees, the industries—all of these things remain to bear witness. But more important is the memory of the man, his courage, his loyalty, and the gracious and fair manner in which he tried to accomplish what he thought was good for Willie Highgrass, his kith and kin.

More telling than the grudging and disparaging remarks from critics about Marvin Griffin's tangible successes are the affection, devotion, and continuing belief with which he is remembered by those with whom he worked, by those who helped him and called him friend.

These things surely have more substance and weight than the vituperative opinion expressed in an anonymous letter to an Atlanta newspaper by no less authority than one disgruntled nonsupporter in Macon, Georgia. Nor does Marvin Griffin need an apology for the failures of his administration, both real and fabricated. It would be ignoble to dismiss all charges of wrongdoing by members of his administration as "nothing more than was done in every administration before and since," but there is a great deal of truth in that proposition.

There were admittedly some wrongdoers. There always are, exposed or unexposed. But whatever the comparable quantity or degree, no administration before or since has been subjected to the intensity or consistency of criticism, scrutiny, allegations, disparagement, opposition, and belittlement as has the Griffin administration because of the long-standing animosity of the Atlanta press and the political opposition allied to or organized by it. Surely, after cataloging the litany of charges and condemnations for more than four years, there could not possibly be even one part-time janitor in the lowest level of the most distant state institution during the Griffin administration who wrongfully used a ten-cent Ticonderoga pencil, but what that miscreant was discovered, charged, duly indicted, and convicted of his crimes. The remainder of the administration should be certifiably honest beyond a shadow of a doubt.

Despite the masses of charges and all allegations, there were few convictions, and no attempt has ever been made to restore the damage to the reputations of those not found guilty of allegations. The record for posterity—created largely by the Atlanta press for political purposes—stands with the allegations. An unwarranted question, once asked, serves its purpose of suggesting political impropriety, regardless of substance. The answers are seldom heard or remembered.

Through all of this, no effort was spared to implicate Marvin Griffin in wrongdoing. The Fulton County Commission was pressured by the Atlanta papers to appropriate $50,000 for Fulton Solicitor General Paul Webb to hire attorney Paul Cadenhead and a task force of investigators to find something on Griffin. Officials who were accused of wrongdoing, guilty or not, were promised leniency if they would implicate Griffin—and some tried, in desperation. Yet a Fulton County grand jury refused to indict Griffin. Despite the continuous and relentless attacks on his honesty, he was never indicted, tried, or convicted of any crime or impropriety. Even a reviewer for the state archives journal has been so conditioned by the Atlanta newspapers' constant litany of Marvin Griffin's corruption that in recent years he wrote of Griffin for an archives journal: "Many officials were indicted by grand jury, including Griffin himself."

That such an assessment of guilt and corruption is assumed by later generations, without knowing the particulars, is not a matter of chance. It grew out of the political animosity begun in the Rivers administration, where the Atlanta newspapers' unproved smears of Griffin's character then became the source they cited for authority in later years—an amusing technique if one doesn't happen to be the victim.

It began in earnest on inauguration day in January 1955 when Charles Pou, a political writer for the Atlanta *Constitution*, pledged to those in a small group within the sound of his voice as he left the ceremony, "I will spend the next four years gutting Marvin Griffin, and I will get him some way." The effort was quite effective, and it continues even now. The constant accusations, distortions, hyperbole, and disparagement of over five years have blended so thoroughly with the minute seasoning soupbone of reality that they are inseparable. And that has become the record.

Marvin Griffin ran on a platform of preserving segregation, preserving the county unit system, paving farm-to-market roads, putting tag sales in the courthouses, and no new taxes. In 1983 State Representative Denmark Groover presented a memorial resolution in honor of Griffin. Groover recalled that, despite campaign pledges against any tax increase, Griffin had the courage to ask, "What is best for Georgians?" and created a State Programs Study Committee to assess the needs of the state. With the committee's report in hand, he convened a special session of the legislature on June 6, 1955, and appealed to a joint session, "Regardless of what I said last summer, let me remind you of these things: I shall not turn my back on progress, I shall not desert our children in their hour of need, I shall not shirk my responsibilities as your chief executive in the task of developing fully our God-given human and natural resources." As a result, the legislature increased the educational and university system budgets by one-third each.

Groover also recalled that Griffin had created the Stone Mountain Authority to purchase Stone Mountain, created the Jekyll Island Authority to remove the property from politics, built the Science Center at the University of Georgia and a nuclear reactor at Georgia Tech. Groover concluded that "Marvin Griffin was proudest of his contributions to education, and probably next for his rural roads program, but his finest hour was probably his decision to ask for a tax increase to meet the needs of Georgians."

The Griffin administration had other significant contributions, many of which were tarnished by the reflex criticism and ridicule of the Atlanta papers. These included: establishment of a State Forestry Center; restoration of the Joseph Vann House; construction of a museum at the Etowah Mounds and a road to the top of Brasstown Bald; restoration of

New Echota; improvements at Kolomoki State Park; completion of the Talmadge Memorial Hospital in Augusta; construction of sixty-two new hospitals and public health facilities through the state/federal Hill-Burton program, as well as a modern facility for retarded children at Gracewood. Among its other accomplishments, the Griffin administration established a $100 floor for teacher retirement for thirty-five years' service; extended Social Security to teachers and financed sick-leave pay for them; enabled Southern Tech to move to Cobb County; began the junior college system in urban areas; helped to bring Continental Can to Augusta and the Monroe Equipment Company to Hartwell; established the "50–50" plan to help advertise the state nationally; created the State Farmers' Market Building Authority; signed $10 million in bonds to finance a new farmers' market south of Atlanta and other farmers' markets where needed; provided $300,000 each of four years to eradicate Bangs disease in cows and hogs; established a probation system; built branch prisons at Leesburg, Bainbridge, Warm Springs, and Waycross; had the capitol dome covered with donated Dahlonega gold; established a Hall of Fame in the capitol rotunda; signed into law a bill establishing the present Georgia flag; created the Georgia Firefighters' Pension Fund; provided $2 million to construct a deep-water port at Brunswick; established an inland port at Bainbridge and began new inland port docks in Augusta; and provided funding for property acquisition in Savannah.

The Bainbridge Inland Port, of course, was a target for ridicule by the Atlanta papers. Ignoring the city's history of river commerce and continuing efforts to reestablish river traffic to the Gulf, the Atlanta *Journal* labeled the proposal a boondoggle. It published a cartoon showing Griffin standing on the bow of an oceangoing steamer moving down a highway toward Bainbridge, with a sign pointing to the Atlantic Ocean 190 miles to the rear. The papers' deficiencies in geography were exceeded only by their lack of honesty and fairness. The deliberately false impression was never corrected. The port at Bainbridge was begun in 1956 and dedicated in May 1958. Later in 1958, two years after the location of a state dock site at Bainbridge, Griffin supported a number of Georgians intrigued with the prospects of developing a shipping company which might eventually utilize the port facility at Bainbridge.

Some fifty Georgians formed a corporation and bought a converted World War II landing ship. Griffin bought one share of stock; his son had two. The Atlanta papers immediately accused him of building the port at Bainbridge to further his own interests. They seldom accused him of that much foresight. This, in the newspaper annals, became another instance of Griffin's corrupt practices to which they could vaguely refer as a scandal—documented because they said it was.

The Rural Roads Authority was a highly successful method of paving farm-to-market roads at low cost. Many highway planners agree a similar plan is needed to implement the Developmental Highway System of the 1980s within an effective time frame. The project was nitpicked and attacked by the Atlanta newspapers as a political boondoggle, and when Griffin attempted to increase the capital of the $100 million authority by an additional $50 million in 1958 Lieutenant Governor Ernest Vandiver selected it as an issue for a political showdown. There was nothing wrong with the program, but Vandiver needed a cause, and he claimed the program would be used by Griffin as patronage to help a Griffin-picked opponent beat him for governor.

Vandiver was the obvious next governor and had political promise for legislators who would be returning. Griffin, a lame duck, had none, and Vandiver won the fight. He blackened the eye of the Rural Roads Program, and when elected had all the signs designating rural roads already built pulled up in an "economy move." But he and succeeding governors quietly adopted similar road-building plans under different names.

Another favorite tactic of the press was to discredit Griffin because of his stand on segregation. He was painted as a rabid racist, and the Georgia Tech–Pittsburgh Sugar Bowl episode of 1955 was pointed out as an example. For Griffin, it was a no-win situation, and, again, the Atlanta newspapers contributed to the problem and generated as much dissension as they could. Tech was scheduled to play Pittsburgh in the Sugar Bowl and someone discovered that Pitt had black team members. They complained to Griffin, reminding him that state law prevented integrated sporting events. Had he not responded, he would have been in trouble with the rigid segregationists; if he did respond—which he did—he would alienate the Tech supporters who wanted to see the team play in the bowl game. Consistency required Griffin to choose the course of protesting the game to the Board of Regents, and the Atlanta press had a field day at his expense. By early afternoon, sound trucks and reporters swarmed onto the Tech campus, encouraging students to a sense of outrage and action. The tradition of the "shirt-tail parade" caught fire, and the march was on.

Griffin was a segregationist. All politicians who wished to be elected were; it was the order of the times. But he was by no means a racist in the sense that he bore or exhibited any hatred, animosity, lack of respect, or ill will toward the black race. To the contrary, in accordance with the "separate but equal" concept of the day, Griffin ensured that black institutions received more than a pro-rata share.

In 1962 Griffin made an unsuccessful effort to return to the governor's office. Any analysis of exactly what defeated him in that race would be likely incomplete, but factors would have to include the repeal of the county unit system, which occurred after Griffin's campaign was underway; the effective political assassination of Griffin by the Atlanta press; the age factor—an older, more "weathered" politician running against a fresh and attractive young man who could use the medium of television better; failure to understand the need to change traditional campaign styles to accommodate the new shift of power to the urban and suburban areas; opposition comprising a powerful coalition of the state's largest financial institution, the sole statewide newspaper and largest television station, and a candidate who better fit the image of the changing times; lack of the experienced campaign team he possessed in 1954.

Of the 1962 race, it has also been said that "his friends" beat him, which contains some truth but is not completely valid. Marvin Griffin loved life and people, and it was difficult for him to believe that anyone would bear him animosity or take advantage of him. His wife, Lib, used to say of him, "The only trouble with Pat is that you'd have to slap him about three times, real hard, before it might occur to him that you did not like him." He was, literally, loyal and believing to a fault. Some of his friends and appointees to whom he remained loyal did violate his confidence for personal gain and hurt his chances, but his real friends, who served ably and honestly, were victimized with him by his adversaries for their association. Nothing they did could have prevented it.

He hated to have to recognize ill-placed confidence in another human being, and seldom said anything when he was deceived. But he knew the difference. It was perhaps the hurt and disappointment that prevented him from confronting those who had used him. But Marvin Griffin enjoyed life. He greeted it and each new person with sincere delight, without cynicism, and with full belief in the basic goodness of his fellow human beings. He was vulnerable and disappointed on some occasions, sometimes with drastic consequences, but he enjoyed an optimistic, rich quality of life that a more cynical and suspicious man would never have experienced. No ordinary disease could fell such a man; it took cancer. And he met that with the same sense of challenge with which he approached every new and interesting idea.

Many of his friends asked why he worked so hard for the people of Georgia—why he was forever helping, befriending, and forgiving. He asked little in return. On the afternoon before his death his son was with him, and he asked for Mary Ann, his daughter-in-law. She came and they asked what they could do for him. "Just put your arms around me and hold me," he answered. That was all he ever wanted.

The authors wish to acknowledge the special contribution of Cathy Cox, who conducted the basic research for this article.

Marvin Griffin Remembers

An Interview by
GENE-GABRIEL MOORE

Editors' Note: The following interview was conducted at Governor Griffin's home in Bainbridge in June 1976. It is published with the permission of Georgia Public Television.

MOORE: Governor Griffin, of all the men that have been governor of our state, none other enjoys the reputation for having the affection of so many people who at the same time consider your administration to have been a controversial one. . . . Every person that I have talked to about you, even people who do not like you politically, who have never voted for you . . . at the same time talk about how splendid . . . a man you are. I wonder . . . if you ever encountered this characterization and if you feel . . . you could tell me where it comes from?

GRIFFIN: Well, Gene, I don't know. I am so glad to know that there is a personal friendship even among the ranks of my former political opponents. But frankly I like people, and I have always liked people, and while I do not agree with them all . . . I do respect them as personal friends—political friends or not. . . .

MOORE: Your son runs the [Bainbridge] *Post-Searchlight* now, but for thirty years you ran the *Post-Searchlight*. The *Post* was founded by your father, a pioneer newspaperman and—as you have told me yourself— someone who had a quick Irish wit and a quick Irish temper. Does your fabled storytelling ability come from your father?

GRIFFIN: Well, I guess it does. If I have any, I guess it does. He had a sense of humor, and I have always tried to maintain a sense of humor and not get too upset or rattled about any political adversities. My basic philosophy was that if a fellow did anything he was going to make some political enemies and become controversial. Now, if he stayed in public life . . . as the old saying goes, "if he takes his pitcher to the well often enough, somebody is going to knock a hole in it and let the water out."

MOORE: Governor Griffin, let's move into your administration. You were in the General Assembly. You were executive secretary in the Ed Rivers administration. You were adjutant general under Ellis Arnall. You were lieutenant governor for six years when Herman Talmadge was governor, and you were elected governor in 1954. It was a very hot campaign with M. E. Thompson and some other political forces in the state. Think back to that year of 1954 and that particular primary campaign and tell me what it was like.

GRIFFIN: Well, it was right hectic. That would be minimizing it. It was really hectic. We had a strong set of people running against us in 1954, and all of them were good men. I have the highest regard for them today, but when you have to run against M. E. Thompson from Valdosta, who had served about two years as acting governor and had been closely identified with the State Department of Education for twenty-five or thirty years, and the Honorable Fred Hand, who had served with distinction as speaker of the House of Representatives and happens to be a neighbor of mine over in Mitchell County, and the Honorable Tom Linder, who served as commissioner of agriculture with a strong personality, and Charlie Gowen, an attorney from Brunswick who moved to Atlanta, a fellow out running against that field, in the vernacular of we Wiregrass Georgians, had to steer his stumps to get by them in 1954. It was a spirited campaign. . . .

MOORE: That was also the year . . . that *Brown vs. The Board of Education* was decided.

GRIFFIN: Yes, that decision came down on May 17, 1954, if my memory serves me correctly . . . three and one-half months before the primary in September. It was certainly important during that campaign.

MOORE: There's always been an element since 1926 in our state called "Talmadgeism" that existed before the two-party system. There were the anti-Talmadge and the Talmadge factions. In that particular race you had been lieutenant governor during the six years that Herman Talmadge was governor. M. E. Thompson was representing the anti-Talmadge people. Tom Linder was very close, and Fred Hand was known to be a close friend of Herman Talmadge. Where did that leave you in relation to the Talmadge influence?

GRIFFIN: I don't think Herman had any intention of taking sides in that primary because, basically, I don't believe he thought the governor should inject himself into a political campaign of a number of friends. I think that perhaps I was successful because I started earlier and I worked harder. I think I can say that without fear of contradiction. I stayed after it for six years. Most of the others had not been in the field that long, and in those days personal contact, shaking hands, visiting homes, visiting rural stores, eating fish and barbecue on the river banks in this state and everything people invited you to, and a few you pumped up yourself, was important. I think I just outlasted them.

MOORE: Well, let's talk about your administration, then. I'd like for you to enumerate the achievements during your administration. I realize that not every politician likes to speak favorably of himself, but maybe you can overcome that inhibition, Governor.

GRIFFIN: Well, I have said this, Gene, out of respect and admiration for my associates who have served as governor of the state of Georgia, and I do respect all of them, and I think each governor who has served has had some beneficial effect upon the progress and development of Georgia. I don't think that my administration killed all of the bears. I don't think that Herman's administration killed all of the bears. I don't think Ellis Arnall's administration killed all of the bears. It is the sum total of the efforts of all of the governors who have served the people of our state.

Now, of course, I was the first governor to be elected as far away from a state capital as I was. It's about 240 miles, and I know . . . you know how far it is. The Florida line is only about fourteen miles south of Bainbridge, and this is down in southwest Georgia where the Flint and Chattahoochee rivers come together. It's a long way from the capital, and an old friend of mine used to say . . . "I tell you, in the state of Georgia the city of Atlanta is the heart. When the heart starts pumping out blood, the farthest member of the body from the heart is the big toe, and that generally stays the coldest because it gets the least amount of blood." So, working on that basis, I was basically committed to improve or develop the resources not only of the urban centers but of rural Georgia, and so I talked with my friends and we got us a plan whereby we could create a Rural Roads Authority and construct about one hundred million dollars or ten thousand hard-surface roads from farm to market.

My idea was that one of the greatest things that Franklin D. Roosevelt did for the rural people of the United States was the creation of the Rural Electrification Administration. Well, the people on the farm got electric power, and that revolutionized the farm business in my opinion. I thought when I became governor . . . that we would pave the . . . rural roads to enable a farmer to get his produce to the market, his family to the doctor in inclement weather, to enable the school buses to run in inclement weather, and things of that nature. Well, we did that, and I guess I'm about as proud of the achievements of the Rural Roads Authority as any other one thing that I was able to do. We got the folks in rural Georgia out of the mud. There's no question about that. We didn't complete the job, and we had a terrific row in 1958 about increasing the capitalization of the Rural Roads Authority by fifty million dollars. I wasn't going to spend it during my administration but the fellahs . . . said, if we give that cracker another fifty million dollars, you'll never get rid of him in politics in Georgia. So the General Assembly failed by about three votes to increase the rural roads capitalization.

MOORE: It could be that in this day and time people are really not aware just how important it was and is to have roads in rural areas.

GRIFFIN: Think of the people in Georgia who lived on a slick clay road or a sandy road and paid six and a half to seven cents a gallon gasoline tax for forty years and didn't have a road to ride on. They felt like they had been forgotten, they'd been mistreated.

MOORE: I suppose everyone knows that M. E. Thompson bought Jekyll Island, but not everyone remembers that Marvin Griffin bought Stone Mountain for the state.

GRIFFIN: Yes, for years when I was adjutant general, and then when I was lieutenant governor, I'd go by Stone Mountain and see that unfinished work there, and I'd want to turn my face away from it. I was a little ashamed because it was in memory of not only a lost cause but it looked like the people of Georgia had fallen down and it was just a failure. So I began to plan some way that the state of Georgia could purchase that property and develop a great state park there and complete that memorial. . . . So, going back to Stone Mountain, I opened my gubernatorial campaign in 1954 at Moultrie with a mammoth crowd, but on the following Monday afternoon I spoke at Stone Mountain, the little town. We had some four or five hundred people, as well as I remember, and I told them that before I came out of the governor's office . . . I would see that Stone Mountain was bought for the people of Georgia and developed for the people of Georgia. I said it's a shame—I'm really ashamed of it. Of course, those people were greatly in favor of it. It was there in their back yard or front yard, and they wanted to see it developed. Well, I think it was the thing to do, you know. That was a great gift of God. God put that big hunk of granite there at Stone Mountain. If our friends down here in Florida, in the Sunshine State, had had something like Stone Mountain, they'd have been wrestling alligators on top of Stone Mountain and charging one dollar a wrestle for a hundred years. There we were letting a great facility, an asset like that, go to waste. . . .

Another thing I'm real proud of is what we were able to do for public education in Georgia, not only in the public schools, elementary and high schools, but for our institutions of higher learning. During my tenure of service as governor, we increased the teacher's salary every year for four straight years. Not only that, but we financed the first sick-leave program. The sick-leave program was on the statute books, but it had never been financed, and then some old dedicated teachers who had taught for thirty-five years and retired were drawing a pension of forty or sixty or fifty-eight dollars, some little trifling sum of that nature, and so we put a floor under it. Every teacher who taught thirty-five years or more would receive not less than a minimum salary of a hundred dollars per month. It took a few hundred thousand dollars to do that; it took a few hundred thousand dollars to finance the sick-leave program. Then we continued to build our public schools under the School Building Authority, which was really the brainchild of my neighbor Fred Hand.

But, in our institutions of higher learning, I'm most proud of the Science Center at the University of Georgia and the atomic reactor at Georgia Tech along with the physics building. Also, on the Tech campus we put the headquarters for the Southern Regional Education Board as a permanent thing. In the other institutions of higher learning we built something of value on every campus of every unit of the university system.

The late Dr. Aderhold wrote me a letter that I keep—one of my keepsakes. He said the building of the Science Center, where we committed about thirteen million dollars at one time, was the first great breakthrough that the University of Georgia had had, and he wanted to thank me. Well, of course, I'm proud too as I go there and see that Science Center. I think we should develop our historical sites and things, and so, with that in mind, I built a museum. The Historical Commission and I had to get up the money for it in tight times. We built a museum at Midway, and a museum near Cartersville at the Etowah Mounds. We found additional money for a museum in Early County. We enlarged the Crawford W. Long Museum. We also began the reconstruction of New Echota in north Georgia, and we renovated the Chief Vann House at Spring Place in Murray County. Those things, plus public parks and other things, were for the benefit of the people.

In industry seeking and building ports, along with the Ports Authority, I got up two million dollars for the deep-water port at Brunswick, and during my administration we bought the ocean steamship facilities from the Central of Georgia [Railroad] and added it to the state port of Savannah. We built an inland port at Bainbridge and started the Augusta one with $150,000 appropriations. I think all those things have enhanced the progress of Georgia.

MOORE: At the same time, Governor Griffin, I think it's fair to say that many people who look back over our state's history and consider the Griffin administration do not consider the things that you have been

saying, and instead consider the parts of it which are considered controversial. Do you feel that you've been given a fair shake?

GRIFFIN: Well, I really have no complaint. In my own heart and
mind I know that we did a good job. Now, sometimes when politics gets
hot and people get after you, they can make the situation look bad until
you have time to back off and look at it. I appreciate the fact that now
many many people have said to me, "I didn't know these things were
done during your administration. I didn't know during your administration that you put the dome on the state capitol from gold that people
donated from Dahlonega." I said, "Yeah, and I looked in the paper sometime ago and they gave another governor credit for that." Well, it wasn't
any use for me to raise sand; but with the people in Dahlonega we refur-
bished the capitol. It cost a few dollars less than a million dollars to
build, and I had to take two million dollars out of a sinking fund, an
equalization fund, and renovate the state capitol. The dome was considered to be hazardous. Well, you know a governor didn't like to take what
little out-of-pocket money he had, especially if he had a budget of only
three hundred million dollars that year, to do all these things. Now the
budget's about a billion eight or nine hundred million.

MOORE: How do you characterize your campaign style?

GRIFFIN: Well, I don't know, Gene. As I get older, sometimes I think
I get extremely slow, but I always liked to read the expressions on the
people in the audience to whom I was speaking. A man who loves people and is out there with them every day can soon . . . tell if his goods
are selling. Now there is a little modification of that. South Georgians
or middle Georgians, I've found, are very enthusiastic if you say something they like. They might throw their hats up as high as a Georgia
pine and holler, "Hurray, tell it like it is!" But when you get up in the
mountains of north Georgia the folks up there are a little more reticent,
and they're not as emotional. They don't show their emotions. First
time I ever spoke at Cleveland, Georgia, in White County, I had about
four hundred, and I made 'em the foot-stompingest, double-barreled, old
wind-up stump speech you ever heard in your life, and they never
changed expression, and I told my benefactor, "My friend, I did not sell
any calico here today." He said, "Don't pay any attention to them not
applauding and so forth. They don't do that anyhow. Let's just wait now.
Don't leave." They came up in ones and twos and shook hands with me.
The biggest promise I got out of anybody that day was one fellow tickled
me on the palm and said, "I won't do you any harm."

MOORE: There's another institution that's been almost copyrighted
by the Griffin years in Georgia politics and that's the barbecue. We don't
have 'em anymore, and I miss having them because when I was a child
and a younger man I've gone to them many a time. I'm sorry to see them

passing, having thousands of people in and having barbecue and brunswick stew and iced tea and talking politics. . . .

GRIFFIN: To tell you the truth, Gene, I am too because I'd go to more
political speeches if they had a barbecue to go along with it. That used
to be the way to rub elbows and to get to know your people better. All
your friends wanted to get up a big crowd, and the way to do that was to
have a nice barbecue and serve all the fringe benefits that went with a
barbecue—pickles and brunswick stew and things of that nature. I
think even my good friend Carl Sanders will say that the Griffin crowds
were the largest. We checked on him, and frankly his crowds didn't look
so large, but they were deceiving. He got the vote and I didn't. I made
the mistake. Everybody that ate my barbecue I don't believe voted for
me.

MOORE: Did you model yourself on any of Eugene Talmadge's platform delivery and style?

GRIFFIN: Well, if I did, I wasn't conscious of it, though I liked his
direct approach. Maybe I got that from him—his direct approach. "Lay
it down," as we used to say. "Lay it down where the cats can get to it. Put
the milk down in the saucer where the cats can get to it." And I believe
to this day in telling it like I think it is.

MOORE: I know a good many newspapermen, having been a newspaperman myself at one time, and from time to time we get together
and talk just like politicians do about people like Marvin Griffin. You're
missed, Governor Griffin, by the press. And the press, the Atlanta newspapers in particular, used to just lay it into you every day.

GRIFFIN: Yeah, well, I liked those fellows, all of them personally.
Some of them could take the hide off of me, there ain't no two ways
about it, and that's their job. I always kept that in mind. That's that
fellow's job, and I got no right to abuse him because our country's
founded on free speech and freedom of the press and I'm in the newspaper business. But I was a little like the fellow who owned the short
line railroad of twenty-five miles. The old railroad presidents in the old
days used to swap annual passes, and the president of the New York
Central wrote him a letter and said, "I can't exchange with you. Your
railroad is too short for the New York Central to exchange an annual
pass." And this friend said, "Well, I tell you, . . . my railroad may not be
as long but it's just as damn wide as yours." Well, all I had was a country
newspaper or two, which couldn't cope with the boys in Atlanta, but
some of my fondest memories come from some of the scuffles we had
up there at press conferences. I named 'em "Jorees." I sent them a stuffed
Joree [a small groundbird that scratches up the dirt] after I came out of
office, and they, in the press club, had a bar and they called it the Joree bar.

MOORE: When you were governor and you were doing things like

buying Stone Mountain and things that would affect generations, were
you aware then that you were making decisions that would put you in
the history books?

GRIFFIN: Well, no, but I did believe at that time that we had to record the past to appreciate the future, and I am proud of my heritage. I
was very anxious to see Stone Mountain purchased by the people of
Georgia and developed as a great park and certainly to complete that
memorial monument on the face of Stone Mountain. . . . I did think in
those terms, I'm sure. I think all other governors in office would have
moments when they thought about the same thing. They had to or they
wouldn't have been committed to certain projects with such zeal and
enthusiasm.

MOORE: In those four years as governor, is there anything . . . you
would not have done had you known at the time what the consequences
would have been?

GRIFFIN: Yeah, there's one or two folks I wouldn't have appointed if
I had it to go over with, but then that's an honest mistake and there's no
need to embarrass anybody at this point about it. But I certainly would
have appointed some other folks. Most of my appointees I was extremely proud of. A few I'm not.

MOORE: What was the tempo and the characteristics of your relationship with Ernest Vandiver, who was lieutenant governor?

GRIFFIN: Well, I was always very friendly to Governor Vandiver. I
don't think we saw eye to eye about everything, naturally. He attacked
me personally when I wasn't eligible to run for reelection, and I never
said anything about him. He didn't need to do that to get elected. He
could've walked into office, but he did attack me personally and I never
have been able to understand why. I don't bear him any ill will . . . but I
don't see why he had to step on me to get the job. I'd never said anything
to or about him, that I know of, except a time or two we may have
crossed swords in an effort I wanted to get done. He delayed the passage
in the Senate of my administration's bill to set up the Stone Mountain
Memorial Commission several times. Finally, I told the floor leader to
go down there and tell him I wasn't interested, I couldn't run for governor in 1958, and that I had no intention of injecting the governor's office
into anybody's race; but they might give it a little thought down there,
that I'd hate like hell to run this summer against Jeff Davis, Robert E.
Lee, and Stonewall Jackson. The weather's too hot. The bill came out
that day.

MOORE: How do you feel the people of the state of Georgia think
about you? I know for a fact you're held in great affection by politicians
and the press.

GRIFFIN: I addressed the Rotary Club in Blakely last Friday, and one of my old friends, Tyge Baker, introduced me, and he said, "I'm gonna' present the man next that doesn't need an introduction." Course, I really didn't. I've spoke at least twenty times in Early County. But he said, "The man that more lies have been told about than any other, but is held as a friend by more folks in Georgia than any other former governor. . . ." Well, I thought that was a great compliment. I didn't deserve it, but I appreciated it. You know, the older folks get, the more they appreciate kindness and compliments.

S. Ernest Vandiver

1959 – 1963

S. Ernest Vandiver
and the Politics
of Change

CHARLES PYLES

In an editorial written near the end of Governor S. Ernest Vandiver's
term, Eugene Patterson, then the editor of the Atlanta *Constitution*,
asked, "Why no statue for Vandiver?"[1] Arguing that the governor deserved one, Patterson asked and answered the question solely on the
economic aspects of Vandiver's administration, but other forces loomed
large during his term that shaped and molded the governor's actions and
had a far-ranging impact on the life and welfare of all Georgians both at
the time and afterwards.[2] Those questions, and how Vandiver responded
to them, must also be considered in any effort to answer Patterson's
rhetorical question.

Two phenomena, the "black belt" and the county unit system, contributed to a rural-urban cleavage in Georgia. The Democratic Party's
power in the state centered in the forty-odd counties where more than
50 percent of the population was black, i.e., the black belt. In those
counties few blacks voted, and the white power structure controlled
most of those who did. The county unit system of voting also favored
the black belt counties. This combination created a hegemony of rural
interests which, in turn, dominated state politics. By the time Vandiver
took office, however, these entrenched conditions were under attack.

In 1949 V. O. Key, Jr., characterized Georgia politics as "The Rule of
the Rustics" and predicted that such factors as urbanization, Negro out-

migration, and the spread of commerce and industry would gradually create conditions favorable to change in the politics of the American South.[3] In the forty years since Key's landmark study, the rural areas have lost population—notably blacks—the cities have grown dramatically, and blacks have become active participants in the political life of the state. Rising educational levels, higher incomes, in-migration, and economic activity have contributed to a far more racially moderate leadership than at any other time in Georgia history. (See Table 1 for evidence of the changing social and economic base of Georgia.)

Vandiver's administration marked the end of much that supported white and rural political and economic hegemony. While this political revolution might well have been conceived in the decade of the forties, Vandiver's administration lay claim to the birth of the new era, for during those years a series of crises forced a young governor and his state to make fateful decisions.[4] This paper will focus on two broad policy areas of substantive importance in the Vandiver years: desegregation and the economic development of the state. Governor Vandiver's role in dealing with these issues will provide the primary emphasis, but his initiatives and responses to other issues will be addressed also.

Samuel Ernest Vandiver, Jr., served Georgia as governor during the years 1959–63. Only forty when elected, he already had experience in state government as adjutant general for six years and as lieutenant governor for four. A native of Franklin County, he attended schools in Lavonia and Rome before entering the University of Georgia where he earned B.A. and LL.B. degrees. During World War II Vandiver served as a bomber pilot. He returned home in 1945 and practiced law, was elected mayor of Lavonia in 1946, and subsequently served as aide to Governor Eugene Talmadge and later to Governor Herman Talmadge. He became adjutant general in 1948, and while in that office he also served as state director of civil defense. His capable leadership as lieutenant governor during the Griffin administration, his political connections to the Talmadge group, and his family ties to Senator Richard B. Russell made him a likely candidate for governor.

As the election year of 1958 approached, rumors persisted that the former chairman of both the Georgia Rural Roads Authority and the State Highway Board would run for governor with Governor Griffin's support. Early in 1958, when Griffin asked the legislature for a $50 million extension in the bond limit of the Rural Roads Authority, supporters of Lieutenant Governor Vandiver, labeling the proposal a "slush fund" to be used against their candidate, rallied to him and defeated the proposal in the House. The House action crushed any hopes of substantial opposition to Vandiver's ultimate campaign, and the Atlanta *Constitution* labeled it the second most important news story of 1958.[5] In-

TABLE I
Georgia Population by Decades and Corresponding Changes in Selected Aspects of That Population

Year	Population	% Non-Whites	Median Family Income	Median Education	% Population in Cities over 10,000	Percent Rural
1940	3,123,723	34.7	a	7.1	28.0	65.6
1950[b]	3,444,578	30.9	1,898	7.8	31.8	54.7
1960	3,943,116	28.6	4,208	9.0	37.4	44.7
1970	4,589,575	26.1	8,165	10.8	36.5	39.7
1980	5,463,105	26.8	12,441	c	29.9	37.6

[a] The 1940 Census gave no figure comparable to median family income.
[b] The 1950 Census of population incorporates a new definition of urban territory. Prior to 1950 the definition was limited to incorporated places having populations of 2,500 or more. The new definition includes unincorporated places having populations of 2,500 or more and densely settled urban fringe around cities of 50,000 or more. The new definition is used for succeeding years.
[c] Not given in the 1982 Georgia Statistical Abstract.

deed, Governor Vandiver himself said that he thought the nomination campaign was decided by that vote in the House, months before the party primary took place.[6]

Vandiver's chief opponents in the 1958 Democratic primary were the Reverend William T. Bodenhamer, a Baptist minister, and Lee Roy Abernathy, a gospel singer. The race concentrated on desegregation, but the debate was not about whether desegregation should occur or not. That was not a debatable question. Public opinion resisted desegregation, and no candidate dared take a moderate stance. Blacks were so ill-organized and the Congress and the president were so reluctant to implement the Supreme Court's desegregation decision that campaigners were free to denounce it.[7] All of the gubernatorial candidates tried to "out-seg" each other, but Bodenhamer attacked Vandiver as weak on segregation, charged him with "race-mixing," and claimed that the National Association for the Advancement of Colored People had endorsed him after whites and Negroes stood together in a line to be served barbecue at a Vandiver rally.[8]

The criticism stung Vandiver, who later admitted that he was too thin-skinned, especially with unjustified and unfair accusations.[9] He claimed that he was best qualified to preserve segregation and the county unit system. The two issues were connected in his mind, and he argued that the county unit system maintained the people's control of their government and thus guaranteed they would never be dictated to and controlled by the NAACP. He promised that he would, as governor, use the "state patrol and national guard troops if needed to maintain segregation," and in a statement, much repeated, he proclaimed that "no school or college classroom [would] be mixed" during his administration.[10]

Recent studies have classified Vandiver as a strong or militant segregationist on the basis of this campaign rhetoric. However, at no time did he attack Negroes themselves. Indeed, he is credited with stopping the "Negro-baiting" rhetoric that had previously come from the governor's office.[11] While desegregation and ways to deal with it were paramount in the voters' minds, Vandiver also campaigned hard on the theme of honesty and decency in government in light of the alleged corruption and wrongdoing of the Griffin administration. He promised to assume full responsibility for the official acts of his department heads.

In a light vote, Vandiver won overwhelmingly, taking 80 percent of the popular vote and 404 of the unit votes—a clear mandate for positions he advocated. Vandiver's victory also signaled a new winning coalition, which ended bifactionalism in Georgia. An examination of the election results reveals that Vandiver showed strength among homeowners, educated, well-to-do people, and in areas with significant population growth. His only weaknesses lay among nonwhites, tenants, agricultural labor, and urban voters who, in the past, had been correlated positively with the Talmadge faction.[12] The end of bifactionalism was occasioned by a combination of factors: there was no U.S. Senate race in Georgia that year, the desegregation crisis forced white Georgians to unite against the "Negro threat," and Herman Talmadge was now sitting in the U.S. Senate.

Shortly after the party primary, the issue of honesty and integrity erupted, creating a crisis of confidence. Headlines announced the indictment of the state revenue commissioner. A judge demanded the purchasing records of seven state departments for presentment to a grand jury. Indiscretions and irregularities surfaced in the education and highway departments, and the state treasurer disclosed that state spending was overrunning income by $12 million a year despite tax increases during the Griffin administration. It was in this environment that Vandiver took office.

In his inaugural address the new governor set forth five guiding principles for his administration: economy, reform, reorganization, integrity, and preservation of Georgia's way of life. Immediately upon gaining office he ordered all departments to slash their spending by 10 percent, excepting only teachers' salaries, health and welfare benefits, and matching funds for federal highway monies. He said that he would make a sincere effort to economize in state business before asking for any raise in taxes.

Early in 1959 Vandiver requested that the General Assembly create a Commission on Economy and Reorganization. The commission was quickly organized and rendered its final report before the end of the year. Under prodding from the governor, many departments had already instituted internal reorganizations and economies, particularly in the fields of purchasing, revenue administration, and public safety. The Highway Department reduced considerably the number of persons employed. Dr. Morris W. H. Collins, Jr., appointed staff director, led the commission to adopt proposals in thirty-four different areas of state government.

The most notable recommendations of the commission called for investment of idle state funds, self-insurance of state property, permanent registration of government vehicles, and destruction of certain obsolete records. The commission also recommended abolition or consolidation of superfluous boards, commissions, and departments and issued a variety of recommendations concerning improvements in revenue administration, treasury management, and purchasing.[13] Pursuing the recommendations of the commission, Vandiver appointed outstanding people to head the Ports Authority, the Parks Department, the Highway Department, and the Purchasing Department.

To the latter position he appointed William R. Bowdoin, an Atlanta banker who had served a previous temporary and exemplary stint on the Ports Authority. Bowdoin served only nine months in purchasing, but he instituted rigorous bidding and contract-letting practices which saved the taxpayers millions of dollars. Interestingly, the Commission on Economy and Reorganization served as impetus for the "Bowdoin Commission," chaired by the same William Bowdoin, during the Sanders administration a few years later. That commission carried on the work begun so effectively during the Vandiver years.

In anticipation of the *Brown v. Board of Education* decision, the Georgia General Assembly had authorized the state to make tuition payments in fulfilling its constitutional obligations for education.[14] The scheme would have replaced public education with private schools. However, the notion of closing public schools was attacked, and alternatives began to surface. Considerable agitation resulted among the populace. Leaders urged calm, and some expressed a cautious optimism that the *Brown* decision could not possibly be implemented in less than a generation. The gubernatorial campaign of 1958, as one would expect, was devoted to the maintenance of segregation in Georgia. There was no debate on alternatives; the debate centered around which candidate could and would ward off the federal onslaught. Vandiver convinced Georgia voters that he was the man.

Just prior to his inauguration the governor-elect stated unequivocally on a television program, "If there is any integration, the schools must be closed under Georgia laws and the constitution of the state." He indicated he would propose legislation providing that individual schools, rather than school systems, be closed. The bill would give the governor discretionary power to close any school which blacks transferred to or from. He further argued that "we must have an arsenal of legislation to deal with the question."[15] Ten months later Vandiver characterized desegregation as "the most overriding internal problem ever to confront the people of Georgia in our lifetime" and attacked the "advocates of surrender."[16]

Georgia's desegregation crisis did not come until the end of Vandiver's first year in office. Meanwhile, that year was spent in widespread debate over the course the state would take when desegregation was finally ordered. A federal court order directed Atlanta to desegregate its schools, but allowed it to delay implementation. Some state leaders called for "massive resistance," but Atlanta leaders doubted the wisdom of closing the public schools, reflecting the economic growth experienced by the city and an acknowledgement of the growing black vote, both of which encouraged moderation. Ivan Allen, Jr., Atlanta civic leader and future mayor, stated, "Atlanta's public schools must stay open . . . and the Chamber [of Commerce] should provide its share of vigorous leadership in seeing that they do."[17]

Atlanta's ministers, university faculty, and public school groups issued manifestos calling for open schools. As massive resistance was increasingly questioned, Vandiver and the legislature called for a special committee of citizens to hold hearings throughout the state. Headed by John A. Sibley, an Atlanta banker and civic leader, the committee ultimately recommended local option choices allowing each community to decide for itself what its policy should be.

While many expected the brunt of the court decision in *Brown* to fall earliest on Atlanta, the scene shifted to Athens, home of the University of Georgia. On January 7, 1961, a federal judge ordered that two qualified black applicants to the university be allowed to register "now" for the winter quarter. "Now" was the last day for registration, which also was the first day the General Assembly convened in regular session. Vandiver would not comment on whether he would cut off funds to the university. An editorial that day stated that "Georgia has no law requiring segregation in its university system," and Judge W. A. Bootle held that actions of university officials amounted to "a tacit policy to that effect."[18]

On January 10 Governor Vandiver, obeying state law as he understood it, closed the university until repeal of the funds cutoff law, stating, "It is the saddest duty of my life."[19] The following day the federal judge barred a funds cutoff and the U.S. Supreme Court denied a stay of the lower court order. On January 12 Vandiver ordered the blacks removed after a wild demonstration, bordering on riot, erupted on the university campus. The black students were actually suspended by university officials. Hal Gulliver, writing for the Atlanta *Constitution* years later, blamed the officials for the disturbance and assessed Vandiver's role:

> There were delays in calling the State Patrol. Governor Ernest Vandiver, who later exercised modern leadership in calling for peaceful school desegregation, felt caught that night by his own rhetoric, his campaign pledges to permit no integration while he was governor. But on that occasion, rather than exercising leadership, the governor ordered the two black students removed from the university for their own "safety."[20]

Two days later the federal judge ordered their reinstatement, and Governor Vandiver promised they would be protected. On January 19, in a courageous "tell-it-like-it-is" speech to the General Assembly, he asked for the repeal of cutoff funds laws at the University of Georgia *and* for the public schools. He also asked for open-school laws, promising that "public education will be preserved . . . [and] our Georgia children will be protected."[21] The legislature passed the proposals, with few votes cast against them, and adopted the Sibley committee recommendations.

After the university crisis Vandiver proved to be a forward-looking governor on civil rights questions and, in the words of Joseph A. Schlesinger, "lent the power of his office to further peaceful integration of the University." Citing Vandiver's campaign rhetoric and his subsequent behavior in aiding integration, Schlesinger wrote that the governor's actions "may be interpreted as a result of the need to change his constituency, if he wished to continue his political career."[22] The victory of moderate forces on the civil rights issue, in the opinion of Numan V. Bartley, was symbolic of the shift of power from rural to urban interests, although the integration struggle was to continue for another decade filled with strife and conflict.[23]

The school crisis was hardly over when there was yet another anticipated attack on one of the state's venerated institutions. Georgia's unique county unit system of nominations for governor and other state officials dated back to the turn of the century.[24] County unit defenders argued that the system protected the state against political machines because it divided them up at county lines. They suggested that city voters included Negroes, Yankees, members of labor unions, agents of the Soviet Union, and other such allegedly sinister and subversive elements.[25]

Earlier attacks on the system had been rebuffed, and rural forces continued triumphant. In 1946 a minority of the popular vote gained the Democratic gubernatorial nomination for Eugene Talmadge. Several citizens sued to invalidate the use of the county unit system in a statewide primary as provided under the Neill Primary Act on the grounds that it violated the equal protection clause of the Fourteenth Amendment. A federal court held that equal protection was not denied in view of the classification of the counties on the basis of population and the constitutional provisions for readjustment after each census, and the U.S. Supreme Court refused to review the decision.[26]

Talmadge forces in 1950 and 1952 proposed a constitutional amendment to place the act in the Georgia constitution. The returns in the 1952 attempt demonstrated the value of the county unit vote in protecting white, rural supremacy. Negroes, labor union members, and city dwellers were able to cast ballots in an important election in which their votes were equal to those cast by the rural citizenry. Predictably, 121 counties supported the amendment and 38, including all of the urban counties, opposed it. The measure failed by fewer than 30,000 votes. If the county unit vote had been operative for the ratification of constitutional amendments, it would have passed 265 to 146. The cities demanded legislative reform, of course, but, as V. O. Key explained in 1949, "Genuine reform of the system by legislative action is virtually impossible because the legislators themselves are the beneficiaries of the malapportionment that would have to be altered."[27]

If the bifactional nature of Georgia's gubernatorial politics died with the failure of the anti-Talmadge faction to field a candidate in 1958, then 1962 was the year that provided the real upset to rural hegemony in the state. The decision of the U.S. Supreme Court in *Baker v. Carr* made the question of apportionment of a state's legislature subject to judicial review.[28] Governor Vandiver was out of the state when that decision was rendered, but upon his return he called a special session of the legislature to convene on April 16, 1962. Meanwhile, a suit attacking the county unit system was scheduled for decision on April 27, which meant the legislature had to act quickly. The governor and others hoped to keep the county unit system in some form while reapportioning the legislature to prevent the courts from doing so. This would be his last-ditch effort to fulfill his campaign promise to preserve the system which had helped sustain rural and, thus, segregationist sentiments.

The plan of the special session of the legislature modified the county unit rule, basing it on the population of the counties rather than county representation in the lower house.[29] Still (as Table 2 illustrates), even

TABLE 2

Contrast Between Sparsely and Heavily Populated Counties Resulting from Modification of County Unit Law, 1962[a]

County	Population	Number of Unit Votes	Population per Unit Vote	Ratio to Fulton County
Fulton	556,326	40	13,908	
DeKalb	256,782	20	12,839	
Chatham	188,299	16	11,760	
Muscogee	158,299	14	11,330	
Webster	3,247	2	1,623	8 to 1
Glascock	2,672	2	1,336	10 to 1
Quitman	2,432	2	1,216	11 to 1
Echols	1,876	2	938	14 to 1

[a]This table was modified from one given in *Sanders v. Gray*, 203 Fed. Supp. 158 (1962).

the revised rule continued the disparity in favor of rural counties. The federal district court took notice of the new arrangement and set guidelines which would have the effect of equalizing rural and urban votes. The legislature made no effort to adjust the disparity to the standard of the decision, and the county unit system became inoperative.

Once the system ceased to exist, Vandiver confessed to an Atlanta newsman, "I think we'll have a better state now that its gone."[30] When asked many years later why he was so adamant in support of the system prior to the courts' action, he flatly replied, "That was where the power was!"[31] The days were gone when the rural counties dominated state politics. Vandiver pragmatically recognized the growth of urban power that the court decisions assured, and he moved to take advantage of it.[32]

Vandiver promised economic development during his campaign in 1958, but he took an essentially conservative position. He stressed economy in government, advised budget cutting, and emphasized an overriding concern with the costs of state government. He did not advocate substantial increases in spending for public education, nor did he emphasize other redistributive economic programs.[33] Yet his administration lay the foundation for significant economic gains. By severely cutting waste, demanding prudent expenditures, and improving enforcement in revenue laws, the state actually raised the budgets in major operating departments. Services were expanded and there was no tax increase. The total state budget grew from $337 million to $419 million—an $82 million increase. Operating budgets were raised $89 million. School support expenditures were increased over $40 million annually—the greatest increase in the state's history in a comparable period. Classrooms grew by 4,500, twenty-two new vocational-technical schools were established, and teachers' salaries were raised.

Thus, while Vandiver "treasured economy in government," to borrow Numan V. Bartley's phrase, he embraced "the economic growth ethos," expanded the vocational-technical programs in the state, and pushed through a new law that permitted local governments "to market revenue bonds for the construction of factory buildings which would be turned over to private companies through lease-purchase agreements."[34] Vandiver became an active promoter of business development. The first Georgia trade mission to seek foreign investment originated in the Vandiver years, and he personally wooed corporate officers to relocate in the state.[35]

Early in the Vandiver administration a series of news articles on mental health and the treatment of patients at mental health facilities prompted the governor and his wife to visit the Milledgeville State Hospital. What they found appalled them, and Vandiver had the hospital transferred from the State Welfare Department to the Health Department, as the Reorganization Commission recommended. As first lady, Mrs. Vandiver worked for the establishment of the chaplaincy program at the hospital and sought funding for a Chapel of All Faiths on the hospital grounds.[36]

During Vandiver's administration the state spent $4 million on the Milledgeville facility. This enabled the hospital to add 575 new personnel and to double the number of physicians on staff, which reduced the doctor-patient ratio. In addition, a 500-bed rehabilitation center was established to speed the discharge of patients to their homes. A 600-bed wing was added to the hospital, and a Georgia Mental Health Center was also created. The press credited the administration for the improvement in mental health programs that these changes brought, and Vandiver proudly claims that his initiatives changed the status of mental health services from a disgrace to one of the best in the country.

Another vow Governor Vandiver made was to restore to the General Assembly the "constitutional powers and prerogatives of the people's elected representatives." At the same time he vigorously opposed any proposal "to diminish the constitutional or statutory authority of the chief executive." Vandiver believed that the most critical imbalance lay in the budget-making process. The legislature had no budgeting system, nor did it provide legislative appropriations. Indeed, Georgia had had only six appropriations bills in the previous twenty-five years. Vandiver argued that the General Assembly would "rubber stamp" his budget proposals without negative votes, and that was wrong.[37]

His recommendations for rectifying this gross imbalance in the principle of separation of powers was a constitutional amendment which would require biennial appropriations. The General Assembly in odd-numbered years would meet for fifteen days to organize and receive the budget and thirty days for an appropriating session. In addition, the amendment would limit appropriations to income and surplus and limit authority debt obligation to 15 percent of the total budget. Vandiver also recommended an act establishing a Budget Bureau. The General Assembly must, he said, "be master in its own house . . . to exercise its constitutional responsibilities [in order to] supply those checks and balances vital to the life of the Republic."[38] Following Vandiver's lead, the General Assembly created the Office of Legislative Counsel—a bill research and drafting unit which had previously been in the executive branch.

Ernest Vandiver proved to be a surprisingly good governor. During his administration he secured essential legislation and increased the power of the General Assembly without diminishing his formal powers. He knew how to pick his legislative leaders and to name persons to high positions to accomplish his purposes. He showed real courage and character, making tough decisions when he had to, even in the face of certain public opposition, and managed to leave office a popular governor. A Lou Harris poll in July 1962 reported that 57 percent of the state's voters thought he was doing a good job.[39]

Without a doubt, the crisis over desegregation was the foremost issue he faced. It was a turning point in Georgia's history, and the future of Georgia politics, social stability, and economic growth depended on how Vandiver handled it. Despite contemporary criticism, Vandiver's ability to resolve the school issue without bloodshed, without standing in the schoolhouse door, and without intervention by federal troops was perhaps his greatest accomplishment, as he himself still believes.

Vandiver grew as governor. He said what he had to say to get elected. His "no, not one" statement haunted him as governor, and he freely admits today that it was a mistake, an unnecessary rhetorical flourish that proved to be an embarrassment.[40] It was only one of several blunders that caused one observer to call him "one of the poorest public relations men I've ever seen."[41] Still, he could not be faulted for lack of courage. Even before he became governor, he took stands that were bold for a Georgia politician with gubernatorial ambitions. In 1957 Governor Orval Faubus of Arkansas came to the Southern Governors' Conference at Sea Island, Georgia, on the eve of the crisis at Little Rock. He met much praise, and most Georgia leaders, including arch-segregationists like Roy V. Harris and Governor Marvin Griffin, urged him to resist desegregation. Vandiver, then lieutenant governor, took a different view of Faubus, saying, "What he is going to do over there in Arkansas is going to speed up integration here and elsewhere in five to ten years. They're cheering him, when actually he's cutting our throats."[42] His candid remarks showed courage and insight, but his friends feared that he might have seriously damaged his chances to run for governor.

Vandiver modified his stand on the race question as his administration took shape. He followed a pragmatic approach, but it was an approach that caused him problems both in Georgia and outside the state. Just days before the desegregation of the University of Georgia, the media reported that he was to be named to President Kennedy's administration as secretary of the army. Senator Russell and Representative Carl Vinson, chairmen of the military committees in their respective houses, were said to have used their influence in his behalf. Because of Vandiver's distinguished service as the state's adjutant general (1948–54), he was regarded as an excellent choice, and most of the speculation centered on what Lieutenant Governor Garland T. Byrd would do when he succeeded to the governorship.[43]

Amidst the speculation, the desegregation crisis broke, and Vandiver later recalled, "I had to make a fundamental decision whether I was going to leave the state in its most distressing situation in modern times. I don't think I could ever have lived with myself if I had left."[44] As it turned out, he did not have to make the choice. Kennedy, citing "pressures," did not appoint Vandiver, and the press claimed that Northern liberals blocked the nomination, "contending his solid, unrelenting support of racial segregation in the armed forces and the public schools had disqualified him to be the civilian chief of an Army that already largely has been racially integrated."[45]

Vandiver faced the crisis, upheld the law, and kept the schools open, but his stand cast him into a totally different political circle. Vandiver wanted to be a United States senator. Both of Georgia's senators had seniority in the Senate and were his personal friends. His wife was a niece of Senator Russell. At the time, Vandiver believed that his decision would dash his hopes of an electoral victory in a Senate race. He felt he had already alienated the blacks (a growing political force) and was certain that conservatives would blame him for not keeping his campaign pledges of massive resistance. The night he decided to keep open the schools, only two men out of one hundred advisers agreed with him. Still, he concluded that he had to do what he could to get Georgia through the crisis.[46]

Vandiver left office with an aura of accomplishment. He had met the problems "with a mixture of dignity and enthusiasm that won him much respect in Georgia; even among those regretting the changes."[47] One observer "put him up there with great ones," arguing that he had "saved the state from . . . national and international disgrace."[48] Bill Harrell, a political writer for the Atlanta *Constitution*, praised Vandiver for keeping the schools open without violence, restoring confidence in state government, enacting honesty in laws, reforming mental health programs, and all of that without increasing taxes. His only criticisms were that Vandiver had not appointed a director of the Division of Mental Health as the Schaefer committee recommended, that he had retained the welfare director, that he had defended Georgia's inadequate penal system and its director, and that he had failed to crack down on speed traps and clip joints. Harrell concluded that Vandiver was an excellent governor who "did a lot of mending, faced many a crisis, and deserves to be ranked among the best chief executives the state has ever had. He should have overcome some of the shortcomings . . . [but] his overall performance has been terrifically good."[49]

Another editorial writer observed, "We look back on the past four years in which the incumbent faced successfully some of the most trying decisions of the century."[50] Eugene Patterson said of Vandiver, "Georgia has had better politicians . . . but [has] not had a better man. . . . Neither has it had a governor who met so many historic decisions so instinctively well. He led the state out of the alley of small things and onto the wide road toward a great tomorrow."[51] Patterson had particular praise for Vandiver's "revolutionary fiscal system" which, he wrote, "resulted in an almost magic ability to raise revenues without raising taxes."[52]

Early in 1966 Vandiver was the front-runner in the gubernatorial campaign of that year. Seventy percent of the electorate favored his return to the governor's office. His administration had been scandal-free. He had averted a financial crisis through sound management. He had raised teachers' salaries and had left a surplus in the treasury of $60 million without raising taxes. In 1966 he still opposed new taxes and preached economy and frugality in government. His target in the area of desegregation was now the federal bureaucracy and its desegregation guidelines.[53] But poor health forced him from the race. He later failed in an effort to win the U.S. Senate seat he wanted and retired to an active private life.

Why no statue for Ernest Vandiver? Indeed, why? At the end of the column in which Eugene Patterson posed the question, Patterson concluded that Vandiver, like Cato, would probably prefer that people ask "Why not?"[54]

Vandiver Takes
the Middle Road

S. ERNEST VANDIVER

Late in 1957, in an effort to lower the tone of racial rhetoric then existent in Georgia, I made a speech to a Dekalb County civic club. The headline writer, in reporting this speech, chose the fateful words "VANDIVER URGES MIDDLE OF ROAD" to describe that speech. My political opposition picked up the headline and printed it in their scurrilous literature, that "VANDIVER WAS WEAK ON SEGREGATION." In 1957 and 1958 to be "weak on segregation" was a political felony. Eighty percent of the population, during that era, liked things the way they were, and would vote to keep them that way. It was obvious from this early cheap shot that the level of the 1958 campaign for governor had been set. The question of who was best qualified to be governor of Georgia was not the issue, but it was who could best maintain the Georgia way of life, which was to preserve segregation.

The 1958 session of the legislature was but a preview of the gubernatorial campaign. The Griffin administration had chosen Roger Lawson, chairman of the State Highway Board, as their candidate for governor. In order to elect him, they proposed an additional hundred-million-dollar rural road bill to trade for votes. With the county unit system still in effect, this was powerful ammunition. The county commissioner was generally the most powerful politician in the county, and if the incumbent state administration could trade with the legislator and commissioner, they could usually swing enough votes to carry a county, and thus take that county's unit votes.

From the first day of the 1958 session this bill became an ordeal for all concerned. The governor, during this period of our history, named the speaker of the House. As lieutenant governor, I controlled the chairmanship of the Senate committees and made the committee assignments in the State Senate. This rural roads bill was introduced in the House of Representatives, and was assigned to the State of the Republic Committee, which was dominated by friends of the administration. Not only did we campaign all day in an effort to defeat this bill, but we usually spent most of the night trying to persuade members of the General Assembly to defeat it. The battle raged for weeks, and finally the speaker of the House and the governor's floor leader advised him that they thought they could pass this legislation.

The lines on both sides of the issue were taut, and the debate lasted all day. Late in the afternoon it was brought to a vote, and when the votes were counted the rural roads bill lost by two votes in the House of Representatives. The members of the Senate breathed a tremendous sigh of relief because they did not have to vote on this controversial legislation. In effect, this was pretty much the governor's race in 1958. Roger Lawson announced that he would not be a candidate, and Denny Groover, the governor's floor leader, but also an old classmate and fraternity brother of mine, pledged his support to my candidacy.

However, T. V. "Red" Williams, the revenue commissioner, and close confidant of Marvin Griffin, determined to make it as rough on me as possible. T. V. Williams persuaded Representative W. T. Bodenhamer, a Baptist minister and the executive director of the States Rights Council, to run as the candidate of the administration. They seized upon the aforementioned newspaper headlines and proceeded to try to persuade the voters that I was "weak on segregation."

It was well known that State Senator Bob Jordan was a friend and school classmate of mine. Bob had a brother, Clarence, also a Baptist minister, who had founded a farm near Americus and had invited disadvantaged whites and blacks to work together in a spiritual environment. Some politicians in southwest Georgia were outraged at this charity, and proceeded to denounce this farm as a Communist plot to advance integration in Georgia. Unlikely as it may seem, there were a great many people who believed this. Bodenhamer charged that since Bob Jordan and I were classmates and friends, I was encouraging Clarence Jordan to promote integration. I had never met Clarence Jordan, nor did I ever meet him. Not only was I harassed, but the entire Jordan family was subjected to this gutter-level attack throughout the entire campaign.

Early during this campaign my advisers and I sat down to plan campaign strategy and my opening speech, which would pretty much be repeated during each speech of the campaign. Unfortunately, my advisers and I let Red Williams and Bodenhamer get under our skin and we took his political goading too seriously. In preparing my speech and my stand on segregation, we put into it these words: "Neither my child nor yours will ever attend an integrated school during my administration— no, not one." Obviously these words were ill-advised. We argued throughout the night about whether or not to insert them into the speech. Some argued that it would have been better to say that "as governor I would use every legal means at my command to maintain segregation." Others contended that sounded weak. Obviously, in the light of history, we chose the wrong phrase, but *"C'est la guerre."*

I have gone into more detail than possibly a governor's campaign deserves, but in order to apprise this and future generations of why certain statements were uttered, it helps to better understand the "temper of the times." After the primary, when the votes were counted, I had received 83 percent of the total, had carried 156 of 159 counties, and had gotten 400 of 410 unit votes. Incidentally, I carried most of the black votes—obviously they considered me the lesser of the evils.

After the landmark *Brown* decision was handed down by the Supreme Court, the two governors who preceded me were fortunate enough not to have any direct confrontations over the issue of segregation. I would be less than honest if I told you that I did not hold out the hope I too would be that fortunate. Such was not the case.

Early in my administration a case which could have been vitally important was filed in the District Court for the Northern District of Georgia and was to be heard by Judge Frank Hooper. After this suit was filed, and seeing the eventual handwriting on the wall, a group of my advisers and I met and discussed what we might do, on the one hand, to delay the decision and, on the other hand, to give the people of Georgia a chance to study their alternatives. Under the laws of this era, they had two choices—either segregated public schools or no schools. The statutes required the governor to close the school if any federal court ordered it integrated.

Griffin Bell, my chief of staff, came up with the idea that we create a committee composed of outstanding citizens who would be required to hold one hearing in each of the state's ten congressional districts. These hearings would allow any person who desired to be heard on this issue to give testimony before the committee. I agreed to this suggestion, provided I could name the chairman in the resolution creating the committee. I then visited Judge John Sibley and asked if he would agree to serve as chairman. I knew that if we could persuade someone of the wisdom and stature of Judge Sibley to chair this committee, he would not let it get out of hand. Out of his love for his state, as well as his friendship for me, he agreed, and we proceeded to ask the legislature to create the committee, which it did. By the way, the youngest member of the Sibley committee was a young legislator named George Busbee, serving his second term in the General Assembly. He told me later that when he was appointed it was the first time he had seen his name in headlines.

What this committee accomplished is now history, but under the leadership of Judge Sibley the people of this state were given an opportunity to do two things: (1) To blow off the steam of their frustrations; (2) To carefully study their alternatives. The Sibley report was completed and filed with the General Assembly—the vote was naturally close, with a minority report also being filed.

After Christmas, and with the new year of 1961 beginning, Judge [William A.] Bootle of the District Court for the Middle District of Georgia ordered the authorities at the University of Georgia to admit two black students. The two had made application to enter during the winter quarter. They were Charlayne Hunter and Hamilton Holmes. These students had been carefully screened and were obviously well qualified. The order of the judge said *now,* and since this was the last day of registration, no time was left to appeal. Under the laws of Georgia I had no choice but to order the University of Georgia closed. Upon petition, the court ordered me to reopen the school and to admit these students.

I sent an assistant attorney general to Macon to ask for a stay of execution of the order, and Judge Bootle granted the request. But Judge [Elbert P.] Tuttle heard about the stay on a newscast and promptly overruled it. The state appealed this order, but before we could get the attorney general of Georgia to Washington—and we flew him up in a state plane— the Supreme Court had already ruled on the case and ordered the students admitted to the University of Georgia. You might wish to compare the speed with which this case was decided by the federal courts with some of the lengthy proceedings taken before and after that time.

After these students had been admitted and assigned to their dormitories, there were some ultra right-wing elements who were determined to cause trouble at the university. They aroused some of the students, and a crowd gathered outside the dormitories and proceeded to throw rocks at the windows. President Clyde Aderhold called the executive mansion and advised me that he believed the two black students to be in danger. I ordered the state patrol to remove them from the dormitories and take them back to the safety of their homes.

In the meantime I asked Aderhold to allow the campus police to maintain order, if possible, and told him that I would send an adequate number of state police to Athens, to stand by in reserve, in case the campus police were unable to maintain the peace and secure the safety of the black students. The federal courts ordered the black students back into school the next day. We kept almost one hundred state patrolmen on duty in the Athens area for the next sixty days.

In the meantime the legislature was convening for the 1960 session, and many of the members, representing their constituents, were frantic. Some legislators had children at the University of Georgia and they feared for their safety. At this time it was obvious that any state law mandating segregation would be immediately struck down, so I recommended that all of the laws dealing with segregation in Georgia be repealed—thereby forestalling a plethora of lawsuits from every direction. This proposal was accepted by the Georgia General Assembly on a vote of approximately 240 to 16.

I then appeared before the legislature and, by television and radio, the people of Georgia in the first night session of the General Assembly and recommended "freedom of choice" legislation and private tuition grants. This too was passed overwhelmingly by the legislature, and although it was eventually struck down by the Supreme Court, it gave us something positive to be *for.*

After all this was over, we had some thoughts about what *could have* happened. Had these students not been admitted to the University of Georgia—and had they been ordered into some other school in Georgia—some dire things could have occurred. Almost every family in Georgia has some connection with the University of Georgia. A father, mother, brother, sister, uncle, or aunt, somebody in the family group had attended. The university would have been more difficult to close down than any other school—the people of our state just could not imagine the University of Georgia being closed.

During those first difficult days, when all of the news media were covering the campus and things were getting pretty much under control, there were some newsmen from national broadcasting systems who were daily urging students to make fiery statements and have their video pictures made with clenched fists and threatening gestures. That convinced people that the national news media would do almost anything to get a story, regardless of the consequences to the schools or to the state.

Another random thought: when I asked a group of department heads, state and legislative leaders whom I had invited to the executive mansion for a conference on the emergency what they would recommend—integrated schools or closed schools—all but two out of fifty recommended that the schools be closed rather than integrated.

I am not embarrassed to say that Betty and I spent a great deal of time during this crisis on our knees, seeking Divine Guidance, and I must say that since the decision was made to reverse my campaign position I have not regretted it. I have had no sleepless nights nor pangs of conscience. I knew that what I had to do was committing political suicide, but I also knew that what I was doing was right, and I don't look back. Perhaps I could have gotten some temporary political gain had I stood in the schoolhouse door or something similar, but I would have had trouble living with myself.

From a review of several administrations, it would seem that I had a propensity for being in a leadership position when lost causes came along. The decision in *Baker vs. Carr*, a case which will live in infamy as far as rural Georgia is concerned, was handed down by the Supreme Court early in 1962. Another of my campaign positions had been to try and preserve the county unit system. This was a method of nominations by the Democratic Party that had become law by virtue of the Neill Primary Act of 1917. Theoretically, a candidate could have the majority of the popular votes and still lose the nomination. It had never happened until 1946, when Jimmy Carmichael polled a majority of the popular votes but lost the nomination to Eugene Talmadge, who had received a majority of the unit votes. The unit system had been patterned after the electoral college used in national presidential elections and until *Baker vs. Carr* had been upheld by the federal courts, even the Supreme Court.

When a suit against the county unit system was filed in Georgia, citing the *Baker* case, we knew that something had to be done if we intended to retain any semblance of a unit system. I called the General Assembly into extraordinary session in an effort to modify the system and still satisfy the federal courts. Try as we might, and we shuffled numbers around mightily, we were unable to mollify the courts, and the result of our efforts was declared unconstitutional. The next elections were held under the popular vote system for the first time in nearly half a century. Still, the electoral vote system for national elections is being used and it seems unlikely that it will be changed.

And now we come to a positive part of the Vandiver administration. This was an area where we were able to accomplish something lasting, and which was not in the field of lost causes. We pledged to reorganize the state government, to do away with useless boards and bureaus, and to institute economy in the operations of state government. This we set about doing immediately—introducing legislation and passing it; doing away with 122 boards, commissions, and bureaus. An amazing thing about these commissions and boards was that they always seemed to have as a member one of our closest political allies who was an opponent of abolishing it.

We introduced and passed the "Vandiver Honesty in Government" laws, which prevented legislators and board members from holding state jobs or doing any kind of business with the state. Under William

Bowdoin and Lieutenant General Alvin Gillam, as directors of purchasing, we reformed the Purchasing Department and made it possible for any Georgian to do business with his state government, in contrast with what had gone on before.

In order to start Georgia on the path to economic progress, we began the first really significant port expansion of our Savannah and Brunswick facilities. We purchased the Whitehall property in Savannah, which gave us room for expansion. We opened Georgia Port Authority offices in Bonn, Germany, and Tokyo, Japan, our first foreign offices. We led state trade missions to New York, Pennsylvania, Los Angeles, and San Francisco. We led the very first trade mission overseas to Europe, where we met with business and governmental leaders in Holland, Belgium, Italy, West Germany, and England. We found that business leaders in these countries had no idea there was a deep-water terminal on the east coast of the United States other than New York.

We accompanied business executives from all over the U.S. on the Chamber of Commerce Red Carpet Tours over Georgia. I suggested that the tour conclude at the Masters Tournament in Augusta. After we started that program, we had no shortage of executives who were anxious to visit Georgia for the tour.

We made the first allocation of state funds to cities. Before the Vandiver administration, only counties received allocated funds from the state. Realizing that Brunswick was hemmed in by water and was inhibited from further industrial development in every direction, we purchased Colonel's Island, which has been a godsend to the Brunswick area and to southeast Georgia. We paid off the debt on the Jekyll toll bridge and allowed Jekyll Island to become a mecca for tourist development.

We began Georgia's welcome center program and programmed welcome centers for every major highway entrance into the state. We introduced and had passed legislation which *saved* Georgia's major highway system. We spent one hundred million dollars rehabilitating our major highway system. I have not heard any complaints about Georgia's main roads since that time.

We hosted Georgia's first conference on trade and commerce, which was supervised by Honorable Ben Gilmer, then the president of Southern Bell. We had attendees from other countries, including the port director of the Port of the City of London, England.

We began and completed twenty-two vocational educational schools in every part of Georgia. Our goal in this program was to have a vocational educational school within fifty miles of any prospective student. As industry began to migrate toward the Sunbelt, we began a program training people to work in the particular industry which was moving to

Georgia. We proposed and had passed legislation which allowed cities and counties to issue industrial revenue bonds. This method has been greatly utilized to promote our industrial development.

We proposed and had passed legislation allowing the state to collect interest on idle state funds. This has increased our state revenue considerably. We began the state program of self-insurance. Up until the Vandiver administration, the state had paid out millions of dollars in insurance premiums. Hundreds of millions of dollars have been saved since.

Early in my administration Jack Nelson, a reporter for the Atlanta *Journal-Constitution*, wrote a series of articles on our state mental institution at Milledgeville. These articles pointed out how our mentally ill had been neglected over the years. At that time we had over 12,000 patients crowded together in inadequate facilities. There were a total of twelve doctors in the hospital to look after these patients. My wife, Betty, and I took a trip to that institution and found incredibly horrible conditions there. Everything that Jack Nelson had written about Milledgeville was true and much more. We found patients eating food prepared by other patients which was so unsanitary that I wouldn't have fed it to my dog. We found retarded children in the same wards as elderly mental patients. We found a woeful lack of medical care. We found common sanitation completely ignored. We found absolutely no spiritual facilities or churches anywhere close to the institution.

If Georgia had been ranked among the states as to its treatment of the mentally ill, I am certain that we would have been close to the last. We brought these shortcomings to the attention of the people of Georgia and to the legislature. We sought and got appropriated funds to change these conditions. We named a committee of distinguished Georgians, headed by Dr. Bruce Schaeffer of Toccoa, to make an in-depth study of our problems and to make recommendations to the governor and the General Assembly. Thus began a movement that brought the state from near the bottom to among the top-ranked states in the field of mental health within a few short years.

Today we have area mental hospitals which allow the patients to be located near their families. We now have six beautiful chapels located on the state hospital grounds where patients can attend churches of their choice. We developed a chaplaincy training program whereby ministers could train at the hospital before going into their ministry at local churches. They are educated to recognize the early symptoms of mental illness so that treatment can be begun earlier. We built central food preparation facilities where food could be prepared away from the patients and served hot and fresh to them.

Today we have adequate medical treatment. Every patient can receive minimal services. We sponsored construction of the Georgia Mental

Health Institute, located in Atlanta, and under the supervision of the Medical School and the Department of Psychiatry of Emory University. Mental health leaders now say that Georgia ranks near the top in the nation in treatment of the mentally ill.

Jack Nelson received a Pulitzer Prize for his reporting on the situation. He advised me that he would not have received it had not Georgia responded to his series of articles. As for me, I received the satisfaction of knowing that Betty and I had taken advantage of the opportunity to be some help to humanity. The people of Georgia responded to our appeals for help. I believe that our Chapel of All Faiths drive was the only occasion in the history of the U.S. where a million dollars of voluntary contributions was raised to provide spiritual facilities for those who were unable to help themselves. Not a dime of tax money was spent on this construction. Practically every Georgian had an opportunity to be a part of this drive and to help the mentally sick.

Again, one of the primary goals of my campaign was to restore to the General Assembly of Georgia some of the historical powers of a government based on a system of checks and balances. Prior to my administration, as I served as lieutenant governor, I observed that the traditional power of appropriating state funds had been abandoned by the General Assembly. The state auditor, working with the governor during that era, prepared an executive budget, presented it to the legislature for adoption, and usually within a thirty to forty-five minute period it was passed just as the governor had presented it. The traditional checks and balances of the three branches of government had gradually been meshed into two branches, and I was determined to leave, as one of my legacies, a stronger legislative branch.

I recommended to the legislature that the budgetary laws be amended to provide for a biennial budget. This recommendation also provided that after the budget was submitted by the governor it be received and studied by the House Committee on Appropriations and by the Senate Finance Committee. The rest of the legislature was to adjourn while the fiscal committees studied the budget request.

I also set up a bureau of the budget in the Executive Department and solicited every department to submit a timely and orderly request to this bureau for appropriations for the next fiscal year. In the off years, amendments would be submitted. This would give the executive branch and the legislative branch ample time to study the requests of the various departments. It would make it less likely that a mistake could be made, or a meritorious request overlooked. I also suggested that we abandon the fiction that the state could not incur debt.

Authorities had been set up for every conceivable purpose, and although legally it was the authority and not the state which was in debt, the state actually could not allow the authorities to default on their obligations, or the state's credit would be jeopardized. By a constitutional amendment, the state was allowed to incur debt and thereby the state's bonds received an AAA rating and reduced interest rates. I recommended, and it is still the law, that the state debt limit is restricted to 15 percent of the annual revenue. Most of these fiscal programs are still in effect, and I think we have a sounder state fiscal system because of it. When I departed the governor's office, I felt that I had given the state a sound, progressive four years. I left sixty million dollars in the Emergency Fund, and operated the state during my term without any increases in taxes.

The changes wrought during those four years were almost incredible.

Carl E. Sanders

1963 – 1967

Carl Sanders
and the Politics
of the Future

JAMES F. COOK

A few days after Carl Sanders's impressive victory over former Governor
Marvin Griffin in the Democratic primary of September 12, 1962, Gene
Britton, a reporter for the Macon *Telegraph*, ruminated about the implications of that election for the future of Georgia. Sanders, he
predicted,

> will, undoubtedly, prove to be a wise guardian of public funds, fol-
> lowing a precedent set by Ernest Vandiver. . . . On race relations, he
> will be a cool-headed moderate, not given to breaking tradition, but
> not given to breaking heads either. He will work to improve Geor-
> gia's industrial climate, bring about significant advances in the
> state's health and welfare programs and, again like Vandiver, do
> some reorganizing and streamlining of the government to make it
> work better for the people. He will, in all probability, be a good
> governor, possibly one of Georgia's best. If Georgians back him in
> office as they backed him in the campaign, Georgia and Carl San-
> ders have much to look forward to in the next four years.[1]

Britton understood the new governor and Georgia politics, for his pre-
dictions were fulfilled with uncanny accuracy as the people of Georgia
backed Sanders as governor even more than they had in the campaign.
Born into a middle-class family in Augusta on May 15, 1925, Sanders

acknowledged that he had "an exceptionally happy and secure child-hood."[2] His parents, not wealthy in material possessions, provided things more valuable: love, encouragement, and discipline. They stressed the importance of hard work, physical fitness, high ethical standards, and the Baptist faith—values that have remained with Sanders ever since. Typical of his class, he earned his own spending money during his school years by delivering newspapers and bagging groceries.[3]

Sometime during his youth Sanders developed an intense desire to excel. Consequently, he became a fierce competitor in the classroom, on the athletic field, and later in the political arena. Not surprisingly, he achieved extraordinary success early in life.[4] His record of accomplishment at the Academy of Richmond County earned him an alternate appointment to West Point. When the primary appointee accepted the position, a disappointed young Sanders, who had also been voted the most valuable player on his football team, accepted a football scholarship to the University of Georgia.[5]

World War II disrupted his studies and he enlisted in the U.S. Air Force in 1943. At age nineteen he was a lieutenant commissioned to pilot B-17 heavy bombers. After the war he returned to the University of Georgia to complete his education. He finished three years of law study in two years, passed the bar exam early in 1947, and completed his course work in December.[6] Active in campus life, he lettered in football and played on the Bulldog team that went to the Oil Bowl. He was a member of Phi Kappa literary society, and was inducted into Sphinx, the highest honor a male student can attain, and Omicron Delta Kappa, a national leadership fraternity for men. He was a member of the debate team, but strangely enough was not interested in campus politics.[7] Somehow, during this period of frenzied activity, he found time to court Betty Foy, a pretty art student from Statesboro he had met at the university. They were married on September 6, 1947.[8]

A crisis struck the newlyweds only nine days after their marriage. Betty suddenly became ill. At first appendicitis was suspected, but the surgeons who operated found a much more serious condition. The doctors were not optimistic. The family was called in as Betty was not expected to live. Miraculously, however, the crisis passed and gradually she began to regain her strength. The recovery was slow. She remained hospitalized for six weeks and bedridden for six months. To meet the staggering medical expenses, Sanders practiced law by day and taught law in his off-hours. Throughout the ordeal his Christian faith was tested and strengthened. "I knew the Lord didn't give her to me only to take her away," he said.[9]

As in other endeavors, Sanders excelled in the field of law. His practice in Augusta flourished. At first he practiced with Judge Henry Hammond, and then he established his own firm of Sanders, Thurmond, Hester and Jolles. It was an ecumenical arrangement, combining a Baptist, a Jew, a Catholic, and an Episcopalian as partners.[10]

Sanders's father had been active in local politics, having served four years on the Richmond County Board of Commissioners, and the son inherited the father's looks, mannerisms, and love of politics.[11] In 1954 Sanders ran for a seat in the Georgia House of Representatives and won. Two years later he advanced to the Senate as the representative of Richmond County. At that time the seat rotated from Richmond County to Jefferson County to Glascock County. Sanders was so popular that the voters of Jefferson County and Glascock County retained him in the Senate in 1958 and 1960. He was the only man ever to serve three consecutive terms from a multicounty senatorial district under the rotation system.[12] In the Senate, Sanders's drive, ability, and political skill impressed Governor Ernest Vandiver, who made him floor leader in 1959. From 1960 to 1962 Sanders served as president pro tempore of the Senate, the highest office open to a member of that body.[13]

Ambitious for higher office, Sanders contemplated running for lieutenant governor in 1962, but he threw caution to the wind and decided to seek the governorship instead. That decision took courage, for urban candidates had not fared well in Georgia in recent decades.[14] The county unit system kept government almost exclusively in the hands of rural politicos. Atlanta, Macon, Columbus, and Augusta had no representation among the power brokers. Still, Sanders launched his campaign confidently. Fortunately for him, the rules of the game changed. Weeks after he began his bid for the nomination, the federal courts declared the county unit system unconstitutional. From that moment, Georgia's governors would be elected by popular vote, and an urbane candidate from Augusta now had a chance of being elected governor.[15]

Sanders started as the underdog, lacking the name recognition of his chief opponent, former Governor Marvin Griffin of Bainbridge. Griffin, who had been associated with the Talmadge faction for years, was an experienced campaigner who had few peers on the stump. With his humorous, engaging personality, he was a formidable opponent. Stressing his opposition to integration, Griffin threatened to put Martin Luther King, Jr., so far back in the jail that "they'll have to shoot peas to feed him."[16] He urged the white people of Georgia to give him a majority because his opponent had "the unqualified support and backing of Ralph McGill, Martin Luther King, and the Atlanta political machine."[17] To handle integrationist agitators, Griffin said: "There ain't but one thing to do and that is to cut down a blackjack sapling and brain 'em and nip 'em in the bud."[18]

Sanders also pledged "to maintain Georgia's traditional separation," but he promised that "violence in any form will not be tolerated."[19] He avoided blatant racism and downplayed racial questions. Sanders was perceived as a moderate on the race issue.[20] He recognized that the forces converging on the South and a growing national mood for change doomed blind resistance to failure. Although he was a segregationist, he saw the futility of the die-hard approach, and he emerged as the voice of reason to many Georgians.

Rivaling the segregation issue in importance in the campaign was the issue of corruption in government. Griffin's term as governor had been notorious for its rampant corruption.[21] A grand jury found "perfidious conduct of state officials" in his administration "heretofore inconceivable in the minds of citizens."[22] The clean-cut young Sanders, untainted by scandal, exploited the issue, which enabled him to appear, as he himself later expressed it, as "a young man on a white horse."[23]

Sanders consistently reminded Georgia voters of the Griffin record. Griffin's administration made Georgia "the laughing stock of the nation," he cried, "and it would again if he ever were given the opportunity to do so."[24] On a television broadcast Sanders said: "We caught old Marvin in the chicken house once, and we're not going to give him the keys to the smoke house again."[25] He accused Griffin of "favoritism, nepotism, rigged bidding, kick-backs and cronyism," and said that during his governorship, "There will be no more rigged bidding, fictitious companies, forged bids or clearing house operations carried on in the state capitol as there were in my opponent's administration."[26]

Despite his strong criticism of the Griffin record, Sanders's campaign was, on the whole, positive in tone. He promised the voters an honest, efficient, frugal administration that would improve education, lure industry to Georgia, and reform several state agencies so that they delivered services more effectively. His emphasis was on the future, not the past. Progress was his favorite theme. The Sanders campaign, he said, "is one which looks to the future. It's one of moving ahead."[27] Believing that Georgia was on the threshold of unprecedented economic advancement, he promised prosperity, progress, and opportunity through strong executive leadership which would make Georgians proud of their governor and their state.[28] Perhaps most importantly, Sanders stressed the "new politics," which shunned the old type political warhorses and used the media effectively.[29]

When Georgia voters went to the polls in September 1962 they had a clear choice between a traditional rural-oriented, race-baiting former governor and a younger, more sophisticated, urban-oriented proponent of the new politics. By an overwhelming margin Georgia voters chose the latter, as Sanders captured 494,978 votes to Griffin's 332,746.[30] Griffin's strength was confined to the rural counties, especially in southwestern Georgia, whereas Sanders ran strongest in the city counties and north Georgia. Indeed, over half of Sanders's statewide vote came from the eleven city counties.[31] His victory over Griffin marked a turning point in Georgia's political history. He was the first man from a city to be elected governor of Georgia since the 1920s, and at thirty-seven he was the youngest governor in the country at that time.[32]

Sanders served as governor during a period of great change and ferment. It was a vibrant, exciting, youth-oriented age, confident in its ability to improve the world. In the field of civil rights, it was the period of Selma, Birmingham, the march on Washington, Martin Luther King's "I Have a Dream" speech, and the passage of federal civil rights laws. It was also a period of black frustration, which saw the emergence of growing militancy, "black power," and devastating urban riots. It was the age of the New Frontier and the Great Society, the Peace Corps and the War on Poverty, the Beatles and Peter, Paul, and Mary, the arrival of the Braves and Falcons in Atlanta, protests and marches, miniskirts and the Counter Culture, full employment and the war in Vietnam. America would never be quite the same again. As Bob Dylan, who captured the spirit of the 1960s better than anyone, put it, "The Times, They Are a-Changin."

In many ways Sanders reflected the ideals and values of that era. He was youthful, energetic, athletic, and urban-oriented, in the manner of John F. Kennedy, who symbolized the 1960s to many Americans. Shortly after his election as governor, Sanders visited Kennedy. He supported his administration, and seems to have been influenced by him.[33] The impact of the New Frontier can be seen in the imagery of Sanders's rhetoric, as, for example, his assertion that his election would launch the state "into a new orbit of progress and opportunity."[34]

Throughout the campaign against Marvin Griffin, and especially in his platform, which he called "a program of progress," Sanders set forth clearly identifiable goals that he hoped to accomplish as governor. Promising an administration that would be both morally and fiscally sound, he made education his top priority. In addition, he intended to reorganize the Highway Department, attract new industry, improve mental health and correctional facilities, reapportion the General Assembly, and pursue research "to build constructively for the future."[35]

It was an ambitious program, but to a surprising extent Sanders accomplished exactly what he set out to do. He suffered few setbacks during his four years as governor, and Georgia made substantial progress in many areas under his forceful leadership.[36] The most significant contributions came in the areas of education, governmental reform, and reapportionment. Moreover, the Sanders administration enhanced Georgia's national image.

Sanders had promised that education would be the top priority of his administration, and it was. He understood that Georgia was shifting from a rather simple agrarian economy to a more complex urbanized and industrialized economy, and in order for the state to attract new high-technology industries and federal research grants he knew that it must transform its educational system quickly or lag behind other states in economic growth. Thus, for Sanders, education was the key that unlocked the door to future growth and prosperity.

At the governor's insistence, the 1963 General Assembly established the Governor's Commission to Improve Education. This blue-ribbon panel of twenty-five members appointed by the governor was charged to conduct "studies, research, investigations and surveys into all facets of public education" and to make recommendations for improvement.[37] Utilizing the findings of the commission, Sanders emphasized education in the 1964 session of the General Assembly. Calling education in Georgia a "modern crisis," he urged the legislature to adopt his education package, which included tax increases of $30 million, a $100 million bond issue to finance construction of new school and college buildings, granting the State Board of Education the authority to establish minimum standards, and increasing local support from 15 to 20 percent. With minor modifications the General Assembly approved the entire program.[38]

In subsequent sessions more educational reforms were adopted, and as more revenue accumulated in the treasury the governor channeled a larger portion of it to education. By the end of his term Sanders could be justly proud of the accomplishments of his administration in the field of education. They included raising teachers' salaries $1,400 per year (more than twice as much as any previous governor), raising university system salaries 32.5 percent, adding 10,000 new teachers, reorganizing the Department of Education, building more schools and classrooms than any previous administration, providing the university system more money for building construction in four years than it had received in the previous thirty-one, establishing additional junior colleges and vocational technical schools, providing scholarships and loans, and creating the Governor's Honors Program.[39] Never before had education received such emphasis in Georgia. It was a remarkable achievement, an investment in Georgia's future which set the tone for the Sanders administration and brought lasting benefits to the state.

Rivaling education in importance was Sanders's determination to modernize Georgia's government and make it operate more efficiently. One of his first—and most important—acts after winning the election was to appoint the Governor's Commission for Efficiency and Improve-

ment in Government. He instituted the commission to "study the organization and operation of the agencies, departments, boards, commissions, and public authorities of the state," and to "submit to him and to
the General Assembly reports of findings with recommendations for a
thorough modernizing of Georgia's governmental structure and procedures."[40]

The commission, composed of seven outstanding business and professional men, was headed by William R. Bowdoin, a highly respected
Atlanta banker, and was commonly referred to as the Bowdoin Commission. Dr. M. W. H. Collins of the University of Georgia served as
executive director. Over the next four years the commission studied the
various departments of Georgia's government. It also encouraged agencies to do self-studies. Whenever possible, it utilized Georgia personnel
and research agencies, but it did not hesitate to go outside the state to
secure competent researchers and consultants. To ensure objective
study and recommendations by the consultants, it released consultants'
reports simultaneously with the commission reports, even though they
were not always in total agreement. Altogether, the commission prepared and distributed more than thirty studies of departments or areas
of state government. Its recommendations dealt with administrative
policies, personnel changes, training, long-range planning, funding, and
related matters in order to provide Georgians "with the most efficient
and economical state government possible."[41]

Governor Sanders supported the Bowdoin Commission enthusiastically. He used his clout to see that its recommendations were implemented, and later suggested that his successor establish a similar
commission.[42] By the end of his administration many of the recommendations had been carried out, and others were implemented later. In his
book *Georgia's Third Force*, published in 1967, Bowdoin noted that of
the fifteen major recommendations in the area of prison reform "all but
one have been implemented either fully or partially" and that of the
more than eighty recommendations relating to the state Highway Department and its administration "approximately 75 percent have now
been implemented fully or partially."[43]

The commission reports, coming out in a steady stream, received favorable publicity from the media, identified obvious weaknesses in government, proposed reasonable remedies, and gave Sanders an agenda for
reform as well as leverage to use against recalcitrant department heads
and the General Assembly. He took full advantage of this opportunity
and results were fortuitous. The most significant reforms occurred in
the Merit System, the Board of Education, the Highway Department,
the Department of Agriculture, the prison system, and the mental

health program. Much remained to be done in modernizing Georgia's government, as Bowdoin readily acknowledged, but substantial progress had been made during the Sanders administration.[44]

While the Bowdoin Commission played a vital role in reforming Georgia's government, it was by no means the only study commission utilized by Sanders. In fact, there were numerous others, including the Governor's Commission on the Status of Women, the Governor's Council on Physical Fitness, the Governor's Commission to Improve Education, the Governor's Special Committee for Statutory Constitutional Coordination, the Commission on Scientific Research and Development, the State Recreation Commission, the State Election Laws Study Committee, the enlarged State Nuclear Advisory Committee, and the Constitutional Revision Committee.[45] Obviously some of these commissions were more important than others, but together they reflect the varied interests of the Sanders administration. Even those that had minimal influence on legislation or administrative reform, such as the Council on Physical Fitness, made positive contributions by utilizing the expertise of competent Georgians, coordinating and disseminating information, and publicizing areas of concern. Sanders was adept at luring outstanding individuals to serve on these commissions, and the commissions helped develop a new image of Georgia as a more progressive state.

Sanders was convinced that Georgia's constitution, adopted in 1945, was no longer adequately meeting the needs of the people. With 381 amendments, it had become a hodgepodge of confusion. At the governor's urging, the General Assembly established a Constitutional Revision Commission of twenty-eight members, consisting of twelve state officials and sixteen members appointed by the governor.[46] The commission, which was organized in May of 1963, held public hearings, made studies, and drafted a new constitution only half as long as the existing one. Sanders called the General Assembly into special session to consider both the proposed constitution and a proposed comprehensive revision of the state election laws. The General Assembly met for nearly two months at a cost of one million dollars and approved both the election code revision and the new constitution, which was then to be voted on by the people in the general election of November 1964.[47]

The new constitution was a modest document that would not have altered the operation of Georgia's government in a drastic manner. It was basically an attempt to make the existing constitution more intelligible and systematic. Governor Sanders was convinced that it had succeeded in doing just that. He described the new constitution as "a responsible product wrought by responsible leaders to obtain responsible results for a responsible people."[48] He customarily praised the legislature at the conclusion of each session, but after this special session his praise was unrestrained. The General Assembly, he said, had been "masterful" in its deliberations and its members constituted "the most dedicated group of public servants" that he had ever known.[49]

Unfortunately, these efforts proved to be fruitless because a United States district court enjoined the secretary of state from placing the new constitution on the ballot because the General Assembly which passed it was malapportioned. However, the court did not invalidate the election laws approved by the same malapportioned General Assembly. This illogical ruling would later be overturned by the United States Supreme Court, but by then the momentum had been lost and the new constitution was dead.[50] Sanders was deeply disappointed in this turn of events, and he could not hide his frustration and disgust at the court's ruling. It would be the major disappointment in his four years as governor.[51]

The federal courts and the reapportionment issue profoundly affected Georgia politics in other ways in the 1960s. The courts began an assault on the state's outmoded system of representation in 1962 when the county unit system was declared unconstitutional. That decision had aided Sanders in the gubernatorial election of 1962, while another ruling during the Vandiver years forced the General Assembly to reapportion the Senate on the basis of population.[52] The furor over the proposed constitution in 1963 signaled that the issue had not been resolved, and on February 17, 1964, the United States Supreme Court extended the reach of the courts when it ruled in *Wesberry v. Georgia* that Georgia's congressional districts would have to be redrawn so that "as nearly as is practicable one man's vote in a congressional election is to be worth as much as another."[53]

With only four days remaining before adjournment, Sanders insisted that the General Assembly act on the issue. As the session drew to a close on February 21, it appeared that no agreement could be reached on reapportionment. The House and Senate conference committees had been deadlocked for fifteen hours. The legislators were tired, angry, and frustrated. The governor's floor leader, Arthur Bolton, and practically everyone else had given up hope. However, Sanders came to the House rostrum and urged the members to try once more.[54]

At 11:50, ten minutes before the mandatory adjournment, Representative Denmark Groover not only stopped the official clock, he literally tore it loose from the wall and smashed it to pieces on the floor. Twenty minutes later, while opponents yelled and cursed and Representative James "Sloppy" Floyd cried in desperation that "the tactics used here are unconstitutional, Communist, and everything else—and I don't like it worth a damn!" the reapportionment bill passed.[55] Actually, there was no written bill. The House had voted on a map with the congressional districts drawn in crayon. The governor quietly instructed an aide to go to the clerk's office when it opened the next morning and write a bill that conformed to the map.[56] By such unorthodox measures, Georgia's congressional districts were reapportioned.

When a federal court subsequently ruled that Georgia's House of Representatives also had to be reapportioned on the basis of population, there was some opposition in the General Assembly, but the change was accomplished in an orderly manner in March of 1965.[57] In reducing the population disparity from 98 to 1 under the old system to 2 to 1 under the new plan, the General Assembly seemed to realize that further resistance to a determined governor and federal court was futile.[58]

Sanders had made reapportionment a campaign issue, but the court decisions accelerated the process. While the court interference derailed his constitutional reforms, in the long run the reapportionment of congressional districts and both houses of the General Assembly mandated by the federal courts made Georgia's government more democratic. Urban Georgia could no longer be ignored. The reforms gave urban residents, many of whom were black, more representation and political opportunities. Sanders, though not always agreeing with the court rulings, consistently argued that the decisions must be obeyed.[59] His calm and effective leadership in this area enabled Georgia to adjust to these new realities with a minimum of trauma and disruption. Near the end of his term Sanders observed that Georgia "is the only State in the Union that has reapportioned its House, Senate and Congressional Districts, and has had every plan passed by the Legislature subsequently ratified by the Federal Courts."[60]

Under Sanders's leadership Georgia began to erase its image as a rural, racist, and reactionary state. Though conservative in many ways, Sanders continually stressed the necessity of change to prepare for the future. Convinced that the complexities of government now required that more accurate information be available in order to plan for the future, he made a strong plea for the establishment of a bureau of planning and programming in the Executive Department.[61] In dealing with the General Assembly, his approach was invariably positive and optimistic, with considerable emphasis on the value of cooperation and teamwork. Sanders, more than any of his recent predecessors as governor, was attuned to the needs of city dwellers. In addition to stressing improvements in education, efficiency in government, and reapportionment, issues which had much urban appeal, he also secured additional funding for municipalities, obtained state funding for planning a rapid transit system in Atlanta, and made Georgia a national leader in the construction of airports.[62]

Sanders did not actively support civil rights, but he faced the issue when he had to face it, and the status of blacks in Georgia improved during his tenure. Although he had campaigned as a segregationist, he was regarded as a moderate on the race issue. He once defined moderate as meaning "I am a segregationist but not a damned fool." Sanders was determined to add one billion dollars of new and expanded industries in his term, and he understood that social upheavals would severely curtail his plans. Consequently, he made it clear from the beginning that "while I am governor we are going to obey the laws, we are not going to resist Federal court orders with violence, and we are not going to close any schools."[63]

Although the Sanders administration did not escape racial turmoil and strife totally, it did avoid the bitter confrontations that Alabama experienced. Sanders defused several potentially explosive situations and compiled a modest record of progress in civil rights. He appointed two blacks to the Governor's Commission to Improve Education as well as the first blacks to the Georgia delegation to the Democratic National Convention. He also appointed the first blacks to the Georgia State Patrol, the National Guard, and the Committee on the Status of Women. Otherwise his administration was white.[64] He appointed no black judges, department heads, or Georgia Bureau of Investigation agents. But, to keep matters in perspective, his predecessors appointed no blacks to these positions and his successors have appointed very few.

Racial tension was so intense in the mid-sixties that the governor's determination and wisdom were tested often. Sanders preferred to resolve disputes through negotiation, and he took no delight in using force. But when violence seemed likely to occur, he did not hesitate to use the threat of force to maintain law and order. When a racial disturbance erupted in Savannah in July 1963, he dispatched state troopers to quell it, and he made it clear that violence would not be tolerated.[65] When a racial dispute in Crawfordville threatened to get out of hand, Sanders refused to have any dealings with black activist Hosea Williams of Atlanta, the self-appointed spokesman for the blacks in Crawfordville. Instead, he brought the local white and black leaders together and they resolved the dispute through negotiation.[66] In the summer of 1966, when Atlanta nearly exploded in a major race riot, Mayor Ivan Allen courageously confronted hostile crowds of angry blacks in the inner-city slums. The governor, cooperating fully with the mayor, stationed state troopers inside Atlanta Stadium, out of sight so their presence would not infuriate the blacks, but still nearby in case the mayor should need them. Fortunately they were not needed.[67]

Sanders attempted to steer a middle course between reactionary racists on the one hand and militant agitators on the other. Both, he felt, were damaging the state. Georgia, he said, "doesn't need any Hosea Williamses or Calvin Craigs. They represent the unreasoning extremes of issues."[68] The governor believed that racial progress could be achieved by working patiently within the system. Consequently, he had contempt for anyone who deliberately violated the law to accomplish an objective. To Sanders, the law was sacrosanct. No state or nation, he asserted, "can give its citizens the 'right' to break the law. There can be no law to which obedience is optional or selective."[69] He regarded both Senator Barry Goldwater and Martin Luther King, Jr., as extremists, and he argued that in essence they held the same philosophy—that the end justifies the means. In contrast to them, Sanders reasoned that moderation was a virtue and extremism a vice. He insisted that grievances must be settled in the courts, not on the streets.[70] To do otherwise, he felt, would jeopardize civilization itself, which rests on the concept of rule by law. In emphasizing the importance of obeying the law, Sanders reminded Georgians that "the only safety in society—the only security for property—the only protection for life—the only hope for the future—is undivided, faithful and honest submission to the law whether we like it or not."[71]

While Sanders consistently stressed the necessity of obeying existing laws, he was not anxious to add new civil rights laws. In fact, he opposed the public accommodations section of the 1964 Civil Rights Act so strenuously that he testified against it in Washington. His speech before the Senate Commerce Committee was a carefully reasoned defense of individualism, property rights, limited government, and voluntary cooperation—all strongly-held principles which Sanders believed the bill violated.[72] His opposition to federal civil rights legislation, as well as his criticism of rioters, generated some negative comments in black and liberal publications, but on the whole they praised his administration.[73]

Civil rights simply was not a high priority for Sanders. It was an issue that could not be avoided so he dealt with it, but it clearly ranked in importance far behind education, industrial development, prison reform, and efficiency in government. Sanders seemed to believe that if his program could be enacted, then all Georgians, blacks included, would benefit. Additionally, he was convinced that lasting progress in race relations would not be achieved by federal coercion. Ultimately, real progress could come only through changing the hearts and minds of the people, and that was more likely to be accomplished through gradual change brought about in an orderly manner.[74]

Sanders revealed his true feelings at the Southern Governors' Conference in September 1965 when, in urging the governors to focus attention on industrial development, he remarked that the race issue was "somewhat passé."[75] For Sanders, it was passé, and he was eager to address other matters. Yet, when all factors are considered, Sanders probably advanced civil rights in Georgia as much as was politically feasible at that time. And he did more than he had promised in his campaign. Near the end of his term, neutral observers concluded that he had managed to keep the lid on the race situation and had maintained good relations both with strong segregationists and with fervent integrationists.[76] That was not an easy political feat to accomplish.

Unlike most Georgia political leaders, Sanders was a loyal Democrat—loyal to both the national as well as the state party. At a time when Georgia's powerful Democratic senators, Richard Russell and Herman Talmadge, were going to great lengths to disassociate themselves from the Democratic administration of Lyndon Johnson, the young governor not only endorsed the president but also actively campaigned for him. Sanders's strong support of President Johnson in 1964 cost him politically and did not prevent Georgia from voting for Goldwater, but it demonstrated his party loyalty and his political courage.[77] That same party loyalty would be demonstrated again in 1966 when he supported Lester Maddox as the party's gubernatorial nominee, though Maddox certainly was not his first choice.[78]

Active in regional and national policymaking bodies, Sanders served as chairman of the Rules Committee at the Democratic National Convention in 1964, served as a member of the Executive Committee of the National Governors' Conference in 1964–65, was chairman of the Appalachian Governors' Conference in 1964–65, and was chairman of the Southern Regional Education Board in 1965.[79] Through his leadership the hostility that often existed between Georgia and the federal agencies was largely dissipated and a more cooperative relationship developed, especially with those federal agencies doling out lucrative grants. By diligent effort he had nudged Georgia into the political mainstream, and in the process had made a name for himself. At the conclusion of his term Sanders was popular nationally, and he was at the crest of his popularity in Georgia. Thus, it was widely believed that higher political positions were in store for him, perhaps even the vice-presidency.[80]

Since Georgia governors could not succeed themselves, their power naturally waned during their last year in office. Sanders was determined that he would not be a lame duck governor in 1966,[81] but many factors combined to make his last year in office less successful than the first three years. As one who had labored diligently to bring people together and to develop a spirit of unity, he was deeply concerned about the growing opposition to the war in Vietnam and the growing militancy of certain civil rights groups. Having toured South Vietnam, he was a confirmed "hawk" on Vietnam, and he became infuriated when protesters desecrated the American flag.[82] Likewise, he had little patience for civil rights activists who resorted to violence. He was especially disturbed by the Student Nonviolent Coordinating Committee (SNCC) and referred publicly to its members as "merchants of discord."[83] Together, the war protesters and the civil rights protesters were, in his eyes, polarizing American society.

In the 1966 legislative session, Sanders and the General Assembly had to confront both forces in the person of Julian Bond. Bond, an articulate young Negro, was elected to the Georgia House of Representatives from a predominately black district of Atlanta by an overwhelming margin. Several other blacks had been elected in the special election following the reapportionment of the House district. The others were seated by the House without any difficulty, but Bond was not.[84] He was not only an active member of SNCC, but also he had supported SNCC's strongly-worded protest against the war in Vietnam. That proved too much for the members of the House to accept. By vote of 184 to 12, they refused to seat him.[85]

Bond then sought redress in the courts. A federal district court upheld the House action but the United States Supreme Court overturned the ruling.[86] Eventually Bond was seated, but not before distracting the General Assembly from issues Sanders considered more important in the waning days of his administration. Sanders had no personal affection for Bond, but he thought that the House had acted unwisely in denying him his seat. He reasoned that ultimately Bond would be seated and that opposition would only enhance his popularity, which is exactly what happened.[87]

Despite the distraction of Bond, Sanders again managed to dominate the General Assembly, which passed his legislative program routinely. The legislature passed a bill allowing the mergers of schools across county lines, a bill regulating billboards on highways, a bill putting members of the General Assembly on a salary of $4,200, and a constitutional amendment permitting the use of state funds for the rapid transit system in Atlanta. In contrast to previous years, it was a rather skimpy program.[88]

As an ambitious young politician nearing the end of an impressive term, Sanders kept his political options open. One possibility that he seriously considered was a race against Georgia's senior senator, Richard B. Russell. Since the venerable senator's health was not good, Sanders thought Russell might be vulnerable. He tested the waters, but was forced to conclude that he could defeat anyone in the state except Russell. In late March of 1966, not willing to challenge the odds, Sanders ended the speculation by announcing he would not run for the Senate.[89]

Sanders well understood that his goals for Georgia could not be fully accomplished in a four-year term. Naturally, he hoped that his successor would share his vision and build on the foundation his administration had laid. When the 1966 gubernatorial campaign began, former Governor Ernest Vandiver appeared to be the front-runner. Sanders knew him well, respected him, and had confidence in his leadership. Unfortunately, when Vandiver's health forced him to withdraw from the race, no one of comparable stature emerged that Sanders could endorse with enthusiasm. The race was wide open from that point on, and it became one of the longest, bitterest, and most unusual races in Georgia's history.[90] Avid segregationist Lester Maddox of Atlanta finally secured the Democratic nomination by defeating former Governor Ellis Arnall in a primary runoff election. He then faced Republican Howard "Bo" Callaway in the general election. Many moderate and liberal voters, however, could not support either candidate, and over 50,000 write-in votes for Arnall prevented either candidate from securing a majority. Since this situation had never occurred before, no one was quite sure of the legal complications. The issue finally was resolved when the Georgia Supreme Court ruled that the General Assembly could choose the governor. Since the legislature was overwhelmingly Democratic, the ruling meant that the inexperienced Maddox would be the next governor.[91]

Sanders had hoped for an orderly transition with the next administration, but the confusion surrounding the election nullified his efforts. In the past, Georgia governors had been able to begin planning their administrations after the Democratic primary in August, since there had been no Republican opposition. In the 1966 election, however, the outcome was not decided until January 10, 1967. Therefore, Sanders prepared a budget, made appointees, and generally tried to keep the ship of state sailing smoothly through the troubled political waters. As it turned out, both the continuity of ideas and programs as well as the orderly transition he wanted were casualties of the chaotic gubernatorial election. Sanders, who had not played an active role in the campaign, was utterly frustrated by the events. When Maddox was chosen, Sanders congratulated him and then quietly slipped out of the governor's office. When asked to comment on the election, he simply remarked, "I have turned over the keys of government to the next governor and am a free man."[92]

By almost any standard of measurement Sanders was a successful governor. His administration was one of the most productive in Georgia's history. He returned to private life reluctant to leave the limelight which he enjoyed, but satisfied with the accomplishments of his administration and pleased with the accolades of the press.[93] In truth, Georgia had advanced economically, politically, and socially under his firm leadership. When he left office, Georgia's schools and colleges were vastly improved, the state agencies in general were operating more efficiently, the prison and mental health systems were substantially better, the congressional and legislative elections were more democratic, and the state treasury had a surplus of $140 million—the largest in its history up to that time. Moreover, as a result of such accomplishments, the state had gained a more favorable national image.[94]

Sanders was fortunate to be governor in the early sixties, and he enjoyed several advantages that few governors have had. Not only were political changes possible at that time, but also they were fashionable, thanks to the climate of reform produced by the Kennedy-Johnson administrations. Sanders was also very lucky that the trauma of racially integrating Georgia's schools had been begun by his predecessor. Had that issue arisen a few years later, his accomplishments probably would have been diminished substantially. In addition to facing the ordeal of integration, the Vandiver administration had also taken preliminary steps to modernize Georgia's government, especially in the area of finances. Without this essential groundwork, Sanders could not have achieved all that he did. Since Sanders and Vandiver respected each other and shared similar political philosophies, there was continuity of ideas and personnel and a smooth transition of power.

The mid-sixties was an extremely prosperous era with full employment, and this also benefited Sanders. State revenues increased from $445,747,368 in 1962–63 to $617,279,294 in 1965–66.[95] Obviously, with more money flowing into the treasury, more programs could be funded. Sanders was the last Georgia governor to totally dominate the General Assembly. He determined the budget, set the legislative agenda, picked the speaker of the House, and chose the committee chairmen. The election of Maddox permitted the General Assembly to assert its independence, and no governor since then has enjoyed as much power over the legislature as Sanders had.[96] No recent governor has benefited from the combination of so many positive forces at work as Sanders. These factors contributed substantially to the success of his administration, but competent, energetic, pragmatic leadership was still required to translate opportunity into reality. That Sanders supplied.

A Time for Progress

CARL E. SANDERS

I don't want to detract from the significance of the "first person" comments of any of us who are former governors, but I think I should make this observation. I had the privilege of playing on two different football teams—one for Richmond Academy and another at the University of Georgia. Through the years, we have had about a half dozen reunions of each team. I've noticed that with each reunion our performances become more heroic. What we used to celebrate as a thirty-yard pass play has now become a fifty-yarder! What was once remembered as a key tackle is now thought to be a goal-line stand that saved the game. I can only conclude that in both football and politics—after a certain number of years—a former player is permitted to remember his successes with far more clarity than his fumbles.

I'd like to divide my time into three areas. First, I want to share with you some of my personal thoughts about the general political climate and atmosphere in our state when I became governor. Then I want to mention a few specific programs or actions that I think have stood the test of time and still have some relevance today. And the third area that I want to mention is the office of governor itself, and what I remember as the basic elements of an effective Executive Department.

On the day I became governor in January 1963 there were a couple of moods or general feelings that I can still recall clearly. First, I had the feeling that something was stirring all across the South that could be an awakening for this region. There was something in the air that said good things were about to happen to this region which had lagged behind the nation in so many ways. And in addition to the normal exhilaration anybody would feel who is about to be sworn in as governor, there was this bona fide optimism which had a major influence on the political climate.

I was interested in what Terry Sanford was doing in North Carolina, what Leroy Collins had already done in Florida, and I had heard a great deal about the public education system in California. The term "Sunbelt" had not been coined at that time, but there was a clear feeling that our region was about to experience an exciting era of growth. I recall that I had a very competitive feeling about my own situation and Georgia's image with relation to other states in the South.

I always had a pleasant relationship with the governors of other states in the region, but I have to confess that after I was sworn in as governor I constantly felt that I was in a competitive situation with the leadership of the surrounding states. In retrospect, I think that feeling of competition had a good deal to do with my agenda and what I considered to be important.

For example, I was very interested in working closely with Ivan Allen as the mayor of Atlanta. To be recognized as a governor who had a great interest in the capital city was not particularly good politics during most of our political history. I like Ivan Allen personally, but I remember having the distinct feeling that if Atlanta could "steal the march" on Birmingham, Charlotte, Nashville, Jacksonville, and Miami and be the first city in the South to have major league sports, it would be a tremendous boost to the image of our state and would in many ways put us in the major leagues.

That may have been a little simplistic, and it might have been a little bit of competitive pride. But the major premise was correct, and I still feel today that every citizen of Georgia benefits when Atlanta progresses. One facet of my administration that I believe was significant was the close relationship between the statehouse and city hall in Atlanta during a crucial period in our history.

Looking back now, I can see other ramifications of the feeling I had as governor that I very much wanted Georgia to be in a strong competitive position. We had an infamous prison known as Buford Rock Quarry. I would like to tell you today that my inherent sense of justice was so strong that I couldn't sleep at night until we got rid of that prison. It would be closer to the truth for me to tell you that I thought that prison was giving us a black eye in the national media, and we closed it. I make no apology for the fact that in prison reform and race relations I simply wanted my administration and my state to come off as handling these difficult and historic problems in a progressive and sensible way. The political climate at that time was very much influenced by where we were in the field of race relations.

I was very fortunate that we had in Atlanta some high quality leadership from Ivan Allen and his administration and some strong leadership in the black community, particularly from the black colleges in Atlanta, both students and faculty. While so much of the South agonized during those four years, Atlanta moved ahead dramatically.

It's impossible to talk about the political climate of that period without mentioning the name Ralph McGill. McGill mostly got slings and arrows from politicians, and I'm sure he would have been very suspect about any plaudits from me or any other elected official, but in retrospect his journalism made the capital city of Georgia a different kind of place to practice politics from any other capital in the South. I was not a close confidant of McGill, and he seldom tried to give me advice, but it was not possible for a person of common sense to live in the same town as Ralph McGill without having some feeling for the moral imperative and practical soundness of racial justice and good race relations.

I worked personally with a number of people in the sixties that I considered to be the founding fathers of modern Atlanta—William Hartsfield, Ivan Allen, Robert Woodruff, Mills Lane, and Richard Rich. But if you ask me the single most influential figure in shaping modern Atlanta, I would have to say Ralph McGill because he told us so often and so well that prejudice was a tragic mistake politically, economically, and morally.

During the first year of my administration we had a feeling which I could only characterize as "official boundless optimism." We were in a period of peace. Inflation was low. The economy was strong. President Kennedy said we were going to the moon. I honestly felt like we could do anything in Georgia that could be done in any other state in America if we just worked hard enough. It was a positive, exciting time.

In my administration, just as today, over half the time of the governor was consumed by what I would call the ceremonial or logistical aspects of serving in that office—presenting proclamations, representing the state in ceremonial functions, and what we might call the daily routine. And every governor is shocked by how little time he has for his main program or his main objective.

I recall very well that after a short time in office what I wanted to do was to bet all of my chips on the basic idea that education was the common denominator of progress. I knew enough about the education system in California to be impressed and envious of what they had. They had a first-rate system of higher education—free community colleges accessible to everybody—and that great attention to higher education seemed to spill over into secondary education.

In retrospect, my aim perhaps was too high, but there was no doubt in my mind that in a reasonable period of time we could have a system of higher education as good as any in the country. It was my basic idea that this would have a dramatic uplifting effect on secondary education.

At that time a great percentage of the people coming out of high school in Georgia simply did not consider higher education to be accessible to them, and it seemed clear to me the top educational priority. We brought in George Simpson to be chancellor of the university system of Georgia, and he was a hard-nosed, tough manager. We put in a system of junior colleges in a very short period of time. The mid-sixties was the golden age of higher education in this state and a number of other states.

Later, during the Vietnam era, higher education lost a lot of its public and political support throughout the nation. Educational strategies seemed to change with the years, but I basically still hold to the view that higher education sets the tone for the whole system of public education and that states with the best colleges always seem to have the best secondary education as well. My basic idea about public education then—and now—is that our colleges should train a steady supply of qualified teachers, that we should pay them enough money to make teaching an attractive career, and that we should leave them alone and let them teach.

Both nationally and on the state level the period of the early sixties is sometimes thought of today in a wistful way as being a time of too much optimism, too many programs, visions that were too expensive, and government that was too expensive. I don't know where it put me on the political spectrum—and I have been active for many years in the business arena dealing with balanced budgets, financial projections, and economic indicators—but I have the strongest personal conviction that government serves best when its agenda includes distant visions such as going to the moon and building excellent colleges all over the state. Every decade should have a different set of dreams and visions.

I have taken a good deal of flak through the years because of my friendship with and respect for Lyndon Johnson, who had the ultimate political dream of a decent life for every inhabitant of his country. It is popular to disparage that kind of optimism today, but I shall always be thankful that my watch at the helm of our state government occurred during a time when it was acceptable for government's reach to exceed its grasp.

I would like to think that in my administration we dealt effectively with the nuts and bolts of operating the state government on a daily basis. The work of the Bowdoin Commission, the extensive involvement we had with reapportionment, and the great amount of time that we invested in writing a new constitution, which unfortunately a federal court prevented from being placed on the general ballot, were all extremely important and time-consuming activities for my administration, but I want to move on to the subject of the office of governor itself.

With these comments I am not attempting to assess the leadership style of other governors or to compare my approach to theirs, but I think if you are seriously studying the impact of governors upon the state of Georgia during the last thirty or forty years some attention has to be directed to the office of governor itself. I want to give an example of the interplay between the person who occupies that office and the policies and priorities of the office. When I was in the military service, I was given the opportunity, so to speak, of learning about aviation. I became a pilot and have always had the point of view that aviation is an important part of our transportation system. When I became governor, I found out there was a federal program through which some assistance could be obtained for building airports where they were not available. Because of this personal interest, I said: "We are going to build an airport everywhere in Georgia that somebody might want to fly an airplane." And we built more than a hundred from Rabun Gap to Tybee Light. We probably got ten times the normal allocation for airport construction simply because I devoted some personal interest to pushing this program.

That is one example of how state policy is influenced simply by the personal views and interests of the person who happens to occupy the governor's office. It was my style and my intent not to be bashful about what I thought was important from the standpoint of the chief executive. That included what today might be referred to probably as interfering in the legislative branch.

It was expected during my time in the capitol that the governor would be the chief executive in a broad sense of that term. I determined who was elected speaker of the House and, in turn, the leadership of the key committees of the House were much more inclined to go along with my program. I had no serious doubt that any program I could put together which was essentially sound and could be financed by the state government would be approved by the legislature. My batting average was not 100 percent—and we had checks and balances—but there was much less of what we now call "bickering and squabbling" between the executive branch and the legislative branch. And the legislative branch made almost no attempts to provide any day-to-day direction through the operating departments of the state government.

Naturally, I am inclined to the view that state government operates much more effectively with a strong governor system, rather than with a system in which the legislature achieves something close to operational responsibility through the budget process and various overview committees. States in the South which have historically been recognized as having less aggressive, less progressive state governments, such as Mississippi and South Carolina, have for decades had a system in which the legislature essentially determines the budget and the governor is only a participant in that process rather than the clear leader of the process.

I fully understand the concept of separation of powers and the concept of checks and balances. But the kind of matters that state governments have to address on a year-to-year basis are the kinds of practical things that there will always be strong difference of opinions about exactly how to accomplish. Therefore, there is the danger that rather than aggressive leadership we will get constant compromise on how to administer education, how to operate the prison system, how to run the health care system, and other practical aspects of state governments.

I am very proud of the overall record of my administration, and I have complete admiration for the people who served in the General Assembly during those years. But there is no doubt in my mind that if it had not been possible for my administration to be operated under what is normally referred to as a "strong governor system," then my agenda would have been less than half as long and our accomplishments would have been cut in half.

The final point I want to make is that one of my basic notions about government has changed with the passing of time. When I was elected, I had the idea that "good government" was something of a promised land and that once we completed some agenda we would have arrived at the promised land of good, efficient, compassionate government. I can see now that good government is not a promised land which we ever really arrive at. It is a process which has to be worked at every day, and those who are working in a vineyard have to constantly adjust their directional bearings to keep moving toward the elusive goal of good government. Every administration and every generation has its own work to do in the ongoing parade.

Lester G. Maddox

1967 – 1971

Lester Maddox
and the Politics
of Populism

BRADLEY R. RICE

Surely it is rare for a political outsider of relatively modest means who lost three races for lower office to reach the governorship of his state on the first try. But Lester Garfield Maddox is a rare individual.

At least three points are necessary to understand the successes and failures of this unlikely governor. First, one must appreciate the flamboyant background that made him a nationally famous, ax-handle-waving symbol of defiant Southern resistance to federally enforced racial integration. Second, one needs to realize the unusual election circumstances that placed this inexperienced outsider in the governor's chair. Finally, one must grasp that, despite his limited vision and his extremist and racist image, Maddox truly did wish to use the powers of state government to make Georgia a better place for all its people.

Of course, if not for his well-publicized ranting about integration and Communist influence, few people other than Atlanta-area fried chicken aficionados whould ever have heard of Lester Maddox. However, if one can overlook his obsession with race and communism, many of the programs and policies championed by Maddox in the 1960s seem forward-looking and progressive.

Maddox often declared that he was no racist and that his policies would be fair to white and black alike. He claimed that his beliefs were based on states' rights, free enterprise, and Christianity—not on racism;

yet, as for many white Southerners, his conception of these values was inextricably bound up with his view of the proper racial order.

Lester Maddox was born and reared in a working-class area of Atlanta near the Georgia Institute of Technology. Yet, even though his father worked in a steel plant, there was a rural-like quality to his urban environment. At various times in Maddox's childhood the family kept hogs, cows, and chickens and sold produce from the garden. This urban-rural mixture produced in Maddox a sort of Populist mentality suggestive of Tom Watson.

The Home Park neighborhood where Maddox was raised exhibited the typical Southern pattern of Negro residence in alleys behind the white-occupied homes, so he grew up in close proximity to blacks and often played with black children. He worked under the supervision of a Negro man in his first regular job. Through a family friend, he managed to land a job at Atlantic Steel, where his father had been fired a couple of years earlier; he also worked around blacks there. These early associations reenforced in Maddox the sort of traditional Jim Crowism that allowed for real warmth toward subservient Negroes but real antagonism toward racial equality.

Maddox dropped out of high school and worked in various odd jobs that sparked his later entrepreneurial spirit. In 1936, after Lester had advanced to a low-level supervisory position at Atlantic Steel, he and Virginia Cox decided to get married. Following a dispute with his boss, Maddox left the company, and at the outbreak of World War II he was living and working in Birmingham, where his father had moved a couple of years earlier. He obtained a civilian job with the Navy Department, and it took him back to Atlanta. (As a father in a war-related job, Maddox was not subject to the draft.) Disliking the travel associated with his Navy position, Maddox quit and quickly was employed at the B-29 factory in Marietta. Soon he left this job too.

Clearly, Lester Maddox was not comfortable as an employee. He longed to be his own boss, and in 1944 he started his first real business—a short-order grill on Fourteenth Street a couple of blocks from the Atlantic Steel plant. A year later he sold this place for a nice profit and worked briefly in groceries and real estate.

In 1947 Maddox began to build the cafeteria-style Pickrick Restaurant that would make him famous. Located on Hemphill Avenue (U.S. Highway 41) near Georgia Tech, the Pickrick was expanded more than a half dozen times until it became one of the largest restaurants in Atlanta. The specialty was good homestyle food, especially fried chicken, at moderate prices. With its highway location and proximity to hungry college students, the Pickrick prospered and the Maddoxes with it.

They had made it. Lester and Virginia built a new home in a fashionable Northside area.[1]

As governor, Maddox once returned to his old neighborhood to address a PTA meeting, and he reminisced about how his dream of owning a prosperous business had come true. "That dream warmed my cold feet and gave strength to tired legs as I pedaled a bicycle over this neighborhood to make a few pennies," he recalled. "It was a long, hard climb from Home Park Avenue to Hemphill Avenue, but my dream came true. I was Mr. Maddox. I was Mr. Pickrick. I was Mr. Somebody."[2]

What brought Lester Maddox into the public eye were his weekly newspaper advertisements headed "Pickrick says." They began in 1949, and after the 1954 school desegregation decisions the homespun messages became much more explicitly political. Thanks to the Pickrick ads, Maddox's position as an anti-integration conservative became well known. Emboldened by a Dale Carnegie course, he decided to take a stab at politics by running an independent candidacy for mayor in 1957 against longtime incumbent William B. Hartsfield. Maddox claimed that his platform was based on issues of "law and order," but racial considerations clearly dominated his campaign. He continually referred to Hartsfield as the NAACP candidate. The federally enforced integration of Little Rock's Central High School happened during the campaign, and Maddox literature declared, "STORM TROOPERS TAKE LITTLE ROCK." He charged that school integration would lead to "widespread racial amalgamation." Drawing from a coalition of affluent whites and blacks, Hartsfield won a comfortable victory. The mayor declared that the results showed that "the people of Atlanta don't want Atlanta's growth and prosperity to be stopped by racial controversy." Close analysis revealed that Maddox may have in fact carried a majority of the white voters.

Maddox stayed active in various anti-integration organizations, and four years later he tried for mayor again. This time, since Hartsfield was retiring, the principal opponent would be Atlanta Chamber of Commerce leader Ivan Allen, Jr., who had helped negotiate the voluntary desegregation of many local businesses. The central focus of the campaign was, of course, once again race, although other matters did come up. Maddox pleaded for the voters not to be influenced by the "race-mixing liberals" of the Atlanta daily newspapers, which backed Allen. One Maddox advertisement made the choice clear: "If you are ready to accept total integration in everything, VOTE FOR IVAN ALLEN, JR.!" Again the moderate coalition prevailed, and Allen won a strong runoff victory.[3]

Having failed to ride the race issue into the Atlanta City Hall, but buoyed by his strong showing among white voters, Maddox decided to try a statewide race for lieutenant governor in 1962. The Democratic primary was wide open because this was the first state election after the demise of the rural-dominated county unit system. Maddox made it through an eight-man race into the runoff against Peter Zack Geer. Since both Geer and Maddox were segregationists, Maddox was not able to use the race issue with the same effectiveness he had against Hartsfield and Allen. Still his anti-integration stance was clear, and his references to such things as "Communist-inspired lawless agitators" were racially tinged. Meanwhile, Geer, who had been Governor Ernest Vandiver's executive secretary, managed to position himself as the responsible conservative facing a "radical extremist." The favored Geer won by over 40,000 votes. Only about half of the 785,520 Georgians who had voted in the regular primary when Carl Sanders won the Democratic nomination bothered to cast ballots in the runoff.[4]

Up to this point racial integration had not threatened Lester Maddox directly. The changing racial order of the South was an assault on his values but not yet on his person or his pocketbook. The token desegregation of Atlanta schools in 1961 had not had an impact on his children, and he had held the Pickrick out of Atlanta's voluntary business desegregation pact. But when the long-discussed prohibitions of discrimination in employment and public accommodations became national law in the Civil Rights Act of 1964, he felt that his business and his property were being directly attacked. His vociferous reaction immediately made him a folk hero to many of the segregationists of Georgia and the South. The events of 1964 and 1965 propelled Lester Maddox from being an "also ran," who would probably have been all but forgotten in Georgia history, to being one of the state's most visible and memorable governors.

After a series of pistol-brandishing, pick-handle-waving confrontations with blacks who wanted to test the Civil Rights Act by eating at the Pickrick, and following a series of defeats in federal court, Maddox closed his restaurant rather than operate on a desegregated basis. (An all-white state jury acquitted him on a criminal charge of actually pointing his gun at the protesters.) One of his spring 1964 Pickrick ads made his position clear: "Just in case some of you Communists, Socialists, and other Integrationists have any doubt—THE PICKRICK WILL NEVER BE INTEGRATED! If you want some fried chicken it will have to be something other than Pickrick chicken." In a swipe at the Lyndon Johnson administration reminiscent of Southern attacks on Eleanor Roosevelt, Maddox wrote, "From the looks of the paper it looks as though the lady birds and the black birds have joined together."[5]

The state and national media gave Maddox and his defiance of national authority so much attention that he decided he would run for governor even though only a couple of years earlier he had been unable to win the number two spot. In the fall of 1965, when he announced his candidacy, his potential Democratic opponents included, among others, three former governors: Ellis Arnall, Ernest Vandiver, and Senator Herman Talmadge. Rational political analysis would have deterred most men from the race, but not Lester Maddox. In typical fashion, he branded his opposition as "cowardly political leaders who ask you to follow their programs of cowardice into the pits of hell and destruction—integration and amalgamation."[6]

Maddox was as much interested in a forum as he was the governorship. He later claimed that he was confident of victory, and perhaps he was, but few others would have shared that optimism. Talmadge decided to remain in the Senate, so Arnall and Vandiver emerged as the leading candidates. Neither of them regarded Maddox's candidacy as a serious threat. In the spring Vandiver withdrew for health reasons, and Talmadge once again flirted with entering the race but did not. With the powerful Talmadge out of the way, segregationist Albany newspaper publisher James Gray, former Lieutenant Governor Garland T. Byrd, and State Senator Jimmy Carter qualified to run against Arnall and Maddox.

The whole process of jockeying for positions in the Democratic primary was shaped by the fact that west Georgia Congressman Howard "Bo" Callaway would be a formidable possibility to become the state's first Republican governor. Callaway had defeated Byrd for Congress, and all the Democrats were well aware that the state had gone for Republican Barry Goldwater for president in 1964.

A voter who paid any attention at all could not have been confused about where Maddox and Ellis Arnall, the leading candidates, stood. Arnall's perceived liberalism and identification with the national Democratic Party was a liability with many voters, but he did not hide it. He unabashedly proclaimed, "I am a local Democrat, a state Democrat, and a national Democrat, and anyone who doesn't like it can go to Hell."[7] Maddox wanted to make sure that the voters understood Arnall's message because he correctly perceived that it was a message that many white Georgians did not want to hear. Arnall was, in Maddox's words, "Earl Warren, Jacob Javits, Nelson Rockefeller, Hubert Humphrey, Lyndon Johnson, and Bobby Kennedy all wrapped up into one, plus Martin Luther King."[8]

Maddox promised that he would chase Martin Luther King, Jr., out of the state and invite George Wallace in. He pledged that he would rather raise taxes than accept the integration guidelines that accompanied federal school aid. He also talked about better education, industrial recruitment, prison reform, and other matters, but it was Lester Maddox the defiant segregationist that his constituency wanted to hear.

Gray's rhetoric was more sophisticated but otherwise not much different from Maddox's; he too wantonly tossed around words such as "socialism," "communism," "left-wing," and "tyranny." (Governor Maddox later designated Gray as chairman of the state Democratic Party despite credible reports that Gray forces had tried to buy Maddox out of the race.)9

Byrd also concentrated on attacking Washington, D.C., and integration, especially school desegregation guidelines. Of the major candidates, Carter's position was the vaguest. He tried to place himself somewhere between Arnall on the left and the Maddox-Gray-Byrd group on the right. It was not a bad strategy, for it put him in a good position for his successful 1970 race. In fact, except for Maddox, all of Georgia's governors since Vandiver have taken positions similar to the one Carter took in 1966.

Maddox's campaign was a shoestring affair constrasting markedly with the well-financed efforts of Arnall and Gray. Maddox tirelessly covered the state in his own station wagon, indefatigably shaking hands, passing out his platform, and tacking up small MADDOX COUNTRY posters. Name recognition was no problem. His 1962 lieutenant governor's race had helped him get somewhat known across the state, but his real fame was as Mr. Pickrick who had stood up to the integrationists.

Maddox led the three segregationists, and his showing (23.5 percent of the vote) was adequate to thrust him into a runoff with Arnall, who polled 29.4 percent. Jimmy Carter was in a suprisingly strong third place with 20.9 percent. Both Arnall and Carter did best in the urban-suburban counties, and it is significant that together the two more liberal candidates won a bare majority of the votes cast.10

In the runoff campaign Arnall attacked Maddox, charging that the election of the "ax handle" candidate would be an embarrassment to the state and an impediment to economic growth. Maddox's position is best summarized by his preposterous but popular declaration that Ellis Arnall was "a wild Socialist who is the grandaddy of forced racial integration."11

The turnout for the runoff was actually higher than in the first primary. Arnall again carried the urban-suburban vote, but his margin there was not sufficient to overcome Maddox's lead in the rest of the state, so Maddox won by about 90,000 votes. The state's blacks and white liberals were devastated, and much of the traditional Democratic power structure was worried. In his memoirs, Atlanta Mayor Ivan Allen, who had defeated Maddox four years earlier, described the typical moderate liberal reaction: "It is deplorable that the combined forces of many Republican voters have thrust upon the State of Georgia Lester Maddox, a totally unqualified individual, as the Democratic nominee for governor. The wisdom, justice and moderation espoused by our founding fathers must not be surrendered to the rabble of prejudice, extremism, buffoonery, and incompetency."[12]

What followed over the next few months was unusual even for a state known for colorful political episodes. Not since the three-governor controversy of 1946–47 had there been such confusion. It was ironic that twenty years later Ellis Arnall would once again be involved in the crisis.

Unlike Maddox, Callaway was a conservative Republican from a wealthy textile family. Like Maddox, he was a segregationist unsympathetic to blacks, although he was not as blatant. His charges against Maddox mirrored those of Arnall. He argued that the Atlantan was irresponsible and inexperienced. In contrast, Callaway stressed his own governmental experience in Congress and appointive positions. During his brief tenure in the House he had had the opportunity to vote against a large dose of Great Society and civil rights legislation, and he was proud of that negative record. Callaway spent about three-quarters of a million dollars on a slick, modern media campaign.

Maddox portrayed Callaway as the silver-spoon candidate, and he continued to play his role as what Reese Cleghorn called "Mr. White Backlash." He counted on the traditional Democratic vote, and he even waved the old bloody shirt, reminding voters that the Republicans had "burned the state once."[13]

Most of the established Democrats gave Maddox at least token support, but some Georgians could not stomach the choice between Callaway and Maddox, so they began to seek alternatives. Several black leaders called Callaway "a silk-stocking segregationist who is no better than Maddox."[14] Disgruntled white liberal and black forces called a mass meeting to consider launching a write-in effort. Several names were considered, but the group settled on Arnall and called itself "Write-In Georgia" or "WIG." Arnall did not endorse the Quixotic campaign, but neither did he disavow it.

The black vote apparently split about evenly between Arnall and Callaway, with only a tiny handful for Maddox. Had Callaway been willing to moderate his stance somewhat to appeal to dedicated Arnall supporters of both races, he might have been able to head off the WIG effort and win without dispute.

So heated was the campaign that about 150,000 more people voted in the general election than in the primary runoff—a phenomenon unknown in a nonpresidential year in traditionally one-party Georgia. Statistics revealed that the dominant cleavage in the electorate was along class lines with Callaway winning in middle- and upper-class areas, especially in the urban-suburban counties, and Maddox racking up heavy margins from blue-collar and rural whites.[15]

The consequence of the WIG campaign was, as several observers had predicted, that neither Maddox nor Callaway received the majority necessary for election. Efforts were mounted in the federal and state court to block legislative selection of the governor. Challengers won the first round in federal district court, but the U.S. Supreme Court in a 5 to 4 ruling upheld the legislature's right to choose the governor as provided in the state constitution. Just three days before the General Assembly was set to convene, the Georgia Supreme Court tossed out the final legal objections.

Most observers, including Callaway, expected that once the legal impediments were removed Maddox's choice by the heavily Democratic General Assembly, which had only 29 Republicans out of 259 members, would be a foregone conclusion. Some legislators started calling him "Mr. Governor" as soon as they heard the news of the U.S. Supreme Court ruling. Last-ditch efforts to get the assembly itself to call a runoff were declared out of order, and the legislature proceeded to make Lester Maddox governor by a vote of 182 to 66. Nine of the eleven black legislators, including recently seated Julian Bond, refused to vote, and the other two split. Maddox rushed into the governor's office quickly to take the oath of office before any legal papers blocking his ascendancy could be filed.[16]

It had been a long and improbable road since Lester Maddox had joked in 1954 that he would like to rock in the governor's chair, but he had made it.[17] Maddox's oft-repeated statement about the nature of the obstacles he had to overcome is substantially accurate, especially regarding the primary and runoff campaigns: "It really wasn't too difficult to be elected. All that was necessary was to defeat the Democrats, the Republicans—on the state and national level—159 courthouses, more than 400 city halls, the railroads, the utility companies, major banks and major industry, and all the daily newspapers and TV stations in Georgia."[18]

At the time he announced for governor, Maddox told John Carlton Huie, Jr., what his goals were: "By running for governor, I can bring to the people of Georgia a program of truth, patriotism, and Americanism. . . . I think we can benefit both our Negro and our white citizens with a program of truth, patriotism, and Americanism."[19]

Such platitudes also characterized his inaugural speech, which surprised many observers by its moderation. Some people thought that they were hearing a "new" Maddox. One liberal politician remarked, "The man was elected like a demagogue but he spoke like a governor."[20]

But it was not a new Maddox. It was just that the new governor had two sides. He could give moderate speeches just as he could engage in demagoguery. He had given lots of calm, sane talks during the campaign urging improvements in education, mental health, prisons, and tourism, but they had not attracted media attention like his more outrageous statements had. Now everybody was listening, and they heard Mr. Pickrick himself declare that he agreed with people who did "not want any extremist organization or group to have any voice of influence in any state programs." He said that he had "a mandate for progress and responsibility."[21]

Maddox later said, "The speech came as no surprise to those who knew me."[22] But neither was it a surprise to those who knew him that arch-segregationists Marvin Griffin and Ross Barnett were seated on the inaugural platform.

Maddox truly was different from the typical governor. For one thing, he was an outsider who lacked a formal education. Profiles from a survey by the Council of State Governments show that Maddox was one of only three sitting governors in 1968 who had not attended college. He was one of only four who had no previous governmental service—two of those were attorneys, and one was listed as an actor and rancher from California. Maddox was one of only eleven state governors without military service. On the other hand, as a married fifty-year-old businessman, he was typical.[23]

Maddox was somewhat defensive about his lack of formal schooling, and in mid-1967 he described his education to a group of principals as follows:

> Wendell Phillips once said that "the best education in the world is the one got by struggling to make a living." If his observation is true, my friends, then Lester Maddox is a well-educated man. As your governor, I hold a degree in hard work and a master's degree in self-reliance. I am now at work on a doctorate thesis called "Excellence in State Government." And I can assure you—as a governor who was not able to get the formal education he wanted as a young man—that a major part of our program for excellence is the finest educational system the State of Georgia has ever known.[24]

Maddox's healthy raises for state teachers and substantial increases in funding for the university system exceeded those of his education-minded predecessors, including Carl Sanders. As in their administrations, however, much of state funding was diluted because of the maintenance of dual systems of effectively segregated schools and colleges. The Pickrick's old neighbors at Georgia Tech were especially pleased with the support Maddox directed toward that institution.[25]

Even under the best of circumstances an outsider like Maddox could have expected to have a difficult time leading a General Assembly dominated by veteran politicians, but Maddox's task as chief legislator was complicated by several factors. The legislature was in a period of change due to reapportionment, which brought into the body more urban-suburban legislators, including blacks, who represented areas not in "Maddox Country." Maddox, of course, owed his very office to the sufferance of the legislators who chose him over Callaway. Moreover, his own idea of the separation of powers called for legislative independence, and he had said so during his campaign.[26]

Historically in Georgia the governor had dominated the legislature, especially the House, since he designated the speaker.[27] That body took advantage of the power vacuum following the 1966 election controversy, and since there was no governor-elect it independently chose George L. Smith as its speaker. Smith's power over committees was enhanced, and committee assignments were made without gubernatorial input. At the end of the 1967 session influential Representative James H. "Sloppy" Floyd said, "This legislative independence has been the greatest thing that has happened in my 15 years in the House."[28] In the Senate, Lieutenant Governor George T. Smith presided with less power than Smith did in the House, but the Senate too stood mostly independent of Maddox influence. In his autobiography Maddox stated that "never once during my years as governor had I so much as called a member of the House or Senate or made even a veiled suggestion as to who should be elected to any legislative office or appointed to any committee. This was the job and responsibility of the legislative branch."[29]

The state's budget procedure requires the outgoing governor to prepare a budget proposal, but normally the governor-elect would have the whole autumn after the Democratic primary to plan his own modifications. Sanders did brief both Maddox and Callaway on his budget presentation, but Maddox had no real chance to put his own brand on the budget.[30]

From the beginning the initiative was out of the new governor's hands. Maddox's biggest victory in his first legislative session was a negative one. He managed to convince the Senate to block a House-passed bill that would have allowed cities and counties to levy a local-option one-cent sales tax, half of which would have gone to support schools. Speaker Smith got the bill passed over the objections of administration floor leader Tom Murphy and other Maddox supporters. One writer said that the governor specifically used his power to sign or veto local bills to influence some senators. At the close of the session Maddox praised the General Assembly and said, "It has been a period of testing for us all."[31]

Maddox was potentially a potent new political force in the South, and during his first few months in office George Wallace came calling by invitation. Vice-President Hubert Humphrey also dropped in at the mansion while he was in town. The Minnesotan declared, "The Democratic Party is like a big house; it has lots of room for all of us."[32]

Big folks like Wallace and Humphrey came to see the new governor, but so did hundreds of "little people," who responded to Maddox's idea of having scheduled times open for anyone to visit the governor and discuss a problem. Maddox kept up the "People's Day" throughout his term, and he regarded it as one of his greatest accomplishments. "It is estimated," Maddox told the Southern Governors' Conference shortly before he left office, "that more people have visited the governor's office and the Governor's Mansion during the past forty-five months than in the rest of this century."[33]

Maddox's administrative appointments calmed many fears. He left quite a few Sanders people in place because, as he later said, "they knew their jobs."[34] His appointment of former State Senator Peyton Hawes as revenue commissioner was generally praised. He hired such moderates as Morgan Redwine, who served as executive secretary for about three months until he resigned, charging among other things that Maddox was refusing to hire blacks in order to keep his "folk hero image with the rednecks."[35] Maddox then lured Tommy Irvin out of the legislature to be his executive secretary (a job later held by Zell Miller after Irvin became commissioner of agriculture). He ran into trouble at first seeking a commissioner of the Board of Industry and Trade, but the eventual choice of recently retired U.S. Army General Louis Truman from Fort MacPherson was effective.

Despite Redwine's charges, Maddox actually put more blacks on advisory boards and into white collar jobs than his supposedly racially enlightened predecessor. By 1968 he had placed twenty-two blacks on draft boards. In 1969, for example, he appointed noted black musician Graham W. Jackson to the Board of Corrections. Still, none of his black appointees were in positions of major responsibility such as department heads or judges.[36]

After Maddox's first year in office *Newsweek* said that he was "fast emerging as America's leading political anti-hero. . . . His style is pure populist." Still, the article pointed out, legislative leaders dominated state government.[37] The 1968 session proved that observation to be perhaps even more true than it had been the previous year, especially in the Senate. In mid-session the governor's Senate floor leader, Bobby Rowan of Enigma, quit in frustration. The Senate rejected one of the governor's nominees to the Board of Pardons and Paroles and extracted concessions on welfare administration before confirming William Burson as Family and Children Services director. Only two minor bills out of a half dozen corrections reform measures advanced by the administration passed. Meanwhile, in the House, Speaker Smith noted a distinct lack of gubernatorial arm-twisting. Some cuts were made in the governor's budget, but the budget passed was very similar to the one proposed, including teacher and professor raises, although their effective date was delayed. Atlanta *Constitution* political editor Remer Tyson blamed Maddox's problems on his suspicion of politicians and his reluctance to engage in political trade-offs. Said Tyson: "You can't wheel if you can't deal, and you can't deal if you can't wheel. And that was Governor Maddox's relationship with the Georgia legislature this year." At least no future General Assembly would have to pick a governor, since they passed a law providing for a runoff.[38]

Shortly after the end of the 1968 legislative session, Georgia and the nation were shocked by the assassination of Martin Luther King, Jr., in Memphis. The killing sparked rioting in many cities around the country, and Governor Maddox correctly feared that disorders might also hit Atlanta, especially since the slain civil rights leader's funeral was sure to attract thousands to the city. Wisely he placed the National Guard on alert and called in state troopers to protect the capitol. Prudence dictated that the state be prepared for violence, and Maddox later defended his actions by pointing out that President Johnson had taken similar precautions in Washington. It went well beyond prudence, however, when Maddox gave the troopers orders to "Shoot them down and stack them up" in case of trouble. His threats, never carried out, to hoist the capitol flags back up to full staff in defiance of a presidential proclamation were spiteful. Whereas Maddox's preparations were all defensive, Mayor Allen and the city police were cooperating with the Southern Christian Leadership Conference and others to provide for what turned out to be an orderly and dignified funeral and procession of some 200,000 people, about half of whom were from out of town. According to Allen, Maddox's phalanx of troopers peered through the capitol windows and cracked racist jokes as King's body was carried by. Maddox continued to say that King had "carried out the policies and programs of Communists."[39]

Later in 1968 Maddox came into the national eye through his actions at the Democratic National Convention and through his support of George Wallace for president. Distressed by the imminent nomination of Hubert Humphrey and desirous of a forum for his pronouncements about the ills of the party, on August 17 Maddox announced for the Democratic nomination. In his televised speech from the Georgia House chambers the governor said, "We have waited and waited and waited. Many of us have prayed. But the void has remained unfilled." He decried violence and civil disobedience and called Johnson's Paris peace talks on Vietnam "nothing but surrender on the installment plan."[40]

Four years earlier Maddox had picketed outside the convention, but now he was inside making a symbolic run at the nomination and trying to send a message to what he called "the socialistic and power-mad politicians in charge of the national party."[41] As he carried his banner and as violent confrontations with Chicago police raged outside, there was a dispute over the Georgia delegation. State Representative Julian Bond, who was symbolically nominated for vice-president, headed a group which argued that the Maddox-led delegation should not be seated since it contained only 2 percent blacks when in fact 23 percent of the Georgia electorate was black. Maddox resigned as a delegate and shortly thereafter as a candidate. The convention came up with a compromise that shared Georgia's votes between the Bond slate and the regulars.[42]

After the convention Maddox campaigned hard for George Wallace across the nation. "By following the blood-and-tear-stained path charted by socialists, communists, anarchists, draft card burners, traitors, flag desecrators, looters, rioters, punks, pinks and polished politicians," Maddox told a group in Oklahoma City, "these 'great leaders' of our two major parties have made it possible, even probable, that on January 1, 1969, Governor George Wallace will be sitting in the White House." At a Wallace fund raiser he engaged in rhetoric that even acerbic Vice-President Spiro Agnew would have been hard-pressed to match: "Lester Maddox and the great majority of other patriotic Americans who are working for a living and who are willing to fight for their liberty are fed up with letting this great, beautiful, hard-earned country be spoiled, spit upon, desecrated and dominated by a bunch of snotty-nosed stringy-haired, red-eyed, LSD-taking young-uns who range in age from thirteen to eighty."[43] Wallace, Agnew, and Maddox did, of course, articulate the frustrations of millions of Americans troubled by the events of the 1960s.

During the fall 1968 campaign Maddox was made the principal character of an irreverent play called *Red, White, and Maddox*. At the play's absurdist conclusion, Maddox has become president and he tells God that he has finally "got rid of all them vermin. All them hippies and yippies and race-mixing Red agitators." So well known was the governor that early in 1969 the play ran for forty-one performances on Broadway.[44]

Maddox was not, of course, popular with liberals and blacks and some others, but a 1968 poll showed that his standing with Georgians was generally good. He lagged behind Senators Herman Talmadge and Richard Russell, but 62 percent of Georgians polled said that he was doing an "excellent" or "pretty good" job of it. Fifty-eight percent also ranked him that way on his handling of race problems. Only on the question concerning dignity and ability in office did less than a majority (47 percent) rate their governor excellent or good.45

He may have been popular with the people, but Maddox's relations with the General Assembly were even more strained in 1969 than they had been in the previous two years. For all his social and racial conservatism, Maddox was often more willing to spend money on the state's education, mental health, and welfare needs than was the legislature. In fact, in 1967 one state official was quoted as saying, "People are all wrong about Governor Maddox in calling him a conservative racist. He is so pro-labor and seems to want to spend so much state money that you would have to describe him as a liberal racist."46 Maddox tended to believe his administrators when they said they needed more money, and as a consequence, Reg Murphy wrote in 1968, his administration "is perhaps the most liberal in Georgia history, though he didn't will it to be."47

"Liberal" is probably not the appropriate word, but Maddox did want to increase appropriations substantially and to pass a one-cent increase in the state sales tax to finance the increase and to help local governments. In his State of the State Message the governor boldly declared, "As one who prides himself upon being a fiscal conservative and a hard-headed businessman, it would be far more popular for Lester Maddox to oppose any new or revised taxes and instead to make loud speeches about 'cutting the fat' out of the budget. But that would only postpone the day of reckoning."48 On the other hand, the General Assembly wanted only to "hold the line."

Even without the passage of the Maddox proposals, 1969 saw the state's largest budget ever—nearly a billion dollars ($933 million). Amid threats of vetoes and the specter of a special session, the legislature went home having cut the budget, especially on urban projects and education, having turned down the sales tax increase the governor wanted, and having passed a gasoline tax hike he did not want. The *Constitution*, normally no friend of the governor, editorialized, "It, frankly, is something of a stand-still budget. . . . Governor Lester Maddox had a program, but he simply did not have enough influence in the legislature to implement his program."49

At the close of the session in late March, Maddox told the legislators to go home and "listen to the people. . . . When you come back," he said in reference to the expected special session, "we can get most of it done." Two weeks later, with characteristic bravado, Maddox promised to resign if the upcoming special session would "pass my program in its entirety."50

The General Assembly gathered in mid-June, and the governor told the lawmakers that they were there "because critical and immediate needs of state demand action now." He conceded, "Deliberations are expected. Compromises may be necessary." In a statesmanlike manner he declared, "The decision to raise taxes is a difficult one, but let us not look at taxes alone . . . for the people will judge us not only by the tax rate, but by the quality and quantity of services which we . . . have provided."[51]

Under the prodding of Majority Leader George Busbee, the House rejected Maddox's tax proposal and went home after two days. Maddox had worked to enlist the support of urban legislators, but it was not enough. Administration House Leader Tom Murphy said he felt sorry for the state and attacked the "lying Atlanta newspapers." Maddox blamed his old enemies Carl Sanders and Ivan Allen. Speaker George L. Smith's assessment was, however, probably most accurate. "The Governor had a good program," he said, "but it was evident that the people did not see that this was such a crisis that it should be passed at this time. I always agree with the people."[52]

Maddox went into the brief 1970 session as a lame duck since he could not succeed himself.[53] Despite this handicap, this session may have been the governor's most effective. He did not stake his overall success or failure on the sales tax bill as he had before. He effectively used the threat of a veto to get the conference committee to restore funding for a women's prison and a work release center he wanted. For the first time the budget broke the billion-dollar barrier ($1.08 billion). At the end, Maddox effused that it had been the "most harmonious and productive session ever to take place in the Georgia Assembly."[54]

Any image of moderation Maddox may have earned in the 1970 session, however, was quickly dissipated a few days later by a widely publicized incident that occurred while he was in Washington, D.C., for the National Governors' Conference. He had also come to testify against the proposed strengthening and extension of the Voting Rights Act of 1965, which he called "ungodly, unworkable, unpatriotic and unconstitutional," adding, using his favorite interjection, "Phooey on anything that says otherwise."[55]

There is some dispute about the precise details of the incident, but the basic story is clear. Maddox brought some of his souvenir pick or ax handles reminiscent of his stand at the Pickrick to the vicinity of the House of Representatives restaurant. Word of his action soon got to Representative Charles Diggs, Jr., of Michigan, and he confronted Maddox in the dining room. The governor told the veteran black congressman that he was "acting more like an ass and a baboon than a member of Congress."[56]

At least three Georgia congressmen suggested that Maddox's antics might damage the efforts of those in Congress who were trying to restrict federal integration efforts, although other spokesmen denied that the incident would have any effect. A black congressman who was present at the confrontation commented with pleasure, "He is hurting his own cause."[57]

During the 1970 General Assembly several legislators introduced bills designed to thwart the progress being made in school desegregation under federal court orders and HEW guidelines. Only one toothless bill on busing managed to pass, however.[58] Maddox endorsed the proposals, but to his credit he did not waste his political capital in the assembly pushing for such futile last-ditch efforts at massive resistance. However, even though the governor did not make school segregation a major legislative battleground, his public pronouncements throughout his term were dominated by scathing attacks on federal efforts to promote racial balance in the public schools. He once told the federal government to take its education money and "ram it."[59]

He praised the move toward private segregation academies and encouraged more of them. Furthermore, he hinted that he would ask the legislature to replace funds lost if schools rejected federal integration guidelines. The governor's interview with *U.S. News and World Report* early in 1970 was, unfortunately, an accurate prediction of what would happen in much of rural small-town Georgia over the next decade as white parents withdrew their children and their support from public schools. "In areas where they do not have the financial means, there is going to be a vast lowering of the level of public education, in addition to an increase in the private-school system," Maddox said. By this point he had given up opposing all racial mixing in schools and was defending so-called "freedom of choice" plans.[60]

Maddox called for and participated in several meetings of Southern officials who were seeking ways to get around federal orders. He seemed unable to comprehend that men of goodwill could favor federally enforced integration—in his version, it had to be a Communist conspiracy and the integrationists had to be either subversives or dupes. Speaking to the state school superintendents' association, he cried, "When the status-seekers and power-mad politicians and do-gooders in the church, labor, business, government and elsewhere tell Georgians they must follow Communist doctrine and place racial amalgamation ahead of our children's welfare and preservation of educational values, then—All should cry out '*We will not. We will never do it.*' " To a PTA group in Lithonia he charged, "These federal officials have placed socialism, racial amalgamation and communism ahead of education." He even used the occasion of a park dedication to call for "hard-headed resistance to the socialistic-communistic edicts of the federal government."[61]

Although Maddox apparently was never an official member, he had close ties to the John Birch Society, and he took his education message to the group in Los Angeles, saying that a "thief" would come "wearing the disguise of 'civil rights,' 'equal opportunities,' 'better schools' and 'law of the land.' But, regardless of what mask he wears, he is the International Communist Conspiracy and he is out to steal the very heart of American strength—our public school system." At other forums he continually referred to federal "tyranny" and "police state" and "gestapo" tactics.[62]

The Lester Maddox that most Americans remember is the Maddox of such bellicose rhetoric—the Maddox who told a Citizens Council leadership conference in 1969, "I'm a segregationist, and proud of it," and the Maddox who pledged to another such meeting in 1970, "If you ever hear that Lester Maddox has given up his fight for racial integrity, for constitutional government, for states' rights, for private property rights, for the private free enterprise system and for freedom of choice and neighborhood schools, then you will know that Lester Maddox is no more."[63]

The Maddox that people remember often associated with Birchers and Klansmen and other disciples of hate, and his rhetoric no doubt sometimes fanned that hatred. Yet Lester Maddox did not seem to be hateful. His deep religious faith allowed him to hate the sin but not the sinner. Of course, to Maddox, racial integration was a sin, and those who advocated it were therefore sinful. Welfare loafing was a sin. Rioting was a sin. Maddox believed that the liberals were encouraging these sins. That loafing and rioting were not the goals of the Great Society failed to dissuade him.

On the other hand, he truly did want to help those who, like himself, came from impoverished backgrounds. Clearly he did think it was time that the state cleaned up its scandalous prison camps. Without a doubt he wanted to make sure that Georgia children could get the good education that he never got. Even Charles Weltner, who had given up a seat in the U.S. House of Representatives in 1966 rather than run on the same ticket with Maddox, admitted two and a half years later, "He really is for the poor folks, and when you do things for the poor folks, it involves black people."[64]

In a 1968 Fourth of July oration the governor proclaimed, "The liberals and the communists of this country, if you can distinguish between them, cannot cope with facts."[65] That half joking statement revealed one of Maddox's intellectual flaws. He did not recognize the legitimate

difference between communism and the sincere belief that federally enforced integration would be good for the country. He did not acknowledge the real distinction between socialism and welfare-state capitalism. He was a master at spotting hypocrisy in others (especially Ivan
Allen, Jr., and the Atlanta daily newspapers), but he could not see it in
himself and those who thought like him. In his constant railings against
federal interference he could never admit that he did not, in fact, oppose
all federal guidelines. He only specifically attacked those he did not
like—especially the ones on race. He often bragged about Georgia's
great economic progress during his administration, but he conveniently
overlooked the statistics that showed that the great bulk of that growth
was occurring in metro Atlanta, which managed to maintain its progressive, "too busy to hate" racial image despite the governor.

But his sincerity was not in question. His honesty was not assailed.
His desire to serve his state well within the limits of his vision was not
doubted, and many other Georgians of his day shared that same flawed
vision. So many shared it that they overwhelmingly elected him lieutenant governor in 1970. By 1974, however, the magic of Pickrick had
finally evaporated, and he lost to George Busbee in his bid to return to
the governorship. Georgia seemed to be ready to leave overtly racial politics behind.[66]

At the end of the 1969 legislative session Tom Murphy, then the governor's floor leader and later speaker of the House, gave what still may
be the best evaluation of Lester Maddox's intentions: "Who among you
will laugh at the efforts of an honest, sincere, dedicated Christian man
whose honest desire is to keep his state ahead?" Another longtime legislator summed up Maddox's political impact, saying, "He wasn't a bad
governor, he didn't rock the boat; he didn't rock the boat."[67]

A Chance for
the Truth

LESTER G. MADDOX

Just as this symposium is historic and the first of its kind, so was my campaign, election, and administration as governor of Georgia. It was that difference that now dictates that my address depart from the norm. In the likely event the print and electronic media continue to exclude the accomplishments of the Maddox administration, and the history books continue to fail to treat Lester Maddox and his term as governor of our great state fairly, honestly, and factually, I would like to have at least one record of the truth. So I am most thankful for this opportunity to tell my side of the story. I have long been convinced that the mass media and authors of our history books are unable to recognize good in those they oppose and bad in those they support, and the facts bear out this contention.

Before I get into the story of why I sought the office of governor of Georgia, which will include my comments as to why the truth about the Maddox administration continues to be ignored and hidden, I must point out several reasons why my election and service in the office of governor was of historical significance.

First of all, I was ignored as a candidate and condemned as an outsider by the entire political establishment. I had no political organization. I was not adequately financed. After announcing my candidacy for governor in September of 1965, it took seven months of hard work before my total contributions reached $1,000. After one year of hard campaigning I had received a total of $18,000 in contributions and, along with $18,000 in borrowed funds, reached the Democratic runoff in September 1966.

On a personal basis, I didn't know the incumbent governor, nor more than ten members of the General Assembly, or other state officials. Neither did I have an acquaintance with elected officials who ran Georgia's city halls and its 159 county courthouses. I knew not one leader in the news media on a personal basis, not one spokesman for the banks, industry, business, labor, religion, education, agriculture, nor did I know the spokesmen for the professionals in medicine, science, and elsewhere.

Second, my campaign, election, and term as governor were historically significant because they were covered not only by the news media in Georgia and other states, but by the international media as well.

Finally, the prognosticators of doom and disgrace for our state were proven to be wrong and deceitful or dishonest in every instance. Led and inspired by the liberal, socialistic, and radical leadership in the mass media, and by state, local, and national Democratic and Republican party leaders, the political establishment in Georgia and other states declared war on Lester Maddox, his family, his friends, and his supporters.

My supporters and I were held in contempt and scorned by media leaders throughout Georgia, the United States, and much of the world. Joining these critics in what appeared to be a conspiracy to mislead were Democrats for Callaway, spokesmen for the Democratic and Republican parties, including Lyndon Johnson and Hubert Humphrey, along with leaders in the church, education, business, industry, and labor and at the city halls and courthouses throughout Georgia. In addition, the biased, prejudiced, dishonest, uninformed, and misinformed members of the NAACP, ACLU, Southern Regional Council, Southern Christian Leadership Conference, and various other liberal and socialist groups, as well as the Communist Party U.S.A. and the Communist Party International, waged a full-time war against Lester Maddox, the truth, freedom of choice, private property rights, and constitutional government.

It seemed all one had to do to get coverage was to attack Lester Maddox. Even though ultimately repudiated, these misrepresentations served to deceive millions of Georgians and other Americans while striking fear into their minds and hearts. This was the plan of the perpetrators, and the media, small and large alike, played right into their hands. These are facts that cannot honorably be disputed. Georgia children and others continue to be denied access to these truths. They are being treated unfairly and history is being treated unfairly.

It was *Time* magazine that said, "Up to 100,000 Republicans voted for 'the balding bigot' over Arnall, feeling it would be easier for Callaway to beat conservative Lester Maddox in the General Election, than for him to beat liberal Ellis Arnall." Honest and informed Georgians knew this statement was untrue. This was just one more example of the thousands of statements published and broadcast that reflected the dishonesty and bias practiced by the mass media and other liberal, radical, socialistic, and communistic groups.

Judge Robert Heard, leader and organizer of Democrats for Callaway, was quoted thousands of times in every city and county of Georgia, saying, "If Georgians vote for Lester Maddox in the General Election, it would be a vote for extremism in all its violent forms, for intemperateness, for provocative acts, for those types of things, which if allowed to fester and influence over four years would absolutely destroy the state as a haven for responsible citizens seeking security and opportunity."

A former governor said, "If Maddox is nominated by the Democratic Party he may well be inaugurated as Georgia's next governor." And he added, "This would be disastrous for the future welfare of our state and our people." On yet another occasion he said: "Lester Maddox has done more to destroy respect for law and order in our state than any other Georgian. It would be a disgrace to Georgia if Lester Maddox were nominated. The entire nation would laugh at us."

Bo Callaway said, "If Lester Maddox is elected, the State of Georgia will never return to leadership in the South." And he added that "four years of martial law and an end to industry coming to Georgia" would be the fate of Georgia and Georgians.

The Atlanta *Journal-Constitution* said, "Maddox's extremism is known throughout the nation. If he should win, it would make mockery of that state's motto, 'Wisdom, Justice and Moderation.' Maddox is altogether unequipped by experience or knowledge to handle the duties of governor." And, on another occasion, the newspaper said: "There can be no choice but Mr. Arnall in the runoff against the dangerous extremism of Lester Maddox."

Other media, other groups throughout Georgia and the nation joined in to mislead, deceive, and frighten Georgia voters. Those who joined in that campaign of fear and deception included Lyndon Johnson, Hubert Humphrey, Ralph McGill, Gene Patterson, Gerald Ford, Charles Weltner, John Sibley, William Bowden, Julian Bond, Martin Luther King, Jr., Roy Wilkins, Ellis Arnall, James Carmichael, Archbishop Paul J. Halliman, and other religious leaders, including my own Southern Baptist denomination.

The list of those campaigning against Lester Maddox also included the AFL-CIO, Jack Anderson, the Washington *Post*, the New York *Times*, the national television and radio networks, every daily newspaper in Georgia, along with the television and radio stations in our state. Not in all the history of Georgia had there ever been such an organized effort to destroy and discredit a candidate for governor.

Martin Luther King, Jr., said, "Mr. Maddox's victory in the Democratic runoff is indicative of a deep corroding cancer in the Georgia body politic. Georgia is a sick state produced by the disease of a sick nation. I must confess that Mr. Maddox's victory causes me to be ashamed to be a Georgian."

After having led both sides of the segregation-integration battle, depending upon which was most politically expedient at the time, former Atlanta Mayor Ivan Allen issued a public statement that called those thousands of Georgians who voted for Lester Maddox "stupid and ignorant." After he made that remark, I offered him a thousand dollars, then fifteen thousand, to call another news conference and make the same statement again. Even though time has vindicated me of all false charges leveled at me by my opponents in high places of leadership throughout the state, not one has had the integrity to come to me and offer an apology for his slander. A few have begrudgingly conceded that Lester Maddox was not as bad as they thought he would be and that he made some good appointments to the courts. However, many rank-and-file Georgians have come to me and said, "I regret not having voted for you but, like so many others, I had been deceived and lied to by the media and spokesmen for the political establishment."

My response to that has always been simply this: "You owe me no apology, for if I had believed what the media printed and broadcast about me, I, too, would have voted for my opponent."

I grew up as an American with a lifelong dream and goal of becoming a successful businessman. I wanted to be a part of the free enterprise system which, more than governors, legislators, presidents, mayors, commissioners, and Democratic and Republican parties, made this nation the greatest and freest ever known.

My decision to seek public office came later in life, when I continued to observe candidates at every level of government campaign one way and, once in office, live in total contradiction of their promises. I wanted to see what one man outside the political establishment could do to promote a government of, for, and by the people, as intended by our forefathers. My major campaign theme and platform was to "promote honest, efficient, and open government" like it had not been promoted in twentieth-century Georgia. The record speaks for itself. I kept that promise.

As I recalled my term as governor of Georgia, a single image continued to stand out: I remembered the face of a loving mother, tears

rolling down her cheeks, her pleading eyes seeking mercy as she talked
with me about her son in prison and what a miracle it would take to get
him home where he belonged. I remember her talking about her distrust
of the Pardon and Parole Board and how you must be rich to even be
considered for parole. That poor woman was a symbol of the have-nots,
the left-outs, the sad and the unfortunate, who had needs and desires
but who had always been ignored and cast aside. She contributed more
than she will ever know to my inspiration and resolution to seek public
office and serve my fellow citizens. I knew, when elected, I should be
able to reach out to these people and all Georgians. I knew that, unlike
other Georgia governors elected in this century, I would have total freedom to be the governor of all the people—the Democrats and the Republicans, the rich and the poor, the weak and the strong, rural Georgians and urban Georgians, the black and the white, and opponents as
well as supporters.

I had grown weary of politicians who, then as now, get along by going
along rather than being the statesmen they should be, and so had many
other Americans.

The 1960s were a time when businessmen were feeling the wrath of
an overzealous federal establishment that penalized them if they failed
to comply with guidelines imposed, mind you, by federal bureaucrats
and not by the Congress. It was a time when state and local officials also
were being harassed and threatened if they did not comply with guide
lines pertaining to their school districts, their classrooms, and their
children. It was a time when children, their parents, and their teachers
were being denied the right to freedom of choice. Education was being
attacked and destroyed by what could only be called a federal police
state. Our government was rewarding failure, mediocrity, and waste in
our society while punishing and penalizing those who worked, produced, and excelled. It was popular then among many in our government, the media, labor, business, the church, the professions, and elsewhere to encourage the American people to forget about America, God,
and morality and to accept socialism and communism.

I had no choice but to give up my business life and neglect my family
and seek public office. To have done otherwise would have made it impossible for me to face my family, friends, and fellow Georgians. Then,
as now, I was convinced that failing to seek the office of governor would
be following the example of cowards who fail to publicly stand and fight
for America. God forbid I should ever follow the path of those who have
failed to serve their God and their country for fear of losing a dollar or a
vote. I had to win. I was the candidate of the people, not one belonging
to and controlled by the special-interest political establishment, which

had nothing to offer but the continued compromise and surrender of the rights of all Georgians to private property, private free enterprise, and the right to be secure in their homes and safe on their streets.

I knew that being the governor of Georgia could be more difficult for me than for my predecessors or those who followed me in that office. I knew full well I would have to be one of the best governors ever to serve our state even to be given credit for being average. However, that caused me no great concern because I knew my platform was one for the people, and that with the help of God and my fellow citizens we would win the fight to make Georgia a safer, cleaner, and better place in which to live. I knew we would practice honesty, efficiency, and morality in government such as had not been witnessed in my lifetime.

So, when I won the Democratic nomination for governor of Georgia, I began to make plans to move into the governor's office and the governor's mansion. I sincerely believed that no Republican at that time, especially one from so high up in the silk-stocking crowd, could be elected. However, as history records, the election was determined by the Georgia General Assembly, as provided by Georgia law. This created a problem, for unlike my predecessors, who historically had some four months to prepare for office, I was given only a few moments.

This was a problem that could, and should, have been prevented, a problem brought about by the mass media and their followers and servants of the political establishment. Through their publications, broadcasts, and statements designed to frighten, deceive, and control the voters of our state, they worked to disrupt an open, fair, and honest election campaign and, in so doing, disrupted the normal process of government. The media were undeniable villains in this election. They inspired the write-in movement approved by my runoff opponent, former Governor Ellis Arnall, who at the time was unable to accept the defeat handed him by the voters of Georgia. I know how he was hurt. I have walked in those shoes more than once. However, I knew, and I believe he must have known, that the write-in candidacy he accepted would probably disrupt the orderly process of the election and the business of state government. Yet he persisted in his refusal to remove his name as a write-in candidate.

I believe Governor Arnall knew, as I knew, that if he discouraged a write-in campaign the write-in movement would collapse and few, if any, liberal, moderate, or conservative Democrats who planned to vote write-in would go to the polls on the day of the general election and vote for the Republican candidate. Had there been no such disruptive diversion, there is no doubt in my mind that the Democratic candidate would have won the election by a substantial margin and the historic election of governor by the Georgia General Assembly would never have taken place.

In spite of the complete absence of the luxury of a transition period, I was far from overwhelmed by becoming an "instant governor." My study of government at every level for more than twenty-five years, along with my industrial management experience and many years of successful owner-management experience in the real estate, restaurant, grocery, and furniture business, gave me the assurance that I could well handle the job of governor of Georgia. I sincerely believed then, as I do now, that any good, successful, and honest business person could make a good governor, president, congressman, legislator, or mayor. But many of those who have proven to be good elected officials would fail miserably in the tough and competitive business of private free enterprise.

However, in spite of the opponents of Lester Maddox making every effort to deny the common people of Georgia the election of their candidate, failing in Georgia courts, as well as the United States Supreme Court, Georgia's "little people," as they came to be called by the media, finally had a governor.

When I accepted the decision of the General Assembly, I did so with a humble heart and a promise that I had no friends to favor and no enemies to punish. I said I would be an independent governor, free from the pressure of the Democratic Party, free from the pressure of the Republican Party, free from the pressure and control of the mass media, and free from the pressure of all individuals and groups making up the political establishment. I can assure you that no twentieth-century Georgia governor has been blessed in that position with the freedom of Lester Maddox.

In stating my personal declaration of independence, I vowed again, as I had so often during the campaign, to work for the restoration and preservation of the separation of the three branches of government. This had been a desire of mine for many years. Thus, upon assuming office, I declared my wishes that the Georgia General Assembly be independent and free from any interference from the governor's office. Contrary to precedent, not one time in four years did Lester Maddox make any attempt, or even request, that any particular representative or senator be named to any committee chairmanship, or as a member of any committee or subcommittee in the Georgia General Assembly. Those who are honest will concede that because of this and other efforts of Lester Maddox to restore representative government, the people of Georgia have benefited greatly, and continue to benefit even today.

In a move that astonished and amazed my opponents, but not my friends and supporters who knew me, I acted promptly to assure Geor-

gians that my efforts and goals for four years would be highlighted by
my determination to promote racial harmony, preserving the peace for
all of our people and all of Georgia, so that we could spend our efforts
and energies in working to help gain improved safety, security, education, health care, and economic opportunity for all.

With this goal in mind, I met with those who represented themselves
as leaders of Georgia's black citizens. I placed no limit on the number of
people who could and did participate in the meeting. Thus, I was not
surprised when State Senator Leroy Johnson, an early spokesman for the
group, stated, in essence, "Governor, our people are behind in our deserved and desired needs because of the policies of this and other governments across America, and we want you to specify just what special
directives you will soon be issuing that will correct some of these things
we believe to be wrong and should be corrected in our state."

It must have surprised Senator Johnson and other members of the
group when I responded, "Gentlemen, you can rest assured that while
serving as governor of Georgia and all her people, I will not be issuing
any special executive directives for the benefit of black or white Georgians, for the rich or poor, for Republicans or Democrats, for labor or for
business, but the executive orders from my administration will be based
on what's best for Georgia and all Georgians."

It was at this time that my visitors admitted not one of them had
voted for me, that they had worked very hard for the election of my
predecessor, but nothing like as hard as they had worked against my
election. I volunteered that, even though they had worked for my predecessor and worked even harder against me, I would do at least as much
for them as had my predecessor. One member of the delegation immediately responded, "Lord God, Governor, please do more than that."

After we all had a good laugh, I told them that if they would work
with my administration and not against me, and if they would help me
preserve racial peace and law and order, I would in return do more for
their people and the rest of the wronged and cheated people of our state
than had been done by all previous administrations in Georgia. I added
that if they failed to work with me they would close the door on my
being able to do more of what they deserved, needed, and wanted in
Georgia.

Those in attendance at that historic meeting agreed that they would
work with my administration and, when called upon to do so, would
work to help prevent any racial strife and violence that would threaten
our state and people. They kept their word, and Lester Maddox kept his.
When I called some of them to my office at a later date and advised that
a long-festering racial problem taking place at a downtown shoe store
might have reached the point where a violent eruption could occur, and

asked them for their help, the store was cleared and the threat of violence was eliminated.

I am convinced that our first meeting did more to resolve Georgia's racial tension than any previous attempts by others, and I rest assured that such a meeting would not have been as productive had it been with any one of my predecessors. It is my opinion that a prior governor with a more moderate or liberal image probably would not have dared to hold such a meeting and make such an agreement. I believe it was my unique administration and the agreement and expression of confidence in my commitment to them, along with the sincere and lasting trust of those Georgians who supported me, that enabled us to break new ground in promoting racial peace and harmony.

As a result of this understanding, while a total of only two black Georgians had been appointed members of the Selective Service draft boards during the previous quarter of a century or more, I was able to appoint thirty-eight black members in less than twenty-five months. Having committed myself to employing any person—black, white, liberal, conservative, Democrat, or Republican—who was qualified for a job opening or appointment, the first blacks were employed as law enforcement officers in our Department of Public Safety, and others were employed and given promotions in other departments throughout state government where in the past they had been excluded. For the first time in Georgia's history, a black man was placed on a state constitutional board. It is a fact that during the Maddox administration more black Georgians were given opportunity to serve in the middle- and upper-level positions in state government than had gained such positions through the combined administrations of all my predecessors. Governors who followed me did not have to plow this new ground, and it made it much easier to continue on the progressive trail we had blazed.

In addition, for the first time in the memory of old-timers at the capitol, Lester Maddox, in order to assure he would find the best person available to serve in sensitive positions in the executive and judicial branches of government, appointed people who campaigned against him as well as those who supported him. I appointed Democrats, Republicans, liberals, conservatives, Democrats for Callaway, those who voted against me in the General Assembly, and those who had supported other candidates. I did this to assure fairness to all people and to assure others that politics would not keep us from doing the best possible job of building a fairer, more representative government in Georgia.

Further, in keeping with the commitment to make the Maddox administration the most open in all of Georgia's history, we invited the public to the governor's office, the various departments of state government, even to the governor's mansion. All law-abiding citizens, regardless of status in life and regardless of race, creed, color, or national origin, were warmly welcomed into their governor's office and to their state government. Some bureaucrats could hardly stand it, but the people, not the bureaucrats, were in charge.

I believe that more Georgia citizens visited the governor's office and the mansion during those four years than during all of the previous years of this century. This is not likely to ever happen again, but while Lester Maddox was governor Georgians and Americans from throughout this great land learned that open, honest, and efficient government was the top priority of the Maddox administration.

One area of state government that cannot be exceeded in importance at any level of government is public education. And what did the purveyors of fear and deception have to say about Lester Maddox and public education in his administration? Listen to some of their deliberately false and deceptive charges, designed to frighten the people of Georgia. It was broadcast and published throughout Georgia, and much of America, that if Lester Maddox became governor of Georgia many of our schools would close, there would be chaos and violence in our schools, and we would experience a great exodus of teachers and professors. They were proven wrong on every point and charge.

Contrary to the doomsayers, we did not experience chaos and violence in our public schools. We had a teacher surplus rather than a teacher shortage, and our emphasis was on opening more and better schools, not closing them.

Some little-known facts that should no longer be kept from Georgians and buried in biased histories of the state and the Maddox administration are:

1. The percentage of budget increase in appropriations for elementary and secondary education during the Maddox administration exceeded the increase of each of the two previous administrations and each of the two that followed.

2. The salary increase for teachers at the entry level was more than that of the two previous administrations combined. The percentage of salary increase for secondary and elementary teachers during the Maddox administration still stands as the largest increase during any four-year term.

3. The Maddox administration appropriated the first million dollars for the construction of the Atlanta School for the Deaf.

4. For the first time, nonteacher personnel—bus drivers, food service workers, and the like—were assured of retirement benefits for their long and faithful service.

5. During the year I left office, as a result of these breakthroughs and

improved and expanded programs in education, Georgia was one of only four states in the nation, and the only one in the South, cited by HEW as having adequate educational programs for the gifted. The other three states were California, Connecticut, and Illinois.

6. We left no stone unturned and held back no available dollar needed to help us achieve noteworthy educational goals. It was during this period that educational television, vocational-technical programs, and instruction for exceptional children received a great thrust.

7. In higher education, the percentage of budget increase for the Board of Regents still stands as the largest increase by far of any four-year term of the past six terms. Research indicates that the percentage of budget increase for higher education in Georgia during the Maddox administration was not exceeded by any other state in the nation during that four-year term.

8. For the first and last time during any four-year term, enrichment funds were appropriated to the Board of Regents, making it possible for the university system to attract and keep some of the nation's top-flight professors in Georgia's system of higher education.

9. Because of the great emphasis placed on higher education, the Board of Regents was able to authorize and establish more than three hundred new degrees and programs.

10. During the Maddox term, we scored the real breakthrough in research funding for general and extramural research. It was this important improvement that helped as much as any other improved program to change the image of the University of Georgia and enable it to be recognized as one of the leading universities in America.

11. During the Maddox term as governor, four junior colleges were established and Georgia State was approved for university status, while Columbus College, Southern Tech, Augusta College, Armstrong State, and Georgia Southwestern all became four-year institutions.

12. When the Maddox administration began in January 1967, the appropriation to the Board of Regents was barely 10 percent of the total state appropriations. By the end of the Maddox administration in January 1971, the appropriation to higher education had risen to over 16 percent of the total. It fell to less than 15 percent the following year, never again to reach the pace set by the Maddox administration.

Georgia was at the bottom of the eight listed Southern states in the acquisition of dollars for new and expanded industry during the year of my campaign for governor, and the State Department of Industry and Trade had discontinued its advertising program. Inefficient and wasteful management had resulted in a fund shortage of more than $200,000. The doomsayers declared that under the Maddox administration existing Georgia industry would close and leave our state, new industrial plants would not come to Georgia, and tens of thousands of Georgians would become unemployed, bringing economic depression to our state.

What really happened for industrial and job growth and job opportunities during the Maddox administration?

1. Dollars gained for new and expanded industry during the Maddox term as governor equaled all the dollars for new and expanded industry for Georgia during the twenty-year period from 1947 through 1966.

2. After assuming office, I promptly removed the director and the chairman of the Board of Industry and Trade and cleared out the deadwood. I refused to agree to several recommendations for a new director made by the board and leaders in business and industry until we could find an extremely capable director who would not be obligated to and under such influence of the board, the governor, or others, which could in any way restrict the new director from providing the efficient and businesslike management necessary to move Georgia from the bottom to a position of leadership. I found the man we needed in the person of General Louis Truman. After his acceptance by the board, I obtained the necessary funds to take, for the first time, the story of Georgia's industrial potential to the nation's business and industrial executives, television and radio, and selected newspapers and other publications. I personally made numerous trips to major American cities to sell our state and its industrial potential. The Maddox administration initiated policies and procedures, while gaining favorable attention and serious interest from America's industrial leaders, that made our four-year term the record breaker it was, and that even today continue to contribute to our phenomenal economic success and our continuing ability as a state to compete with the rest of the world and win.

Going back to the three previous four-year terms, and forward through the three following four-year terms, the percentage of budget appropriation increase during the Maddox administration for Department of Human Resources/Division of Medical Assistance has never again been equaled. Our commitment to do all within our power to expand and improve health-care delivery services for Georgia's citizens was carried out with vigor as we requested and obtained appropriations necessary to schedule the opening, construction, expansion, and improvement of all regional and central health services/care units, including both inpatient and outpatient services. Under the Maddox administration, Georgia became one of the first states to implement Medicare, which has been of great benefit to hundreds of thousands of Georgia's senior citizens. We saved more than three million dollars by implementing Medicare two and one-half years prior to being required to do so by the federal government.

Under the Maddox administration, history was made in the field of corrections in that there was a breakthrough in the planning and construction of new penal institutions, plus advancements and improvements such as real penal reform relating to nutrition, working conditions, visiting hours, health care, sanitation, building care and quality, etc.—more than had been accomplished by all of my predecessors combined. The following are documented facts:

1. The Maddox administration closed twenty-eight county work camps, which in most instances were nothing more than destructive hellholes for those confined in them. Not in all the history of Georgia had this many such camps been forced to close by state government. Only the unique freedom and determination of Lester Maddox made this possible.

2. The Work Release and Early Release programs, which still bring new joy, hope, and opportunity to many deserving inmates and their loved ones, were initiated during the Maddox administration.

3. The Board of Pardons and Paroles, under the watchful, dedicated, and able leadership of Judge J. O. Partain, Jr. (a Maddox appointee), became a national model no longer controlled and influenced by the whims and demands of the politicians and/or the wealthy and influential.

4. The Wayne County Prison and the Diagnostic Center at Jackson, started by Governor Carl Sanders, were funded and placed in operation. We also obtained the necessary land and financing to construct the Montgomery County and Walker County regional penal institutions. The Georgia Diagnostic Center was the first facility of its kind in Georgia and the three regional penal institutions were the first to be constructed in modern-day Georgia.

5. The Maddox administration opened the state's first vo-tech schools in the Georgia Industrial Institute at Alto. It has since been accredited by the Southern Association of Colleges and Schools. Also, Georgia became the first state in the nation to use statewide educational TV in its penal system. Through the program of TV High School, hundreds of young Georgians who had brought tragedy into their lives and heartbreak to those who loved them have prepared themselves for and passed the General Education Test. This program has helped many of them return to a free society and become hardworking, law-abiding, and productive citizens.

6. The Maddox administration brought the basic essentials of health care, nutrition, clothing, housing, education, and hope to an element of our society which in many instances had been discarded and often treated with less kindness than is normally afforded stray animals.

Similar progress occurred in the Highway Department:

1. The true priority of need for the accelerated construction and opening of I-75 north of Atlanta and I-285, Atlanta's perimeter highway, had, due to political priorities, fallen secondary to other portions of Georgia's federal interstate system. Because of this condition, the Maddox administration insisted that greater emphasis be placed on awarding contracts for increased construction on these projects.

2. Contrary to what others have said and what you may have been told, it was during my term in office that funds were appropriated for beginning the Appalachian Highway. At my request the General Assembly approved the spending of $16 million from surplus funds, *not from the usual motor fuel tax.* This was another first and was an amount equal to 2-1/2 percent of the total state budget, which today would amount to some $125 million being taken from the current surplus to start construction of a highway. In addition, this was the first major commitment of surplus funds to one-shot appropriations.

3. Shortly after I became governor the late President Lyndon Johnson froze $1 billion in highway construction funds. I made a special trip to the White House to inform him of how the holding back of these funds would affect the safety of motorists on our highways and how we would be harmed economically. Although he did not agree to promptly release any of the funds, he did promise to give serious consideration to what I said and promised to be in touch with me later. In March 1967, not long after I had returned to Georgia, the White House called and informed me that President Johnson wanted me to know he would release $500 million of the funds within thirty days.

The Maddox administration was successful in getting the budget appropriations for the Department of Public Safety increased by an astounding 87 percent during my term of office. Also:

1. Being aware of the rapid growth of highway mileage and the growing number of motorists on our streets and highways, I succeeded in getting the General Assembly to appropriate funds for the employment of one hundred new uniformed patrolmen. And in order to free up many others who should be patrolling the highways, I was successful in getting funding for seventy-five full-time radio operators, which relieved the troopers for full-time law enforcement duties.

2. We secured the first funding for start-up of the Georgia Crime Information Center, which has proven to be one of the most helpful law enforcement programs ever for local and state governments. Today it has expanded to such size and effectiveness for the benefit of all law enforcement agencies in Georgia, and for the added security and safety of our citizens and their property, that we would be crippled without it.

3. Insisting that the highway patrol be increased by large numbers, improving their mobility, and continually improving the skill and pro-

fessionalism of the enforcement officers of this state paid the taxpayers big dividends. The Georgia State Patrol helped to clean up Long County, restore law and order to Augusta, and prevent violence and preserve peace throughout Georgia when in the late sixties much of the nation was being burned and looted.

The story of what we accomplished to improve and protect our environment and improve and expand our parks and recreation facilities, while constantly taking steps to protect the beauty of our coastal areas and coastal islands, has never been compiled and broadcast or published. Some of these accomplishments were:

1. We acquired seven additional state parks.

2. We began negotiating for four additional parks which subsequently became state parks, including Sweetwater Creek, Panola Mountain, Skidaway Island, and John Tanner Park.

3. We established the North Georgia Mountains Authority and Commission, the forerunner of Unicoi State Park.

4. We stopped Kerr-McGee's plans to mine phosphates on Little Tybee Island, thus protecting and preserving a vast area of the coastal environment as well as the fresh water supply.

5. We acquired the northern three-fourths of Sapelo Island with $660,000 in federal funds that were about to lapse and only $138,000 in state funds. Today it is estimated that this $138,000 has multiplied in value to some $25 million or more.

6. During the Maddox administration the Georgia Surface Mining Act, the Air Quality Control Bill, the Georgia Scenic Rivers Act, the Coastal Marshland Protection Act, the Preservation of Historic Sites, the State Archaeologist Bill, etc., all became law in Georgia.

The true story of the Metropolitan Atlanta Rapid Transit Authority (MARTA) has never been broadcast or published. All the people have been told is about my veto of the first legislation to provide financing for the system. Here is the rest of the story. When I vetoed the MARTA bill which required that all local financing would be borne by the ad valorem taxpayers of Fulton and Dekalb counties (the two counties in Georgia already with the highest ad valorem tax rates), you would have thought from what the media and the proponents of MARTA had to say about Lester Maddox that General Sherman had again marched through Georgia and burned Atlanta. What they did not tell is that I stated I would never allow the ad valorem taxpayers to be unduly and unjustly burdened with this tax. I stated that if sufficient ad valorem taxes were collected to provide for the local share of MARTA financing, this would help to destroy local home ownership for many. It would also make it difficult for the affected local governments to obtain the essential tax revenues for education, sanitation, public safety, streets and roads, etc.

Such a program would cripple government in general and the MARTA program in particular.

I insisted that a local option sales tax be used by the affected counties, thus protecting and preserving the ad valorem tax base for essential needs to meet government's responsibility to the people. I argued that not just the ad valorem taxpayers but all of the citizens of Fulton and Dekalb, as well as visitors from elsewhere in Georgia and from outside the state, would support the program financed with the sales tax.

After leaving the office of governor and becoming lieutenant governor, I still refused to allow any MARTA bill of financing to be passed that would burden only the ad valorem taxpayers. Finally, MARTA financing was introduced as I had demanded. It was passed, and today MARTA is in the process of collecting hundreds of millions of dollars that could never be collected otherwise. People from all over Georgia, the nation, and much of the world are helping to finance Atlanta's mass transit, and officials from throughout the world are coming to see what has been accomplished.

Wherever I went in Georgia, both before and after assuming office, people in all walks of life were concerned about what they sincerely believed to be a low level of honesty, morality, and efficiency within state government. A state employee from Clayton County asked why nothing was ever done about the $130,000 that had been taken from the Employees' Credit Union. Office supply and equipment sales and service people wanted to know why their companies could not offer bids on state purchases. A private citizen from Douglas County wanted to know why the state paid out tens of millions of dollars each year to private legal firms as retainers and legal fees for handling bond issues and other routine matters when the state had its own well-qualified staff of legal experts.

These few but dramatic examples were only the tip of the iceberg. However, they show conclusively that the state capitol needed a mighty dose of sound management if we were to wage war on the dishonesty and inefficiency that was prevalent throughout the maze that made up state government. But, mind you, Georgia was not an island to itself. It is my belief that such waste and dishonesty is prevalent in local and state government generally, especially in the federal government, and in too many of the large utility and industrial corporations.

What was needed in state government, the Maddox administration provided. I relished the opportunity to wade in. I attacked the graft, corruption, and mismanagement with great zeal. What I was unable to find, I had the "Governor's Committee of One Thousand" finding throughout Georgia. It was one of the most enjoyable tasks I attempted as governor. We corrected the deliberate mismanagement of construction contracts such as the one where a private contractor had occupied free office and storage space on Capitol Hill for a number of years and had been given over $6 million in capitol construction contracts without ever having to meet one competitive bid. Against the wishes of the capitol status quo leadership, we appointed a new director of the Georgia Building Authority. We installed a businesslike management plan to ensure that taxpayers received fair value for every dollar spent. We followed this practice into every nook and crook possible for years. My "Committee of One Thousand" (and I had in excess of this number) really upset the parasites, the special-interest groups, and the liberal media. Nevertheless, I did not falter in my goal to make Georgia's government perform responsibly for the good people who had been cheated far too long. And there is no doubt in my mind that the "Governor's Committee of One Thousand" saved the taxpayers millions of dollars.

When a prison warden was found to be using food, supplies, clothing, linens, etc. in his home and business which were paid for by the taxpayers and purchased for the prison and its inmates, and when a district highway engineer was found to be using state personnel, supplies, and equipment in his own construction firm, they along with others who were caught paid the price.

For the very first time state agencies were forced to accept bids for computer rentals and purchases, and the old practice of buying gasoline, oil, etc. on a political patronage basis with no real evidence of concern for price, quality, or quantity ended.

One of the most outrageous practices was discovered shortly after I assumed my duties as governor. When traveling from the capitol to the mansion one afternoon during my first week in office, I overheard a highway patrol dispatcher ordering patrol cars to the governor's office. Upon inquiring, I learned that it was the practice and policy in state government for the state patrol to provide free taxi service for just about anybody who had influence.

I immediately had my driver call the patrol office and advise them to cancel that call and to never provide such services again. Prior to that order, I learned that Patrol Post No. 9, in Atlanta, was not being used for traffic enforcement but only for the pleasure and comfort of the influential. I was really burning. By the time I cleaned up this intolerable mess, Patrol Post No. 9 was writing more traffic tickets than any other patrol post in Georgia.

Ludowici, Georgia, in the mid-sixties was known throughout the United States as possibly the nation's most abusive and corrupt speed trap and clip joint. The Maddox administration decided to tar and feather the corrupt leadership that was hurting all of Georgia, especially the law-abiding citizens in Long County. The speed trap and clip joint operations, along with other criminal activities involving prostitution, gambling, stealing, alcohol, etc., brought shame to their good citizens and shame to our state and region. The criminal and corrupt leadership in Long County was under the control of a scum of a man, neither appointed nor elected to public office, who not only controlled the local citizens and local government but appeared to have more influence and control over state operations and services in his county than the authorities at the state capitol, including the governor. And everybody was powerless to help until Lester Maddox, with the help of God and the good people of Georgia, brought his evil reign to a halt.

I went in there without warning—didn't even inform people in state government—and told the rats, along with the business owners and operators who were either willingly or unwillingly a part of the rotten and corrupt machine, what I intended to do if they did not shape up. For a short while they eased off, but soon returned to the same old practice of entrapping the helpless with their criminal and immoral activities. It was then that I had billboards placed at the north and south boundaries of Long County to warn travelers they were entering Ludowici, Long County, and to be aware of speed traps and clip joints. I placed twenty-four-hour highway patrol officers around the signs so the Chief Rat could not have them burned or torn down. This decision really paid off because within a very few days "Boss Dawson" had arranged to have his Georgia legislators set up a meeting with me. So, along with his legislators, Ralph Dawson and some twenty-five Dawson puppets (county, city, school officials, ministers, etc.) arrived at the governor's office.

Dawson's first words were, "Governor, what you are doing to us is hurting and embarrassing our people and our county." I was literally infuriated. My immediate response was, "You no-good dirty rascal, you are the one who is hurting Long County, and all of Georgia and all Georgians. Your corrupt and criminal activities keep industry and jobs out of Long County, denying your citizens the economic opportunities that should be theirs. Young people have no choice but to grow up in such a corrupt atmosphere and get out of town as soon as they finish school. It is my sincere belief you are the nastiest and most corrupt individual ever to enter the office of the governor and the longer you stay here the longer it will take us to clean up after you leave." With that, I grabbed him by the arm and as I started dragging him to the door, his last words were, "Wait a minute, I have got to get my hat." I never even hesitated and kept dragging as I answered, "I'll throw your hat out next." And I did.

Upon returning to my office I informed the entire group that if they believed as Ralph Dawson believed, then everything I said to the chief of the scums I also intended for each of his devoted followers. Whereupon, they assured me, "Naw, Governor, we are on your side." Thereupon I dismissed class, knowing full well some of them were lying. But we really cleaned up Long County, thank God, and I am as proud of that accomplishment as anything I was able to do in fighting waste and corruption.

Well, that's it. I have only scratched the surface, but have been too long already. As I said earlier, my campaign, election, and term in the office of governor made history. I promised the people of Georgia I would promote open, honest, efficient, and moral government like had not been witnessed in twentieth-century Georgia. I kept that promise. The true facts about the campaign, election, and public service of Lester Maddox presented here are, for the most part, achievements which most Georgians have never heard broadcast or read. I suppose one reason the media will not tell the facts and full story about the Maddox administration is that their diet of crow would last until eternity. Unless you publish and broadcast what you have read and heard today, the true story about Lester Maddox's public service will always be a secret. It will be history lost. It will always be truth lost. And it will always be an opportunity lost—an opportunity at last to be honest and fair to the one Georgia governor who dared to serve the people . . . all the people.

Jimmy Carter

1971 – 1975

Jimmy Carter
and the Politics
of Transition

GARY M. FINK

The continuing growth of urban centers, accelerated economic growth, the U.S. Supreme Court's "one man, one vote" dictum in *Baker v. Carr*, and, above all, the Voting Rights Act of 1965 all had the effect of transforming the character of Southern politics.[1] In Georgia that transformation was further exaggerated by *Sanders v. Gray*, which ended the county unit system of primary elections that had enabled Eugene Talmadge and his son Herman to build a nearly invincible electoral machine.[2] The game rules of Southern politics had been drastically altered and the consequences of those changes were felt almost immediately. But it was not until Jimmy Carter took the oath of office as Georgia's seventy-sixth governor in January 1971 that the total implications of those changes became fully apparent.

Following the swearing-in ceremonies, Carter delivered one of the shortest yet most memorable inaugural addresses in the state's long history. Shortly after beginning the twelve-minute speech, Carter surveyed the large gathering before him and then almost casually informed the assemblage that the time for racial discrimination had passed. "No poor, rural, weak, or black person," he declared, "should ever have to bear the additional burden of being deprived of the opportunity of an education, a job, or simple justice."[3] With those words Carter recognized and at the same time contributed to an important transition occurring in Georgia political history.

Students of Southern politics have already begun chronicling and analyzing the changes in electoral politics that have occurred in the South as a result of altered game rules.[4] Although more difficult to document, related and equally important changes have occurred in state legislative politics, particularly the relationship between the executive and legislative branches of state government and the policy content of state legislative decision-making. Changes in this area have been almost as profound as those in electoral politics, albeit slower and less dramatic. Moreover, changes in legislative politics were less uniform between states in the South, depending upon previous institutional structures and arrangements as well as customs, traditions, and the character of the personalities involved in the transition.

In Georgia the relationship between the legislative and executive branches of state government was greatly influenced by events surrounding and flowing from the gubernatorial election of 1966.[5] The election controversy that year had a profound impact on legislative relations. For the first time in many years House members organized their own chamber and elected their own leaders. It was a prerogative they never again relinquished, thus greatly altering the previous relationship between the governor and the lower house of the state legislature.[6]

Similarly, the 1966 election controversy greatly eroded the governor's influence over Senate affairs, and the members of that body, like their counterparts in the House, jealously guarded their newfound independence in subsequent years.[7] These legislators found in Lester Maddox, the state's new chief executive, a pliant administrator who exhibited little interest in the concerns of the legislature. Maddox had little time or inclination to get involved in the humdrum, everyday responsibilities of constructive legislative leadership.[8] Although unorthodox, he still reflected an essentially traditional style of Southern politics grounded more in the past than in the present or the future. Having no real program, Maddox did not initiate policy, but rather reacted to it, usually in a negative and obstructionist manner.

Maddox's successor, Jimmy Carter, exhibited a very different style of political leadership. Like most Georgians, Carter respected custom and tradition, and he gloried in the positive aspects of the state's historical heritage, but he also was strongly committed to the future rather than defending the past or denying the present. Hoping to sensitize Georgia citizens to the importance of long-term planning, Carter launched a "Goals for Georgia" program shortly after becoming governor. He assumed the average Georgian could play a constructive role in government, and through the "Goals" program he initiated a limited form of participatory democracy as a vehicle to facilitate citizen participation in the determination of public policy. Fifty-one public meetings were held throughout the state, enabling participants to establish goals in such areas as mental and physical health, tax equalization, education, prison reform, transportation, criminal justice, preservation of historic sites and natural areas, environmental quality, and industrial development.[9] Reforms in these areas formed the basis of the extensive legislative package that Carter set before the General Assembly during his governorship.

Carter inherited an executive office much weakened by his predecessor. The Georgia General Assembly had elected Lester Maddox, and it dominated state government during his governorship.[10] By the end of Maddox's term the power and influence of particular legislative leaders had grown tremendously, and they zealously protected and defended that independence. In this endeavor they found in Lester Maddox a willing accomplice. Banned by constitutional provision from seeking a second term in 1970, he ran instead for lieutenant governor and scored a stunning triumph, winning the Democratic nomination against a popular incumbent without the necessity of a runoff. Most political observers assumed Maddox would recapture the governorship four years later. Consequently, the new governor, Jimmy Carter, confronted in his lieutenant governor a legislative leader who was not only a popular former chief executive but a likely future governor. Moreover, besides presiding over the Senate, under Senate rules the lieutenant governor referred bills and appointed the members of standing and ad hoc committees.

Maddox might have been leaving the governor's office, but he was determined to retain as much power and influence as possible. In explaining his decision to run for lieutenant governor in 1970, he reasoned, "As lieutenant governor I would have an official position from which to help keep alive the work of the previous four years, a forum from which I could be heard and from which I could exert a positive influence on the direction of state government."[11] Obviously, Maddox intended to play a role in legislative leadership as lieutenant governor that he had failed to exercise while governor. This ultimately placed him on a collision course with Jimmy Carter, who had his own legislative agenda he hoped to push through the state legislature.

Conflict between the two strong-willed political leaders was inevitable. Although both were deeply religious and had a Populist-conservative political philosophy, their religious convictions, conservative principles, and Populist ideals differed significantly. The governor-elect simply rejected Maddox's race-conscious religious fundamentalism, his anti-intellectual, reactionary political ideology, and his demagoguery in the Southern Populist tradition.

Other equally important differences divided them. Carter was an activist reformer with an extensive legislative program, and his reform agenda contained the suggestion that much was wrong with state government as then constituted and an implicit criticism of the incumbent administration. Proud of his accomplishments while in office, Maddox bristled at the suggestion that state government needed a fundamental overhauling. Moreover, like most persons in his situation, he resented the man who took over his office and assumed his lease on the governor's mansion.

Even before Carter's inauguration, he and Maddox were totally estranged. During the campaign the press had noted several occasions during which Maddox appeared to be baiting Carter, contradicting him, and at times making the nominee appear foolish. Although both men denied differences, real problems existed and grew in intensity as the campaign progressed. At a meeting of the State Democratic Convention shortly after the primary runoff election, Maddox seemed bent on picking a fight with the party's gubernatorial nominee. He warned Carter not to get involved in the affairs of the General Assembly, particularly the Senate, over which the lieutenant governor would preside. Maddox added that he would be watching the new governor to see that he kept his campaign promises. "When I put my pennies into a peanut machine," he declared, "I don't expect to get bubble gum, and neither do the people."[12]

Shortly after the first primary, Maddox had attempted to solicit a pledge from the two Democrats in the gubernatorial runoff, Carter and former Governor Carl Sanders, that they would not interfere in any way with the functions of the General Assembly. Sanders agreed but Carter refused, informing the man who expected to preside over the Senate that he wanted some voice in naming Senate committee chairmen.[13] The two men clashed over the election of the president pro tem of the Senate shortly after the November 1970 elections and again before the General Assembly convened in January. By August of 1971 the lieutenant governor charged Carter with trying to destroy him and create a dictatorship, and by autumn Maddox wished the governor would stop "riding my back and trying to cut my throat."[14] In a letter to Carter released earlier to the press, the lieutenant governor said he had attempted to cooperate with the governor despite his "open and sometimes undercover attempts to ridicule and discredit me."[15]

Thus the battle between the old and the new politics had been joined in the Georgia Assembly. Carter had two possible options in dealing with state legislators—conciliation and compromise or confrontation. In the House of Representatives, the new governor developed good relationships with the leadership and was able to practice the former.

Speaker Smith, House Majority Leader George Busbee, and most other members of the House Democratic leadership were generally able to muster majority votes in support of their policy commitments. Thus in the lower chamber Carter needed only to win the support of House leaders for his policy initiatives.[16] Conciliation and compromise worked well in the lower house, but Lester Maddox and a number of powerful and resourceful factional leaders in the Senate left him no alternative to confrontation politics in the fifty-six-member upper house.

The ensuing battle between the governor and the lieutenant governor polarized the Senate into two hostile factions. The Maddox bloc consisted of twenty-two senators who voted consistently against administrative measures and five additional lawmakers who usually voted with the lieutenant governor. This left the Maddox forces only two votes short of exercising an absolute veto over the governor's program. The administration's bloc consisted of fourteen consistent and four fringe supporters along with a satellite cluster of five Republicans. Ultimately, a small group of six swing senators decided the fate of most administration measures, and Carter won their support often enough to get most of his reform proposals through the General Assembly.[17]

The success of Carter's governorship was qualified and conditioned by a number of other circumstances, some of which he shared with his predecessors and others of which were unique to Jimmy Carter. One such circumstance was the constitutional provision limiting governors to one nonconsecutive term in the governor's mansion. This forced Carter to consider the future of his political career earlier in his governorship than he otherwise might have done, and it undoubtedly conditioned not only the reform proposals he advanced but the timetable he established to accomplish them. A second factor that influenced the character of Carter's gubernatorial performance was his very active involvement in national Democratic Party politics, and closely related to this, his early decision to seek the Democratic nomination for president.

Largely as a result of his dramatic inaugural address, Carter found himself being projected nationally as the vanguard of yet another "New South." Carter's portrait graced the cover of *Time* magazine, and the editors profiled a new breed of Southern governor—Linwood Holton, John West, Reuben Askew, Dale Bumpers—who rejected racism, instead advocating a reform agenda and projecting a business-progressive image designed to bring the South into the national mainstream and, not incidentally, to appeal to both foreign and domestic investors.[18]

The legal prohibition against Carter's running for a second gubernatorial term in 1974 forced him to accelerate national political ambitions, the seeds of which had been planted by the *Time* cover story, and the reality of which had germinated during the 1972 presidential campaign. Along with other moderate/progressive Southern Democratic leaders, Carter sought to influence the selection of a Democratic nominee who would be acceptable to the South. Ultimately, he agreed to nominate Senator Henry "Scoop" Jackson of Washington at the Democratic National Convention and probably cherished hopes that, if successful, Jackson would find in Jimmy Carter the perfect vice-presidential candidate to balance the ticket geographically and ideologically.[19]

The nomination of George McGovern obviously frustrated whatever national hopes and ambitions Carter might have had for 1972, but his involvement in national Democratic Party politics had a marked influence on him. He had closely observed the steady stream of Democratic candidates in 1972 who called upon the Georgia governor, seeking his support while spending a few days visiting and talking at the governor's mansion. After observing the best the party had to offer, Carter concluded he was as good as any of them; henceforth, he thought less about second place on the Democratic ticket and began contemplating a run for the presidency itself.[20] Shortly thereafter, Hamilton Jordan was relieved of his duties as Carter's executive secretary and sequestered in a small basement office in the state capitol, where he developed the blueprint for the 1976 campaign. The McGovern debacle of 1972 simply reinforced Carter's rather critical assessment of the quality of prospective Democratic nominees for 1976, and the Watergate scandal provided the issue that would help catapult him into national office.

All of that aside, Carter's political ambitions, particularly the pursuit of the presidency, would necessarily be greatly influenced by the record he made as governor of Georgia. Most immediately, then, Carter needed to neutralize Lester Maddox and overcome the race issue, which had sounded the death knell to the national ambitions of so many talented (but often bigoted) Southern politicians. In the end, Carter managed not only to offset the race issue but to turn it to his advantage.[21]

Before assessing Carter's civil rights activities, however, by any objective measure a survey of his other accomplishments during the four years of his governorship reveals an impressive record of change and reform. Friend and foe alike agreed that the state government he left behind was significantly different from the one he had inherited in 1971. Shortly after this election Carter developed a lengthy reform agenda, including initiatives in such volatile areas as welfare reform, conservation, tax policy and budget reform, education, consumer protection, and judicial reform. Beyond all of that, he informed legislators shortly before they convened in January 1971 that he intended to develop the state's first comprehensive government reorganization plan since Richard Russell's administration in the early thirties.[22] Four General Assembly terms later, to a surprising degree, the Carter Agenda had been accomplished. Carter and most of those close to him agreed that government reorganization had been the most significant accomplishment of his governorship.[23]

The reorganization struggle reflected much about Carter's executive leadership style. Anticipating fierce resistance to change regardless of merit, Carter sought to give as many people as possible a vested interest in reorganization. This became especially obvious as the formation of the reorganization management team began to take shape. Tom M. Linder, the youthful director of the Bureau of State Planning and Community Affairs, was nominated to head the reorganization project. The Linder family had long been prominent in south Georgia politics, and Tom Linder's grandfather had served for many years as commissioner of agriculture prior to his defeat by Marvin Griffin for the governorship in 1954. Linder reported to an executive committee chaired by Governor Carter that included two state legislators and two state administrative officers.

After a careful study, the administration contracted with Arthur Anderson and Company, a management consultant firm which had previously assisted in state government reorganization in Wisconsin, to assist in the reform study. Project Director Linder then wrote major business firms located in the Atlanta area asking them to contribute personnel to reorganization study teams for periods ranging from two to six months. Forty-eight businesses contributed a total of sixty-five individuals to the effort. Carter similarly solicited volunteers from state government agencies. In the end 117 people, including state employees, business volunteers, and Arthur Anderson representatives, worked full-time on the Reorganization and Management Improvement Study.

Following the completion of the study, Carter began an intensive lobbying effort to win support for the plan that resulted. This included an elaborate public awareness campaign designed to convince state legislators, government bureaucrats, and the electorate at large of the wisdom of reorganization. Ultimately, Carter got most of what he wanted. To be sure, he did not get the whole loaf and probably never thought he would, but he did manage to retain the main features of the plan despite the hostility of Lieutenant Governor Maddox and the fierce opposition of powerful and influential legislators and state constitutional officers who perceived themselves to be losers in the reorganization sweepstakes.[24]

Carter was similarly successful in achieving a substantial and long overdue reform of the state's criminal justice system. Although receiving less publicity than the reorganization effort, a majority of the reforms recommended by the Governor's Commission on Judicial Processes, which he had appointed in 1971 to make recommendations for improvements, had been implemented through legislative enactment, executive order, or constitutional amendment before he left office. These reforms initiated the movement toward a unified court system, a merit system for the selection of judges, and a constitutional method of regulating judicial conduct.[25]

Carter also took important initiatives in the closely related area of penal reform, although these were less successful. The number of inmates in overcrowded prisons was not significantly reduced, but prison education and treatment programs were increased, as was the number of professionally trained counselors. Meanwhile, educational standards for state prison system employees were raised and current employees, particularly wardens, were urged to upgrade their credentials. Carter then persuaded Ellis MacDougall, a professionally trained, nationally known criminologist, to leave his post as the head of the Connecticut prison system to accept a similar position in Georgia. While problems in the state's prison system could not be solved in four years, Carter took important initiatives upon which his successor could build.[26]

State government reorganization and, to a lesser extent, judicial reform, two of the most important items on Carter's reform agenda, are excellent examples of the type of change Carter championed—highly visible, relatively low-cost reform. Another example of such change was the creation of the Georgia Heritage Trust, designed to preserve the state's natural and cultural resources. Before Carter left the governor's mansion, more than two thousand such sites had been identified and nineteen acquired, including 141 precious acres along the Chattahoochee River in Atlanta.[27] As the latter suggests, Carter was a dedicated conservationist who not only worked hard to prevent developers from despoiling the Chattahoochee but also checked the U.S. Army Corps of Engineers' plans to dam the Flint River, Georgia's only remaining wild river.[28]

Carter was also able to use his appointment power to affect political and social change in Georgia. He greatly increased the number of minorities and women appointed to major state boards and agencies. Appointments of blacks to such positions, for example, increased from 3 when he took office to 53 when he left, while the aggregate number of state black employees increased from 4,850 to 6,684.[29] He also appointed qualified women to governmental positions, including the appointment of the first woman to the state bench. Along similar lines, he established a Commission on the Status of Women to look after the interests of women and strongly supported passage of the equal rights amendment.[30]

Upgrading the state's notoriously weak educational system was another of Carter's major goals as governor. While a member of the General Assembly during the early sixties, he had chaired the standing Senate Committee on Education and in that capacity had been responsible for successfully updating and revising the Minimum Foundation Program for Education inaugurated by Herman Talmadge in 1949.[31] As governor, Carter secured passage of legislation implementing his Adequate Program for Education in Georgia (APEG), a program that increased the state's commitment to preschool education, and inaugurated a campaign for a statewide kindergarten program that was ultimately implemented by his successor. The APEG also provided funds for special and vocational education, to reduce pupil-teacher ratios, and to equalize funding for schools throughout the state regardless of the relative wealth of the particular school district.[32]

The Carter administration made similarly significant strides in mental health programs, where his (and Rosalynn's) interest and emphasis on programs for the mentally handicapped were, in the words of one observer, "revered in professional circles."[33] Drug and alcohol addiction, prenatal health care, sickle-cell anemia screening programs, and educational programs providing instruction in basic skills to the mentally retarded were among the more notable concerns of the governor in the physical and mental health fields. Meanwhile, an improved delivery system for health care was an important objective of his government reorganization effort.

Among other important reforms advocated by Carter, changes in the budgeting procedure probably received more attention than any of the others. Here Carter developed a concept called "zero-based budgeting." Under this proposal, rather than routinely submitting an aggregate budget figure that usually represented an inflation-inspired percentage increase over the previous year's budget, state departments and agencies were supposed to start from scratch, evaluating and justifying every dollar appropriated. While in reality zero-based budgeting was something of a gimmick that was never fully implemented, it did lead to periodic reexaminations of budget priorities. Moreover, through his use of the Office of Planning and Budget, Carter was able to rationalize and regularize budgeting procedures.

Consumer protection was another area in which Carter's hopes for reform were frustrated. With one of the weakest consumer protection laws in the nation, Georgia, in the governor's words, had become "a dumping ground for con artists, shysters, and unscrupulous businessmen."[34] Nevertheless, special-interest hostility to consumer protection, Carter's failure to develop a consumer protection package until the third year of his governorship, and his choice of an unenthusiastic administration floor leader on the issue all conspired to stymie consumer legislation during his governorship.[35]

If the failure to secure consumer protection legislation was Carter's greatest disappointment, the General Assembly's mangling of his property tax relief measure was his greatest frustration. The governor had promised property tax relief during his campaign and in 1973 the General Assembly passed a bill providing a $50 million rebate to all property taxpayers. The intent of Carter's original bill, however, was badly abused in the legislative process and it soon became apparent that the primary beneficiaries of the tax relief measure were the state's major corporations. As a consequence, Carter vetoed a continuation of the tax rebate the following year.[36] As the foregoing makes clear, while he failed to achieve reform in all areas, his recognition of the need for reform and the publicity he gave it were significant. Recognition of the need for change is an important element of wise and enlightened political leadership, and such was not always in abundant supply in Georgia during the mid-twentieth century.[37]

Nowhere was the need for leadership more obvious and nowhere was reform more necessary or important than in the broad area of race relations and civil rights—again, a relatively low-cost but much-needed reform the support of which sets Carter apart from his gubernatorial peers and makes him the crucial figure in the evolution of modern Georgia. Carter, of course, had used his inaugural address to announce the dawning of a new day in Georgia, and he followed the courageous words he spoke that January day with a series of deeds that gave them meaning and substance. Of a more immediate and substantive nature, he appointed qualified blacks to his own staff and to major state policy boards. Carter named to a judgeship a state senator who several years earlier had been denied admittance to the University of Georgia Law School because of race. The governor replaced a powerful, unreconstructed segregationist on the university system Board of Regents with a black man, and he arranged to have the portraits of three black Georgians, one of them Martin Luther King, Jr., hung in the state capitol. A year earlier Carter had proclaimed January 15, 1973, Martin Luther King, Jr., Day, and on the first anniversary of that occasion "King's portrait was hung in the state capitol as Carter and an integrated audience sang, 'We shall Overcome,' and the Ku Klux Klan staged a demonstration outside." He also appointed a biracial Civil Disorder Unit which helped to quell racial disturbances that had accelerated to a point that in one Georgia community machine-gun-carrying rival groups engaged in an arms race that threatened to convert the Georgia countryside into a war zone. At the same time, he appointed six blacks and six whites to a

Governor's Council on Human Relations to promote racial justice and harmony.[38]

Carter's civil rights activities as governor of Georgia contained both symbolism and substance, and in this particular matter at this particular time, perhaps the symbolism was at least as important as the substance. Georgia had a recognized leadership role in the South; it was, after all, the home of Henry Grady, who first proclaimed a "New South," and it was only fitting and proper that another son of Georgia, Jimmy Carter, should sever the umbilical cord that had so nourished race as the central theme of Southern and, more specifically, Georgia history.

Certainly, Georgia gubernatorial politics after Carter differed remarkably from that practiced before him. In the pre-Carter years, race, either implicitly or explicitly, was an issue in every campaign and a factor in every gubernatorial administration since Reconstruction. Every campaign, especially in the years following World War II and the *Brown* decision, featured at least one self-styled segregationist and even hard-liners on the issue worried about being "out niggered." After Carter's term in office and the defeat of Lester Maddox, his most adamant critic, in the 1974 Democratic gubernatorial primary, race became, at best, a subterranean issue in Georgia gubernatorial politics as most serious candidates (and all successful ones) made an overt appeal to the black vote and sought to avoid the stigma that had become attached to too blatant an appeal to racial prejudice.

Even if Jimmy Carter's governorship was only partially as significant as has been suggested above, it would still have to rank as a crucially important turning point in Georgia history. Yet few observers, even among professional historians and political activists, are much inclined to give Carter high marks for political leadership or for precipitating this important watershed in Georgia history. When a group of historians in Georgia were surveyed concerning their perceptions of the gubernatorial effectiveness of Carter along with eight other post-World War II Georgia governors, they rated Carter as, at best, an average governor. A selected sampling of the membership of the Georgia Association of Historians ranked Carter no better than fourth among those being studied—higher than Herman Talmadge, Lester Maddox, Ernest Vandiver, and Marvin Griffin, but substantially lower than Ellis Arnall, Carl Sanders, and George Busbee. Moreover, 50 percent of those polled speculated that Carter could not have been reelected governor at the conclusion of his first term; only Ernest Vandiver, in the eyes of these Georgia historians, appeared to have been less popular after four years in the governor's mansion.[39]

Despite this rather middling assessment of his governorship, however, those same historians gave the future president good marks for his recognition of and response to the important issues confronting the state during his term. Along similar lines, Carter received the highest rating of the eight governors examined for the quality of his administrative and judicial appointments, and even more impressive, considering his obvious political ambition, Carter was ranked second only to Ellis Arnall on what might be termed the "Courage Index"—that is, his willingness and his ability to pursue important policy objectives even when those objectives were fraught with potential political danger.

While Carter generally was viewed as a fiscal conservative, a commitment requiring relatively little courage or political leadership in Georgia, he was also perceived as a social liberal and a racial moderate. These were positions that did not come naturally in Georgia Democratic politics, particularly to one born and bred in southwest Georgia's Sumter County. Nevertheless, more than anything else, it was that racial and social liberalism which resulted in Carter's being listed along with Arnall as the Georgia governor with the most positive national reputation. This becomes especially obvious when examining Carter's position vis-a-vis other governors on several policy issues. In the broad area of civil rights and civil liberties, Carter had no peer among recent Georgia governors. Similarly, he ranked high on health, welfare, and urban reform issues. Ironically, his lowest ranking was in the area of support for education. In fact, as pointed out earlier, Carter made significant inroads toward reforming the state's inadequate educational system, but his opposition to raises during a period of high inflation antagonized teachers and undoubtedly contributed to his low rating on that issue.

To summarize, then, on key policy issues Georgia historians concluded that Carter not only recognized the most significant issues confronting the state during his term but addressed them relatively effectively, even those issues which were not particularly popular and the advocacy of which carried with it substantial political risk. He was a strong advocate of fiscal conservatism, social liberalism, and racial moderation, and he made relatively high quality appointments to the executive and judicial branches of state government. Nevertheless, despite this very positive assessment, Carter was rated, at best, as a marginally effective governor who would have had difficulty getting reelected had a second term option been available to him.

Why, then, is Carter ranked by Georgia historians as being a rather insignificant or unimportant governor, even when compared to other recent governors, most of whom exhibited more concern with maintaining the "Lost Cause" and preserving segregation than in providing constructive and enlightened leadership?[40] One explanation revolves around Carter's perceived absence of communication and interpersonal relations skills. Regarding the ability to communicate positions on issues effectively to the public, only Ernest Vandiver received a more negative rating than Carter from those historians surveyed. Similarly, only Lester Maddox was considered to be less effective in working with legislative leaders or in his ability to command the respect of state government administrators and to secure their compliance with executive decisions. In two other areas of communication, Carter was given somewhat better marks but was still significantly below such governors as Arnall, Busbee, and Sanders. These two areas involved press relations and the ability to gain special interest support of major policy initiatives. In terms of overall communication and interpersonal skills, Carter ranked fifth among the eight governors studied—higher than Vandiver, Griffin, and Maddox, but substantially below Busbee, Arnall, Talmadge, and Sanders. Yet Carter's perceived lack of communications skills gives rise to another of the many dilemmas one must consider in attempting to evaluate the future president's political career. How can a politician with such apparently deficient communication skills be so effective on the campaign trail?

Style and personality have much to do with it. Just as Carl Sanders's urbane and dignified manner of leadership projected an image of substance, Carter's "controversial, aggressive, and combative administration" left an unjustified aura of failure, frustration, and, at times, foolishness.[41] One of the most frequent observations about Carter's style concerned his perceived intractableness and refusal to compromise. "I have never seen a man so rigid," State Senator Julian Bond complained. "He just won't give in."[42] Representative Grace Hamilton, noting that Carter had served in the Navy, observed: "He thinks that he's commander of a submarine, and you give the orders and everything falls into line."[43] Another legislator put it more bluntly: "If your [sic] not with him, he'll cut your throat."[44]

But, again, the record is at odds with the perception. In reality, compromise was an integral part of Carter's leadership strategy. At one point during the early stages of the government reorganization effort, for example, he told those drafting the measure to write the best plan possible. He told them he would make the necessary compromises to get it passed. Indeed, there is evidence to suggest that he consciously included in his legislative proposals items that he would later "reluctantly" abandon. Carter seems to have consciously projected a hard-line attitude on compromise as a tactic which permitted him to maximize the possible in a given situation.[45] After repeatedly vowing not to compromise, however, when he finally did so it not only damaged his credibility but also carried with it the unfortunate and largely erroneous aura of failure and defeat rather than success and achievement.[46]

Certainly, Carter would have won few popularity contests among state legislators and constitutional officers after his four years in the governorship. His floor manager in the lower house of the General Assembly, Al Burrus, in responding to a newspaper reporter's query about the governor's most faithful supporters, quipped: "It's not going to be a long article is it?" Burrus's sentiments were echoed by another veteran representative. "Your [sic] not gonna find too many in the House you could classify as his friends. Even Lester [Maddox] could boast more friends."[47]

It would be unwise, however, to conclude that because Carter was not popular among state legislators he accomplished little. Indeed, there appears to be an inverse relationship between the two, especially in the post-Maddox years. The less governors do, or try to do, the more likely they are to get along with key legislative leaders. The most commonly used tactic in overcoming this resistance to legislative proposals is the logrolling technique that often creates such strange bedfellows in support of legislative reform. But solving one problem by creating another violated Carter's sense of rationality and order, and he opposed such horse trading both in principle and in practice.[48]

Along with his opposition to logrolling, Carter was also reluctant to use his appointment power to grease the tracks for his legislative proposals. "Jimmy never rewards his friends," one disappointed supporter lamented. "Instead he looks to the most qualified people."[49] Similarly, while exhibiting little hesitancy to use patronage to build support for his proposals, he nevertheless refused to make deals that violated the principle of reforms he was advocating. Some loyal legislators believed he simply went too far in this regard—that he was out of touch with reality. "Jimmy's his own worst enemy as far as getting something done is concerned," groused one frustrated legislator. "He feels he's right and he's got a lot of integrity, but he just doesn't communicate."[50]

How, then, did Carter manage to get so much substantive reform through a state legislature indifferent, if not hostile, to his reform proposals (as well as to the governor himself)? Part of the answer involves Carter's success in practicing a new style of legislative leadership. More than any other governor before or after him, Carter appealed to the Georgia citizenry over the heads of its elected representatives in the state legislature. He employed public relations firms, polling organizations, and media consultants to identify, dissect, measure, and ultimately to influence public opinion. Likewise, he used the Goals for Georgia program, conducted town meetings, held regional press conferences—which somewhat qualified the influence of the often critical capitol press corps—and he occasionally moved the governor's office for a day outside Atlanta to the outstate areas in a symbolic effort to take the government to the people. Before his term ended, Carter had become perhaps the most visible governor in the state's history, and the traditional politicos who controlled the General Assembly and managed state executive departments were seemingly uncertain how to handle this departure from the traditional executive leadership to which they had become comfortably indifferent. As politicians are wont to do in such situations, they "ran scared" until acquiring a more certain grasp of the implications of this new style of politics. During the first two years of his governorship, Carter managed to leverage that indecision into a number of significant legislative victories.[51]

Other than substance and style, conditions peculiar to time and circumstance influenced perceptions of Carter's governorship. Carter's term coincided with major domestic and international crises—especially Watergate and the Arab oil embargo—that had political and economic repercussions at the state as well as the national level. In addition, as noted earlier, Carter had inherited an office much weakened by his predecessor, Lester Maddox, who rejected any responsibility for legislative leadership. As a consequence, the power and influence of a few well-entrenched state legislators grew enormously, and they fiercely resisted the new governor's efforts to resurrect the traditional gubernatorial-leadership model in state government. Carter created other long-lived enmities as well. The supporters of Jim Gillis, the longtime czar of the State Transportation Department, for example, vowed to avenge Carter's firing of their friend and benefactor. The state's doctors and physicians deplored their diminished influence in the creation and operation of state health programs as a result of government reorganization and the introduction of some laypersons on supervisory boards. Other losers in the reorganization effort were equally bitter and resentful. Most of these critics, along with some of the governor's most resourceful antagonists in the General Assembly and in state government, coalesced around Lester Maddox in their efforts to frustrate Carter's programs.[52]

Ultimately, the constant state of verbal warfare that characterized relationships between the governor and the lieutenant governor during Carter's administration influenced perceptions about his style and effectiveness in a negative fashion. Put in its most brutal form, it was difficult to maintain any sense of dignity and decorum while doing battle on a daily basis with Lester Maddox, the clown prince of Georgia gubernatorial politics. Even though Carter prevailed in most instances, the conflict left him battered and scarred to such an extent that the identity of the victor was not always apparent.[53] After four years of such acrimonious bickering, both men lost favor with Georgia voters. In 1970 Maddox had won a landslide victory in the lieutenant governor's race over a popular incumbent; four years later he was crushed by a candidate who consciously projected himself as a noncharismatic, lackluster politician—"a workhorse, not a showhorse."

Beyond the historical accident of his predecessor, however, Carter's own personality and style created confusion. While cultivating a casual, down-home image, he often practiced a distancing and aloofness that led the editors of the Atlanta *Constitution* to suggest that a "touch of the quarterdeck manner remained from his USN days."[54] Similarly, while projecting an intellectual demeanor he could be dogmatic, sometimes resolutely refusing to admit to even the most obvious error. "Jimmy has always hated to apologize or admit he was wrong," wrote his cousin, Hugh Carter, somewhat later.[55] Although occasionally exhibiting a ruthlessness and pettiness that seemed to compromise the moral code he professed, Carter usually claimed the moral and ethical high ground; meanwhile, whether out of arrogance or ignorance, he sometimes practiced a style of politics based on exaggeration, disingenuousness, and at times outright deception.[56]

In electoral contests he gave no evidence of recognizing any precise relationship between the campaign for office and the problems of governing once the campaign was over. Perhaps nothing better illustrates this than his 1970 gubernatorial campaign. It would be difficult to find anything high-minded about Carter's campaign. He stirred up both class and race prejudices to skewer his primary opponent, Carl Sanders.[57] Then, a few weeks later, he delivered his startling inaugural address unabashedly proclaiming an end to segregation. If Georgia voters were a bit mystified by it all, they had every right to be. Too often Jimmy Carter seemed to subscribe to the old political adage of "Watch what we do, not what we say." The inconsistency between Carter's rhetoric and his actions, along with a weakness for hyperbole, eventually created credibility problems that were often wrongly attributed to poor communication skills. Moreover, those credibility problems, when combined with Carter's tendency toward self-righteousness and moral posturing, bred disillusionment if not contempt among many.

Jimmy Carter was not perceived by the public as a particularly warm and personable individual, nor did his public persona generate feelings of awe or apprehension in the manner of a Richard Russell. Nevertheless, as the distance between his gubernatorial tenure and memories of his political personality grows, the evaluation of his performance in office should become increasingly positive. The unfortunate fact is that Jimmy Carter was a better governor than he has led us to believe.

Jimmy Carter:
Years of Challenge,
Years of Change

An Interview by
GARY L. ROBERTS

Editors' Note: The following interview was conducted at the office of former President Jimmy Carter on September 20, 1985, based upon questions submitted in advance by participants in the symposium.

ROBERTS: Good afternoon, President Carter. I'd like to begin by asking you what you consider to be your most significant accomplishment as governor of Georgia?

CARTER: Well, when we went into office we had a very broad agenda and at the top of our agenda was to reorganize the structure of state government, which involved a lot of things. One was to make it more streamlined, more efficient, more fiscally responsible, both in matters of organizational structure and also in general obligation bonds, moving from a Minimum Foundation Program of education to what we called an Adequate Foundation Program, and a judicial reform with merit selection of judges. And so I am proud of all those things. I think we were surprisingly successful in spite of the controversial nature of them. Finally, I served at a time of racial unrest, and I always felt a heavy responsibility to try to leave the governor's office at the end of four years with as much harmony and common purpose established among our black and white citizens as possible. Those are the kinds of things that come to my mind as accomplishments.

ROBERTS: What do you think about disappointments? Are there any things that stand out as being particularly disappointing to you about those four years?

CARTER: Well, of course, in none of those things were we 100 percent successful. You never can be in a political world. In general, the thing that was most disappointing to me was my failure to accomplish a major goal of eliminating the unwarranted influence of very powerful special-interest groups in Atlanta and the state government and throughout the government structure. This involved a lot of things concerning lob-byists—special tax privileges that are carved in the law that we were not able to get out, a pack of consumer protection, things of that kind. We had some success, but I would say that would be the most disappointing thing

ROBERTS: As you reflect back on your governorship, are there any things that you would do differently now, after the benefits of reflection?

CARTER: The most common criticism of our administration is one that I shared, at the time and maybe even now, many years later, and that is that we tried to do too much too quickly. But then you have to remember that there was no second term possible. And so we had a very heavy agenda in the beginning and knew that we only had four years to do it. I didn't have to worry about carving out a basis for a reelection campaign; I was able to confront controversial issues without much fear of the political consequences. I think that we left behind an image of some confusion because we didn't single out just one or two issues and concentrate on them. Ours was a highly activist administration, with a lot of controversy involved. And so I think that if I had been a better communicator and been more careful about the political consequences of some of my positions I could have left more harmony within the state government, as it related to me. That's a regret, but I'm not sure that it is consistent with my own political nature to do it differently if I had it to do all over again. But that's a commonly accepted failure with which I certainly wouldn't disagree.

ROBERTS: You spoke earlier of the reorganization efforts. What were the main ingredients of government reorganization, and after nearly a decade how do you assess the overall success of reorganization?

CARTER: The main ingredients, of course, were to eliminate a whole multiplicity of dozens, even hundreds, of unnecessary little agencies, departments, bureaus, commissions that had become individual fief-doms. Each one had its own status in the government, sometimes with a large staff and many employees, sometimes with just a few. Each one of them had special privileges that they had carved out for themselves. They had a certain degree of political influence in the legislature and it was highly wasteful of taxpayers' money. So we streamlined the government and eliminated a lot of those extra and nonessential functions.

When we—that is, I and the legislature together—decided that these particular functions ought to be preserved, we generally put them under a broader departmental structure, like Human Resources or Natural Resources. In the same period we tended to professionalize the service of America's and Georgia's public servants. The GBI [Georgia Bureau of Investigation] was taken out of politics. GBI agents were no longer just sheriff's aides—they became highly professional.

We did the same thing with prison officials. And in many ways this was the case in departments like Game and Fish, which then became Natural Resources. We removed employees from the political influence of a multiplicity of people and put them under a tighter merit system.

One of the most difficult things I had to do was to eliminate the wide range of different agencies in Georgia that could issue bonds, in order to circumvent the state constitutional prohibition against debt. We consolidated all these different bonds issued by many authorities into one general obligation bond, and in the process we got a triple A rating, which Georgia has been receiving ever since. We were quite proud that this has saved the taxpayers millions of dollars in unnecessary interest payments.

So you can see that in the process of government reorganization a lot of people were shaken up, a lot of people were aggravated. It was a highly controversial debate and vote and political campaign within the House and Senate to get some of these things accomplished. The budgeting procedures were clarified and the principle of zero-based budgeting was established. Although all this was not perpetuated by my successors, the theory of it has been very good: each time a budgeting process came up, to make sure that we not only considered new additions to the budget but also assessed the need for expenditures that had been approved in previous years.

And the final part of your question—ten years later how does it look? I was lucky in having George Busbee succeed me in the governor's office. He never blamed any problems that he faced on me, but he tended to fine-tune the reorganization decisions that we had made. (He was majority leader when I was governor.) There were no revolutionary changes; nothing was repealed that was significant, so the reorganization decisions made by me and the legislature together have been preserved in a remarkably intact way and have been very beneficial to the state.

ROBERTS: You spoke earlier too of the area of race relations. Are there any particular things that stand out in your memory as accomplishments in that area?

CARTER: One of the most memorable things was the statement I made when I took the oath of office in January 1971. It is difficult even now to think back on the years that preceded me when people would run for public office promising to close down the public school system before blacks and whites could go to school together. Blacks were excluded from restaurants and voting booths and things of that kind. The race problem was one that permeated the entire Southeast and the rest of the country as well. George Wallace was in his ascendancy as a spokesman for so-called states' rights, which had a clear racial connotation, so I made a statement in the inaugural address, which was only about eight minutes long, that the time for racial discrimination was over in my state. This set a tone that was beneficial to me and that was generally accepted by the people.

This was followed by appointing multiracial committees, with 50 percent black and 50 percent white—a small task force that worked directly for me that could go into a community when there was a highly controversial race argument. In the past a substantial portion of the time of the state patrol and the GBI agents had been devoted to going into troubled communities. We practically eliminated that need by sending in a small, highly trained group to resolve differences peacefully, and I think the blacks and whites felt they were getting a fair shake. So you know you don't ever have, as I said earlier, complete success, but that was something that I believe was acknowledged to be successful while I was governor, and I don't think my successors in office have had any particular problem with race issues.

ROBERTS: Would you comment briefly on your decision to enter the governor's race in 1970?

CARTER: I ran for governor in 1966. I had been running for Congress in 1966 against a Republican, Bo Callaway. I can't say I would have beaten him had he stayed in the race, but he decided to change and run for governor, which almost left me with a clear field in the Third District congressional race. However, I felt after considering it a few days that I would rather change also and run for governor—for several reasons that I need not go into. And so I decided to run for governor in '66 at the very last minute, and I came in a close third. And only a day after I was defeated in 1966 I decided to run in 1970.

So for four years I tried to pay off my '66 debts and make myself known around the state, to learn from the mistakes I made in '66; to get an early start, and to consolidate my position in every county in Georgia. I visited, shook hands, made speeches in six hundred towns and cities in our state, and during the last few months in the campaign my wife campaigned also, separate from me but on the same days. So we had a very carefully prepared campaign in 1970—after an ill-prepared or nonprepared campaign in 1966. And another thing that gave me the advantage in 1970 was that at the beginning of that race, although I had run before, no one thought I had a chance in the world to win, and it was an advantage being an underdog. That was a very pleasant experience in '70, and not so pleasant in '66.

The fact that I didn't have the choice of running or not running for reelection in 1974 gave me a great deal of freedom, and I don't think hurt me much as a so-called lame duck. The record will show that the last year I was in office we were just as successful in dealing with the legislature as we were the first or second year in office. But I might add, parenthetically—you haven't asked me about it—I think it was a good move in our state, subsequently, to authorize two terms for governor.

ROBERTS: In 1970 it appeared to many people that the Atlanta newspapers were rather hostile to your candidacy. Why do you think that was?

CARTER: That's putting it mildly. They were more than hostile. In the first place, I was a south Georgian and I was looked upon as a fiscal conservative, and the Atlanta newspapers quite erroneously, because they didn't know anything about me or my background here in Plains, decided that I was also a racial conservative. That's one of the factors, and it was very difficult for me to change their concept because it was a prefixed, unshakable belief. The second thing was that they had endorsed former Governor Carl Sanders. He was their man, and they saw me as a challenger to him, not only who was not worthy of their support, but also who had no chance to win, and who was just stirring up the political waters to the detriment of their own chosen candidate. The editors of the newspapers could probably tell you other reasons, but those are two that stick in my mind. I think at least in those days, the lack of support from Atlanta newspapers was probably a benefit to me in the rest of the state, and perhaps even in Atlanta too. The endorsement of the Atlanta *Constitution* and Atlanta *Journal* was not a particularly great boon to the candidate who received the endorsement.

ROBERTS: I was going to ask you about that. How about after you became governor? How do you feel about the Atlanta newspapers' treatment of your administration during the time you were governor?

CARTER: I would say it was fair. You know, no incumbent governor or president is ever completely satisfied with his news treatment. It would be nice if your press secretary could write all the news stories. But the statewide papers and almost all the local papers in Georgia treated my administration quite fairly. We dealt with them fairly. We briefed them probably more than they wanted on key issues that we had to present to the legislature—judicial reform, reorganization, the Adequate Foundation Program for Education, conservation matters. I learned a lot from not having press support in the campaign that helped me to correct this some when I was governor.

ROBERTS: Most of us who remember your administration remember the battles between yourself and Lester Maddox. Would you comment on that, on the problems in that area?

CARTER: I recall that also! That was the most unpleasant aspect of my experience as governor. There would have been a dramatically different environment in the state capitol if I had had a supportive lieutenant governor who would have talked to me rationally about a common goal and worked out our differences privately—and after that cooperated in the passage of legislation. But this was not the case, unfortunately, and it was something with which I had to live. And I think that in the political arena it hurt both of us, because the Georgia people after four years of this kind of lack of cooperation felt that both of us ought to be criticized.

I certainly don't claim that all the blame was on Maddox's side and none on my side, but as everyone knows, he is a very difficult person when he believes something and you disagree, and I felt as governor I had to set the basic agenda for the state and my hope was that he would cooperate on occasion. But those occasions were quite rare. Also, he had been my predecessor, remember, in the governor's office, chosen by the legislature after a deadlock in the 1966 campaign. I think a former governor becoming the immediate lieutenant governor still feels he ought to have a role to play in state government that is probably much greater than his successor feels ought to be the case. So we didn't get along politically at all, and I do regret it very much; I think it did hurt the state to some degree. But let me add quickly that even in spite of that unpleasantness, when anyone asked me at the White House or asks me now, "What were your best times in the political world?" I always say, "As governor." And when I've talked to other people who served in Washington, like Senator Ed Muskie, or Senator Herman Talmadge, or some of the other Southern U.S. senators, and ask, "What was your best time in the political world?" they always say, "When I was governor."

ROBERTS: Would you discuss some of the ways and means that you used to get your program through the legislature? What were your tactics, your approach to getting things done with the legislature?

CARTER: Anyone who reads carefully the history of our four years there would see the highly controversial nature of almost every issue we put forward. We were trying to revise what was there, to change what was there, to improve what was there, and this, as I said, rocked the boat. Some of it disturbed people very deeply, and some of those people were highly effective, very knowledgeable, very senior, and also very influential politicians. So what we did was work out with some of the more cooperative members of the legislature a basic program, then launched a very carefully prescribed procedure to get that passed through the legislature, in two or three phases.

First of all was the bringing together of distinguished advisers, both from within the state government and outside. If it involved a change in the computer programs, we brought in people who knew the most in our state about computers. If it involved transportation, we did the same thing; if it involved printing, we did the same thing. If it involved judicial reform, we brought in some of the most distinguished jurists and lawyers in our state, whose reputations were beyond criticism, and let them consult with us so they would feel legitimately that they were part of the planning process. Then later it became their baby as well as mine and they were supportive. We encouraged them not only to help us devise the reforms that we needed, but also to let their opinions be known through the press.

This brings up the second phase, and that was to acquaint the members of the press, not only in Atlanta but throughout the state—large and small newspapers, radio stations, TV managers—about what our goals were. I would bring them to the governor's mansion, which is a very beautiful place to entertain, show them through slide presentations and other means what we had how and what we hoped to achieve in the process that I would use to make the change—ask for their advice, their criticisms, and their questions. I hoped when they left the governor's mansion that they would be allies of mine when the matter became a public altercation or debate.

And then the next thing, of course, was to bring in large groups of Georgia citizens who were not in politics or not directly related to the political world. We had probably more than 50,000 Georgians who participated in our program to define what they wanted our state to be. This was headed by Tom Linder, whose grandfather was a distinguished Georgia public servant, commissioner of agriculture for years. Tom Linder coordinated these programs. We went into many communities in Georgia and said, "What do you think about our state government? How can it be better in your eyes?" to try to get the Georgia people involved in it. Then, when we did reach the point of confrontation in the legislature, we hoped that we had the press, distinguished Georgians, plus the Georgia populace, on our side. That was the reason, I think, that the reorganization plan, for instance, had a surprising degree of acceptance.

ROBERTS: How would you assess your place in the historical scheme of things? How do you fit in Georgia as governor in the long view?

CARTER: The previous governor who had completely reorganized the state government structure was Senator Richard Russell, during the few years that he served before he went to the U.S. Senate. And I thought when I was running for governor that it was time for another, if you'll pardon the expression, revolutionary approach to government structure. I think history will show that we were successful. At the same time, this was very costly politically, because it made it very difficult for me to get along as harmoniously as I would have liked with the legislature, with other state officials, and with lobbying groups and so forth because we did shake up some of the existing patterns that had been formed. That's one place that I will fit in, as kind of a turning point in the organizational structure of the government.

I think another one, of course, that I mentioned earlier, is the race pattern. Without any derogation at all of my predecessors, I think while it is fair to say that many of them were progressive on the race issue, some had the image of not being enlightened on the race issue, and the time I came there was a time when the South was ready to put the race question behind us and move forward as an accepted part of the nation in every respect. In the political world, that was kind of a turning point, not because it was I in the office but because it was time for it. John West in South Carolina and Reuben Askew in Florida and Dale Bumpers in Arkansas are other governors who served at the same time I did who had basically the same nonracist philosophy. It wasn't because we felt that way that we were elected; it was because the people felt that way that we were elected. And we represented, I think, an inclination in the South: "Let's put the race segregation obsession behind us; let's turn now to other things."

One thing that we haven't mentioned in this interview that I think is important is a responsibility the Georgia governors have accepted to benefit the state, to improve the economic status of our people. I spent a lot of time bringing foreign investments into Georgia. By "foreign" I mean from other states and from overseas. We also worked to market Georgia products in foreign countries. And so this was another thing that we accomplished.

ROBERTS: Do you feel in any sense, then, that your administration was a kind of turning point in Georgia's history that represented a shift away from the past in new directions?

CARTER: I think so, but mine wasn't the only time. Obviously in the term of Ellis Arnall he gave Georgia a nationwide image of progress and innovation that was quite startling in his time. And I think less than he did, I presented to the rest of the nation an image of Georgia that was attractive and acceptable. I say this hesitantly because I am not trying to cast aspersions on the governors who came before and served in a different time or different period. And I've been grateful that the governors who came after me, both Joe Frank Harris and George Busbee, built upon what I did and improved upon what I did and I have been really grateful to them for honoring my own contributions in a positive fashion.

George D. Busbee

1975 – 1983

George Busbee
and the Politics
of Consensus

ELEANOR C. MAIN &
GERARD S. GRYSKI

When George Busbee was campaigning for governor, a political writer depicted him as a man "whose dreams lie more in the immediate task to be performed than in the shaping of destiny, more in the present than in the future. Busbee is more the engineer than the architect, more the craftsman than the designer."[1] Busbee the journeyman had spent eighteen years in the Georgia legislature, mastering the political process and the details of Georgia government. In spite of his role in the House leadership as chairman of the House Judiciary Committee, vice-chairman of the powerful Rules Committee and majority leader, Busbee was relatively unknown when he entered the race for the Democratic gubernatorial nomination in 1974.

However, Busbee's "workhorse, not a showhorse" campaign barely eased out the big-spending Bert Lance and earned him a spot in the runoff against the flamboyant Lester Maddox. The sensible, modest, businesslike Busbee trounced Maddox, winning three-fifths of the votes. In 1983 George Busbee, the first Georgia governor to serve eight consecutive years, was hailed as leaving office "with an enviable record of progress and stability. . . . Busbee's legacy of achievement and sound government should serve as a model for future state chief executives.

Georgia is indeed fortunate to have had the Busbee brand of leadership for the past eight years."[2]

During those eight years Georgians fought a recession, then soaring inflation accompanied by a slowdown in the economy. Georgia's population ballooned from 4.9 million to 5.6 million, the fifth fastest growing population among the states. Half of the 700,000 increase was attributable to in-migration. Although Georgia's population remained more rural (37.6 percent) than the nation's (26.3 percent), it continued to become urban. The number of people working in nonagricultural jobs increased by 37.6 percent. Much of the growth was in the Atlanta metropolitan area, but only ten counties failed to gain population during the 1970s. Georgians were becoming more educated. The median years of schooling for the state (12.3 years) was close to the national median of 12.5 years and represented a significant increase over the 1960 median level of nine years for Georgians. The state remained predominantly white (72.25 percent).[3] Obviously, the changes in the state's population precipitated demands on state government; in some cases the changes may have resulted from state policy decisions.

When George Busbee became governor he had more legislative experience than the preceding eight governors. He was a highly respected member of the House who had been a protégé of the powerful Speaker George L. Smith. Smith's style of careful negotiating and bargaining in long legislative meetings behind closed doors was compatible with Busbee's. Many thought that Busbee was a likely successor, and indeed the personal choice of George L. Smith, to be speaker. When Smith died unexpectedly in 1973, some of Busbee's supporters pressured him to seek the post in the legislature and abandon the more risky race for chief executive. Busbee addressed the problems of executive-legislative relations forthrightly in his inaugural speech:

> If we are to spend our energies and resources on the things that matter most to the people of Georgia we must work hard and above all we must work together. Responsible and healthy debate over issues is a hallmark of our system, but the people are tired of personal bickering, petty in-fighting and political chatter. That kind of gamesman has no place in the serious times in which we find ourselves today and I ask that we put it aside for the next four years.[4]

The test of legislative-executive harmony involved one of the governor's most important programs during his first year in office. Busbee had specified that "the number one priority of my administration is education."[5] The hallmark of that program was a statewide kindergarten funded by the state. Before Busbee's inauguration, Tom Murphy, the mercurial speaker of the House, announced his opposition to the kindergarten program, hoping to convince Busbee that the governor's proposed reduction of the pupil-teacher ratio should be his major goal. Murphy estimated the cost of the program to be $300 million and questioned whether the state could afford such an expenditure.[6] Realizing that legislative opposition and budgetary restraints would not allow him to get through a full-fledged program in one year, the governor estimated the full costs at $65 million and proposed a program to serve 25 percent of the state's five-year-olds at a figure of $10.4 million. In addition to the opposition of the House leadership, the governor could not depend on constituent pressures to influence the legislators. Busbee was in fact confronted with the unnerving fact that there was no overt lobbying for the kindergarten program by the teachers. The powerful Georgia Association of Educators had placed the program fifth on its list of legislative priorities.[7] School board members also were worried that the program would add additional local costs for them, that there were hidden costs which would be passed on to the localities.[8] The governor set about trying to persuade individual legislators by meeting with them in small groups, either in his office or at the mansion.

The kindergarten program and a proposal for tax relief became entangled. Initially the governor had supported a plan for tax relief, but when revenue estimates dropped he abandoned the plan and continued to press for his kindergarten program. Conversely, the speaker rejected the kindergarten plan and supported a circuit-breaker tax relief plan of about $50 million. The governor's strongest allies were in the Senate, where Lieutenant Governor Zell Miller called the tax relief a "cruel hoax" and argued that it favored upper income taxpayers and did not provide enough relief for the lower and middle income taxpayer. Busbee, who had based his opposition to the plan on the ground that it could not be funded, accepted and elaborated upon Miller's criticisms while contending that support was increasing for the kindergarten proposal as part of the total education package.[9]

The House leadership then devised a less expensive $35 million tax relief plan. The governor, in response, began to hammer out some changes to ensure that the new plan was constitutionally sound. Although he attempted to separate the kindergarten program from tax relief by insisting that "one is exclusive of the other," some observers argued that they were tied together, that Busbee could exercise his gubernatorial veto on tax relief if there were no kindergarten.[10] Busbee was said to have been convinced by advisers to support the plan in order to avoid any further conflict in the session.

The lieutenant governor, in what he labeled a "spirit of cooperation with the governor," was forced to capitulate and withdraw his opposition from a plan he considered a "monstrosity."[11] In exchange for his support, Busbee succeeded in having his kindergarten program funded by both houses under the title of "selective pre-school training." The governor, who was criticized by some during the session for acting more like a legislator and not exerting enough leadership, played both roles with the members of the appropriations conference committee and won his priority programs.[12] He had also used his prerogative and postponed for several weeks signing the supplemental budget bill for the remainder of the 1975 fiscal year, keeping both departmental heads and key legislators in the dark about whether or not he would line-item veto some of their programs until he knew the status of his own legislation.

The governor's victory was short-lived. Faced with declining revenues, Busbee called legislative leaders together in June 1975. He estimated that there would be a $108 million budget deficit. The first step he wanted to take to erase the deficit was to repeal the tax relief bill, which the House leadership considered to be its prime accomplishment in the 1975 session. Utilizing a tool now familiar to chief executives, the state-wide television address, the governor went directly to the people to explain his plans for coping with what he said "may be the most crucial problem confronting your state in the past 40 years." Busbee justified his proposal to eliminate the tax relief program: "The facts are that under present economic conditions this program would not be real tax relief. It would be an illusion of tax relief, a political hoax." While the lieutenant governor, who had held out the longest against tax relief, supported the governor's plan, Speaker Murphy rejected it, stating that the deficit could be erased through other means. "Property tax relief is not a hoax for the people who need it most," he said.[13]

The governor also proposed deferring the pay raises for teachers and state employees until January 1, 1976. Groups such as the Georgia Association of Educators and the Association of County Commissioners of Georgia rallied to protect the respective gains they had made during the regular session. The House leadership proposed retaining part of the tax relief plan and making deeper cuts in the operating budgets of state government. The Senate refused this plan, arguing that the proposed cuts would eliminate needed state services and that tax relief in light of the deficit did not make sense.

Discussions of cutting out the governor's hard-won kindergarten program ensued. The House became more fragmented as the impasse continued. Finally, it became apparent to the House leadership that there would be a revolt among its members to kill the tax relief measure. The House leadership then proposed and its members voted overwhelmingly to discard the kindergarten program, the pay hikes, and property tax relief. The Senate balked at deleting the pay raises for the entire fiscal year and was reticent about eliminating the kindergarten program.

However, Governor Busbee once again broke the bottleneck in the conference committee by working out a compromise budget plan abandoning state pay raises and kindergarten funding at least until the next session of the General Assembly.

Some members of the Senate were visibly upset at this compromise. Terrell Starr, the governor's Senate floor leader, urged support, noting that the Senate was "being forced into an untenable position. But we must do what we are being called on to do."[14] Later Busbee managed to get enough federal funding to reinstate some of the kindergarten funding. The governor emerged from the special session as a decisive, responsible leader. He had prevented the House leadership from seizing the initiative and had kept control over his budget. Although some in the Senate felt betrayed, they could not be obstructionists and were somewhat comforted by the elimination of the tax relief measure.

Throughout Busbee's tenure, disagreements with the legislature tended to center on budgetary and tax matters. A pattern seemed to develop: the House and Senate would disagree over the governor's budget or tax proposal; most often the Senate would support Busbee and the House would oppose him; there would be an impasse; Governor Busbee would author a compromise that both houses could accept.

One exception to this pattern developed from the withdrawal of the teacher pay raises for the 1976 fiscal year. Immediately after the legislative session, the Georgia Association of Educators and the Georgia Conference of the American Association of University Professors filed separate suits to win back some $41.4 million in promised pay raises.[15] The court subsequently combined the actions into one suit. First a Fulton County Superior Court judge and then the Georgia Supreme Court ruled that the Board of Regents must pay university professors the salary increase they were promised. The decision in December 1975 would cost the state $11.5 million.

The court reasoned that the regents had violated their contracts with university professors that had been entered into between April 25 and July 3, 1975.[16] The governor and the board agreed that all university employees, not just those who had signed contracts, would get raises. However, he warned that their proposed raises for the next fiscal year would be reduced. Notably, the state primary and secondary teachers, who had not signed contracts before the budget revision, did not have their raises reinstated. Busbee did meet with members of the Georgia Association of Educators to work on education reforms and salary raises in the succeeding legislative sessions.

By the 1979 General Assembly session, the teachers decided they had some catching up to do. They pushed for a 13 percent pay raise and were stunned when the governor recommended a 5 percent increase. The

Georgia Association of Educators immediately organized one of the most intensive lobbying efforts ever seen in the General Assembly. There were rumors that the association was prepared to strike when it was discovered that the organization had taken a poll of its members to ascertain what they might do if they did not get the desired raise. The GAE did not release the results and its president insisted that the survey "was never intended to be a strike vote."[17]

The House Appropriations Committee passed out a 6.5 percent raise. On the floor, rebelling against the leadership and responding to the teachers, House members approved a 9 percent salary increase. Busbee sought the advice of Alfred E. Kahn, President Carter's chief inflation adviser, who urged him to reject the 9 percent raise because it violated the voluntary 7 percent guideline maximum for prices and wages.[18] The Senate leaders indicated they were unwilling to violate the guidelines, and the governor proposed a 6.5 percent increase for teachers and university system instructors effective September 1 and an additional 2.5 percent pay raise to go into effect January 1. The GAE indicated this was unsatisfactory.

In a surprise move the Senate raised the entire budget, including the estimate of funds available for spending. The action, which passed a budget $25 million above the House version, set the governor against the Senate. Furthermore, the Senate locked itself into its position by instructing its members on the conference committee not to abandon the 10 percent raise for university system personnel and teachers and the 9 percent raise for state employees. The governor cited the attorney general in warning both houses that such a budget would be unconstitutional because raising the revenue projection was within the power of the executive branch of government, not the legislative branch.[19]

After weeks of fighting and on-again, off-again negotiations, the House and Senate passed a two-step 9.5 percent increase for the state's teachers and university system personnel and an 8.5 percent increase for other state employees. Busbee, unhappy with the budget, warned that he might use the line-item veto. The final version of the budget had been drawn in such a way that the governor could veto the second phase of the pay raise.[20] When he confirmed two weeks later that he would approve the $131 million in raises for state teachers and employees, Busbee insisted that he was not reacting to political pressures. In what might be interpreted as uncharacteristic criticism of an interest group, Busbee observed that Georgians "do not countenance loose and militant talk about leaving the classrooms and taking up picket signs."[21]

Although he had lost this particular battle in the session, he won others. He had managed to obtain full funding for a statewide kindergarten program. By using his arbitration skills, he was able to fulfill a

1978 reelection campaign promise by persuading the feuding House and Senate to agree on a $75 million property tax relief measure which would benefit the schools.[22]

Less frequently, executive-legislative relations during the Busbee years were tested on nonbudgetary issues. George Busbee supported constitutional revision in both his campaigns. In 1974 the Georgia constitution was the longest in the nation, containing 500,000 words and 831 amendments. In many cases the constitution was so specific that an amendment, often concerning local matters, was needed to make changes. The articles were also so interdependent that altering one article by constitutional amendment could necessitate changes in others. Therefore, in 1976 a reedited version of the constitution was on the ballot. The purpose of this exercise was to put the existing constitution in a coherent form so that true constitutional revision could take place.

Ironically, also on the 1976 ballot was an additional amendment that would allow a Georgia governor to serve two consecutive four-year terms. The proposed constitutional amendment passed the legislature early in the 1976 session. Most observers thought the lack of opposition there was due to the popularity of the incumbent governor. Some thought that Busbee, who had proven himself as a fiscal conservative, was so constrained by the economy that he deserved another term to develop his programs.[23]

After the amendment easily passed the legislature, relations between the governor and the lieutenant governor were strained. Before the proposed amendment, many presumed that Zell Miller would run for governor in 1978. Although he maintained his support for the amendment, Miller criticized the governor for permitting members of his staff to pressure legislators and others to work for and help finance the passage of the amendment in November. At one point Miller promised to resign if Busbee could prove his charges wrong; at another time he said that both he and Busbee should declare they would not run for governor in 1978.[24] The governor did admit that he knew of the actions of his staff and supporters in behalf of the amendment, but denied that he personally was lobbying others or that state employees were using work time to push for the two-term provision. Although at times the exchange between Miller and Busbee became so heated that it was compared to the Maddox and Carter feud, the entire dispute lasted for a relatively short two months.

Along with the succession amendment, the "editorial" revision of the 1945 constitution won at the polls. The plan then was to submit revisions of the constitution to the public a few articles at a time. Two revised articles were defeated in 1978 because of an apparent backlash of voters against the large number of proposed amendments (thirty-six) on the ballot.[25] Any revision had to pass two-thirds of each house of the legislature before being submitted to the voters. During the regular session of the General Assembly in 1981, difficulties between the House and Senate on such issues as a limit on the size of the House and four-year terms for senators killed revisions. The governor's commitment to constitutional revision was evidenced by the fact that he personally chaired the biweekly meetings of the Legislative Overview Committee, a group of sixty senators and representatives revising the constitution on an article-by-article basis during the summer of 1981. In spite of the fact that these meetings often resulted in deadlocks and the need to send proposals to House-Senate conference committees, Busbee remained optimistic and planned to include constitutional revision on the agenda for the special session later in the summer which would also reapportion Georgia's legislative and congressional seats.[26]

However, in August 1981 an angry George Busbee struck constitutional revision from his call for a special session two weeks later. At a press conference Busbee told reporters that "it is not my intention to be a part of the creation of a two-headed monster."[27] He was reacting to a vote the day before in the Legislative Overview Committee which would allow the General Assembly, by a simple majority vote, to set up different classes of property and prescribe different tax assessments for each. The existing constitution banned such practices without a two-thirds vote in both houses. According to Busbee, the proposed change "would give every special interest group in the state the opportunity to come and put pressure on the Legislature" for special tax breaks.[28]

After the vote in committee, the governor had quickly adjourned the meeting for lack of a proper quorum. Property classification designed to give the farmers of the state a break had been brought up often in the General Assembly, but failed because there were disagreements over the specifics and the constitutionality of such a classification. Marcus Collins, chairman of the House Ways and Means Committee, indicated that he was willing to compromise on the wording as long as "agricultural and forest lands" were included. Four days before the scheduled start of the special session the Legislative Overview Committee deleted the controversial provision and the governor agreed to include consideration of a revised state constitution in his call for the session.[29] As part of the compromise, Busbee also added two separate potential constitutional amendments to the list of issues on the legislature's agenda: a possible land classification plan to help farmers with their property taxes and the consideration of restoring the two-term provision for governors dropped in the revised constitution.[30]

Hours after the beginning of the session the governor addressed a joint session of the General Assembly and warned the legislators to leave "controversial matters" out of the proposed constitution to enhance its chances for voter approval. Representative Collins won approval from a House committee to include a provision allowing farms of less than two thousand acres to be taxed at only 75 percent of the taxable value of surrounding property. Senators protested this violation of the agreement carefully worked out before the session.[31] The governor eventually became so disgusted with the legislative deliberations that he had his supporters lobby the House to defeat the document. In an uncharacteristic public pique at the legislature, Busbee angrily castigated them for wasting the taxpayers' money and urged them to finish reapportionment and go home. The governor expressed disappointment "that my idealistic dream of a good, sound constitution has turned into a nightmare . . . replete with regressive amendments which amount to a leap into the past."[32]

However, one week later, when the speaker and the lieutenant governor were discouraged and wanted to delay further consideration of the new constitution until the next regular session, the governor, afraid that it was now or never, urged the legislature to perfect a new document in conference committee. The committee's work received Busbee's support and he commended it to the General Assembly. Although a tightened section on property classification remained, most of the provisions the governor had faulted were either deleted or modified. The Senate by a single vote and the House by an overwhelming margin submitted the new constitution for the electorate's ratification. Governor Busbee had been successful in achieving one of the prime goals of his administration.

Busbee's chief managerial chore was to manage the budget. Although he had to rely on the legislature for support, it was his responsibility to present the plan for how Georgia would face the fiscal crisis. Admitting the overestimation of state revenues and calling a special session during the first year of his administration instead of trying to resolve the deficit solely through cuts in services signaled a hallmark of Busbee's style. He was prepared to seize the initiative and assume charge. In assessing that year, Governor Busbee observed that the initial crises gave him the "idea of trying to use the budget as a tool in itself to restructure and streamline the operation in government. . . . I got enthused again. . . [t]here were some things I could do during this period of time that would have some real meaningful benefits to the state."[33] For example, the governor emphasized performance evaluations and instructed department heads that only extraordinary necessary hiring be done.[34]

The Department of Human Resources was the subject of criticism by many in the legislature. Busbee asked for and received legislative authority to restructure the massive department almost immediately. He did not plan to separate the basic welfare, health, and vocational programs. However, he did find it necessary by the end of 1976 to sever the Medicaid program from the Department of Human Resources and place it under a new commission with its own director.[35] But before and after that decision, the Medicaid program presented major problems for the administration. The program was running an estimated deficit of $5 million per month, and many providers had been waiting for more than a year for reimbursement from the state. The governor suspended Medicaid payments for dental and optometric services and instituted a small fee for doctor's visits. Neither of these actions was popular with recipients or providers.

In addition, the state's method of paying Medicaid bills was declared unconstitutional because it violated the Georgia constitution's ban on deficit spending. Since the program began, it had been customary for the Department of Human Resources to carry over expenditures/reimbursements from the last month of one fiscal year and pay them with money appropriated for the next fiscal year. The practice came into question when for the first time the state prepared legally binding contracts with providers of Medicaid services. Because of the possibility that there would be a $30 to $35 million shortfall in the Medicaid budget, the contracts gave the state the option to reduce pay for Medicaid services if the money ran out. Obviously, the Medicaid hospital and nursing home associations protested and the state faced the real possibility that there would not be enough health providers for the poor.[36]

Governor Busbee, fearful that he would either have to eliminate Medicaid funding for prescription drugs and for care in "intermediate care" nursing home facilities or begin by October to pay the providers only 64 cents for every dollar of their bills to the state, proposed a plan to U.S. Secretary of Health, Education, and Welfare David Mathews. Georgia would be able to meet most of its Medicaid deficit if the federal government would interpret some of its regulations so that the state could charge recipients or their families a "co-payment" for a number of services the federal government required the state to provide as part of the Medicaid program.[37] Mathews granted the waiver on the only grounds possible: the payment-for-services plan was viewed as an "experimental or demonstration program" which would assist in promoting the objectives of several public-aid statutes. Attorneys representing Medicaid patients brought suit.[38] U.S. District Judge Charles A. Moye, Jr., ruled that the state's co-payment plan could be continued, but because of its "experimental" nature it had to be submitted to a review board. Much to the consternation of Busbee and other state officials, the twelve-person Institutional Review Board composed of ten DHR employees and two college professors declared that the co-payment plan for hospitals and physicians placed Medicaid recipients "at risk" and could not continue.[39]

Given these problems, the separation of Medicaid from DHR appeared administratively sound and the General Assembly ratified the creation of the Department of Medicaid Services in 1979. The Medicaid budget would have to stand on its own and could no longer depend on being rescued by drawing funds from the DHR budget. The governor and the agency instituted reforms to make sure that charges were based on the norm for that category of services and facilities, enabling the state to predict, analyze, and audit claims. The implementation of a computerized Medicaid Management Information System reduced the time necessary to process claims to an average of two weeks. However, Busbee warned that in spite of increased administrative efficiency "the most significant reason for the alarming growth of the Medicaid program is overutilization and outright fraud."[40] He battled the escalating Medicaid costs during his entire governorship. But Georgia expenses were reflective of the rising charges nationally. As chairman of the National Governors' Conference, Busbee lobbied the Reagan administration to alter their planned reductions in the federal share of funding.[41] Medicaid had changed from a crisis administrative problem to a recurring one that had to be scrutinized continuously. The governor's reorganization and emergency fiscal management eliminated the crisis; the continued growth had to be met incrementally.

George Busbee also faced a crisis in the prison system as soon as he took office. He requested a special prisons appropriations bill even before the supplemental budget for fiscal year 1975 was considered. This emergency measure funding for repairs, medical supplies, clothing, food, and plans for new prisons and youthful offender centers was the first piece of legislation passed that year. Georgia's prison system in 1975 was not very different from those in most of the other Southern states. Outdated, inadequate facilities, coupled with mandatory sentences, an increase in arrests, and a lack of alternative programs, were straining the system and increasing the chance of federal intervention and regulations. In fact, Alabama, Florida, Louisiana, and Mississippi were already under federal court orders to improve conditions. By 1975 the Georgia prison system was averaging an increase of 300 prisoners a month. More than 11,000 prisoners were housed in a system designed for 8,000 inmates; at Reidsville, the maximum security facility, 3,000 men were packed into space for 1,000.[42]

Three years earlier, in 1972, a group of black prisoners had initiated a suit on behalf of about 2,000 black inmates, charging that the prison was overcrowded, that it provided inadequate medical aid and sanitary facilities, that it practiced racial discrimination, and that it employed too few blacks in responsible positions. The case, known as the "Guthrie case" after one of the plaintiffs, resulted in U.S. District Court Judge Anthony Alaimo ordering desegregation of the Georgia prison system, implemented at Reidsville in 1974.[43] State officials were fighting the case, fearful that a decision favoring the inmates would be too expensive. In order to stave off an adverse decision and to relieve the poor conditions, Governor Busbee continued his budget requests for prison improvements and for the most part received cooperation from the legislature. The governor supported development of the prototype housing concept for new prison construction. He also initiated a new system permitting inmates to earn release. The twofold objective of the plan was to relieve overcrowding and to emphasize rehabilitation.[44] Prerelease programs for some prisoners in halfway houses were also introduced, and the governor used his discretionary powers to allocate all of the $8.1 million state share of the federal job-creating public works grants to the Georgia prison system. The largest portion of these funds, $5 million, was designated for improved job training for youthful offenders and first-time prisoners at the Georgia Industrial Institute at Alto.[45]

In spite of this series of incremental decisions to spend increased amounts of money and to develop programs alleviating overcrowding and targeted toward a reduction in the recidivism rate, prison problems seemed to climax in 1978. A series of clashes, some full-scale riots, left one guard and five inmates dead. Prison officials and inmates characterized the violence as racial, contributed to and exacerbated by court-ordered integration. Busbee agreed with this assessment.[46] A Tattnall County grand jury issued a special report reiterating the charge that the 1974 court order had contributed to the racial clashes. The grand jury urged the court to lift the order and allow prison officials the discretion to make assignments of the prison population. In separate action, the Inmate Unity Committee that had been recognized by Warden Joe Hooper to allow prisoners to negotiate their grievances formally with authorities was abolished. Some observers think that Governor Busbee pressured Hooper to withdraw legitimacy from this group after 150 Reidsville guards hired an attorney to protest that the prisoners had more influence with the authorities than they did.[47]

In an important and unexpected move, Judge Alaimo ordered that for a period not to exceed 90 days inmates should be assigned to the dormitories in a checkerboard fashion in order to ease racial tensions. He also specified that the Department of Corrections must reduce the state inmate population by three hundred within a period of less than two weeks.[48] The violence at Reidsville continued, but prison officials and the governor urged that the segregation order be extended. Busbee also insisted that all allegations by prisoners and outside groups implicating guards in the violence be investigated. Judge Alaimo did extend his segregation order. Attorneys from the NAACP Legal Defense Fund and the state attorney general's office negotiated the reintegration of the prison population, which began without incident in February 1979.

However, the prison population and its attendant problems continued to grow. In 1982 the governor presented and received approval for legislation to construct modular housing to expand the state's prison capacity. Agreements had to be worked out with local governments so their facilities were not overcrowded because they were holding state prisoners. In eight years, while the total state budget had increased by 119 percent, the budget for the Department of Offender Rehabilitation had grown by 293 percent. Although the number of state employees had expanded by only 5.6 percent, the Department of Defender Rehabilitation enlarged from 2,466 to 5,359, or 117 percent. Alternative programs for incarceration were introduced and new facilities were built. Yet Governor Busbee described the inability to bring any permanent solution to the prison problem as one of his biggest disappointments in office: "Prison overcrowding problems have hounded me since the day I took office . . . . There is scant satisfaction to being able to boast that I was the governor who built more prisons than any governor in history."[49]

Busbee ranked economic development as a priority second only to educational advancement when he took office. Later he described the term as "providing those things that make it possible for the people of the State to have a better life. Education is a part of it . . . transportation is a part of it . . . the quality of government is a part of it . . . the number of industrial jobs in the State and the number of tourist dollars spent in the State . . . are big parts of it."[50]

Busbee's approach to economic development was aggressive.[51] Recognizing that the state could no longer depend on agriculture and textiles as its major industries, he sought to attract high-technology companies and disperse these industries in small as well as large communities. To reinforce this emphasis, the governor had the Department of Community Development relabeled its original designation as the Department of Industry and Trade. Busbee did not believe that the state could afford to "give away" much to attract business. The incentives used were carefully chosen and placed the state in partnership with local governments and industry. The governor asked the General Assembly to approve the local option freeport constitutional amendment and campaigned for its passage by the electorate in 1976. Under terms of the freeport amendment, counties and municipalities by local referendum can exempt certain goods in transit and stored in warehouses from property taxes. The localities offset the loss of the revenue through the income derived from higher employment and the income it generates. By 1983 about one-third of the counties had enacted some form of freeport legislation. Federal money was used initially to give state grants to communities to upgrade water and sewer services. The Department of Industry and Trade divided the state into seven regions and assigned representatives to advise localities on tourism and industrial development.

The governor's personal efforts to attract industry were probably the most visible aspects of his economic development program. Busbee's 1976 legislative package included a statute to permit international banks to operate within Georgia; sixteen international banks had offices in Georgia at the end of his administration. Busbee traveled extensively throughout the country and abroad, most often to the Far East and Europe. For each of his administration's eight years, the governor, the Department of Industry and Trade, and local communities attracted an average of over $1 billion investment and 18,000 new jobs. Industry and Trade's increased budget was targeted to promote Georgia as a center of foreign business and trade in the Southeast. Total employment in foreign-owned workplaces in 1982 exceeded 41,000, compared to 12,000 employees in 1974. The state established foreign offices in Athens, Bonn, Brussels, Hong Kong, Tokyo, and Toronto to encourage firms there to do business in Georgia and to provide access in the countries for Georgia industries. The Department of Industry and Trade's international division created a Trade Lead Program to inform Georgia business of trade opportunities abroad and to give technical assistance to companies engaged in or wishing to become involved in international trade.

The state had to improve its own infrastructure and facilities. The Savannah and Brunswick ports were developed and expanded through extensive state investment. The state highway system was an integral part of the economic development plan. The governor, the Department of Transportation, and the General Assembly expedited completion of the interstate system through the use of bonds and other funding mechanisms. The system was completed five years ahead of time. The World Congress Center, which had been authorized when Busbee was in the legislature, would promote trade and business by hosting international trade shows and conventions. Busbee later asked, and the General Assembly agreed, that this successful center be doubled in size. It brought in over $12 million a year in state taxes and employed over 7,500 persons. Expansion was projected to yield over $1.3 billion in additional revenues during the twenty years after 1983. The governor's plans for economic development generally seemed to be well received and noncontroversial. Busbee's determination to diversify and build the economy reflected his perceptions of the role of government: government's investment is wise and justified if it yields an expanded dividend to the private sector that provides opportunities for the citizens and the development of the state.

George Busbee became very involved in and concerned about the nature of state-federal relations in his eight years as governor. Economic conditions, coupled with the constraints that he felt federal regulations placed on his ability to solve problems, appear to have precipitated Busbee's immersion in this area. He developed a clear articulation of what he believed federalism should be by the time he left office.

One of the first forays the governor took into the federal-state arena was to attack the distribution of funds to the states. In a speech to the Southern Governors' Conference, Busbee charged that the South was "being raped" by Northern congressmen who were trying to change the federal formula for grants to the states.[52] As chairman of the Southern Growth Policies Board, he made the "Sunbelt-Snowbelt issue" a rallying point for the Southern governors.[53] Historically the South, disadvantaged economically, had been the favored recipient of federal tax dollars; most federal programs designed to help the poor would apply relatively to more people in the Sunbelt. However, because of the decline in their economic prosperity and their increasing loss of population, the Snowbelt states had become more aggressive about changing the grant formulas and redefining the distribution of federal funds.[54]

Reflective of his style not to preclude further cooperation, Governor Busbee emphasized: "I despise regionalism, but I think we ought to put our shoulder to the wheel to create some regionalism to help ourselves . . . as a definitive pattern."[55] Busbee and Massachusetts Representative Michael Harrington, chairman of the Northern-Midwest Coalition of Congressmen, agreed that neither side would benefit from an "all-out political war over the disbursement of federal funds."[56] In 1978 the governor participated in a "North-South Summit" in Boston between Sunbelt and Snowbelt officials to defuse the conflict. However, under Busbee the Southern Growth Policies Board did expand its Washington staff lobbying efforts and cooperation with Congress. It received credit for the Southern states not losing funds. When Busbee finished his term as chairman of the newly revitalized board, he reiterated his philosophy that the states had a responsibility to initiate domestic policies and not to just react to Washington. Further, he believed that "any new initiative ought to strive to better allocate and coordinate resources to people and places in need regardless of where they reside or might be. To do otherwise . . . would further fuel the fires of negative regionalism."[57]

Governor Busbee's belief in an active role for the states in the federal system propelled him to a national role among the governors. In addition to his prominence as a spokesman for Southern governors, he was an active member of the National Governors' Association, serving as chairman of its Transportation, Commerce, and Technology Committee and of the International Trade and Foreign Relations Committee as well as chair of its Task Force on Medicaid. When Busbee assumed the elected position of chairman of the National Governors' Association in August 1980, he immediately called for a reassessment of state and federal roles. He expressed fear that future governors would be reduced to being "mere clerks of the federal establishment."[58] The proliferation of categorical grants and the absence of accountability because of the lack of division of responsibilities among the levels of governments were the major targets of his criticisms. Often, the states had no choice but to participate in the programs and when emphases changed they had to continue the programs at their own expense.[59]

When Busbee ran for the Democratic nomination in 1974, he appealed directly for the support of black voters. Some analysts credit the strength of his endorsement by black leaders in Chatham County as a major contribution to his victory over Bert Lance in the first primary. Immediately Lester Maddox, who had won the most votes in the election, interjected the race issue into the primary. Maddox particularly tried to picture Busbee as beholden to State Representative Julian Bond, whose antiwar and civil rights positions had made him a well-known figure. Maddox accused Busbee of "buying a lot of votes." Busbee replied that he was "appealing to all Georgians" for their votes.[60] When he trounced Maddox in the runoff, John Lewis, executive director of the Voter Education Project, claimed that "a coalition of Georgia voters, black and white, [had] rejected the gubernatorial candidate who symbolized the segregationist views of the old South."[61]

After winning the general election, Busbee addressed the biracial Hungry Club, an Atlanta-based group which works toward racial harmony, and told the group that "the atmosphere which surrounded the political process in Georgia this year simply did not permit any political profit from catering to racial fears."[62] He said he did not think any person or group deserved credit for the absence of racial politics. Instead, he described it as "simply a quiet happening in our history which probably deserves little notice, but which I think represents a step forward in which every Georgian can take pride."[63]

During the Busbee administration the Board of Regents modified and developed the Special Desegregation Plan which it had originally adopted in 1974. New degree programs were added at the three predominantly black schools. However, neither blacks nor whites were particularly pleased when the Department of Health and Human Services approved a plan merging predominantly black Albany State College with largely white Albany Junior College and providing for the sharing of educational programs by black Fort Valley State College and Savannah State College with nearby white institutions. Although black leaders feared the loss of the black colleges, the plan was implemented.[64] Minority enrollment in the university system increased from 13 percent to 17 percent. In 1979 Governor Busbee recommended, as part of the desegregation plan, the Regents Opportunity Grant Program, which consisted of one hundred grants of $5,000 to assist minority students in professional and graduate programs.[65]

The governor precluded action by the Equal Employment Opportunity Commission against the State Merit System when he issued an executive order in 1976. The order required agencies to develop plans for increasing black employment. Two years later the members of the legislative black caucus told the governor they were very dissatisfied with his commitment to minority hiring in state agencies. Busbee responded by describing a bill he had drafted to encourage the hiring of blacks which contained civil penalties for state officials who practiced discrimination in hiring and promoting blacks.[66] When he signed the Fair Employment Practices Act, he emphasized cooperation among all groups: "Improvements won't come through threats, coercion, unruly demonstrations or through nuisance court actions, but they will come through the type of working relationship already established and because our people want to do what is right."[67] The Office of Fair Employment Practices, established as a separate state agency, was to facilitate fair employment practices throughout the state and to receive, investigate, and conciliate complaints of employment discrimination in state government, not in private businesses or in local government. Although the first director of the agency was very controversial, it continued to function under the supervision of a nine-member advisory board.[68] The state also established an Office of Minority Business Enterprise, which would help minority businesses obtain contracts to provide goods and services to state agencies.[69]

These advances on the part of the Busbee administration were not announced with any fanfare; they were pressed for and expected by minority groups and there was not any great resistance from opponents. Race politics in Georgia had entered a different era. Busbee had openly appealed to blacks for support in his election campaign and yet did not lose the support of white conservatives. He campaigned for and implemented equal opportunity and affirmative action programs. The pace of the gains was not swift, and black legislators and groups often pressured the governor. However, George Busbee recognized the black political program as a legitimate part of the overall political agenda. At times he met their demands; in some situations he did not.

Busbee's tenure in office is the portrait of a chief executive who set an agenda, tackled problems, realized limitations, and worked within them. Economic and budgetary difficulties were a constant. Some of the restrictions, such as two election-year campaign promises not to raise taxes, were self-imposed; others, including federal regulations and state and federal court decisions, were not. Governor Busbee was a realist who achieved his goals incrementally. Leadership often meant working out compromises and mediating and minimizing political conflict to make partial gains. His political agenda had to be adjusted and reconciled with other demands. The education program was delayed, but statewide kindergarten did become a reality. Not every phrase in the new constitution was one he would have authored, but constitutional revision was achieved. Busbee realized that decisions to break roadblocks by making some concessions did not mean an abrogation of authority; in fact, they often gave a chief executive more political clout in the next battle.

The separation of the executive and legislative branches continued in Georgia. Although there were differences between the legislature and the governor, hostility was minimized and a pattern of respectful accommodation and cooperation developed. Busbee attacked problems. There was no doubt he knew state government, the scope and the nature of the policies and the difficulties before he made a decision. Although much of his time was spent as a problem solver, he did present a vision for Georgia as an economically progressive state whose government's primary role was to provide services efficiently and raise the quality of life of its citizens. As Georgia became more urbanized and more industrialized, it was to become a leader in the Southeast. Governor Busbee aggressively marketed the state. Educational improvements, economic development, fiscal responsibility, and racial harmony were all elements of an integrated plan for the state's advancement. Busbee was firm about the partnership role of the states in the nation, and he played a prominent role among the nation's governors. In a time when the media had become so important to shaping political leadership and popularity, George Busbee was not a media star. His leadership style was low-keyed, often operating behind closed doors, but decisive. Yet the public opinion polls consistently revealed that his governorship was rated very highly by Georgians.[70]

Building a
New Economic
Order

GEORGE D. BUSBEE

When I became governor in 1975, Georgia was a state in transition. We were becoming more urbanized. Our people were getting older and our households were decreasing in size. As a percentage of the national average, we had almost closed the gap on the median number of school years completed, and our workers were steadily improving their per capita income.

While these social, educational, and economic changes were revolutionizing our life-styles, our population growth was taking off like a rocket, creating further demands to be met by government. All told, 700,000 new people would come during my administration, and the number of new jobs would grow at an even faster rate than our population—a 60 percent faster rate, in fact, over the next eight years.

We would be faced in the coming years with the highest inflation rates in modern times, averaging in double figures through all of the mid-years of my two terms. Also, the changing federal-state relationship, as a result of "New Federalism" and federal budget-cutting policies, would force us to reevaluate entire programs and many of our spending habits. All these issues had to be dealt with, in addition to trying to implement policies that allowed us to continue catching-up to the national average in so many areas in which we had trailed for decades.

In responding to these and other problems, a lot of changes were made in Georgia's state government between January 1975 and January 1983. A few new programs were necessary, the roles within some agencies were changed, some directions were shifted, and some programs were abolished or reduced in scope. But mostly we tried to improve the programs in place to make them more efficient and responsive to the citizens they serve.

I feel that, where possible, gradual change is much better for program recipients than sudden, dramatic changes that confuse everyone. We methodically went about our objectives, removing problems one by one as best we could. I guess you could say that the key word in describing my administration would be "methodical." And despite the fact that my administration started with the worst recession in four decades and ended with another recession underway, I believe the record reveals that we met with some measure of success.

I said at the outset that I would stress two extremely high priorities during my time in office—the first being public education. Public education—elementary schools, middle schools, high schools, and vocational-technical schools, as well as colleges and universities—is the largest enterprise in the state of Georgia. It involves every citizen at one time or another, and approximately one in every four individuals in the state is now either a student or an employee of this massive undertaking. Over one-half of every state and local tax dollar is used to finance public education. The quality of life for the state as a whole and for almost every citizen individually is dependent, in a large measure, on the quality and productivity of this enterprise.

In 1975, the state did not provide any funds for kindergarten. Today every school in Georgia is provided state funds for a kindergarten program. At that time less than 25 percent of Georgia high schools had a vocational education program. We were able to increase the number of comprehensive high schools from 89 to 193, or 49 percent of all high schools, with more planned for the future. More importantly, 75 percent of all students in 1982 attended comprehensive high schools which provided vocational education training as well as college preparation courses.

When I began my tenure, there was grave concern that Georgia was losing many of its best university and college professors because of low salaries. During the next eight years we were able to increase faculty salaries by 84 percent, giving Georgia a rank above the Southern college average. We worked to establish equality of opportunity, to increase student growth and achievement, to improve staff and curriculum, and to provide a more acceptable physical climate for learning. We strove to increase student aid, to provide medical education improvements, and to ensure that Georgia institutions received the maximum in research funds. Of course, no amount of improvement is ever enough, but I feel that we did make great strides in the field of education, and I am immeasurably proud of my part in establishing the kindergarten program.

The other priority that I established—second only to education—was economic development, and I can say to you without a shadow of modesty that my eight-year administration was a period of unprecedented growth in Georgia. I say this without modesty because I sincerely believe that this impressive growth was the result of a lot of hard work by a group of dedicated people who shared my vision that Georgia could become a leader in attracting international business.

Our goal was jobs for Georgians, and we pursued this objective in two ways—first, by working to attract new top-quality companies requiring highly skilled workers rather than the old traditional, nonskilled industries; and second, by arranging for a dispersal of industry throughout the state, in small as well as large communities.

Working through the Department of Industry and Trade, we achieved our growth objectives by creating and maintaining what is best termed as a "favorable business climate," one in which a prospective industry knows it is welcome and is assisted by a partnership of business and government working hand in hand. Some of our earliest efforts to improve our business climate were in support of freeport legislation to exempt certain manufacturing inventory from taxation. Freeport was not enacted on a statewide basis but was, instead, made an option in individual cities and counties. By the end of the administration, over one-third of our counties had enacted some form of freeport legislation.

We knew that the most precious of all our resources was the 2.2 million people who made up the work force. To provide workers with quality training, we vigorously supported the Office of Vocational Education's "Quick Start" program, an innovative plan which enabled the state to assist new industries with training programs geared to their individual needs.

We also made a commitment to a clean, healthy environment. The Georgia Environmental Protection Division is the agency invested with the authority not only to issue most federal and state environmental permits for industry but also to ensure that we are well protected in the areas of ground and surface water management, water and air pollution control, and solid waste management. The efforts we made in this area proved conclusively that regulation and development are not incompatible.

We realized that Georgia could not prosper without the proper infrastructure, and we were able—here again, through the dedication and hard work of some enormously talented people—to put this infrastructure in place: the early completion of the interstate highway system years ahead of schedule, particularly that portion which surrounds and crisscrosses the city of Atlanta; a magnificent international airport which much of the time is the busiest in the world; a system of international banks; a grant program whereby communities lacking in essential water and sewer services to attract industry could be assisted in financing such facilities; an expansion in the Georgia port facilities which saw the tonnage handled at the Georgia Ports Authority increase from 2.7 million tons in 1975 to 5.5 million tons in 1982.

Once the infrastructure was in the planning stages, I began my travels. These trips were carefully planned and orchestrated by the Department of Industry and Trade, and I traveled extensively throughout the United States, to Mexico, Central America, twice to Canada, six times to the Far East, and seven times to Europe. I called on scores of companies to express my personal interest in having them come to Georgia and to sing the praises of the state and all we had to offer.

The results of these trips were rather dramatic in that an average of over $1 billion in investment and 18,000 new jobs were attracted to Georgia during each year of my administration. The number of international companies in the state increased from 150 in 1975 to 680 at the end of 1982; the number of international banks rose from zero to 18; and the number of international flights out of the Atlanta Airport went from none to six.

Georgia's per capita income rose from $4,753 to $9,350 over the eight-year period, and the Gross State Product increased more than twofold from $29.6 billion to $68 billion. I'm proud of this.

And there are other areas in which I feel some satisfactory sense of accomplishment. When I took office, Medicaid was an administrative nightmare, with claims being paid on an average of four months after being filed. Providers were overpaid, underpaid, paid for the same services more than once, and paid for services which were not rendered. We were able to straighten out many of the problems and reach a point where providers were paid within an average of 13.4 days from the date the claims were received. A significant number of Georgia counties did not have even one doctor at that time, and many more had fewer doctors than needed. I was able to launch two separate programs to correct this problem, and we actually placed 171 family doctors in rural counties, with more in training for the future.

In 1975 state expenditures for the arts totaled only $178,000. By 1983 we were spending nearly $1.6 million to make the arts more available to

Georgians throughout the entire state, especially to our school children. The state's program to make Georgia a major site for the production of movies for theaters and television was in its infancy. By the end of my administration Georgia had become one of the three leading states in the nation as a site for filming movies.

I feel particularly grateful for the role I was able to play in the area of Georgia's intergovernmental relations. My involvement had four distinct dimensions: (1) protecting and advancing the state's singular interests in federal legislative and administrative decisions; (2) developing a regional coalition to prevent federal discrimination against the Southern or Sunbelt states; (3) mobilizing state officials to secure modifications in federal policies thwarting state economic development efforts, especially in the transportation and international trade areas; and (4) working to unite the states around an agenda of short-term and long-term reforms of the overall structure of federal-state relations.

From the beginning I placed great emphasis on working with the Georgia congressional delegation and with federal agency officials to ensure that Georgia's interests were promoted in federal legislative and administrative decisions—with some notable results. For example, in 1975 we discovered that the Ford administration was about to release $9 billion in previously impounded water pollution control funds, to be distributed under a formula which concentrated funding in a handful of states. After close consultation with the Georgia congressional delegation and the National Governors' Association, we were able to put together a coalition to amend the formula to ensure a more equitable distribution of funds among the states. These Talmadge-Nunn amendments—as they became known nationally—saved Georgia $27 million immediately and untold millions in later years, and provided something of a model for state-congressional cooperation.

In working to protect Georgia's interests in administrative decisions made by federal agencies, for instance, I met with five different secretaries of health and human services to secure regulatory modifications allowing the state more flexibility in administering the costly Medicaid federal-state entitlement program.

I was happy to have the challenge of serving as chairman of the National Governors' Association from August 1980 to August 1981. This gave me the opportunity to increase Georgia's national exposure as a prime supporter of reforms in national policies which are diametrically opposed to the best interests of the states.

I feel great satisfaction in the fact that I was able to be involved in virtually every significant piece of federal trade legislation considered during the last four years of my administration—an involvement which grew out of my position as the first chairman of the Governors' Association's Committee on International Trade and Foreign Relations, a committee which was created at the request of President Carter.

This successful stance on federal-state relations encouraged me to devote a lot of effort to strengthening relations between the state and its local governments and between the federal and local governments. My commitment was to ensure the best possible relationship between state government and the constituent local governments.

And last, but certainly by no means least, I am proud of my contribution to the passage of a new, streamlined constitution for Georgia. The road to this new document was long and often bumpy, involving a special session of the legislature, many heated discussions, much give-and-take, and pressured compromise. But this is what government is all about, and it is a measure of the people involved in this venture that they were able to finalize a document that would well serve all the people of this state.

But let's come now to the song's second verse. I would be remiss if I did not say that, despite the many advances made, there were many problems left for my successor. That is the way of government. As you resolve one problem, another is created to take its place, because we live in a time of fast-paced changes in life-styles. It is not in the nature of our society for governments to be free of problems.

One of the major crises left was in our prison system, and this represents one of my greatest disappointments. Despite the fact that prison overcrowding was the first problem I faced as governor, and despite the fact that we worked on a solution every year, the problem seemed to intensify instead of getting better. Our prison system had about 9,800 inmates when I took office, and its population was close to 16,000 when I left office. It remains one of the thorniest of problems for our state.

Despite tremendous advances in education, we were still not satisfied that the best educational opportunities were being given our children. Of particular concern was the inequity in financing our system of public education. Many problems remained. The cost of medical services continued to be a concern, and I left with the feeling that dramatic changes must occur over the next years to restrict the cost of health care. The loss of federal funds for our state and local governments plagued me, and I knew as I left office that this worry would continue throughout the decade of the eighties.

But through it all, Georgia continued to improve services to its citizens. During the recession of 1981 and 1982 our economy continued to produce state revenue growth in the range of 8 percent. While other states had to raise taxes, reduce state employment, and cut programs drastically, we continued to expand our programs. This is one of the strongest testimonials to the vitality and strength of our economy and the way we operate our state government.

I know for an assured fact that the eight years from 1975 to 1983 were the most pleasurable of my twenty-six years in public life. I hope that my administration served the state well. I think it did. And I pray that Georgia will continue toward the goal of excellence among all states.

Georgia Politics:
Retrospect and Prospect

Georgia Governors
in an Age of Change

NUMAN V. BARTLEY

In a book on Georgia history that appeared fairly recently, I related two stories that seemed to me to illustrate the kinds of political change that have taken place in the state during the past half century. The first of these events occurred in the middle years of the 1930s, a time that would serve as well as any other for dating the beginning of the collapse of the economic and social order that underlay the Georgia political system during the late nineteenth and early twentieth centuries. Although the Great Depression and World War II fundamentally redirected Georgia's development—after 1945 it would have been impossible to turn back—it required several decades for the completion of the process. Following the great social and political upheavals of the 1960s, however, Georgia had by the 1970s completed the transition. Therefore, the second of these two stories took place in the early 1970s.

In 1933 Governor Eugene Talmadge set about to reorganize aspects of Georgia state government. Serving his first term in the statehouse, the new governor asked the General Assembly for legislation strengthening the governor's authority over the Public Service Commission and the State Highway Board. Talmadge had promised in his gubernatorial campaign to lower utility rates, yet the governor had no control over the state's popularly elected regulatory commission. Similarly, the Highway Department disposed of approximately one-half of the state budget, yet its governing board consisted of long-term appointees who were essentially independent from the governor. Relatively high on Talmadge's list was the fulfillment of a campaign promise to lower the cost of automobile license tags to three dollars. The Georgia legislature, many members of which had already clashed with the flamboyant wild man from Sugar Creek during the years he served as state commissioner of agriculture, rejected these and other administration recommendations.

Undeterred, Talmadge waited until the legislature adjourned and then reorganized state government. Under the authority of an obscure early-nineteenth-century state law, Talmadge suspended the collection of license tag fees except for a charge of three dollars. Then the governor called out the National Guard and declared martial law in the state capitol. He dismissed the Public Service Commission and two of the three Highway Board members. When the powerful Highway Board stood its ground and sought injunctions restraining Talmadge, the governor growled a warrant and outmaneuvered his opponents in federal court. Talmadge appointed friends and relatives to both commissions and released the National Guard. Georgia's government had, in a sense, been reorganized.

Four decades later, in the early 1970s, Governor Jimmy Carter set about to reorganize Georgia state government. The newly elected first-term chief executive employed a management consultant firm, created a Reorganization and Management-Improvement Study team, and asked businesses and corporations in Atlanta to contribute personnel. Of the 117 full-time members of the reorganization study group, 65 were Atlanta business and corporation employees, mainly executives, 48 were academicians and other state employees, and 4 were members of the management consultant company. These "experts" produced more than twenty-five hundred pages of recommendations.

To promote legislative acceptance of the plan, the Carter administration organized a public awareness program to sell reorganization to Georgia citizens. The public awareness advisory committee and staff included top media executives, high-level corporation and state employees, an Atlanta Gas Light Company lobbyist, and the Rafshoon Advertising Agency. The public awareness staff worked closely with the Georgia Chamber of Commerce, the state Jaycees, and other uptown groups. The campaign to "sell" reorganization was largely successful, and the reorganization plan survived legislative scrutiny relatively intact.[1]

These two approaches to governmental reorganization suggest the nature of the political transformation in Georgia, as does another example drawn from the administrations of the same two governors. In 1935 the Georgia legislature, once again feuding with Governor Eugene Talmadge, adjourned without passing an appropriations bill, thus depriving the state government of a budget. Talmadge simply ignored the legislature's oversight and ran the state without an authorized budget. This achievement required the heavy-handed replacement of the state comptroller general and the state treasurer, the latter of whom had to be forcibly removed from his position. Governor Talmadge sent the state adjutant general and six other men to the state treasurer's office, where they, in the words of Talmadge's biographer, "lifted him from his chair and carried him out of the capitol to the street." After a lengthy period of conflict and considerable confusion, Talmadge as usual got his way—he did collect taxes and expend public funds without normal budget authorization. Some four decades later, Governor Jimmy Carter faced budgetary problems. He responded by rationalizing and centralizing monetary procedures, introducing the concept of zero-based budgeting, and creating the Office of Planning and Budget to serve as a watchdog agency.[2]

The purpose in retelling these well-known stories is *not* specifically to compare the gubernatorial politics of Gene Talmadge and Jimmy Carter. Talmadge did, however, personify—in an exaggerated form, to be sure—the unstructured and personalized approach to gubernatorial politics common in the first half of the twentieth century, while Carter exemplified the rationalizing and bureaucratizing procedures that have marked recent gubernatorial administrations.

Such changes have not been confined to gubernatorial reorganization and budgets. They have affected electoral politics as well. For example, consider Georgia's response to two gubernatorial succession crises. In December 1946 Gene Talmadge died after being elected but before being inaugurated as governor of Georgia. That event touched off a succession crisis that at various times had three different people claiming to be governor of the state. Herman Talmadge occupied the office of governor at the state capitol (and promptly changed the locks on the doors). Whether because of ambiguities in the state constitution or because of the rather logical proposition that in a personalized and family-oriented political environment the office that Gene Talmadge won but was unable to occupy should properly go to his son, the legislature supported the younger Talmadge, as did the state police and the National Guard. Ellis Arnall, the incumbent governor, refused to surrender his position to Talmadge and, deprived of the governor's office and lacking keys to the new locks, set up his governorship in the halls of the capitol, operating mainly from the information booth. M. E. Thompson, the incoming lieutenant governor, who upon Eugene Talmadge's death had a logical claim to be chief executive, established a government in exile in a downtown Atlanta office. Ultimately the Georgia Supreme Court settled the issue and Thompson became governor, but it is little wonder that national journalists wrote with a touch of amazement of Georgia's banana republic politics and V. O. Key, when he completed his masterful study of Southern politics two years later, titled his Georgia chapter "The Rule of the Rustics." In the mid-1960s Georgia faced another gubernatorial succession crisis. In a hotly contested election, no candidate received a majority of the votes. The Georgia legislature sedately assembled and decorously declared Lester Maddox, who had finished a very close second in the balloting, to be governor of the state.[3]

In a real sense these types of Georgia political war stories better describe the profound changes in Georgia governmental and specifically gubernatorial procedures than does more conventional academic analysis. Nevertheless, only the hastiest glance at statistical evidence would make abundantly clear that the Georgia presided over by Eugene Talmadge was a very different state from the one headed by Governor Harris. When Gene Talmadge reorganized Georgia's government, approximately one-half of Georgia's families lived on farms, and only three of every ten resided in urban communities of 2,500 or more people. Georgia was overwhelmingly a rural and agricultural state. By the time Joe Frank Harris became governor, approximately one-half of all Georgians lived in metropolitan areas and the farm population had shrunk from a million and a half people to less than 200,000, which meant that only 3 percent of Georgia's people were farmers.

Scarlett O'Hara observed in *Gone With the Wind* that she "had never seen a factory, or known anyone who had ever seen a factory." Georgia is now arriving at a point in history when an increasing number of people have never met a farmer and, quite possibly, know no one who has ever met a farmer, a strange state of affairs, given Georgia's agrarian past. Massive economic and demographic upheavals did bring prosperity to the state. Measured in constant 1972 dollars, Georgia's gross state product increased from approximately $8 billion in 1950 to more than $32 billion in 1980. Such changes also made ever greater demands on Georgia state government. In 1940 the state expended approximately $72,000,000; in 1980 state governmental expenditures were approximately $5 billion, and by that time well over 400,000 Georgians were government employees.[4]

Such statistics reflect a truly profound transformation marked by the awesome demographic upheavals that depopulated the countryside and peopled the cities; by a virtual economic revolution that changed the way Georgians earned their living, and indeed the way they conceived of work; by social conflict that among other things pulled down the elaborate edifice of Jim Crow racial segregation; and by political shifts that brought an end to such venerable institutions as disfranchisement, legislative malapportionment, one-party politics, and the county unit system. These traumatic and often socially painful developments structured the public agenda in Georgia and defined the fundamental issues faced by Georgia's governors during the period. Doubtless because of Georgia's gubernatorial leadership—only the most hardened and disreputable cynic would say in spite of Georgia's gubernatorial leadership—Georgia came through this hectic era more constructively than most other states that faced similar problems. The governors who served Georgia during these years can look back to a period of considerable achievement.

Among the most profound political changes that occurred during these decades was a transformation of the public ideology. Following the Civil War, carpetbaggers and Republican congressmen (along with change-oriented native Georgians) sought to reconstruct the state's social system. In turning back that threat, Georgia's leadership absorbed the lesson that the most fundamental purpose of state government was to protect the state from outside intervention. That philosophy hardened over the years, and in the backwash of the Populist Revolt the public ideology came to visualize the central task of Georgia state government to be the maintenance of social stability, most particularly segregation, and the protection of these social conventions from outside intervention. Set in the hard concrete of custom and socioeconomic reality, this ideology established the basic parameters for Georgia's gubernatorial leadership. In the modern period it was challenged and ultimately decimated by the transformation taking place in Georgia, by federal intervention, and most of all by the changing self-perceptions of Georgia's black citizens.

From the collapse of that philosophy gradually emerged a different public ideology that stressed the role of state government in promoting economic growth. In a period of demographic and social upheaval in a poor and underdeveloped state, it is little wonder that a number of Georgia governors sought salvation in new factories, new office parks, and new shopping malls. In a land that had long been severely burdened not so much by unemployment as by massive underemployment, it is hardly surprising that the public ideology came to be perceived in terms of economic growth.[5] It is from this perspective of competing ideologies that I would like very briefly and in very general terms to examine some aspects of this transformation.

The New Deal and World War II were of course crucial episodes in the creation of modern Georgia, and in that regard the administrations of E. D. Rivers, who brought the Little New Deal to Georgia, and Ellis Arnall, who served through the mid-1940s, marked an important transition period in the state's political history. During the Arnall years Georgia created a state merit system, which was an important factor in the gradual shift from personalized to bureaucratized government procedures. In 1943 came the formation of the Agricultural and Industrial Development Board, which was the first time Georgia had established an agency specifically designed to attract new industry to the state. It was of course the forerunner of today's Department of Industry and Trade. Both Rivers and Arnall were leaders in the Southern attack on discriminatory freight rates, a railroad pricing system that discouraged Southern manufacturing. Given the declining role railroads played in the industrial life of the nation, Georgia's victory in the freight-rate controversy may have been to a considerable degree symbolic; nevertheless, the fight was significant if only as a symbol of the growing refusal of Georgia's leadership to accept second-class colonial dependency status in the national economy. These and other developments suggested important new trends in the state's political outlook.

During the 1950s and 1960s social and political practices in Georgia came under sustained attack from the federal government and increasingly from an aroused black citizenry at home. This frontal assault on a declining but still potent public ideology put enormous pressure on a series of gubernatorial administrations. Georgia was a leader in the Southwide massive resistance to desegregation, a movement that on occasion went to some extremes. At one point die-hard racial segregationists attempted to convince Governor Marvin Griffin that he should deliberately disobey federal court orders and thereby force the federal government either to surrender on the issue or to imprison the governor of a sovereign state, an act that presumably would arouse concern for states' rights throughout the nation. Griffin responded with the rather thoughtful observation: "Bein' in jail kind of crimps a governor's style."6 Griffin stayed out of jail and Georgia ultimately desegregated.

Ernest Vandiver was governor when Georgia actually experienced its first school desegregation, and, indeed, Vandiver was governor when the sit-in movement began, when the county unit system and legislative malapportionment came under fatal attack, and when the Voter Education Project launched a major effort to register black voters in the state. Soon after Vandiver left office Barry Goldwater became the first Republican presidential candidate to carry Georgia. While dealing with these epic developments, the Vandiver administration also found time to promote a post–high school vocational-technical system, a municipal industrial revenue bond program, and other initiatives designed to encourage industrial growth.

Governor Carl E. Sanders, who succeeded Vandiver, vigorously articulated the emerging consensus. In his inaugural address in January 1963, Sanders stated: "This is a new Georgia. This is a new day. This is a new era. A Georgia on the threshold of new greatness."7 Governors promoted the "new era" of economic progress with a variety of "modernizing" reforms, perhaps most significantly in the field of education. The Minimum Foundation Program sponsored by Herman Talmadge's administration revolutionized popular education by creating, really for the first time in the state's history, a true system of public education; the educational reforms of Governor Sanders's administration launched the university system on a quest for national excellence; and, most recently, the Harris administration has initiated a promising Quality Basic Education Program.

As such examples suggest, Georgia's governors were in the main forceful leaders who sponsored broad legislative programs. In this context, Governor Lester Maddox was perhaps something of an exception. I do not for a moment agree with the prominent Atlanta journalist who stated: "Lester Maddox has successfully demonstrated that Georgia does not need a governor." But it is true that Governor Maddox did not push a general legislative program, on the rather sensible grounds that "we've got more laws now than we know what to do with." Governor Maddox took evident pride in his "open" administration, and his "Little People's Days" at the state capitol proved popular. Probably more than any other chief executive in Georgia's history, Maddox evidenced genuine concern for the state's prison population. At the same time Maddox helped to keep racial controversy alive by condemning federal school desegregation efforts as "un-American, un-Godly and even criminal."[8]

Governor Jimmy Carter was, it seems to me, Georgia's first modern governor. In a memorable inaugural address Carter stated, "I say to you quite frankly that the time for racial discrimination is over. Our people have already made this major and difficult decision." Carter thus publicly denounced an older and an increasingly discredited public ideology and thereafter devoted his administration to promoting economic growth, reorganizing state government, and other similar programs. By the end of Carter's gubernatorial tenure, incoming Governor George Busbee could observe: "The politics of race has gone with the wind."[9]

During the years of the Busbee administration, the South that in the E. D. Rivers era had been correctly labeled "the nation's number one economic problem" was promoted to the ranks of Southern California and Las Vegas as a part of the Sunbelt. The "Southern way of life," with its overtones of racial segregation, elitism, and provincialism, now became the "Southern style of life," with its emphasis on graceful living, good manners, and year-round barbecue cookouts. A public ideology stressing social stability had fully given way to a public ideology stressing economic progress, and Governor Busbee, in one journalist's words, was "a frequent international traveler in quest of new industry."[10]

If a generalization can be drawn from such a brief and tentative overview of gubernatorial leadership in modern Georgia, it might be the importance of periodically reexamining conventional wisdom. Following the sharp social and political conflict of the 1960s, Georgians reached an apparent consensus on the virtues of material progress and the assumption that economic growth would ameliorate the state's social problems. To some extent developments have vindicated this commitment to a growth ethos. At the same time, the Georgia economic success story has been an uneven one. Metropolitan and most especially Atlanta-area suburban counties have expanded to the point that one wonders just how much yet another office park or shopping center in Cobb County would contribute to the general welfare. In much of the rest of the state (including inner-city metropolitan areas) economic opportunities remain relatively limited. Long ago Georgia deemphasized its search for just any factory to focus on attracting high-wage, high-technology enterprises. More recently, if I understand it correctly, the Harris administration is proposing to shift from economic progress per se to state promotion of economic growth in the poorer and less developed parts of the state. This concern for balanced economic progress promises to be an important modification of the prevailing public philosophy and perhaps a step toward a general policy of managed economic growth.

But however one perceives current trends, the gubernatorial administrations of modern Georgia can in considerable measure be defined by their responses to the sweeping economic, social, and political transformations taking place in the state. Some governors appear to have been suspicious of these developments and endeavored to halt or impede them. Other governors were in general sympathy with the main thrust of change and sought to encourage or promote it. At any rate, Georgia seems to have survived a difficult era, and the state's citizens are more prosperous than ever before. Finding methods to manage further economic expansion and its accompanying social changes on behalf of the general welfare may be a central task for Georgia's next generation of governors.

Visions for a
Better Georgia

JOE FRANK HARRIS

It is truly an honor to have been invited to keynote this first Abraham Baldwin Symposium on History and Government. I want to commend the faculty members at Abraham Baldwin Agricultural College for conceptualizing this conference, and I look forward to other seminars in the future which will no doubt increase the knowledge and understanding of our state's political history for the benefit of all Georgians. The subject of the symposium, "Georgia Governors in an Age of Change: From Ellis Arnall to George Busbee," is particularly apropos because it was during this period that Georgia evolved from a bastion of Southern traditionalism to the Empire State of the South it is today.

The forty years covered by the administrations of Governors Arnall, Thompson, Herman Talmadge, Griffin, Vandiver, Sanders, Maddox, Carter, and Busbee were perhaps the most critical in our state's history since the Civil War, and each in his own way contributed to a pattern of growth and development that has Georgia pacing the Southeast today. It was a building process, a balancing process, and each of these governors is to be recognized and commended for his efforts.

The 1940s marked the beginning of the end of the plantation agricultural economy in Georgia as we began to evolve into a multifaceted state with a diversified economic base. With this transformation has come Georgia's growth from a lackluster regional distribution center to a respectable nationwide commercial hub to the burgeoning young international state it is today. Each of the administrations played an important role in this metamorphosis, and I would like to begin by taking a closer look at Georgia's development over the last forty-odd years.

It was in the early 1940s that President Franklin Roosevelt labeled the South the nation's number one economic problem. And it was in the early 1940s that Governor Ellis Arnall and others viewed this epithet in an entirely different light. To the Georgia progressives of the 1940s, Georgia was not the nation's number one economic problem but the nation's number one economic opportunity—and so began a new impetus and direction in the state's development.

Each of these governors had distinct priorities and agendas of his own—personal dreams and visions of a "certain" Georgia, a greater Georgia—and it has been the sum of these dreams, visions, and accomplishments that has formed Georgia's solid foundation for the future. It is clear that the common thread among these nine administrations, and the key to Georgia's growth and prosperity, has been and will continue to be development of the state's public school system. "Education," Ellis Arnall said, "is the hope of the future. It is the salvation of our people. It is the cure for ignorance, poverty, prejudice, hatred, and demagoguery."

It was Governor George Gilmer, in 1837, who first announced plans to correct the defects in public education, but it was more than a century later, in 1946, that a special committee charged with studying the state's educational needs began to take a comprehensive look at the public schools. Initiated in the Arnall years, the Georgia Minimum Foundation Program for Education was finally approved during Herman Talmadge's administration. The major incentive for passing the 1949 MFPE Act was equalizing educational opportunities among the school systems of the state—an integral concept in the Quality Basic Education Program of my administration.

A decade later Carl Sanders commissioned a new group to evaluate Georgia's public educational system. This committee wrote: "Georgia's present and prospective educational needs grow out of the rapidly changing demands of the space age, rather than out of past negligence." The MFPE Act of 1949 had been a grand beginning, but the times dictated that it be radically improved—so was born the MFPE Act of 1964 during the Sanders years.

Ten years later Jimmy Carter perceived a need for another restructuring of the public school system, and oversaw passage of the Adequate Plan for Education. Once again, Georgia's growth and development spawned education reform.

With the arrival of the technological advances of the eighties came a need for further reform, and thus was born the Quality Basic Education Program passed by the General Assembly in 1985. So we evolved from the need for a *minimum* plan for education to the need for an *adequate* plan to the need for a *quality* plan with a goal of excellence. As Georgia progressed, so did the demand for a stronger, more competitive public school system, and Georgia's leadership responded.

These three programs represent milestones in the development of the state's educational system. Education is the common thread that runs throughout Georgia's executive leadership in recent history. Governor Griffin expanded the state's teacher work force; Governor Vandiver saw the need to expand the state's vocational-technical training program; Governor Maddox awarded teachers substantial increases in salary; and

Governor Busbee, an early advocate of the Minimum Foundation Program, continued the progressive move forward. In his inaugural address Busbee said, "Every child in Georgia must have the opportunity for the fullest development of his mind and skills no matter how poor his family, how great his handicap or where he lives. We can make a major movement forward in education in this administration and this we must."

The interdependence of education and economic development is evident as educational reform throughout the last forty years has progressed hand in hand with the state's economic growth and development. Out of necessity, Georgia has strived to keep its educational system a step ahead of its economic growth because education itself cannot relate only to the present, but must always be looking down the road to the future. We can no longer merely respond to the situation of the present. We must search for solutions to the challenges of the future.

While education serves as the linchpin between Georgia's past and present, there are other factors over the last four decades which have contributed to the state's rise to the top in the Southeast. For the sake of simplicity, I have traced the evolution of Georgia's public educational development. The same transformation has taken place in our economic system, but the important factor to remember is that all of the changes that have taken place are the result of one governor building upon a foundation laid by his predecessors. It has been a team effort, a gradual movement forward—the sum of many years of successive accomplishments.

Prior to the Arnall years, the principal purpose of state government in Georgia was the protection and promotion of white supremacy and social stability—maintenance of the status quo. Since that time, Georgia gradually has evolved into a state where the protection and promotion of economic and industrial progress has become the agenda of the day.

It was in 1971 that Jimmy Carter said in his inaugural address that "the time for racial discrimination is over." Three years later Governor Carter hung the portraits of Martin Luther King, Jr., Lucy Laney, and Bishop Henry McNeal Turner in the state capitol. The time for race to be an issue in Georgia politics was over, and Georgia had rid itself of the last barrier to becoming a world-class state. The stumbling blocks to educational, economic, and social progress in Georgia were falling.

I can look back and point to several other building blocks to Georgia's economic and social foundation: Ellis Arnall's trust-busting of the railroads; Melvin Thompson's purchase of Jekyll Island; Herman Talmadge's reorganization of the State Highway Department; Marvin Griffin's construction of dock facilities at Brunswick and Bainbridge;

Ernest Vandiver's advances in care for the mentally ill; Carl Sanders's community development programs; Lester Maddox's commitment to openness in state government; Jimmy Carter's reorganization of state agencies; and George Busbee's international trade promotion, just to name a few.

Georgia's transformation from a backward, stagnant state to the dynamic, progressive state it is today was a gradual evolution steered by our state's governors during this "age of change." And that brings us to where we are today.

When I was elected the seventy-eighth governor of our great state, I inherited a solid foundation that was already in place, a steady pattern of growth and a legacy of outstanding leadership in the governor's office. My objective was to build on this strong foundation and make the state of Georgia a better place to live, work, and raise children.

To meet these challenges, I recognized two areas in which I would place priority emphasis—two important areas where we could set the course for the future of our state. Education and economic development are the cornerstones of my administration, and I am proud to report to you that Georgia is taking bold steps forward under these initiatives, continuing the efforts undertaken over the past forty years.

I had my objectives clearly identified, and I had to assemble the best organization to get where we wanted to go. As a businessman, I realized that to meet the challenges our state was facing in our ever-changing, business-oriented world, state government would have to be run more like a business. Today efficiency is not only important, it is essential to the economic, social, and educational welfare of our state.

Education and economic development are closely related, married to each other, if you will, in three important ways: a quality education system improves the training of your work force, which greatly enhances your economic development; a quality education system is a major attraction to outside investors; and you cannot fund a quality education system without substantial revenues, revenues which are generated by a sound business climate and progressive economic development.

Former President Lyndon Johnson once said, "We must open the doors of opportunity, but we must also equip our children to walk through those doors."

I have taken a businesslike, coordinated approach to state government. We have stressed the team concept, and it is a concept that is growing stronger each day. Through a strategy of building partnerships between state agencies—partnerships between state government and local governments and partnerships between state government and an enthusiastic private sector—a new spirit of cooperation and sense of unity has emerged all across our state.

I stand before you today to tell you every major success of my administration has resulted because of what I like to call our team concept. I can in no way overstate this fact. Success cannot be achieved by one man alone; he must have the help of others working together. I am certain the former governors here will attest to that fact.

The subject of this symposium—Georgia's governors over the last four decades—also speaks of teamwork. As a team, these governors have carried, and then passed, the torch leading the way—a guiding light for the future of Georgia.

As a candidate for governor in June of 1982, I stood in the rotunda of the state capitol and announced my intention—if elected—to provide a quality education for every child in Georgia. Not many people listened that day, but now, three and a half years later, that dream is fast becoming a reality. Demonstrating my commitment to the program, I broke with tradition and delivered a special education address to the General Assembly. I felt education was that important to the future of our state.

The Quality Basic Education Act, the most comprehensive, all-inclusive education reform to date, passed the General Assembly without a single negative vote—unprecedented for such a major piece of legislation. (You know, you can't even have a motion for adjournment in the General Assembly without someone voting against it!) But, seriously, I believe QBE passed without a dissenting vote for two reasons: first, the comprehensiveness of the QBE Program, and second, the need—which all Georgians had begun to recognize—to dramatically improve public education in our state.

There is a general theme woven throughout the QBE Program, and it is a direct reflection on my administration, a trend in society and a trend in the public education reform movement being led by Georgia and some of the other Southern states. It is a concept borrowed from business: accountability. We have taken a businesslike approach to education, holding everyone associated with the educational process accountable for achieving the desired result: a quality basic education. Accountability is a trend we are seeing more of in all walks of life. Elected officials, in particular, are being held more accountable for their actions, and this is healthy. Accountability is healthy for education and society as a whole. It is a trend which I see growing ever stronger in the future. The times are demanding it.

Because of our strong economy, we've been able to begin implementation of Quality Basic Education without a tax increase. In my first three budgets I have recommended—and the General Assembly has appropriated—over $1 billion in new money for education. As long as I am governor I intend for this financial support for education to continue. Education has changed and improved with the times, and it must continue to change and improve to carry our state into the next century.

We have also been aggressive in our approach to economic development. This approach has been in large part an extension of my common-sense ideals for state government. We have recognized what we have to offer, and enhanced these strengths to attract new businesses and expand existing ones. It has been effective. Georgia has a great deal to offer, and we have mounted a successful effort to publicize our assets. We have a probusiness attitude, an excellent quality of life, and an educated, dedicated work force.

Our capital city, Atlanta, has emerged as the transportation, commercial, and financial center of the Southeast and, with its central location, has come by much of its economic development naturally. However, the nonmetro areas of Georgia have not been ignored, and my administration is committed to stimulating economic growth in all parts of the state. An impressive economic development highway system is presently under construction which will provide a more direct link between the cities and towns of Georgia, and should be a great boon to economic development. Our education program will serve the needs of every child in the state, no matter where he or she lives, and through a state/local partnership it will equalize funding for education all across Georgia.

Furthermore, our State Department of Community Affairs is directing numerous programs toward rural Georgia. They have been working with local leaders and stressing the team concept, and it is being effective.

The development of Georgia's economy has been an evolution—an evolution of the state's leadership, the state's education and transportation systems, the state's business climate, and the state's people. It has been an evolution which has helped to create new jobs, new and expanded investment, and unprecedented revenue growth.

I take particular pride in the internationalization of Georgia's economy. This is a trend that was begun by Governors Carter and Busbee and a trend that my administration has continued. Shortly before this conference, I led an economic mission to the Far East, my third to that region and my sixth foreign mission since I've been governor. We officially opened a Georgia Trade Office in Seoul, Korea, in order to build on a budding economic relationship with that nation. I also visited Japan, where we relocated our Tokyo office in the most active business district in that city.

A decade ago there were 150 foreign companies with facilities in

Georgia. By the end of this year we hope to have over a thousand, which is solid evidence of Georgia's stature in the international marketplace. The times have dictated the extension of Georgia's borders, and I am enjoying opening our doors even further. I am committed to helping this globalization continue, because foreign investment has certainly played a vital role in our state's economic health.

We've also fully replenished our revenue shortfall reserve—the state's rainy-day fund. The shortfall reserve is a vital element in preparing for the future of Georgia.

I inherited a strong foundation and intend to leave a stronger foundation for my successor—one which he or she can build upon, one that allows for flexibility and diversity. The key to Georgia's success has been the ability to change with the times. When the times dictated that we expand from the growing fields to the factories, we did. When the times dictated that we move into the information and service industries, we did. When the times dictated that we join the technological revolution, we did. We have the ability and capacity to move into any direction we deem necessary, and for this reason Georgia will continue to lead the Southeast.

Like the previous nine governors Georgia has had over the past forty years, I am continuing to look forward and give the state an agenda for the future. We have evolved from an agrarian society to a highly technological and service-oriented society, and this has been necessary for us to establish and maintain a competitive place in the world's economy.

We have involved the private sector, on a partnership basis, in our efforts and this has produced economic prosperity unprecedented in our state's history. These are the sorts of changes that futures are built upon and this is the approach that the Harris administration takes—one that will lead, one that will produce results . . . results that will set the course for the future of Georgia and that will spawn change for a new age.

APPENDIX

Georgia Association of Historians
Survey of Georgia Governors, May 1985

I. GENERAL EVALUATION

A. *On a scale of 1 to 8 (1 being the most positive), please rank the following Georgia governors based on your percent of their effectiveness in the gubernatorial office.*

Ellis G. Arnall	1.92	(N = 48)
Carl E. Sanders	2.79	(N = 48)
George D. Busbee	2.80	(N = 50)
Jimmy Carter	3.40	(N = 50)
Herman E. Talmadge	3.74	(N = 46)
Lester G. Maddox	4.40	(N = 50)
S. Ernest Vandiver	4.61	(N = 46)
S. Marvin Griffin	5.43	(N = 46)

B. *Assuming they were eligible to run for a second term in office at the end of their first term, which of the following governors do you believe could have won reelection?*

Herman E. Talmadge	96% Positive	(N = 48)
Carl E. Sanders	67% Positive	(N = 48)
Ellis G. Arnall	64% Positive	(N = 44)
Lester G. Maddox	50% Positive	(N = 48)
S. Marvin Griffin	50% Positive	(N = 44)
Jimmy Carter	50% Positive	(N = 44)
S. Ernest Vandiver	43% Positive	(N = 42)
George D. Busbee (not listed—won reelection)		

C. *On a scale of 1 to 5 (1 being the most positive), rank the degree to which each of the governors listed below had a positive national reputation.*

Ellis G. Arnall	1.75	(N = 48)
Jimmy Carter	1.76	(N = 49)
Carl E. Sanders	2.00	(N = 50)
George D. Busbee	2.24	(N = 50)
S. Ernest Vandiver	3.29	(N = 49)
Herman E. Talmadge	4.00	(N = 49)

S. Marvin Griffin	4.63	(N = 49)
Lester G. Maddox	4.67	(N = 49)

D. *If effective political leadership, among other things, can be defined as the ability to get others to do that which they do not necessarily want to do, how would you rate the following Georgia governors with regard to their political leadership abilities on a scale of 1 to 5 (1 represents the most effective political leadership)?*

Ellis G. Arnall	1.96	(N = 45)
George D. Busbee	2.21	(N = 50)
Jimmy Carter	2.29	(N = 49)
Carl E. Sanders	2.29	(N = 46)
Herman E. Talmadge	2.30	(N = 46)
S. Ernest Vandiver	2.86	(N = 45)
S. Marvin Griffin	3.14	(N = 43)
Lester G. Maddox	3.50	(N = 48)

II. CHARACTERIZING RECENT GEORGIA GOVERNORS

On a scale of 1 to 5 (1 being the most positive), evaluate the extent to which each of the governors identified below exhibited the trait identified.

A. *Fiscal Conservative*

George D. Busbee	2.04	(N = 50)
S. Ernest Vandiver	2.22	(N = 47)
Jimmy Carter	2.28	(N = 50)
Lester G. Maddox	2.36	(N = 50)
Herman E. Talmadge	2.36	(N = 45)
S. Marvin Griffin	2.39	(N = 47)
Carl E. Sanders	2.42	(N = 47)
Ellis G. Arnall	2.59	(N = 45)

B. *Social Liberal*

Ellis G. Arnall	1.78	(N = 47)
Jimmy Carter	1.92	(N = 50)
Carl E. Sanders	2.60	(N = 50)
George D. Busbee	2.76	(N = 50)
S. Ernest Vandiver	3.78	(N = 47)
Lester G. Maddox	4.48	(N = 50)
Herman E. Talmadge	4.50	(N = 44)
S. Marvin Griffin	4.70	(N = 46)

C. *Racial Liberal*

Jimmy Carter	1.44	(N = 50)
George D. Busbee	2.44	(N = 50)
Carl E. Sanders	2.58	(N = 49)

Ellis G. Arnall	2.67	(N = 49)
S. Ernest Vandiver	3.87	(N = 46)
Lester G. Maddox	4.71	(N = 49)
Herman E. Talmadge	4.83	(N = 47)
S. Marvin Griffin	4.91	(N = 49)

E.   *Anti-intellectual*

S. Marvin Griffin	1.91	(N = 45)
Lester G. Maddox	2.04	(N = 47)
Herman E. Talmadge	2.23	(N = 46)
S. Ernest Vandiver	2.48	(N = 42)
George D. Busbee	3.23	(N = 48)
Carl E. Sanders	3.48	(N = 47)
Jimmy Carter	3.83	(N = 48)
Ellis G. Arnall	3.83	(N = 46)

III. COMMUNICATION AND INTERPERSONAL SKILLS

On a scale of 1 to 5 (1 being the most positive), please rank the Georgia governors listed below on the following items:

A.   *Ability to communicate positions on issues effectively to the public*

Herman E. Talmadge	1.87	(N = 45)
Ellis G. Arnall	2.04	(N = 46)
George D. Busbee	2.20	(N = 50)
Carl E. Sanders	2.32	(N = 50)
Lester G. Maddox	2.48	(N = 50)
S. Marvin Griffin	2.71	(N = 47)
Jimmy Carter	2.72	(N = 50)
S. Ernest Vandiver	3.09	(N = 48)

B.   *Ability to work effectively with legislative leaders*

George D. Busbee	1.64	(N = 50)
Herman E. Talmadge	1.74	(N = 47)
Ellis G. Arnall	2.26	(N = 46)
Carl E. Sanders	2.32	(N = 50)
S. Ernest Vandiver	2.59	(N = 44)
S. Marvin Griffin	2.64	(N = 45)
Jimmy Carter	2.76	(N = 50)
Lester C. Maddox	3.24	(N = 50)

C.   *Ability to command the respect of state government bureaucrats and secure their compliance with executive decisions*

George D. Busbee	1.90	(N = 42)
Herman E. Talmadge	1.94	(N = 37)
Ellis G. Arnall	2.22	(N = 37)

Carl E. Sanders   2.45   (N = 40)
S. Ernest Vandiver   2.67   (N = 37)
S. Marvin Griffin   2.78   (N = 37)
Jimmy Carter   2.90   (N = 42)
Lester G. Maddox   3.65   (N = 40)

D. *Relationship with the press*
Ellis G. Arnall   1.68   (N = 45)
George D. Busbee   1.83   (N = 48)
Carl E. Sanders   1.87   (N = 45)
Jimmy Carter   2.39   (N = 45)
S. Ernest Vandiver   2.95   (N = 43)
Herman E. Talmadge   3.09   (N = 44)
S. Marvin Griffin   3.76   (N = 42)
Lester G. Maddox   4.08   (N = 48)

E. *Ability to secure special interest support of program (as opposed to special interest hostility)*
George D. Busbee   1.89   (N = 39)
Herman E. Talmadge   1.94   (N = 35)
Carl E. Sanders   2.35   (N = 35)
Ellis G. Arnall   2.35   (N = 35)
Jimmy Carter   2.53   (N = 37)
S. Ernest Vandiver   3.06   (N = 32)
S. Marvin Griffin   3.13   (N = 32)
Lester G. Maddox   3.82   (N = 35)

F. *Overall communication and interpersonal skills (average of items A–E)*
George D. Busbee   1.83
Ellis G. Arnall   2.17
Herman E. Talmadge   2.21
Carl E. Sanders   2.24
Jimmy Carter   2.63
S. Ernest Vandiver   2.91
S. Marvin Griffin   3.06
Lester G. Maddox   3.55

IV. POLICY ISSUES

On a scale of 1 to 5 (1 being the most positive), please rank the Georgia governors listed below on the following items:

A. *To what extent do you feel each governor recognized and confronted the most historically significant issues of his term(s)?*
Ellis G. Arnall   1.71   (N = 48)
Jimmy Carter   1.96   (N = 48)

Carl E. Sanders	2.25	(N = 48)
George D. Busbee	2.50	(N = 48)
S. Ernest Vandiver	3.23	(N = 44)
Herman E. Talmadge	3.48	(N = 47)
Lester G. Maddox	3.67	(N = 48)
S. Marvin Griffin	4.09	(N = 47)

B. *How effective was each governor in addressing the major issues of his term in office?*

Ellis G. Arnall	1.70	(N = 47)
George D. Busbee	2.29	(N = 48)
Jimmy Carter	2.33	(N = 48)
Carl E. Sanders	2.39	(N = 47)
Herman E. Talmadge	3.00	(N = 44)
Lester G. Maddox	3.22	(N = 45)
S. Ernest Vandiver	3.23	(N = 44)
S. Marvin Griffin	3.50	(N = 44)

C. *How would you rate the quality of each governor's administrative appointees?*

Jimmy Carter	2.12	(N = 35)
Ellis G. Arnall	2.13	(N = 30)
George D. Busbee	2.18	(N = 35)
Carl E. Sanders	2.35	(N = 35)
Herman E. Talmadge	3.20	(N = 30)
S. Ernest Vandiver	3.20	(N = 30)
Lester G. Maddox	3.41	(N = 35)
S. Marvin Griffin	4.40	(N = 30)

D. *How would you rate the quality of each governor's judicial appointments?*

Jimmy Carter	1.67	(N = 24)
George D. Busbee	2.00	(N = 24)
Ellis G. Arnall	2.27	(N = 23)
Carl E. Sanders	2.73	(N = 23)
S. Ernest Vandiver	3.10	(N = 20)
Herman E. Talmadge	3.27	(N = 23)
Lester G. Maddox	3.45	(N = 23)
S. Marvin Griffin	3.91	(N = 23)

E. *On a scale of 1 to 5 (1 being the most positive), assess the degree to which each of the governors listed below was willing and able to pursue important policy objectives even when such objectives were considered a political liability.*

Ellis G. Arnall	1.53	(N = 39)
Jimmy Carter	1.85	(N = 40)
Carl E. Sanders	2.50	(N = 40)

George D. Busbee	2.80	(N = 40)
Lester G. Maddox	3.15	(N = 40)
S. Ernest Vandiver	3.37	(N = 39)
Herman E. Talmadge	3.67	(N = 38)
S. Marvin Griffin	4.32	(N = 39)

F. *In the field of agriculture?*

Herman E. Talmadge	1.94	(N = 35)
S. Marvin Griffin	2.25	(N = 32)
Jimmy Carter	2.47	(N = 35)
George D. Busbee	2.88	(N = 35)
S. Ernest Vandiver	2.88	(N = 32)
Ellis G. Arnall	2.93	(N = 30)
Lester G. Maddox	2.94	(N = 32)
Carl E. Sanders	3.12	(N = 35)

G. *On issues of health and welfare?*

Jimmy Carter	2.00	(N = 39)
Ellis G. Arnall	2.12	(N = 35)
George D. Busbee	2.47	(N = 39)
Carl E. Sanders	2.63	(N = 39)
Lester G. Maddox	3.16	(N = 39)
S. Ernest Vandiver	3.71	(N = 35)
Herman E. Talmadge	3.76	(N = 35)
S. Marvin Griffin	4.06	(N = 35)

H. *In the areas of civil rights and civil liberties?*

Jimmy Carter	1.68	(N = 45)
Ellis G. Arnall	1.95	(N = 43)
George D. Busbee	2.45	(N = 45)
Carl E. Sanders	2.59	(N = 44)
S. Ernest Vandiver	3.67	(N = 43)
Lester G. Maddox	4.36	(N = 44)
Herman E. Talmadge	4.71	(N = 43)
S. Marvin Griffin	4.81	(N = 43)

I. *In the field of education?*

Ellis G. Arnall	1.82	(N = 44)
Carl E. Sanders	1.88	(N = 44)
Lester G. Maddox	2.50	(N = 48)
Jimmy Carter	2.54	(N = 48)
George D. Busbee	2.58	(N = 48)
Herman E. Talmadge	2.81	(N = 43)
S. Ernest Vandiver	3.41	(N = 43)
S. Marvin Griffin	3.55	(N = 44)

J. *On urban affairs issues?*

Carl E. Sanders	2.05	(N = 40)
Jimmy Carter	2.05	(N = 40)
George D. Busbee	2.05	(N = 40)
Ellis G. Arnall	2.32	(N = 39)
Lester G. Maddox	3.80	(N = 40)
S. Ernest Vandiver	3.89	(N = 39)
Herman E. Talmadge	4.32	(N = 39)
S. Marvin Griffin	4.63	(N = 39)

NOTES

Ellis Arnall and the Politics of Progress
by Harold P. Henderson

1. For a discussion of the 1942 campaign, see James F. Cook, "The Georgia Gubernatorial Election of 1942," *Atlanta Historical Bulletin* 18 (1973): 7–19.

2. Mrs. J. E. Hayes, comp., *Georgia's Official Register, 1939–1941–1943* (Atlanta: Georgia Department of Archives and History, n.d.), 6–7. Talmadge had been defeated in a state representative race in 1920 and in U.S. senatorial campaigns in 1936 and 1938.

3. William Anderson, *The Wild Man from Sugar Creek: The Political Career of Eugene Talmadge* (Baton Rouge: Louisiana State University Press, 1975), 88–95, 144–45.

4. For a discussion of Talmadge and the Board of Regents, see James F. Cook, "Politics and Education in the Talmadge Era: The Controversy Over the University System of Georgia, 1941–1942" (Ph.D. dissertation, University of Georgia, 1972).

5. Thomas Elkin Taylor, "A Political Biography of Ellis Arnall" (M.A. thesis, Emory University, 1959), 1–37; John Chamberlain, "Arnall of Georgia," *Life*, August 6, 1945, 68–76; Ellis Gibbs Arnall, *The Shore Dimly Seen* (Philadelphia: J. B. Lippincott, 1946), 29–32; James F. Cook, *Governors of Georgia* (Huntsville, Ala.: Strode Publishers, 1979), 257–58.

6. Interview with Ellis Arnall, Atlanta, Ga., July 19, 1985.

7. Atlanta *Constitution*, November 2, 1941.

8. For the text of Arnall's opening address, see Atlanta *Constitution*, November 2, 1941.

9. *Official Register, 1939–1941–1943*, 656; Arnall interview; Anderson, *Wild Man*, 211.

10. Chamberlain, "Arnall," 69.

11. Taylor, "Ellis Arnall," 94–252; Arnall interview.

12. Ellis Merton Coulter, *Georgia: A Short History*, rev. ed. (Chapel Hill: University of North Carolina Press, 1947), 450.

13. Georgia Association of Historians Survey of Georgia Governors, May 1985. See Appendix.

14. *From Thurmond to Wallace: Political Tendencies in Georgia, 1948–1968* (Baltimore: Johns Hopkins University Press, 1970), 71.

15. Cook, *Georgia Governors*, 257.

16. V. O. Key, Jr., *Southern Politics in State and Nation* (New York: Alfred A. Knopf, 1949), 128.

17. Coulter, *Georgia*, 449.

18. Taylor, "Ellis Arnall," 378.

19. *Messages and Addresses of Governor Ellis Arnall, 1943–1946* (Atlanta: Executive Department of the State of Georgia, n.d.), 4; *Acts and Resolutions of the General Assembly of the State of Georgia, 1943,* 670–72, 66–68; *Journal of the Senate of the State of Georgia of the Regular Session of the General Assembly, 1943,* 105, 160–61; *Journal of the House of Representatives of the State of Georgia of the Regular Session of the General Assembly, 1943,* 133–34, 152, 155; Atlanta *Journal,* January 31, 1943; *Official Register, 1945–1950,* 274.

20. *Acts and Resolutions, 1943,* 636–39, 56–57; *Senate Journal, 1943,* 80–83; *House Journal, 1943,* 197, 327–30; *Official Register, 1945–1950,* 374.

21. *Messages,* 4.

22. Jane Walker Herndon, "Eurith Dickinson Rivers: A Political Biography" (Ph.D. dissertation, University of Georgia, 1974), 331–36; Atlanta *Constitution,* July 17, 1946; Augusta *Chronicle,* June 21, 1946.

23. *Messages,* 4; *Acts and Resolutions, 1943,* 225, 399–400; *Senate Journal, 1943,* 254; *House Journal, 1943,* 368–69.

24. *Messages,* 4; *Acts and Resolutions, 1943,* 225, 399–400; *Senate Journal, 1943,* 83, 178; *House Journal, 1943,* 385–86.

25. *Messages,* 4; *Acts and Resolutions, 1943,* 361–63; *Senate Journal, 1943,* 106–108; *House Journal, 1943,* 227.

26. *Acts and Resolutions, 1943,* 142–43; *Senate Journal, 1943,* 83; *House Journal, 1943,* 197–98.

27. *Acts and Resolutions, 1943,* 298–302; *Senate Journal, 1943,* 94; *House Journal, 1943,* 280.

28. Atlanta *Constitution,* March 19, 1943; *Acts and Resolutions, 1943,* 84; *Messages,* 11; *Senate Journal, 1943,* 104, 162–63; *House Journal, 1943,* 134–36, 185–88; Atlanta *Journal,* February 6, 1943. The legislature also unanimously approved the remaining two points of Arnall's ten-point program. The first was a resolution of support for the war effort. The second limited the authority of the governor to remove state employees.

29. *Messages,* 5; *Senate Journal, 1943,* 941–42, 1239–42, 774–75; *House Journal, 1943,* 1379–80, 185–86, 923–24; *Acts and Resolutions, 1943,* 64–65; *Official Register, 1945–1950,* 374; *Messages,* 104.

30. *Messages,* 4; *Acts and Resolutions, 1943,* 441–42; *Messages,* 5; *Senate Journal, 1943,* 201–203; *House Journal, 1943,* 129–34; *Messages,* 7; Arnall interview.

31. *Messages,* 5; Atlanta *Constitution,* November 2, 1941; *Acts and Resolutions, 1943,* 128–34, 28–30; *Official Register, 1945–1950,* 378–79.

32. *Acts and Resolutions, 1943,* 171–77.

33. *Acts and Resolutions, 1943,* 216–22; *Senate Journal, 1943,* 581–86; *House Journal, 1943,* 1314–16; Arnall interview.

34. Ellis Arnall, "Without a Dissenting Vote," *Atlanta Journal Magazine,* March 7, 1943, 1; *Senate Journal, 1943,* 356–58; *House Journal, 1943,* 912–15, 943–45; *Official Register, 1945–1950,* 374; Arnall, *Shore Dimly Seen,* 54.

35. *Senate Journal, 1943,* 1008.

36. Editorials in the Atlanta *Journal* and the Atlanta *Constitution*, March 19, 1943.

37. Taylor, "Ellis Arnall," 94.

38. "Unanimous Arnall," *Collier's*, July 24, 1943, 16.

39. Cleveland *Plain Dealer* editorial quoted in Atlanta *Journal*, February 28, 1943.

40. Cullen B. Gosnell and C. David Anderson, *The Government and Administration of Georgia* (New York: Thomas Y. Crowell, 1956), 25–26.

41. *Acts and Resolutions, 1943*, 1680–83.

42. Albert B. Saye, ed., *Records of the Commission of 1943–1944 to Revise the Constitution of Georgia* (Published by authority of the State, 1946): 1:5, 23.

43. Arnall, *Shore Dimly Seen*, 251.

44. *Records of the Commission* 2:337.

45. Atlanta *Constitution*, August 15, 1944. These included limited local home rule, abolishment of the allocation system, a statewide merit system, and reapportionment of the legislature based on population.

46. *Records of the Commission* 2:338, 478–520, 464–75, 533–39, 475–77.

47. Atlanta *Constitution*, August 6, 1945.

48. Albert B. Saye, *A Constitutional History of Georgia, 1732–1968*, rev. ed. (Athens: University of Georgia Press, 1970), 397.

49. For a complete listing of the changes, see Ellis Arnall, "Arnall Describes Provisions to Eliminate Dictatorships," Atlanta *Constitution*, April 1, 1945. See also Saye, *Constitutional History*, 397–400; Gosnell and Anderson, *Government of Georgia*, 27–32; and Arnall, *Shore Dimly Seen*, 252–58.

50. Atlanta *Journal*, March 4, 1945.

51. Editorials in the Atlanta *Constitution* and the Atlanta *Journal*, December 10, 1944.

52. Harold Paulk Henderson, "The 1946 Gubernatorial Election in Georgia" (M.A. thesis, Georgia Southern College, 1967), 16–18; *Official Register, 1945–1950*, 473.

53. Saye, *Constitutional History*, 426–29. For a brief history of the new constitution, see George D. Busbee, "An Overview of the New Georgia Constitution," *Mercer Law Review* 35 (Fall 1983): 1–17.

54. Taylor, "Ellis Arnall," 117.

55. Arnall, *Shore Dimly Seen*, 238–40. For the Gross-Harris report, see *House Journal, 1943*, 20–35.

56. *Messages*, 21–23, 25–26.

57. *Senate Journal, Extraordinary Session, 1943*, 17; *House Journal, Extraordinary Session, 1943*, 40–42; Arnall, *Shore Dimly Seen*, 243. For Arnall's discussion of the penal problem, see *Shore Dimly Seen*, 236–42.

58. Anderson, *Wild Man*, 205.

59. Quoted in Willis A. Sutton, Jr., "The Talmadge Campaigns: A Sociological Analysis of Political Power" (Ph.D. dissertation, University of North Carolina, 1952), 255.

60. Atlanta *Constitution*, November 2, 1941.

61. Quoted in Sutton, "Talmadge Campaigns," 256.

62. Atlanta *Constitution*, August 30, 1942.

63. Arnall interview.

64. *Records of the Commission* 2:100–101. The Supreme Court decision was *Smith v. Allwright* 321 U.S. 649 (1944).

65. *Records of the Commission*, 2:540.

66. Atlanta *Constitution*, December 21, 1944.

67. Frederic D. Ogden, *The Poll Tax in the South* (University, Ala.: University of Alabama Press, 1958), 181–87.

68. Atlanta *Constitution*, January 5, 1945. For statements of George and Russell on the poll tax, see the Atlanta *Journal* editorial "The Discredited Poll Tax," January 8, 1945. While both favored state abolishment of the tax, they opposed federal intervention in the matter.

69. Atlanta *Constitution*, January 4, 1945.

70. *Messages*, 46.

71. Atlanta *Journal*, January 23, 1945.

72. Taylor, "Arnall," 161.

73. Arnall interview.

74. *Senate Journal, 1945,* 137, 142–43; Atlanta *Constitution*, January 25, 1945; *House Journal, 1945,* 318.

75. Key, *Southern Politics,* 607.

76. Ogden, *Poll Tax,* 187.

77. Editorial in the Atlanta *Journal*, February 1, 1945.

78. Key, *Southern Politics,* 618.

79. Atlanta *Journal*, January 28, 1944.

80. The Supreme Court held in the Texas case that state legislation had made the Democratic primary an integral part of the election process. See *Smith v. Allwright* 321 U.S. 649 (1944).

81. *King v. Chapman* et al., 62 Fed. Supp. 639; *Chapman et al. v. King,* 154 F. 2d 460. The U.S. Supreme Court on April 1, 1946, refused to review the appellate court's decision. *Chapman et al. v. King,* 327 U.S. 800 (1946).

82. *Chapman et al. v. King,* 154 F 2d 460.

83. Atlanta *Constitution*, March 19, 28, 1946.

84. Ibid., April 5, 1946.

85. This contention proved true. South Carolina led the way in repealing state primary laws and converting state political parties into private organizations. The federal courts still stood firm in the demand that blacks be allowed to participate in primary elections. See *Rice v. Elmore,* 33 U.S. 875 (1948).

86. Augusta *Chronicle*, April 5, 1946.

87. Savannah *Morning News*, July 2, 1946.

88. *Statesman*, June 27, 1946.

89. Savannah *Morning News*, April 7, 1946.

90. Arnall interview.

91. Atlanta *Constitution*, June 26, 1946.

92. Atlanta *Journal*, June 6, 1946. For similar statements, see Henderson, "1946 Gubernatorial Election," 46–47.

93. Arnall, *Shore Dimly Seen*, 96–106; Arnall interview.
94. Arnall, *Shore Dimly Seen*, 291–92.
95. Henderson, "1946 Gubernatorial Election," 10–14, 20–23, 51, 63, 70, 92–94.
96. Key, *Southern Politics*, 128.
97. Arnall interview.
98. Taylor, "Ellis Arnall," 338–41; Numan V. Bartley, *The Rise of Massive Resistance: Race and Politics in the South During the 1950's* (Baton Rouge: Louisiana State University Press, 1969), 333–34.
99. Harold Paulk Henderson, "The 1966 Gubernatorial Election in Georgia" (Ph.D. dissertation, University of Southern Mississippi, 1982), 94–95, 160–73.

M. E. Thompson and the Politics of Succession
by Harold P. Henderson

1. Mrs. J. E. Hayes, comp., *Georgia's Official Register, 1945–1950* (Atlanta: Georgia Department of Archives and History, n.d.), 543. The office of lieutenant governor was created by the Constitution of 1945.
2. Physicians attributed Talmadge's death to acute hepatitis and hemorrhaging of the stomach and intestinal tract. Atlanta *Constitution*, December 22, 1946.
3. James F. Cook, *Governors of Georgia* (Huntsville, Ala.: Strode Publishers, 1979), 260–63; Joseph A. Tomberlin, "Melvin Ernest Thompson," in *Dictionary of Georgia Biography*, edited by Kenneth Coleman and Charles Stephen Gurr (Athens: University of Georgia Press, 1983), 2:973–74.
4. Interview with Ellis Arnall, Atlanta, Ga., December 12, 1985.
5. Hartwell *Sun*, July 5, 1946; Augusta *Chronicle*, April 16, 1946; *Georgia Voter: Facts About Candidates Offering for State Positions Compiled by Georgia League of Women Voters*, reprinted in the Cartersville *Daily Tribune News*, July 4, 1946. For a discussion of the white primary issue in the 1946 primary, see Harold Paulk Henderson, "The 1946 Gubernatorial Election in Georgia" (M.A. thesis, Georgia Southern College, 1967), 4–5, 18, 25–31, 42–53.
6. *Official Register, 1945–1950*, 497.
7. Savannah *Morning News*, December 24, 1946.
8. Atlanta *Journal*, December 27, 1946.
9. *Journal of the Senate of the General Assembly of the State of Georgia, 1947*, 34–35; Atlanta *Journal*, December 27, 1946.
10. Atlanta *Constitution*, December 28, 1946. For an in-depth discussion of Talmadge's legal arguments, see chapter 3 of James B. Sanders, "The Georgia Gubernatorial Controversy of 1947" (Unpublished manuscript, Emory University, 1948).
11. Americus *Times-Recorder*, December 24, 1946. For an in-depth discussion of Thompson's legal arguments, see chapter 4 of Sanders, "Gubernatorial Controversy."

12. Savannah *Morning News*, December 29, 1946.

13. Valdosta *Daily Times*, January 2, 11, 1947.

14. Atlanta *Constitution*, January 12, 1947.

15. Atlanta *Journal*, January 13, 1947.

16. Atlanta *Constitution*, January 5, 1947.

17. Savannah *Morning News*, January 7, 1947.

18. Ibid., January 14, 1947.

19. *Opinions of the Attorney-General, August 1945–December, 1947, Eugene Cook Attorney General* (Hapeville, Ga.: Tyler and Company, n.d.), 303–305.

20. Atlanta *Constitution*, January 5, 1947.

21. Valdosta *Daily Times*, December 21, 1946; Atlanta *Journal*, January 3, 1947.

22. Savannah *Morning News*, January 7, 1947.

23. Atlanta *Constitution*, January 8, 1947.

24. Savannah *Morning News*, January 9, 1947.

25. Valdosta *Daily Times*, January 1, 1947; Atlanta *Journal*, January 8, 1947.

26. Americus *Times-Recorder*, December 23, 1946.

27. Atlanta *Constitution*, January 14, 1947.

28. *Georgia House Journal, 1947*, 37.

29. Ibid., 29–34; Atlanta *Journal*, January 15, 1947.

30. Americus *Times-Recorder*, January 31, 1947. Ralph McGill and Talmadge also claimed that Arnall had reversed his position. For McGill's statement, see Atlanta *Constitution*, January 26, 1947. For Talmadge's, see *Constitution*, January 20, 1947.

31. Arnall interview.

32. Atlanta *Journal*, January 15, March 2, 1947; Atlanta *Constitution*, January 15, 1947. The Atlanta *Journal* investigated the write-ins in Talmadge's native county of Telfair and concluded the votes were a "prima facie case of conspiracy and fraud." For a discussion of these write-in votes, see Henderson, "The 1946 Gubernatorial Election," 120–21.

33. Atlanta *Constitution*, January 16, 1947.

34. *House Journal, 1947*, 36–43; Atlanta *Journal*, January 15, 1947.

35. Atlanta *Journal*, January 15, 1947; Savannah *Morning News*, January 15, 1947; "Wool Hat Rebellion," *Newsweek*, January 27, 1947, 23.

36. Atlanta *Journal*, January 15, 1947; Augusta *Chronicle*, January 16, 1947.

37. Atlanta *Constitution*, January 16, 1947.

38. *House Journal, 1947*, 51–53; *Senate Journal, 1947*, 45–46.

39. Atlanta *Journal*, January 16, 1947; Atlanta *Constitution*, January 18, 1947.

40. Henderson, "The 1946 Gubernatorial Election," 101–104.

41. Atlanta *Journal*, January 18, 1947.

42. *Minutes of the Executive Department of the State of Georgia, 1947*. File located at the Georgia Department of Archives and History, 1.

43. Atlanta *Journal*, January 17, 1947.

44. Ibid., January 16, 1947.

45. Letter from Roy V. Harris to Ed Stephens, January 31, 1947. Box 4 (Lamar-Sumter). Correspondence by Georgia Counties and Miscellaneous Correspondence, 1947. M. E. Thompson Collection. Valdosta State College Library, Valdosta, Ga.

46. Atlanta *Journal*, January 22, 1947.

47. Ibid., January 19, 1947.

48. Atlanta *Constitution*, January 19, 1947.

49. Savannah *Morning News*, January 20, 1947.

50. "Strictly from Dixie," *Time*, January 27, 1947, 21.

51. *Executive Minutes, 1947*, 2–4; Atlanta *Journal*, January 19, 1947.

52. Atlanta *Constitution*, January 19, 1947. Arnall insisted that he refused to continue as governor for two reasons: first, he believed that "the governor should be elected by the people"; second, he had planned to go on the lecture circuit after leaving the governorship and had speaking engagements lined up all over the country. According to Arnall, "I was up to my neck in contracts and I couldn't continue it [staying in the governor's office] even if I had wanted to and I didn't want to." Arnall interview.

53. Savannah *Morning News*, January 20, 1947.

54. Ibid., January 19, 1947.

55. Atlanta *Journal*, January 20, 1947.

56. *Senate Journal, 1947*, 47.

57. Savannah *Morning News*, January 21, 1947.

58. *Senate Journal, 1947*, 51; *House Journal, 1947*, 57; Atlanta *Constitution*, January 21, 1947.

59. Savannah *Morning News*, January 21, 1947.

60. Atlanta *Journal*, January 21, 1947.

61. *Senate Journal, 1947*, 63, 67.

62. Atlanta *Constitution*, January 22, 1947.

63. *Senate Journal, 1947*, 68–69.

64. Savannah *Morning News*, January 23, 1947.

65. Atlanta *Journal*, January 26, 1947; *House Journal, 1947*, 134; *Senate Journal, 1947*, 77, 80–82.

66. Savannah *Morning News*, January 28, 1947.

67. Atlanta *Constitution*, February 16, 1947.

68. "Fly Time," *Time*, February 17, 1947, 25; A. G. Mezerik, "Georgians Have Had Enough," *The Nation*, February 15, 1947, 174–75. For the press reaction, see Henderson, "The 1946 Gubernatorial Election," 112.

69. *House Journal, 1947*, 169.

70. *House Journal, 1947*, 182; Atlanta *Constitution*, January 31, 1947.

71. *House Journal, 1947*, 563; *Senate Journal, 1947*, 216.

72. *House Journal, 1947*, 369–70; *Senate Journal, 1947*, 231–32; Atlanta *Journal*, February 20, 1947.

73. Atlanta *Constitution*, March 6, 14, 1947.

74. *Ellis Arnall (M. E. Thompson) v. Herman Talmadge* (decision reprinted

in Atlanta *Journal*, February 12, 1947); *Thompson* v. *Byers et al.* (decision reprinted in Atlanta *Journal*, February 12, 1947); *Fulton National Bank of Atlanta* v. *Philip Landrum, Herman Talmadge, and M. E. Thompson* (decision reprinted in Atlanta *Journal*, February 16, 1947).

75. *Thompson Lieutenant Governor* v. *Talmadge*, 201 Ga. 867, 871–907 (1947).

76. Atlanta *Journal*, March 19, 1947; Arnall interview.

77. Americus *Times-Recorder*, March 19, 1947.

78. "Georgia: 'Honey, Pack Up,'" *Newsweek*, March 31, 1947, 23. Talmadge later stated, "I knew the majority of the Supreme Court had been appointed by Ed [Rivers] or Ellis [Arnall] or both of them. But I didn't think their political persuasion would affect them." Interview with Herman E. Talmadge, Lovejoy, Ga., March 24, 1986.

79. "Untangled," *New Republic*, March 31, 1947, 9.

80. Atlanta *Journal*, March 19, 1947; *Senate Journal, 1947*, 596.

81. *Opinions of the Attorney General*, 305–309.

82. Macon *Telegraph*, March 20, 1947.

83. Augusta *Chronicle*, March 20, 1947.

84. *Executive Minutes, 1947*, 19–20.

85. *Senate Journal, 1947*, 653–54.

86. Atlanta *Constitution*, March 21, 1947.

87. *Senate Journal, 1947*, 654–59, 663–64.

88. Atlanta *Journal*, March 22, 1947.

89. Valdosta *Daily Times*, March 21, 1947; Atlanta *Journal*, March 20, 23, 1947; Atlanta *Constitution*, March 20, 1947.

90. Atlanta *Constitution*, March 22, 1947.

91. Savannah *Morning News*, March 26, 1947; Valdosta *Daily Times*, March 29, 1947.

92. Atlanta *Journal*, March 28, 1947; Atlanta *Constitution*, March 28, 1947.

93. Atlanta *Journal*, March 23, 1947.

94. Ibid., July 11, 1948.

95. Ibid., August 6, 1948.

96. Ibid., July 24, 1948.

97. Atlanta *Constitution*, May 26, 1948; Jane Walker Herndon, "Eurith Dickinson Rivers: A Political Biography" (Ph.D. dissertation, University of Georgia, 1974), 385.

98. Atlanta *Journal*, July 11, 1948.

99. Joseph L. Bernd, *Grass Roots Politics in Georgia: The County Unit System and the Importance of the Individual Voting Community in Bifactional Elections, 1942–1954* (Atlanta: Emory University Research Committee, 1960), 13.

100. Atlanta *Journal*, July 11, 1948.

101. Robert Sherrill, *Gothic Politics in the Deep South: Stars of the New Confederacy* (New York: Grossman Publishers, 1968), 49.

102. Atlanta *Journal*, August 11, 1948.

103. Atlanta *Constitution*, May 26, 1948.

104. Atlanta *Journal*, July 11, 1948.

105. For a discussion of the 1948, 1950, and 1954 campaigns, see Joseph L. Bernd, "A Study of Primary Elections in Georgia, 1946–1954" (Ph.D. dissertation, Duke University, 1957), 116–46.

106. *Official Register, 1945–1950*, 577, 681.

107. *Official Register, 1953–1954*, 630.

108. *Official Register, 1955–1956*, 758.

109. Tomberlin, "Melvin Ernest Thompson," 974.

Herman E. Talmadge and the Politics of Power
by *Roger N. Pajari*

1. Numan V. Bartley, "1940 to the Present," in *A History of Georgia* (Athens: University of Georgia Press, 1977), 388.

2. Thad L. Beyle and Lynn Muchmore, *Being Governor: The View from the Office* (Durham: Duke University Press, 1983), 206–207.

3. Martha Wagner Weinberg, *Managing the State* (Cambridge, Mass.: MIT Press, 1977).

4. James F. Cook, *Governors of Georgia* (Huntsville, Ala.: Strode Publishers, 1979), 265; Arna R. Jordon, *Dreams Come True: Accomplishments of Governor Herman Talmadge* (Atlanta, 1954).

5. Cook, *Governors*, 388.

6. Robert Sherrill, *Gothic Politics in the Deep South: Stars of the New Confederacy* (New York: Grossman Publishers, 1968), 42–44.

7. Mary Givens Bryan, comp., *Georgia's Official Register: 1951–1952* (Atlanta: Department of Archives and History, n.d.), 19.

8. Kenneth Coleman, *Georgia History in Outline* (Athens: University of Georgia Press, 1960), 102.

9. Numan V. Bartley, *The Rise of Massive Resistance: Race and Politics in the South During the 1950's* (Baton Rouge: Louisiana State University Press, 1969), 41.

10. Jack Bass and Walter DeVries, *The Transformation of Southern Politics* (New York: Basic Books, 1977), 140.

11. Joseph L. Bernd, "Georgia Static and Dynamic," in *The Changing Politics of the South*, edited by William C. Havard (Baton Rouge: Louisiana State University Press, 1972), 294.

12. V. O. Key, Jr., *Southern Politics in State and Nation* (New York: Alfred A. Knopf, 1949), 116–17; Bartley, "1940 to the Present," 375.

13. Bartley "1940 to the Present," 394–95.

14. Bartley, *The Rise of Massive Resistance*, 26.

15. Ibid., 19.

16. Bernd, "Static and Dynamic," 304–308.

17. Interview with Herman E. Talmadge, Lovejoy, Ga., September 9, 1985; Georgia McMillan, "Talmadge—The Best Southern Governor?" *Harper's Magazine*, December 1954, 38.

18. Bernd, "Static and Dynamic," 315, 319–20; Sherrill, *Gothic Politics,* 48–50, 54–55.

19. Cook, *Governors,* 266; Bernd, "Static and Dynamic," 318–19.

20. Jordon, *Dreams Come True.*

21. Zell Miller, *Great Georgians* (Franklin Springs, Ga.: Advocate Press, 1983), 182, 185.

22. James David Barber, *The Presidential Character,* 2d rev. ed. (Englewood Cliffs, N.J.: Prentice Hall, 1977).

23. Talmadge interview.

24. Savannah *Morning News,* November 18, 1948.

25. Atlanta *Constitution,* January 12, 1954.

26. Cullen B. Gosnell and David C. Anderson, *The Government and Administration of Georgia* (New York: Thomas Y. Crowell, 1956), 113.

27. Val Gene Mixon, "The Growth of the Legislative Power of the Governor of Georgia: A Survey of the Legislative Program of Governor Herman Talmadge (1949–1954)" (M.A. thesis, Emory University, 1959), 56–57.

28. Gosnell and Anderson, *Government of Georgia,* 109, 118–19.

29. Savannah *Morning News,* January 9, 1951.

30. Ibid., December 7, 1949, November 18, 1948.

31. Cook, *Governors,* 267–76; McMillan, "Best Southern Governor?" 37; Savannah *Morning News,* June 13, 1949, April 19, 1949.

32. Mixon, "Growth of Legislative Power," 66; Savannah *Morning News,* January 10, 1951, July 13, 1950.

33. Frank Daniel, ed., *Addresses and Public Papers of Carl Edward Sanders* (Atlanta: Georgia Department of Archives and History, 1968), 174; Coleman, "Society and Culture," 382.

34. Gosnell and Anderson, *Government of Georgia,* 234.

35. Savannah *Morning News,* January 10, 1951.

36. Mixon, "Growth of Legislative Power," 66; Gosnell and Anderson, *Government of Georgia,* 80.

37. McMillan, "Best Southern Governor?" 36–37; Cook, *Governors,* 267–68.

38. McMillan, "Best Southern Governor?" 37.

39. Mixon, "Growth of Legislative Power," 97; Gosnell and Anderson, *Government of Georgia,* 80; Savannah *Morning News,* July 29, 1949.

40. Neal R. Peirce, *The Deep South States of America* (New York: W. W. Norton, 1974), 315.

41. Numan V. Bartley and Hugh D. Graham, *Southern Politics and the Second Reconstruction* (Baltimore: Johns Hopkins University Press, 1975), 69; and Gosnell and Anderson, *Government of Georgia,* 204.

42. Gosnell and Anderson, *Government of Georgia,* 191.

43. Savannah *Morning News,* April 19, June 4, 1949.

44. Atlanta *Constitution,* January 13, 1954.

45. Sherrill, *Gothic Politics,* 55; Mixon, "Growth of Legislative Power," 15–16; Gosnell and Anderson, *Government of Georgia,* 89.

46. Mixon, "Growth of Legislative Power," 53–54.

47. Peirce, *Deep South States,* 324; Gosnell and Anderson, *Government of Georgia,* 90.

48. Savannah *Morning News,* June 1, 1950; New York *Times,* June 23, 1953; Birmingham *News,* June 23, 1953.

49. McMillan, "Best Southern Governor?" 35.

50. Sherrill, *Gothic Politics.*

51. Savannah *Morning News,* August 21, 1951.

52. Mixon, "Growth of Legislative Power, 78; *Senate Journal, 1951,* 566, 571; *House Journal, 1951,* 770; Bernd, "Static and Dynamic," 302.

53. Gosnell and Anderson, *Government of Georgia,* 66; Numan V. Bartley, *The Creation of Modern Georgia* (Athens: University of Georgia Press, 1983), 188–89; Sherrill, *Gothic Politics,* 39; Bernd, "Static and Dynamic," 312–13; Cook, *Governors,* 266; E. Merton Coulter, *Georgia: A Short History,* rev. ed. (Chapel Hill: University of North Carolina Press, 1960), 460; Key, *Southern Politics,* 125.

54. Atlanta *Constitution,* June 30, 1950; Bernd, "Static and Dynamic," 299.

55. Mixon, "Growth of Legislative Powers," 50; *Georgia Laws 1949,* 1204–27; *Elmore v. Rice,* 72 Fed. Supp. 516 (1947); *Davis v. Schnell,* 81 F. Supp. 872 (1949).

56. McMillan, "Best Southern Governor?" 39; Mixon, "Growth of Legislative Power," 50.

57. *Georgia Laws, 1949,* 1291–93; Bernd, 299.

58. Atlanta *Constitution,* January 11, 1949; Mixon, "Growth of Legislative Power," 46–53, 63.

59. Atlanta *Journal,* September 6, 1953; Savannah *Morning News,* November 18, 1948; Mixon, "Growth of Legislative Power," 42–43; Cecil David Anderson, "The Organization, Functions, and Operations of the Georgia State Merit System of Personnel Administration" (M.A. thesis, Emory University, 1956), 90; Gosnell and Anderson, *Government of Georgia,* 162–64.

60. Sherrill, *Gothic Politics,* 56–57.

61. *Brown v. Board of Education of Topeka.* 347 U.S. 497 (1954); Bernd, 297.

62. Savannah *Morning News,* August 21, October 26, 1951; Bartley and Graham, *Southern Politics and the Second Reconstruction,* 68; Louis T. Rigdon, *Georgia's County Unit System* (Decatur, Ga.: Selective Books, 1961), 38–39; Atlanta *Constitution,* February 6, 1951; *Senate Journal, 1951,* 27.

63. Bartley, *Massive Resistance,* 42–43; Bernd, "Static and Dynamic," 297; *Gray v. Sanders* 373, U.S. 368 (1963).

64. Talmadge interview.

65. Herman E. Talmadge, *You and Segregation* (Birmingham: Vulcan Press, 1955); Bass and DeVries, *Transformation of Southern Politics,* 137; Birmingham *News,* June 23, 1955; Bartley, *Massive Resistance,* 43, 186; Savannah *Morning News,* April 9, 1948, December 9, 1949; Atlanta *Constitution,* July 4, 11, 18, 1948; Bernd, "Static and Dynamic," 314–15.

Marvin Griffin and the Politics of the Stump
by Robert W. Dubay

1. "Out of the Smoke House," *Time,* September 21, 1962, 24–25.

2. "Trend of the Times," *Newsweek,* September 24, 1962, 18.

3. Numan V. Bartley, "1940 to the Present," in Kenneth Coleman et al., *A History of Georgia* (Athens: University of Georgia Press, 1977), 395. For a complete understanding of the county unit method of voting, see Louis T. Rigdon, *Georgia's County Unit System* (Decatur, Ga: Selective Books, 1961).

4. Ordinary Georgians, as well as observers elsewhere, harbored a negative view of Griffin's gubernatorial term due to the seemingly high number of incidents of wrongdoing which were made public during and after the time he was in office. One writer, as an example, saw the Griffin administration this way: "His [Griffin's] thieving created so much space in the state treasury that it has taken four years to recover from the state bankruptcy in which he left us. If he is allowed to get his filthy hands in the public till again, it will probably require a whole generation to recover from the losses we will suffer." See Anonymous Macon Resident to Carl Sanders, August 30, 1962, in Carl E. Sanders Papers, Candler Building, Atlanta, Ga.

5. Sanders and his strategists placed considerable stress on the Griffin administration's negative aspects, although this was done in subtle ways. See Robert R. Richardson interview, November 10, 1976; Carl E. Sanders interview, June 1, 1976.

6. Numan V. Bartley, *The Creation of Modern Georgia* (Athens: University of Georgia Press, 1983), 200.

7. S. Marvin Griffin interview, April 13, 1976.

8. Bainbridge *Post-Searchlight,* July 5, 1934; S. Marvin Griffin, "Autobiographical Notes," (c. 1960s), in Marvin Griffin Collection, Bainbridge Junior College, Bainbridge, Ga.

9. Atlanta *Constitution,* December 22, 1940, January 15, 1941, August 4, 8, 1954.

10. This unit was soon busy on maneuvers in Georgia and North Carolina. S. Marvin Griffin interviews, April 20, June 14, 1976.

11. Movement Order No. 13, April 27, 1942, in Charlie Camp Papers (private possession); Charlie F. Camp interview, October 14, 1976.

12. Ellis G. Arnall interview, July 6, 1976; Atlanta *Constitution,* September 29, 1944.

13. Griffin interview, April 20, 1976.

14. Bainbridge *Post-Searchlight,* April 25, 1946; Announcement for Governor, in Griffin Collection.

15. Bainbridge *Post-Searchlight,* June 28, 1978; James D. Pippen interview, July 6, 1976.

16. Bainbridge *Post-Searchlight,* May 16, 1946. For voting returns, see Mrs. J. E. Hayes, comp., *Georgia's Official Register, 1945–1950* (Atlanta: Georgia Department of Archives and History, n.d.).

17. For an analysis of this interesting episode, consult Ralph McGill,

"How It Happened Down in Georgia," *New Republic*, January 27, 1947, 14; William L. Belvin, "The Georgia Gubernatorial Primary of 1946," *Georgia Historical Quarterly* 50 (1966): 37–53.

18. Arnall interview, July 6, 1976.

19. Pippen interview, July 6, 1976; Ramsey Simmons interview, February 28, 1980; Atlanta *Constitution*, December 8, 1946; Steve B. Campbell, "Hollocaust on Peachtree: The Story of the Winecoff Fire," *Atlanta Historical Bulletin* 14 (1969): 14.

20. Herman E. Talmadge interview, June 1, 1976; *Official Register, 1945–1950*, 581, 685.

21. For a representative cross-section of Griffin's activities during those years, see Sumter *Tri-County News*, January 10, 1951; Waycross *Journal-Herald*, April 12, 1951; Bulloch *Herald*, September 27, 1951; Macon *News*, April 24, 1953; Cobb County *News*, August 6, 1953.

22. Moultrie *Observer*, July 12, 1954.

23. Bainbridge *Post-Searchlight*, July 1, 1954; Marvin Griffin Inaugural Address, January 11, 1955, in *Marvin Griffin Speeches*, vol. 1, Bainbridge Junior College Library.

24. Mrs. Mary Givens Bryan, comp., *Georgia's Official Register, 1953–1954* (Atlanta: Georgia Department of Archives and History, n.d.).

25. Atlanta *Constitution*, February 3, 1955; Ernest Vandiver to Ben Wiggins, January 13, Carlton Mobley to Wiggins, January 21, T. V. Williams to J. Loyd Ewing, January 24, Bill Kilgore to Marvin Griffin, February 2, 1955, in Griffin Collection. See also Insurance Lists with classifications, Griffin Collection.

26. Robert A. Griffin interview, October 19, 1978.

27. Georgia McMillan, "Talmadge—The Best Southern Governor?" *Harper's Magazine*, December 1954, 36–37; *Progress Report by the Governor to the General Assembly, January 1959*, 3–4.

28. The Minimum Foundation Program was actually enacted in 1949. However, it was not funded until after Talmadge took office. Basically, the plan called for "providing state support sufficient to assure all school districts a minimal level of funding per student." Coleman, *A History of Georgia*, 377.

29. Construction of the science center was the project of one-time House Speaker and Board of Regents member Roy V. Harris. The idea of a nuclear reactor for Georgia Tech came from Atlanta banker Freeman Strickland. Roy V. Harris interview, August 3, 1976; S. Marvin Griffin interview, November 6, 1979.

30. *Progress Report by the Governor, 1959*, 3–4.

31. Georgia *Recorder*, April 22, 1958.

32. Cullen B. Gosnell and C. David Anderson, *The Government and Administration of Georgia* (New York: Thomas Y. Crowell, 1956), 125, 127–31, explains this fund; Harris interview, August 3, 1976.

33. Atlanta *Constitution*, July 28, 1962.

34. Ibid., June 1, 4, 7, 1955; John E. Sims interview, October 5, 1978; *Progress Report by the Governor, 1959*, 3–4.

35. Griffin to Carole Wingate, May 26, 1962, in Griffin Collection; Augusta *Herald,* October 21, 1958; *Progress Report by the Governor, 1957,* 6.

36. Lester E. Waterburg to E. W. Stetson, January 21, Morris M. Bryan to Griffin, March 15, Griffin to Norman B. Oppenheimer, April 13, 1955, in Executive Department Correspondence, Marvin Griffin, Group 1, Series 5, Georgia Department of Archives and History, Atlanta; Griffin Speech, January 18, 1955, in Griffin Speeches, vol. 1.

37. Dalton *News,* November 6, 1955; Atlanta *Constitution,* November 2, 1955; Bainbridge *Post-Searchlight,* June 27, 1979.

38. Griffin Speech, January 10, 1956, in Griffin Speeches, vol. 2; Atlanta *Constitution,* August 4, 8, 1955.

39. Atlanta *Constitution,* January 10, 1956, June 28, 1957; Atlanta *Journal-Constitution,* June 28, 1964; Atlanta *Journal,* February 10, 1958.

40. Andrew Sparks, "What Marvin Plans to Do as Governor," *Atlanta Journal and Constitution Magazine,* January 9, 1955, 10–12; Ben W. Fortson, Jr., interview, June 15, 1976; *Progress Report by the Governor, 1959,* 6, 10, 12, 15; C. E. Gregory Report of the Georgia Historical Commission, December 5, 1958, in Griffin Collection.

41. Lester Velie, "Strange Case of the Country Slickers vs. The City Rubes," *Reader's Digest,* April 1960, 108.

42. William Anderson, *The Wild Man from Sugar Creek: The Political Career of Eugene Talmadge* (Baton Rouge: Louisiana State University Press, 1975), 228–29.

43. Atlanta *Constitution,* May 16, 1958; January 31, 1956.

44. Trammel McIntyre interview, January 11, 1979.

45. Atlanta *Constitution,* February 2, 4–5, 11, 1958.

46. *Wall Street Journal,* June 4, 1959.

47. Acworth *Progress,* November 1, 1957; Atlanta *Constitution,* April 23–24, 1958; Huey Ledbetter interview, January 14, 1979.

48. Atlanta *Constitution,* February 4, 1958.

49. Proposed Fulton County Grand Jury Six-Count Indictment, S. Marvin Griffin, December 14; Affidavit, E. Thurston Brown, October 7; Affidavit, William C. Massee, November 2, 1960, in Griffin Collection.

50. Atlanta *Journal-Constitution,* January 1, 1961.

51. Atlanta *Constitution,* May 21, 1959.

52. Fletcher Knebel, "The Real Little Rock Story," *Look,* November 12, 1957, 32; Virgil T. Blossom, *It Has Happened Here* (New York, 1959), 54; "Who *Is* Stirring Up the South," *Newsweek,* September 23, 1957, 32.

53. Neal Peirce, *The Deep South States of America* (New York: W. W. Norton, 1974), 132.

54. "Rebels at Georgia Tech," *Newsweek,* December 12, 1955, 104; "Armageddon to Go," *Time,* December 12, 1955, 24; "When Symbols Clash," *Commonweal,* December 16, 1955, 274.

55. "Springhill Survivors on Segregated Spree," *Life,* December 8, 1958, 49–50; Sam Caldwell interview, December 12, 1978.

56. Robert Griffin interview, October 19, 1978.

57. Samuel Marvin Griffin, Sr., File, Federal Bureau of Investigation, U.S. Department of Justice, Washington, D.C.

58. Atlanta *Constitution,* October 31, November 1, 5, 1957; Gene Roberts and Jack Nelson, *The Censors and the Schools* (Boston: Little, Brown, 1963), 154.

59. George P. Dillard to Griffin, November 16, 1956, H. A. Poole Memo to File, June 20, 1956, George P. Dillard to Griffin, June 21, November 16, 1956, Roger Lawson to B. D. Murphy, October 13, 1958, in Griffin Collection.

S. Ernest Vandiver and the Politics of Change
by Charles Pyles

1. Atlanta *Constitution,* July 2, 1962.

2. See Numan V. Bartley, *The Creation of Modern Georgia* (Athens: University of Georgia Press, 1983).

3. V. O. Key, Jr., *Southern Politics in State and Nation* (New York: Alfred A. Knopf, 1949), 674.

4. Earl Black, "Southern Governors and Political Change: Campaign Stances on Racial Segregation and Economic Development," *Journal of Politics* 33 (August 1971): 703–34.

5. Atlanta *Constitution,* January 1, 1959.

6. Interview with S. Ernest Vandiver, Lavonia, Ga., July 29, 1985.

7. Black, "Southern Governors and Political Change," 715.

8. Charles Boykin Pyles, "Race and Ruralism in Georgia Elections, 1948–1966" (Ph.D. dissertation, University of Georgia, 1976), 103; Atlanta *Constitution,* September 2, 1958.

9. Vandiver interview.

10. Atlanta *Constitution,* September 1, 1958.

11. Interview with Harold Davis, former aide to Senator Richard B. Russell and former editor of the Atlanta *Journal,* May 30, 1985.

12. Pyles, "Race and Ruralism," 107–109.

13. *Final Report by the Governor's Commission on Economy and Reorganization,* Atlanta, December 28, 1959.

14. A constitutional amendment proposed in November 1953 and ratified by the voters November 2, 1954.

15. Atlanta *Constitution,* January 12, 1959.

16. Ibid., January 14, 1959.

17. Ibid., November 29, 1960.

18. Ibid., January 7, 1961.

19. Ibid., January 10, 1961.

20. Ibid., September 24, 1980.

21. Ibid., January 19, 1961.

22. Joseph A. Schlesinger, "A Comparison of the Relative Positions of Governors," in Herbert Jacobs and Kenneth Vines, eds., *Politics in the American States,* 2d ed. (New York: Little, Brown, 1971), 224. Schlesinger's article

was useful in formulating a model for examining the Vandiver administration. He emphasized organization devices—tenure, appointment, budget control, and veto power—to determine the relative strength of governors in terms of formal powers. By his approach, Georgia is a "weak-governor" state, but Schlesinger also observed that "the state legislatures are still weaker in policy leadership" and that this allows governors to dominate on policy matters. Thad L. Beyle, "The Governor's Formal Powers: A View from the Governor's Chair," *Public Administration Review* 38 (November 1978): 540–45, confirmed Schlesinger's index through research on the perspectives of governors themselves. Nelson C. Dometrius, "Measuring Gubernatorial Power," *Journal of Politics* 41 (May 1979): 589–610, challenges some of Schlesinger's conclusions.

23. Bartley, *The Creation of Modern Georgia*, 196.

24. Numan V. Bartley and Hugh D. Graham, *Southern Politics and the Second Reconstruction* (Baltimore: Johns Hopkins University Press, 1975), 49. See also Bartley, *From Thurmond to Wallace* (Baltimore: Johns Hopkins University Press, 1970); Joseph L. Bernd, *Grass Roots Politics in Georgia* (Atlanta: Emory University Research Committee, 1960); Louis T. Rigdon, *Georgia's County Unit System* (Decatur, Ga.: Selective Books, 1961).

25. Bernd, *Grass Roots Politics*, 16.

26. *Turman V. Duckworth*, 68 Fed. Supp. 744 (1946).

27. Key, *Southern Politics*, 121.

28. 369 U.S. 186 (1962).

29. Albert B. Saye, *Election Laws of Georgia*, 2d ed. (Athens: University of Georgia Press, 1963), 97–102. *Georgia Code* 34-3212 to 34-3217.

30. Charles Pou, "Epilogue: The Vandiver Years," *Atlanta Magazine*, December 1962, 56.

31. Vandiver interview.

32. V. O. Key, Jr., *American State Politics* (New York: Alfred A. Knopf, 1956), 76.

33. Black, "Southern Governors and Political Change," 720.

34. Bartley, *The Creation of Modern Georgia*, 199.

35. Leslie W. Dunbar, "The Changing Mind of the South: The Exposed Nerve," *Journal of Politics* 25 (February 1964): 20; Vandiver interview. Dunbar notes, "Southern governors have become *de facto* executive directors of the state chambers of commerce, and spend their time competing with each other as supplicants for new plants."

36. Vandiver interview.

37. Atlanta *Constitution*, January 11, 1962.

38. Ibid.

39. Pou, "The Vandiver Years," 63.

40. Vandiver interview.

41. Pou, "The Vandiver Years," 43.

42. Ibid., 45.

43. Atlanta *Constitution*, January 2, 1961.

44. Pou, "The Vandiver Years," 46.

45. Atlanta *Constitution*, January 2, 1961.

46. Vandiver interview; Pou, "The Vandiver Years," 52.

47. Bruce Galphin, *The Riddle of Lester Maddox* (Atlanta: Camelot Publishing Co., 1968), 106. Useful for evaluating Vandiver's term are several methodological works, including E. Lee Bernick, "Gubernatorial Tools: Formal or Informal," *Journal of Politics* 41 (May 1979): 656–64; Thomas R. Dye, "Executive Power and Public Policy in the United States," in *The American Governor in Behavioral Perspective*, edited by Thad Beyle and J. Oliver Williams (New York: Harper and Row, 1972), 245–55; Larry Sabato, *Goodbye to Good-time Charlie* (Lexington: D. C. Heath, 1978), 50–53; Joseph E. Kallenbach, *The American Chief Executive* (New York: Harper and Row, 1966), 257–67; and Lee Sigelman and Roland Smith, "Personal, Office and State Characteristics as Predictors of Gubernatorial Performance," *Journal of Politics* 43 (Fall 1981): 169–80.

48. Pou, "The Vandiver Years," 43.

49. Atlanta *Constitution*, December 7, 1962.

50. Ibid., December 24, 1962.

51. Ibid., December 18, 1962.

52. Ibid., July 2, 1962.

53. Ibid., April 1, 1966.

54. Ibid., July 2, 1962.

Carl Sanders and the Politics of the Future
by James F. Cook

1. Macon *Telegraph*, September 17, 1962.

2. Charlotte Hale Smith, "Boyhood of Governor Sanders," *Atlanta Journal and Constitution Magazine*, September 13, 1964, 12.

3. Ibid., 12, 14, 54; Robert Coram and Remer Tyson, "The Loser Who Won," *Atlanta Magazine*, November 10, 1970, 43.

4. Coram and Tyson, "The Loser Who Won," 43.

5. Lynda Stewart, "The Possible Dream," *Georgia Alumni Record* (Summer 1969), 4.

6. Andrew Sparks, "Hopes and Dreams of the Sanders Family," *Atlanta Journal and Constitution Magazine*, January 13, 1963, 25.

7. Margaret Spears Lyons, "A Comparison of Carl Sanders' Gubernatorial Campaigns: 1962 and 1970" (M.A. thesis, University of Georgia, 1971), 10–11.

8. Virginia W. Atwell, ed., *Georgia's Official Register, 1963–1964* (Atlanta: Department of Archives and History, 1965), 26; Sparks, "Hopes and Dreams," 25.

9. Smith, "Boyhood of Governor Sanders," 54; Augusta *Chronicle-Herald*, July 8, 1962; Press Releases, July 1964, Carl Sanders Papers, Executive Department Correspondence, Georgia Department of Archives and History.

10. Augusta *Chronicle-Herald*, July 8, 1962.

11. Smith, "Boyhood of Governor Sanders," 14; *Official Register, 1963–1964*, 26.

12. Coram and Tyson, "The Loser Who Won," 43.

13. *Official Register, 1963–1964*, 26.

14. Macon *Telegraph*, April 22, 1962; Atlanta *Journal*, April 22, 1962.

15. "Jubilation in Atlanta," *New Republic*, May 7, 1962, 6; Albert B. Saye, *A Constitutional History of Georgia, 1732–1968*, rev. ed. (Athens: University of Georgia Press, 1970), 417–18.

16. "Politics," *Time*, August 24, 1962, 11–12.

17. Atlanta *Journal*, May 6, 1962.

18. "Out of the Smoke House," *Time*, September 21, 1962, 25.

19. Ibid.

20. Earl Black, *Southern Governors and Civil Rights* (Cambridge, Mass.: Harvard University Press, 1976), 14–15, 68, 178.

21. Lester Velie, "Strange Case of the Country Slickers vs. the City Rubes," *Reader's Digest*, April 1960, 108–12; Ben Hibbs, "Progress Goes Marching Through Georgia," *Saturday Evening Post*, February 16, 1963, 70.

22. "Politics," 11.

23. Lyons, "Comparison of Sanders' Campaigns," 24.

24. "Out of the Smoke House," 25.

25. Ibid.

26. Thomasville *Times-Enterprise*, July 7, 1962.

27. Lyons, "Comparison of Sanders' Campaigns," 69–81 (quote, p. 73).

28. Atlanta *Journal-Constitution*, July 1, 1962; Augusta *Chronicle*, May 11, 1962.

29. Joseph L. Bernd, "Georgia, Static and Dynamic," in *The Changing Politics of the South*, edited by William C. Havard (Baton Rouge: Louisiana State University Press, 1972), 332–33.

30. *Official Register, 1961–1962*, 1436.

31. Bernd, "Georgia, Static and Dynamic," 333–34.

32. Macon *Telegraph*, September 17, 1962; Coram and Tyson, "The Loser Who Won," 60.

33. Atlanta *Constitution*, November 16, 1962; Press Releases, January 19, 1963, Sanders Papers; Interview with Carl E. Sanders, Atlanta, Ga., August 15, 1985; Interview with Nathan Dean, Rockmart, Ga., October 8, 1985.

34. Atlanta *Constitution*, July 1, 1962.

35. Ibid.

36. E. Merton Coulter, "The Sanders Administration," in *Addresses and Public Papers of Carl Edward Sanders*, edited by Frank Daniel (Atlanta: Georgia Department of Archives and History, 1968), xxiii–xxvii; Numan V. Bartley and Hugh D. Graham, *Southern Politics and the Second Reconstruction* (Baltimore: Johns Hopkins University Press, 1975), 148–49; Larry Sabato, *Goodbye to Good-time Charlie: The American Governor Transformed, 1950–1975* (Lexington, Mass.: D. C. Heath, 1978), 52; Ivan Allen, Jr., *Mayor: Notes on the Sixties* (New York: Simon and Schuster, 1971), 135–38; *Christian Science Monitor*, January 23, 1970; Atlanta *Constitution*, January 10, 1967.

37. Press Releases, June 12, 1963, Sanders Papers; *Acts and Resolutions of the General Assembly of the State of Georgia, 1963* (Atlanta: State Printers, 1964), 394–96.

38. *Acts and Resolutions, 1964*, 3–49.

39. Carl E. Sanders, *Age of Change, Time of Decision: A Report to the General Assembly and the People of Georgia on the Administration of Governor Carl E. Sanders, 1963–1967* (Atlanta: State Printers, 1967), 5, 15–20.

40. William R. Bowdoin, *Georgia's Third Force* (Atlanta: Foote & Davies, 1967), 13.

41. Ibid.

42. Sanders interview; Athens *Banner-Herald*, January 12, 1967.

43. Bowdoin, *Georgia's Third Force*, 18, 22.

44. Ibid., 27–35.

45. Press Releases, January 21, April 23, June 12, 19, 29, July 26, September 5, October 8, December 19, 22, 1963, Sanders Papers.

46. *Acts and Resolutions, 1963*, 402–409.

47. *Acts and Resolutions, 1964 Extraordinary Session*, 234–356; Saye, *Constitutional History*, 427–29.

48. Press Releases, June 24, 1964, Sanders Papers.

49. Ibid., June 25, 1964.

50. Saye, *Constitutional History*, 429.

51. Rome *News-Tribune*, November 7, 1966.

52. Numan V. Bartley, "1940 to the Present," in Kenneth Coleman et al., *A History of Georgia* (Athens: University of Georgia Press, 1977), 395–96.

53. "Redrawing the Lines," *Time*, February 28, 1964, 19.

54. Augusta *Chronicle-Herald*, January 1, 1967; Rome *News-Tribune*, February 16, 1964.

55. "Redrawing the Lines," 19.

56. Atlanta *Journal*, October 8, 1978.

57. Rome *News-Tribune*, March 3, 4, 10, 1965; *Acts and Resolutions, 1965*, 127–74.

58. Saye, *Constitutional History*, 423.

59. Press Releases, March 18, 1963, March 3, August 23, September 30, 1965, Sanders Papers.

60. Ibid., May 16, 1966.

61. Ibid., November 8, 1966.

62. *Acts and Resolutions, 1965*, 63; Press Releases, December 21, 1966, Sanders Papers; Sanders, *Age of Change*, 3, 7, 8, 30.

63. Hibbs, "Progress Goes Marching Through Georgia," 69, 70.

64. Press Releases, July 26, 1963, Sanders Papers; "Georgia Elects Negro Delegates," New York *Times*, July 29, 1964.

65. Press Releases, July 12, 1963, Sanders Papers.

66. Ibid., October 6, 1965; Sanders interview; Atlanta *Journal*, October 8, 1978.

67. Sanders interview; Allen, *Mayor*, 182.

68. Press Releases, October 4, 1965, Sanders Papers.

69. Ibid., August 23, 1965.

70. Ibid., July 20, 1964, August 23, 1965.

71. Ibid., July 20, 1964.

72. Daniel, *Addresses of Carl Sanders*, 81–88.

73. Atlanta *Inquirer*, August 21, 28, 1965; Montgomery *Monitor*, June 4, 1965.

74. Daniel, *Addresses of Carl Sanders*, 81–88.
75. New York *Times*, September 13, 1965.
76. Atlanta *Journal*, January 2, 1966.
77. "Goldwater Is Victor in Georgia Despite Gov. Sanders' Appeals," New York *Times*, November 4, 1964; Augusta *Chronicle*, August 7, 1966.
78. Daniel, *Addresses of Carl Sanders*, 218–20.
79. Ibid., xxi.
80. Atlanta *Constitution*, January 10, 1967, August 8, 1968; Athens *Daily News*, August 24, 1968.
81. Atlanta *Constitution*, January 10, 1966.
82. Press Releases, February 11, April 1, 1966, Sanders Papers.
83. Ibid., September 13, 1966.
84. Reese Cleghorn, "No Seat for the Negro Who Won," *New Republic*, January 29, 1966, 11–12; "Times Have Changed," *Newsweek*, June 28, 1965, 24–27.
85. "One Word Too Many," *Time*, January 21, 1966, 20; "Two-Time Loser," *Newsweek*, January 24, 1966, 26–28.
86. "The Bond Issue," *Time*, February 18, 1966, 24; "Bond's Word," *Newsweek*, December 19, 1966, 27.
87. Sanders interview.
88. Rome *News-Tribune*, February 20, 1966.
89. Senatorial Campaign 1966, Political Series, Richard B. Russell Collection, Russell Memorial Library, University of Georgia, Athens; "Pulling a 'Huhmun,'" *Newsweek*, September 20, 1965, 26–28; Savannah *Morning-News*, March 31, 1966.
90. Harold Paulk Henderson, "The 1966 Gubernatorial Election in Georgia" (Ph.D. dissertation, University of Southern Mississippi, 1982).
91. "Winners Wanted," *Time*, November 25, 1966, 32–33; "Picking Maddox," *Newsweek*, December 26, 1966, 20; James F. Cook, *Governors of Georgia* (Huntsville, Ala.: Strode Publishers, 1979), 289–95.
92. Savannah *Morning-News*, December 12, 1966, January 11, 1967.
93. Columbus *Enquirer*, January 13, 1967; Rome *News-Tribune*, January 15, 1967; Atlanta *Constitution*, January 10, 1967.
94. Atlanta *Constitution*; Sanders, *Age of Change*.
95. Sanders, *Age of Change*, 11.
96. Interview with Henry Neal, Atlanta, Ga., August 28, 1985; Dean interview; "Tom Murphy Speaks Out," *System Summary* 21 (October–November 1985): 1, 12.

Lester Maddox and the Politics of Populism
by Bradley R. Rice

1. John Carlton Huie, Jr., "The Dream of Lester Maddox" (M.A. thesis, Emory University, 1966), 2–3; Robert Coles, "Maddox of Georgia," *New Republic*, August 5, 1967, 22; Marshall Frady, "How Lester Maddox at Last Became 'Mr. Somebody,'" in Frady, *Southerners: A Journalist's Odyssey* (New York: New American Library, 1980), 44. For general biographical information, see also Bruce Galphin, *The Riddle of Lester Maddox* (Atlanta:

Camelot Publishing Co., 1968), and Lester Garfield Maddox, *Speaking Out: The Autobiography of Lester Garfield Maddox* (Garden City, N.Y.: Doubleday, 1975).

2. Frank Daniel, ed., *Addresses of Lester Garfield Maddox, Governor of Georgia, 1967–1971* (Atlanta: Georgia Department of Archives and History, 1971), 164.

3. Bradley R. Rice, "Lester Maddox and the 'Liberal' Mayors," *Proceedings and Papers of the Georgia Association of Historians, 1983*, 78–87.

4. Galphin, *Riddle*, 38–46; Huie, "Dream of Maddox," 21–22; Atlanta *Constitution*, August–September 1962.

5. Atlanta *Constitution*, May 16, 1964, in Huie, "Dream of Maddox."

6. Atlanta *Constitution*, September 15, 1965, quoted in Harold Paulk Henderson, "The 1966 Gubernatorial Election in Georgia" (Ph.D. dissertation, University of Southern Mississippi, 1982).

7. Atlanta *Constitution*, July 7, 1966.

8. Ibid., Sept. 18, 1966.

9. "Georgia: The Great Payoff," *Newsweek*, December 12, 1966, 34–35; Galphin, *Riddle*, 112–14; Maddox, *Autobiography*, 74–80; Henderson, "1966 Gubernatorial Election," 129–30; Interview with Sam Hopkins, Atlanta *Journal-Constitution* reporter, Tifton, Ga., October 31, 1985. A sixth candidate, Hoke O'Kelly, was no factor. On Gray, see Millard B. Grimes, *The Last Linotype: The Story of Georgia and Its Newspapers Since World War II* (Macon: Mercer University Press, 1985), 377–79.

10. See Henderson, "1966 Gubernatorial Election"; Numan V. Bartley, *From Thurmond to Wallace: Political Tendencies in Georgia, 1948–1968* (Baltimore: Johns Hopkins University Press, 1970); Numan V. Bartley and Hugh D. Graham, *Southern Politics and the Second Reconstruction* (Baltimore: Johns Hopkins University Press, 1970). Some observers suggested that Arnall would have won without a runoff if Carter had not entered the race. Such speculation overlooks the fact that the combined Arnall-Maddox total was only 4,132 above the total of the other four contenders, and the probability is that considerably more than 5,000 of Carter votes would have gone to Gray, Byrd, and even Maddox. Arnall himself realized that he would have faced a runoff with or without Carter in the race.

11. Atlanta *Constitution*, September 21, 1966, quoted in Henderson, "1966 Gubernatorial Election."

12. Ivan Allen, Jr., *Mayor: Notes on the Sixties* (New York: Simon and Schuster, 1971), 140. Some Republicans and Democrats who were both anti-Maddox and anti-Arnall may have voted for Maddox in the runoff under the assumption that he would be an easy mark for the sophisticated, well-financed Callaway. Close analysis of the returns by Henderson and Bartley, however, indicates that it is unlikely that such voters were responsible for the Maddox victory. Some criticized Carter for not endorsing Arnall in the runoff. See Grimes, *Last Linotype*; Henderson, "1966 Gubernatorial Election," and Bartley, *Thurmond to Wallace*.

13. *New York Times Magazine*, November 6, 1966, 27–29; Atlanta *Journal*, October 19, 1966, quoted in Henderson, "1966 Gubernatorial Election."

14. Atlanta *Journal*, November 5, 1966.

15. Bartley and Graham, *Southern Politics and the Second Reconstruction.*

16. Henderson, "1966 Gubernatorial Election," 246–63; "Supreme Court: Picking Maddox," *Newsweek,* December 26, 1966, 20; Galphin, *Riddle,* 164–67; Maddox *Autobiography,* 88–93. Some have claimed that Callaway could have won if he had courted the members of the General Assembly. See Jasper Dorsey column, Atlanta *Journal-Constitution,* September 9, 1979.

17. Galphin, *Riddle,* 15.

18. *Addresses,* 143. See similar versions in Maddox, *Autobiography,* 93; Coles, "Maddox," 22; Frady, "Mr. Somebody," 46; and "Surprise from Maddox," *U.S. News & World Report,* January 23, 1967, 14.

19. Huie, "Dream of Maddox," 52.

20. "Georgia: Lester Leaps In," *Newsweek,* January 23, 1967, 29–30. See "Surprise from Maddox," 14; Coles, "Maddox," 21; Frady, "Mr. Somebody," 60; Atlanta *Journal-Constitution,* March 19, 1967.

21. *Addresses,* 6.

22. Maddox, *Autobiography,* 96. See also Coles, "Maddox," 21.

23. Council of State Governments, *The American Governors: Their Backgrounds, Occupation, and Governmental Experience* (Chicago: July 1968), tables 1–3.

24. *Addresses,* 69.

25. Robert McMath et al., *Engineering the New South: Georgia Tech, 1885–1985* (Athens: University of Georgia Press, 1985), 404.

26. Atlanta *Constitution,* March 19, 1967; Maddox *Autobiography,* 136–37; *Addresses,* 115. See University of Georgia Institute of Government, *Reapportionment in Georgia* (Athens, 1970).

27. Atlanta *Constitution,* March 19, 1967.

28. Ibid.

29. Maddox, *Autobiography,* 136.

30. Atlanta *Constitution,* March 18, 1967; Maddox, *Autobiography,* 104; Galphin, *Riddle,* 161; Interview with Carl Sanders, October 31, 1985.

31. Atlanta *Journal-Constitution,* March 18, 19, 1967.

32. *Facts on File, 1967,* 134.

33. *Addresses,* 508.

34. *Facts on File, 1967.*

35. Maddox, *Autobiography,* 108, 113–16; Galphin, *Riddle,* 189.

36. *Facts on File, 1967.* "Georgia: The People's Choice," *Newsweek,* January 8, 1968, 24; Galphin, *Riddle,* 206; Reg Murphy, "The Maddox Administration Is Perhaps the Most Liberal in Georgia's History," *New York Times Magazine,* November 11, 1968, 81.

37. "Georgia: The People's Choice," 24.

38. Atlanta *Constitution,* March 9, 1966. See Atlanta *Journal-Constitution,* March 10, 1968; Galphin, *Riddle,* 190; Murphy "Maddox Administration," 128–33.

39. Reese Cleghorn, *Radicalism: Southern Style* (Atlanta: Southern Regional Council, 1968), 9; Allen, *Mayor,* 196–218; Maddox, *Autobiography,* 126–30; Galphin, *Riddle,* 207–10; Murphy, "Maddox Administration," 82.

40. *Addresses,* 197–200. See Maddox, *Autobiography,* 131; *Facts on File, 1968,* 345–46.

41. Maddox, *Autobiography*, 132.
42. *Facts on File*, *1968*, 358–59.
43. *Addresses*, 213, 226.
44. Murphy, "Maddox Administration," 81; *Facts on File*, *1969*, 247.
45. Murphy, "Maddox Administration," 83.
46. Atlanta *Constitution*, March 20, 1967.
47. Murphy, "Maddox Administration," 81.
48. *Addresses*, 248.
49. Atlanta *Constitution*, March 27, 1969. See also March 8, 28, 1969.
50. Ibid.; New York *Times* April 12, 1969.
51. *Addresses*, 303–306.
52. Atlanta *Constitution*, June 14, 1969. See also June 15, 1969.
53. Maddox's legal effort to overturn the one-term limitation was unsuccessful, and, despite early rumors to the contrary, he decided not to follow the Wallace example and have Virginia run as a surrogate. See "The Maddox Case—Broad Impact?" *U.S. News & World Report*, January 19, 1970, 10–11; Maddox, *Autobiography*, 156; Atlanta *Constitution*, March 9, 1969.
54. Atlanta *Journal-Constitution*, February 22, 1970.
55. "Governors: Give 'em the Ax," *Newsweek*, March 9, 1970, 20.
56. Ibid.; *Facts on File*, *1970*, 124.
57. Atlanta *Journal-Constitution*, March 1, 1970. See Atlanta *Constitution*, February 26, March 6, 8, 1970; New York *Times*, March 1, 1970.
58. Atlanta *Journal-Constitution*, February 22, 1970.
59. "Georgia: Lester's Itching Jaw," *Newsweek*, September 4, 1967, 30.
60. "Crisis in Southern Schools—Six Governors Speak Out," *U.S. News & World Report*, February 16, 1970, 42. See *Addresses*, 77, 80, 492; New York *Times*, July 25, 1969.
61. *Addresses*, 190, 272, 331, 342.
62. Ibid., 442, 492, 499. College agitators were also a favorite Maddox target. See Atlanta *Constitution*, March 9, 1969.
63. *Addresses*, 342, 498.
64. New York *Times*, March 17, 1969.
65. *Addresses*, 185.
66. Numan V. Bartley, "Moderation in Maddox Country?" *Georgia Historical Quarterly* 58 (February 1974): 340–48. On Maddox as lieutenant governor, see Gary M. Fink, *Prelude to the Presidency: The Political Character and Legislative Leadership Style of Governor Jimmy Carter* (Westport, Conn.: Greenwood Press, 1980).
67. Atlanta *Constitution*, June 14, 1969; Interview with William "Bill" Lee, October 28, 1985.

Jimmy Carter and the Politics of Transition
by Gary M. Fink

1. V. O. Key, Jr., *Southern Politics in State and Nation* (New York: Alfred A. Knopf, 1949).

2. Numan V. Bartley, "1940 to the Present," in Kenneth Coleman et al., *A History of Georgia* (Athens: University of Georgia Press, 1977), 295, 389, 395; Joseph L. Bernd, *Grass Roots Politics in Georgia: The County Unit System and the Importance of the Individual Voting Community in Bifactional Elections, 1942–1954* (Atlanta: Emory University Research Committee, 1960); Val B. Mixon, "The Growth of the Legislative Powers of the Governor of Georgia: A Survey of the Legislative Program of Governor Herman Talmadge, 1949–1954" (M.A. thesis, Emory University, 1959).

3. Frank Daniel, comp., *Addresses of Jimmy Carter* (Atlanta: Georgia Department of Archives and History, 1975), 79–81.

4. See, for example, Numan V. Bartley and Hugh D. Graham, *Southern Politics and the Second Reconstruction* (Baltimore: Johns Hopkins University Press, 1975); Numan V. Bartley, *From Thurmond to Wallace: Political Tendencies in Georgia, 1948–1968* (Baltimore: Johns Hopkins University Press, 1970); Neal R. Peirce, *The Deep South States of America: People, Politics and Power in the Seven States of the Deep South* (New York: W. W. Norton, 1974); Jack Bass and Walter DeVries, *The Transformation of Southern Politics: Social Change and Political Consequences Since 1945* (New York: Basic Books, 1976); and Pat Watters and Reese Cleghorn, *Climbing Jacob's Ladder: The Arrival of Negroes in Southern Politics* (New York: Harcourt, Brace & World, 1967).

5. Charles Longstreet Weltner, *Southerner* (Philadelphia: Lippincott, 1966), 37–38; Write-In Georgia Papers, Southern Labor Archives, Atlanta; Conversation with Elmer T. Kehrer, Southern director, AFL-CIO Civil Rights Department, February 28, 1979.

6. Peirce, *Deep South States*, 324–25.

7. Interview with Senator A. W. Holloway, president pro tem, Georgia Senate, November 8, 1978.

8. For an elaboration of Maddox's point of view, see Lester Garfield Maddox, *Speaking Out: The Autobiography of Lester Garfield Maddox* (Garden City, N.Y.: Doubleday, 1975), 136–37. The best assessment of Maddox's politics is contained in Bruce Galphin, *The Riddle of Lester Maddox* (Atlanta: Camelot Publishing Co., 1968).

9. Mattie S. Anderson, "Governor Jimmy Carter: Idealist or Realist: A Study of Carter's Commitment to Citizen Participation and Planning in the Goals for Georgia Program" (M.A. thesis, Georgia State University, 1979).

10. Peirce, *Deep South States*, 324–25.

11. Maddox, *Speaking Out*, 135.

12. Atlanta *Journal*, October 7, 1970.

13. Maddox, *Speaking Out*, 136–38.

14. Atlanta *Constitution*, August 25, 1971.

15. Maddox to Carter, November 22, 1971, Record Group 1, Subgroup 1, Series 5, Carter Gubernatorial Papers, State of Georgia, Department of Archives and History, Atlanta; Macon *News*, November 23, 1971.

16. See Carter's correspondence with such influential House leaders as George Smith, George Busbee, Al Burrus, Sam Nunn, Elliott Levitas, and

Tom Murphy, Record Group 1, Subgroup 1, Series 5, Carter Papers. See also Gary M. Fink, *Prelude to the Presidency: The Political Character and Legislative Leadership Style of Governor Jimmy Carter* (Westport, Conn.: Greenwood Press, 1980), part 3. The death of Smith in December 1973 greatly altered Carter's relationship with the House leadership. Smith was replaced by Tom Murphy, who had previously served as Maddox's floor leader in the House.

17. See Fink, *Prelude to the Presidency*, chapter 7.

18. *Time*, March 31, 1971.

19. Leslie Wheeler, *Jimmy Who? An Examination of Presidential Candidate Jimmy Carter the Man, His Career, His Stands on the Issues* (Woodbury, N.Y.: Barron's Educational Series, 1976), 93; Rosalynn Carter, *First Lady from Plains* (New York: Houghton Mifflin, 1984) 105–106.

20. Jimmy Carter, *Why Not the Best?* (Nashville: Broadman Press, 1975), 177; Rosalynn Carter, *First Lady*, 100–101; Conversations with James E. "Chip" Carter III, January, February 1973.

21. The black vote contributed significantly to Carter's successful pursuit of the Democratic presidential nomination in 1976.

22. Fink, *Prelude to the Presidency*, 10. Ellis Arnall sponsored some reorganization proposals, and Carl Sanders also gave lip service to the idea, but little was done until Carter took office. For Carter, the association of reorganization with Richard Russell's governorship and his own interest in orderly procedure, good management, and efficiency made it a very attractive reform.

23. For evaluations of Carter's governorship, see Wheeler, *Jimmy Who?* 63–109; Carter, *Why Not the Best?* 137–59; Carter, *First Lady from Plains*, 71–196; Bass and DeVries, *The Transformation of Southern Politics*, 146–47.

24. For an extended discussion and analysis of the reorganization program, see my *Prelude to the Presidency*. See also T. McNeil Simpson, "Georgia State Administration: Jimmy Carter's Contribution" (Paper delivered at the 1973 annual meeting of the Southern Political Science Association, Knoxville, Tenn.), Carter Papers.

25. Wheeler, *Jimmy Who?* 76–77; Interview with James L. Maddex, Jr., December 7, 1978 (Maddex was a member of the Judicial Review Study Team).

26. Wheeler, *Jimmy Who?* 76–77; Carter, *Why Not the Best?* 140–41.

27. Fink, *Prelude to the Presidency*, 10–11; Carter, *First Lady*, 104; Carter, *Why Not the Best?* 154–55.

28. Carter, *Why Not the Best?* 155; Fink, *Prelude to the Presidency*, 12–13; Record Group 1 Subgroup 1, Series 5, Carter Papers.

29. Wheeler, *Jimmy Who?* 80.

30. Carter, *First Lady*, 94–96; Dorothy J. Tracy to Gary Fink, n.d.

31. Fink, *Prelude to the Presidency*, 10; Carter, *Why Not the Best?* 118–20.

32. Carter, *Why Not the Best?* 118–20.

33. Tracy to Fink, n.d.

34. Quoted in Wheeler, *Jimmy Who?* 82.

35. Fink, *Prelude to the Presidency,* 203.

36. Wheeler, *Jimmy Who?* 81–82; Coleman, *A History of Georgia,* 403.

37. See, for example, Numan V. Bartley, *The Rise of Massive Resistance: Race and Politics in the South During the 1950's* (Baton Rouge: Louisiana State University Press, 1969).

38. Carter, *Why Not the Best?* 138–43; Wheeler, *Jimmy Who?* 80; Bass and DeVries, *Transformation of Southern Politics,* 145.

39. The results of the survey are reported in the Appendix. The questionnaire was sent to ninety-two selected members of the Georgia Association of Historians. Forty-eight questionnaires were returned. It was not anticipated that those completing the survey had any special knowledge of the gubernatorial administrations under review. The objective of the survey was simply to ascertain the perceptions of an informed, interested, and historically minded group of observers.

40. See Bartley, "1940 to the Present," 389–403, and Numan V. Bartley, *The Creation of Modern Georgia* (Athens: University of Georgia Press, 1983), 190–201, for his discussion of recent Georgia governors.

41. Carter described his administration as "controversial, aggressive, and combative" in his autobiography, *Why Not the Best?* 137. The authors of *A History of Georgia* characterized the Sanders administration as follows: "Other than presiding over the hectic mid-1960s with a refreshing dignity, his [Sanders's] administration found little time or energy to deal with other basic problems," 401.

42. Quoted in Wheeler, *Jimmy Who?* 86.

43. Bass and DeVries, *Transformation of Southern Politics,* 145.

44. Wheeler, *Jimmy Who?* 85.

45. Bass and DeVries, *Transformation of Southern Politics,* 145; Fink, *Prelude to the Presidency,* 152, 156–58.

46. Fink, *Prelude to the Presidency,* 166–69, 172–74, passim.

47. Quoted in ibid., 169.

48. Ibid., 166–67; Wheeler, *Jimmy Who?* 85.

49. Wheeler, *Jimmy Who?* 83–84.

50. Fink, *Prelude to the Presidency,* 163.

51. See ibid., particularly part 2.

52. Ibid., chapter 1; Wheeler, *Jimmy Who?* 77–87.

53. Bass and DeVries, *Transformation of Southern Politics,* 145; Fink, *Prelude to the Presidency,* 152, 156–58, passim.

54. Atlanta *Constitution,* January 9, 1972.

55. Hugh Carter, *Cousin Beedie and Cousin Hot: My Life with the Carter Family of Plains, Georgia* (Englewood Cliffs, N.J.: Prentice-Hall, 1978), 138.

56. In one case he infuriated his wife, Rosalynn, by telling a group of anti-ERA demonstrators that he supported the equal rights amendment but that his wife did not. In recounting the story several years later, Mrs. Carter was still obviously miffed. *First Lady,* 95–96.

57. For a discussion of the 1970 campaign, see Bass and DeVries, *Transfor-*

mation of Southern Politics, 144; Wheeler, *Jimmy Who?* chapter 4; Reg Murphy and Hal Gulliver, *The Southern Strategy* (New York: Charles Scribner's Sons, 1971), 176, 186–94; Atlanta *Constitution,* November 8, 11, 1970.

George Busbee and the Politics of Consensus
by Eleanor C. Main and Gerard S. Gryski

1. Atlanta *Journal,* September 4, 1975.

2. "Busbee, A Tough Act to Follow" editorial in Atlanta *Constitution,* January 10, 1983.

3. *Governor's Policy Statement, 1975–1983* (Atlanta: Georgia Office of Planning and Budget, 1983) 138–41.

4. George D. Busbee, "Inauguration Speech," *Senate Journal, Regular Session, 1975,* 53.

5. George D. Busbee, "State of the State Speech," *Journal of the Senate of the State of Georgia, Regular Session, 1975,* 69.

6. Atlanta *Journal,* November 7, 1974.

7. Ibid., February 16, 1975.

8. Atlanta *Constitution,* January 29, 1975.

9. Ibid., February 6, 10, 28, 1975.

10. Ibid., March 7, 1975.

11. Ibid., March 20, 1975.

12. Ibid., March 17, 1975.

13. Ibid., June 20, 1975.

14. Ibid., July 3, 1975.

15. Ibid., August 8, 1975.

16. Ibid., December 5, 1975. The professors had also challenged the legality of the entire state appropriations act as amended in special session, but the court did not accept that argument.

17. Atlanta *Journal-Constitution,* March 11, 1979.

18. Ibid.

19. Ibid., March 17, 1979. During the 1980 legislative session, the governor appeared to have agreed to a plan that would have allowed the legislature to set the state's revenue estimate. The attorney general reminded him that this could not be done. Atlanta *Constitution,* March 18, 1980.

20. Atlanta *Constitution,* March 28, 1979.

21. Ibid., April 13, 1979.

22. Ibid., April 26, 1979.

23. Atlanta *Journal-Constitution,* January 18, 1976.

24. Atlanta *Constitution,* September 3, October 21, 1976.

25. Atlanta *Journal-Constitution,* December 3, 1978.

26. Ibid., March 22, 1981.

27. Atlanta *Journal,* August 13, 1981.

28. Ibid.

29. Atlanta *Constitution,* August 21, 1981.

30. Ibid., August 22, 1981.

31. Ibid., August 26, 1981.

32. Ibid., September 5, 1981.

33. Atlanta *Journal*, December 18, 1975.

34. Over his eight years, there was an annual increase of 286 new positions as compared to 2,000 each year in the prior eight years. Most of the increase was due to the expansion of staff in the Department of Offender Rehabilitation. *Governor's Policy Statement, 1975–1983*, 119.

35. Many of the legislators who had fought the Carter reorganization plan urged Busbee to go back to the structure before Carter's amalgamation of the divisions. Then, during 1976, Busbee's plans to restructure DHR became a minor issue in the presidential campaign. Atlanta *Constitution*, October 8, 1976.

36. Ibid., August 1, 1975.

37. Ibid., August 22, 1975.

38. Ibid., November 29, 1975, December 24, 1975. HEW did not agree to all the co-payments Busbee suggested, specifically those affecting maternity, emergency and inelastic care.

39. Atlanta *Journal*, July 8, 1976. The board said the plan was poorly designed and compared it to patients being put in risk for medical experiments. Atlanta *Constitution*, July 9, 1976.

40. Atlanta *Constitution*, November 17, 1977. The governor had pursued his concern about Medicaid as chairman of a task force of the National Governors' Association to investigate Medicaid abuses and problems in 1976.

41. Ibid., August 11, 1981.

42. Ibid., August 8, 11, October 5, 1975; Atlanta *Journal-Constitution*, October 12, 1975.

43. Atlanta *Constitution*, June 5, 1977.

44. Ibid., January 30, 1976.

45. Ibid., July 1, 1977.

46. Ibid., April 7, 1978.

47. Ibid., May 4, 22, 1978.

48. Ibid., July 7, 1978. "Checkerboarding" means segregating and alternating dorms by race.

49. Atlanta *Journal*, June 18, 1982.

50. George D. Busbee, "State of the State Speech," *Senate Journal, Regular Session, 1977*, 55.

51. This section is based largely on *Governor's Policy Statement, 1975–1983*.

52. Atlanta *Constitution*, August 31, 1971.

53. The Sunbelt states are generally considered those in the traditional South, plus the Southwestern states across to California. The snowbelt states are the Midwestern states and the Northeastern states.

54. Atlanta *Constitution*, September 25, 1977.

55. Ibid., April 26, 1978.

56. Atlanta *Journal-Constitution*, April 30, 1978.

57. Atlanta *Journal*, December 12, 1978.

58. Atlanta *Constitution*, August 6, 1980.

59. In 1978, Governor Busbee had rejected $50,000 in funds from the Department of Education to initiate Educational Information Centers in Georgia. In a letter to the U.S. commissioner of education he wrote that the programs would probably depend on promised future federal funding, but that the state would wind up carrying most of the federal burden. Atlanta *Journal*, February 28, 1978.

60. Atlanta *Constitution*, August 15, 1974.

61. Ibid., September 5, 1974.

62. Ibid., November 21, 1974.

63. Ibid.

64. Ibid., October 18, 1978, July 9, 1979.

65. *Governor's Policy Statement, 1975–1983*, 29–30.

66. Atlanta *Constitution*, January 19, 1978.

67. Atlanta *Journal*, March 10, 1978.

68. Ibid., February 11, 1979.

69. Atlanta *Constitution*, January 12, 1978.

70. When Busbee was leaving office, a poll listed him as "the second most popular politician in Georgia." U.S. Senator Sam Nunn came in first with a 712.4 rating to Busbee's 704.6. Atlanta *Journal-Constitution*, December 26, 1982. In early 1979 a poll conducted by Darden Research Corporation in Atlanta found that Busbee would beat then U.S. Senator Herman Talmadge by more than a 2 to 1 margin. Busbee's strength was distributed throughout the state. Atlanta *Constitution*, February 23, 1979.

Georgia Governors in an Age of Change
by Numan V. Bartley

1. Numan V. Bartley, *The Creation of Modern Georgia* (Athens: University of Georgia Press, 1983), 179–81. William Anderson, *The Wild Man from Sugar Creek: The Political Career of Eugene Talmadge* (Baton Rouge: Louisiana State University Press, 1975), is the standard biography of Talmadge; Gary M. Fink, *Prelude to the Presidency: The Political and Legislative Leadership Style of Governor Jimmy Carter* (Westport, Conn.: Greenwood Press, 1980), is a thorough study of Carter's reorganization program.

2. Anderson, *Wild Man from Sugar Creek*, 141–52; Elizabeth G. Bowden, "The Gubernatorial Administration of Jimmy Carter" (M.A. thesis, University of Georgia, 1979), 24–29 passim.

3. Numan V. Bartley, "1940 to the Present," in Kenneth Coleman et al., *A History of Georgia* (Athens: University of Georgia Press, 1977), 388–400; Bruce Galphin, *The Riddle of Lester Maddox* (Atlanta: Camelot, 1968), 105–67.

4. Lorena M. Akioka, ed., *1982 Georgia Statistical Abstract* (Athens: Col-

lege of Business Administration, 1982), 2–26, 403–25; *Georgia: Descriptions in Data, 1983* (Atlanta: State Government, 1983), 9–11, 236–39.

5. Detailed treatments of these developments include the following works by Numan V. Bartley: "1940 to the Present"; *The Creation of Modern Georgia,* 147–207; *From Thurmond to Wallace: Political Tendencies in Georgia, 1948–1968* (Baltimore: Johns Hopkins University Press, 1970); and "The Era of the New Deal as a Turning Point in Southern History," in James C. Cobb and Michael V. Namorato, eds., *The New Deal and the South* (Jackson: University Press of Mississippi, 1984), 135–46.

6. Quoted in Robert Sherrill, *Gothic Politics in the Deep South* (New York: Grossman, 1968), 3.

7. Frank Daniel, ed., *Addresses and Public Papers of Carl Edward Sanders* (Atlanta: Department of Archives and History, 1968), 3.

8. Quoted in Neal R. Peirce, *The Deep South States of America: People, Politics, and Power in the Seven Deep South States* (New York: W. W. Norton, 1974), 325, and Galphin, *Riddle,* 212.

9. Frank Daniel, ed., *Addresses of James Earl Carter* (Atlanta: Department of Archives and History, 1975), 78; Busbee quoted in Jack Bass and Walter DeVries, *The Transformation of Southern Politics: Social Change and Political Consequences Since 1945* (New York: Basic Books, 1976), 148.

10. Dick Pettys, in *Savannah News-Press,* October 10, 1982.

CONTRIBUTORS

NUMAN V. BARTLEY, Professor of History, University of Georgia, is widely regarded as the leading scholar in the field of recent Georgia politics. Bartley is the author of *The Creation of Modern Georgia, From Thurmond to Wallace: Political Tendencies in Georgia, 1948–1968, Rise of Massive Resistance: Race and Politics in the South in the 1950's,* and *Southern Politics and the Second Reconstruction* (with Hugh D. Graham) as well as several noteworthy articles in professional journals. He was the editor of *The Evolution of Southern Culture.*

ROY F. CHALKER, SR., publisher emeritus of the Waynesboro *True Citizen,* is a distinguished Georgia journalist who once served as president of the Georgia Press Association and is a close friend and political ally of Marvin Griffin. Governor Griffin appointed him Director of State Parks in 1955. In 1956, he was named to the State Highway Board, and the next year he became its chairman. He was also chairman of the Rural Roads Authority and the Bridge Building Authority.

JAMES F. COOK, Professor of History, Floyd College, is well known in the field of Georgia gubernatorial politics. His doctoral dissertation, "Politics and Education in the Talmadge Era: The Controversy Over the University of Georgia," treats a significant episode in the evolution of the modern governorship. His book, *The Governors of Georgia,* is the standard introduction to the subject. Dr. Cook has also published several important articles in historical journals.

ROBERT F. DUBAY, Professor of History, Bainbridge College, is perhaps the leading authority on Governor Griffin's career. His biography of Governor Griffin, *Stump King: Marvin Griffin, a Political History,* is currently in press. Dr. Dubay is the author of *John Jones Pettus: Mississippi Fireeater* and has published extensively in such journals as the *Georgia Historical Quarterly,* the *Community College Social Science Quarterly,* and the *Southern Historian.*

GARY M. FINK, Professor of History and Chairman of the Department of History, Georgia State University, is the author of *Prelude to the Presidency: The Political Character and Legislative Style of Governor Jimmy Carter* and the founder of the university's important Georgia Government Documentation Project, which promises to preserve a vital link to the state's political past.

SAM M. GRIFFIN, JR., publisher of the Bainbridge *Post-Searchlight*, is the son of Governor S. Marvin Griffin. A graduate of Georgia Tech and a veteran of the U.S. Navy, he is the third generation of Griffins to edit the Bainbridge newspaper. A former president of the Georgia Press Association, he was vice-chairman of the State Board of Education during the Maddox administration.

GERARD S. GRYSKI, Associate Professor of Political Science, Auburn University, is the author of *Bureaucratic Policy Making* and numerous articles in political science journals and anthologies. He is a member of the editorial board of the *Journal of Politics* and the winner of the Western Political Science Association Award for the best paper on women and politics presented at major conferences in 1984.

HAROLD PAULK HENDERSON, Professor of Political Science, Abraham Baldwin Agricultural College, is a leading authority on the career of Governor Ellis Arnall. His master's thesis, "The 1946 Gubernatorial Election in Georgia," and his doctoral dissertation, "The 1966 Gubernatorial Election in Georgia," concern two of the most controversial elections in modern Georgia history. He is currently writing a biography of Governor Arnall.

ELEANOR C. MAIN, Associate Professor of Political Science and Associate Dean of Emory College at Emory University, has done extensive research on recent Georgia politics. She wrote the chapter on Georgia in *The 1984 Presidential Election in the South*, edited by Robert Steed, Laundre Moreland, and Todd Baker. Among her other credits are the articles "Different Perspectives: Seven State Legislators' Attitudes about Women and Politics," in the *Social Science Journal*, and "Differences in Recruitment of Male and Female Southern State Legislators," in the *Southern Political Review*.

GENE-GABRIEL MOORE is a free-lance journalist from Atlanta who conducted a series of interviews with former governors in 1976 for Georgia Public Television. He was then the host of a weekly talk show called "Byline" on GPTV. He is also the former editor of a weekly newspaper called *Creative Loafing*. His articles appear frequently in newspapers and magazines.

ROBERT J. PAJARI, Professor of Political Science, Georgia Southern College, specializes in state and local government. His dissertation, "A Comparative Analysis of Orientations to Change in Twenty-Four Southeast Georgia Cities," provides significant insights into the dynamics of change in recent Georgia history. He has published widely in journals such as the *Southeastern Political Review, The Journal of Political Science*, and the *Georgia Political Science Journal*.

CHARLES B. PYLES, Professor of Political Science, Georgia State University, is widely respected as an authority on Georgia politics. His doctoral dissertation, "Race and Pluralism in Georgia Elections, 1948–1966," is an important study. He is the book review editor for *Southeastern Political Review*, the journal of the Georgia Political Science Association.

BRADLEY R. RICE, Professor of History, Clayton College, is an acknowledged expert on the Maddox years. His article "Lester Maddox and the 'Liberal' Mayors" appeared in the *Papers of the Georgia Association of Historians*. Dr. Rice is also the author of *Progressive Cities: Commission Government in America, 1901–1920*. He edited, along with Richard M. Bernard, a volume entitled *Sunbelt Cities: Growth and Politics Since World War II* and since 1983 has been the editor of *Atlanta History: A Journal of Georgia and the South*.

GARY L. ROBERTS, Professor of History, Abraham Baldwin Agricultural College, is a lifelong student of Georgia politics, although this is his first publishing venture in the field. He has published widely on the history of the Trans-Mississippi West, the American Indian, and American violence. He is currently working on a study of the Sand Creek Massacre to be published by the University of Oklahoma Press. In 1978 he received the Vivian A. Paladin Award for the best article appearing in *Montana, The Magazine of Western History*. For several years he was a member of the Board of Consultants for the Education Division of the National Endowment for the Humanities.

INDEX